WARS FOR EMPIRE

WARS FOR
EMPIRE

APACHES, THE UNITED STATES, AND THE SOUTHWEST BORDERLANDS

JANNE LAHTI

UNIVERSITY OF OKLAHOMA PRESS : NORMAN

Library of Congress Cataloging-in-Publication Data

Name: Lahti, Janne, author.

Title: Wars for empire : Apaches, the United States, and the Southwest borderlands / Janne Lahti.

Description: Norman : University of Oklahoma Press, 2017. | Includes bibliographical references and index.

Identifiers: LCCN 2016058960 | ISBN 978-0-8061-5742-9 (hardcover : alk. paper)

Subjects: LCSH: Apache Indians—Wars, 1883–1886. | Apache Indians—Warfare. | Violence—Southwest, New—History—19th century. | Military art and science— United States—History—19th century. | Southwest, New—History, Military—19th century. | United States. Army—History—19th century.

Classification: LCC E83.88 .L34 2017 | DDC 979.004/9725—dc23

LC record available at https://lccn.loc.gov/2016058960

1 2 3 4 5 6 7 8 9 10

CONTENTS

v

ILLUSTRATIONS

Figures

Map

ACKNOWLEDGMENTS

Like most scholarly books, this one owes debts to numerous people and several institutions. If I have missed some who helped me along the way, it is not intentional but can be blamed on a flawed memory. The bulk of the research and writing for this book was done between 2011 and 2014 when I was lucky enough to land a three-year postdoc fellowship from the Academy of Finland. It enabled me to split my time between the University of Helsinki and the University of Arizona, which was extremely beneficial in my development as a scholar. For once there was enough time for writing, pursuing archival research, visiting many of the places I write about, and networking.

In Helsinki, Markku Peltonen was very encouraging and supportive toward my work, and Hannes Saarinen provided me an academic home. I shared office space as well as many laughs and discussions on academia and life with my colleagues Ilkka Levä, Markku Kekäläinen, Antti Ruotsala, and Erkki Teräväinen. In Arizona, Kevin Gosner made me feel most welcome at the History Department, as did Jadwiga Pieper-Mooney, Jeremy Vetter, Douglas Weiner, and many others. Most profound thanks go Roger and Marilyn Nichols, whose warmhearted support and kindness toward me and my family will never be forgotten. I also wish to extend my thanks to staff members who proved invaluable in steering my journey in the bureaucratic maze of modern universities: especially Leena Viitaniemi, Kirsti Nymark, and Jaana Gluschkoff in Helsinki, and Debbie Jackson and Victoria Parker in Arizona. At the Arizona Historical Society, Bruce Dinges and Caitlin Lampman aided the project in many ways, as did the helpful staff at the Arizona State Museum Archives and at the University of Arizona Special Collections. Those reading earlier drafts of the chapters and/or supporting me in my research and academic life this time around included Michael Coleman, Bruce Dinges, Durwood Ball, Robert Wooster, and Margaret Jacobs. At the University of Oklahoma Press, Adam Kane, whose advice and suggestions I mostly managed to follow despite my chronic stubbornness, got the project under contract in record time and proved a wise and skillful editor. I also wish to thanks Stephanie Evans and Kelly Parker for their work. During the latter stages of this project, I have enjoyed much-appreciated financial support from the Finnish Cultural Foundation.

Last, but certainly not least, my wife, Sanna, and our two kids, Sofia and Juho, have provided a strong emotional base as well as constant and much-needed reality checks ensuring that history would not overtake my life completely. They accompanied me to Tucson for a memorable year. Among other things, they endured numerous hours and a few thousand miles in the car because of my obsession with visiting a plethora of historic sites and nature parks spread across the broad vistas of the Southwest. As a result, the kids have a box full of junior ranger badges, as well as a healthy skepticism toward any kind of ruins. I was then and I am now very proud of my family.

WARS FOR EMPIRE

INTRODUCTION

*Stealing horses was fun. I was not quite old enough to get in on that,
and how I envied those who were! It was usually the boys, too, who shot the
firearrows to set houses ablaze. I never saw that done but twice, though.
I did see many, many people killed. I wish I could forget it.
Even babies were killed; and I love babies.*
—Charlie Smith, Chiricahua Apache

*Repeated depredations have so thoroughly aroused the animosity of
the settlers that a war of extermination has in fact already begun.
Indians [Apaches] are shot wherever seen.*
—Joseph Pratt Allyn, associate justice, Arizona Territory

A region of deserts and rugged mountain ranges with little rainfall, the area the
United States claimed in the mid-1800s had an explosive history and an equally
volatile present. It was a borderlands, a space of multiple sovereignties characterized by intricate networks of amity and enmity between vibrant Hispanic
and Native American groups, foremost among them the many communities
identified by outsiders as Apaches. It was very much an unstable zone, where
diplomatic overtures, economic dependencies, social and cultural mixing, and
fiercely violent competition for resources and status had shaped the imperatives
of its residents long before the United States made its advances.[1]

American imperial rule leaped forward as the U.S.-Mexican War (1846–48)
brought the Southwest borderlands under nominal United States rule in a relatively short span of time. However, as highlighted recently by several scholars
studying empires and borderlands, resistance, accommodation, and violence
frequently disrupted and undermined the attempts to make borderlands into
bordered spaces.[2] Control of imperial borderlands proved habitually unstable,
elusive, and subject to constant negotiation. In the Southwest it took several
decades for the United States to advance its influence by diplomacy and violence

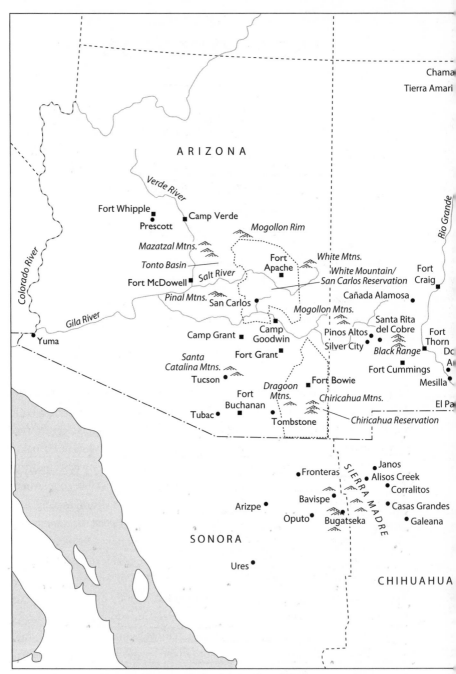

ARIZONA

Verde River

Fort Whipple
Prescott
Camp Verde

Mogollon Rim

Mazatzal Mtns.

Tonto Basin

Fort McDowell

Salt River

Fort Apache

White Mtns.

White Mountain/
San Carlos Reservation

Fort Craig

Rio Grande

Colorado River

Gila River

Pinal Mtns.

San Carlos

Mogollon Mtns.

Cañada Alamosa

Yuma

Camp Grant

Camp Goodwin

Pinos Altos

Silver City

Santa Rita del Cobre

Black Range

Fort Thorn

Santa Catalina Mtns.

Fort Grant

Fort Cummings

Mesilla

Tucson

Dragoon Mtns.

Fort Bowie

Chiricahua Mtns.

El Pa

Fort Buchanan

Tubac

Tombstone

Chiricahua Reservation

Janos

Fronteras

Alisos Creek

Corralitos

SIERRA MADRE

Bavispe

Casas Grandes

Arizpe

Oputo

Bugatseka

Galeana

SONORA

Ures

CHIHUAHUA

Chama
Tierra Amari

Do
A

The Southwest Borderlands. Map by Bill Nelson.
Copyright © 2017 by the University of Oklahoma Press.

4

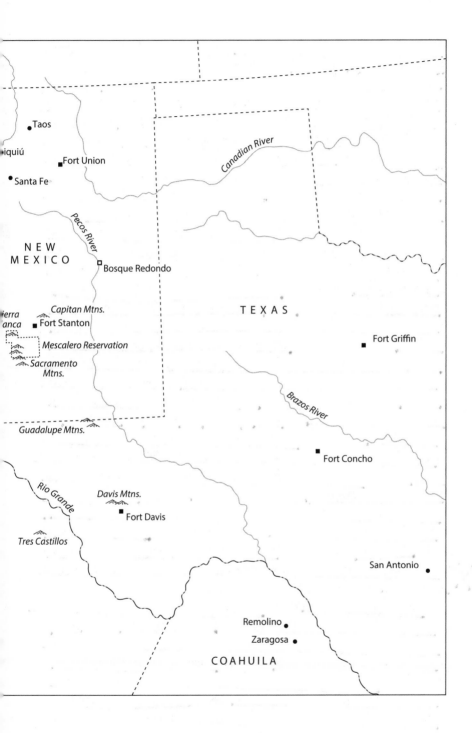

by containing, destroying, segregating, and deporting indigenous peoples it saw as competitors. Only the forced removal of the Chiricahua Apaches in 1886 brought something like a victory for the American regime.[3] It is the strands and shapes of violence comprising this splintered and intricate encounter between the United States and the Apaches that this book sets to chart. While these wars for the Southwest borderlands showcased the vulnerabilities and inconsistencies of empires, they represented an important act in the worldwide development of settler colonialism by which fluid multiethnic borderlands of plural sovereignty were turned into more hegemonic and racially stratified spaces where the modern state sought to categorize, order, restrict, and control peoples and land.[4]

Throughout North America, indigenous groups like the Cherokees, Creeks, Seminoles, Lakotas, Comanches, and others created strong cultures of violence and carved out opportunities and power for themselves in the junctures of imperial rivalries.[5] Some of the militarily more ingenious and astute peoples were known by whites as "Apaches." A fragmented, multilayered, and dynamic galaxy of extended families, local groups, bands, and clans sharing a similar culture and language, and, by and large, an interconnected living space that reached eastward from the intersection of the Gila and Salt Rivers beyond the Rio Grande, the Apaches had no overarching political system or social sphere that would have united them. They also had no army. Five main divisions of Apaches are usually identified in the mid-1800s: the Lipans, Jicarillas, Mescaleros, Chiricahuas, and Western Apaches. While some Apache communities sought peaceful accommodation from their early contact with the Anglos onward, many never got the chance. They either perished in the face of Anglo violence or endured diasporic lives of constant insecurity as borderlands refugees. Still other Apaches turned the invaders and their material property from potential threats into objects of personal and group empowerment. The actions of these cells of knowledgeable and skilled raiders brought the United States to a temporary standstill, exposed the limitations of its power, frustrated its efforts, and countered its attempts at domination.

How did the Apaches do it? Their small population base (all Apaches combined probably did not exceed ten thousand people in the mid-1800s) and diffused sociopolitical structures certainly disqualified any notions of achieving quantitative equality with the United States, whose population reached tens of millions. Instead, the Apaches honed the martial skills of the individual in a quest to outdo the American fighters man to man. Then, by relying on the methodically trained individual fighting for his own and his community's prosperity and position, the Apaches frustrated the United States by wisely avoiding potentially disastrous standing battles. As an alternative, they perfected a mode of combat reliant on fast and deft movement over the roughest terrain, expertise over their natural surroundings, command of skirmishes and ambushes, and meticulous preparation. Designed to shock and awe, the energetic hit-and-run operations of the Apaches and their equally swift evasive moves compelled those seeking their quick destruction and/or capitulation—federal (usually known as "regular") U.S. Army soldiers, Confederate troops, volunteer Californians, as well as local Anglo, Hispanic, and indigenous fighters—into protracted, ferocious, painful, and splintered wars.

Along with the Seminole conflicts in Florida, the U.S.-Apache wars constitute the longest military encounter in U.S. history. Although the confrontation involved parties that were highly uneven in their overall resources and manpower, on the ground the everyday realities proved often very unpredictable and confusing. The wars included multiple more or less interlinked theaters of operations (from West Texas to New Mexico and from central Arizona to northern Mexico) and shifting phases of intensity (from diplomacy to carnage). Moreover, not only were the boundaries between "us" and "them" ambiguous and fluid, but the struggle involved several communities and actors who seldom understood or valued the others' behavior and who held divergent agendas, methods, and notions regarding the parameters of violence. The wars took many shapes of violence, from raiding to massacre to destructive campaigns targeting whole societies, their material bases, and the environment.

Driven by perceptions of racial superiority and eager to replace the indigenous peoples and capture their lands, some whites yearned to exterminate the Apaches, while others wanted to subjugate, segregate, and civilize them. It seems that many local civilians and volunteers regularly favored more merciless variations of violence, whereas the regular army, which repeatedly experienced exceptional difficulties in finding or catching the Apaches, let alone in making them fight, undertook endless chases, quick skirmishes, as well as sackings of villages and material property as a less honorable but often necessary substitute for standing battles. What the often disharmonious Americans could agree on was that they wanted to end Apache raiding and military sovereignty. But their efforts were frequently compromised, and not only by a capable adversary. The U.S. Army tackled shortcomings in transportation and logistics, motivational issues, difficulties in acclimatizing, as well as incompatible and poor quality equipment. Too much manual labor and too little military training for the enlisted soldiers did not help either. Trying to legitimize their invasion and use of violence, as well as find an outlet for their dissatisfactions, scores of American fighters demonized the Apaches as cruel predators. Many military officers and soldiers also wanted to represent themselves as powerful empire builders who struggled against the elements in an unwelcoming region and liberated it from horrific Apache rule. Yet, behind their seemingly unwavering belief in their own superiority lay hidden tangible frustrations, painful insecurities, and agonizing fears of annihilation at the hands of their enemy. Countless disillusioned whites cursed their whole military experience in the borderlands. While more than a few soldiers deserted, others turned their attention away from war. The officers' attempts to transplant Victorian middle-class culture, leisure practices, and ideas of public space and domesticity to the borderlands—all designed to increase their sense of privilege—complemented their fighter identity and acted as a substitute for military success, proving a welcome diversion from the unpleasant and emasculating inadequacies exposed by a skillful enemy.[6]

An overview of the U.S.-Apache wars, this study describes a multicentered borderlands regenerated by war into a realm where the monopoly of violence was grasped and jealously guarded by a powerful empire. Connecting the U.S.-Apache wars to recent revisionist borderlands histories, it applies violence and military culture as its interpretive framework.[7] It holds that war and violence, paraphrasing a sentence from a classic work of military history, constitute expressions of culture determined by cultural forms and norms. This work pays close attention to expressions and modes of military ethos, training, leadership, organization, commitment, adaptation, force projection, rhetoric, and face of battle in order to more deeply understand how Apaches and the United States valued, approached, understood, and engaged in war and violence. Discussing how motives, goals, and methods differed and why, it traces the process of how one society was able to break the power of another and occupy its space.[8]

Importantly, a cultural approach to war and violence requires openness to understanding variety and complexity, and also non–Euro-Americans. For one, the types of violence as well as organizations of fighters are dynamic entities that change over time, and the course and final outcome of any violent conflict, no matter how uneven the sides appear in their level of technology, material resources, or demography, should not be seen as inevitable or preordained. If anything, the forty years it took for an industrial giant, the United States, to gain dominance over loosely connected raiders, the Apaches, offers ample evidence of that. Second, in this framework models that juxtapose the "real war" by Euro-American masses relying on industrial technology against guerrilla warfare by non-Europeans are utterly antiquated. So are claims that ascribe normativeness and dynamism to Euro-American war making and that describe indigenous modes of combat as stagnant and tradition-bound, ceremonial, or something akin to a game among individuals competing for acts and regalia of merit.[9] Regardless of how plausible an idea the "western way of war" might be, every violent conflict, armed force, and military culture deserves to be scrutinized on its own terms as well as in comparison with others.[10]

If the United States enjoyed unquestionable potential for conquering far-off lands, the Apaches in turn excelled in individual sharpness and speed, yet held no promise for the takeover of distant places. For Apaches, violence and armed conflict constituted localized efforts in finding ways to enhance individual and collective (family and local communities) material prosperity and status in relation to other borderlands communities. Wanting to minimize risks and avoid casualties at all costs, Apaches saw the relatively soft and secluded targets—tiny mining communities, small hamlets, isolated ranches, freight wagons, stagecoaches, and other travelers and rural residents—as the most enticing military objectives for extracting resources or taking revenge. Furthermore, as the indigenous, Hispanic, and Anglo neighbors acted both as suppliers of raiding booty and avid traders of it, it was central to safeguard an elusive balance between exploiting their neighbors successfully from year to year without driving them away, killing them off, or allowing them to become too strong so as to threaten Apache survival. Maintaining the relative weakness, both mental and physical, of the habitually incensed neighbors who typically both feared and hated the Apaches often required some killing. It also called for diplomacy as well as social mixing. In fact, killing was something of a secondary concern for Apaches. It was sometimes necessary for fulfilling short-term economic goals, for retaliating, for securing one's own safety, and for sustaining band, family, clan, or personal reputation and standing.

While the military influence of the Apaches relied on a reputation of fierceness that in turn was built on terrifying demonstrations of efficiency and on a historical record of excellence, enabling the Apaches' success was the premium given to individual military skills. Meticulous training from an early age not only reflected a community-wide effort of making all males superior fighters, but resulted in a cadre of highly ambitious, knowledgeable, and independent, as well as extraordinary fit, combatants whose sense of masculinity was closely linked to success in armed conflict. Organizing small units of fighters who knew the terrain and who were familiar with the climate, Apache outfits moved smoothly from their mountain homes, using the high ground as much as possible to conduct quick and sharp operations. Running or riding horses, their pace, skills, and knowledge often enabled the Apaches to advance undetected to their target area. Of course, it also helped that the borderlands were relatively sparsely populated. Flexible nonauthoritative leadership further encouraged individual initiative and the demonstration of personal skills. Kin ties, shared experience in training and in everyday life, and a system of apprenticeship for youngsters also knit the fighting groups together and instilled a spirit of camaraderie. Moreover, emphasis on planning, patience, preparation for different scenarios, escape plans, and prevention of losses (meaning that retreat or escape was not regarded shameful) made every combatant feel important and valued and increased the likelihood of success.

Still, the military muscle and ambition of the Apaches was also acutely restricted. Narrow extent of geographical knowledge of places more distant from the Southwest borderlands, limited aspiration for the acquisition of other peoples' real estate, exposed noncombatants, desire for accommodation, skeletal material base, shortcomings in manufacturing, unregulated military organization, lack of centralized leadership, heightened individual freedom, and shortage of manpower add to the list that explains why the Apaches were ill-suited for unremitting the military pressure often necessary for the conquest of large populated territories and/or distant lands. There is little doubt that regionally—within their own comfort zone—the Apaches were capable of organizing penetrating military expeditions. Some of their raids had the geographical reach of hundreds of miles, closing on central Mexico and reaching the shores of the Pacific Ocean on Sonora's coastline. But still, whether or not the Apaches were blocked by formidable powers, such as the Comanches, Apaches' operations proved limited, as a successful or unsuccessful military maneuver was always followed by a period of recuperation. Even when it seemed that some Apaches raided incessantly or fought constantly, they always tried to find opportunities for respites, seeing those as essential not only for personal welfare but for community well-being. Frequently, this meant hiding or attempting to open diplomatic talks with the enemy in order to draft a temporary peace and/or find opportunities for trade. Time and again it also denoted a retreat back home at the moment when a sufficient quantity of captured goods—that could be safely transported home, consumed by one's own community, or easily traded with outsiders—had been secured. Safe relocation of these goods was vital, as losing them on transport would undermine the success of the whole expedition and the reputation of those involved. Furthermore, raiding left the families of Apache fighters exposed, and thus an urgent return back home was essential to ensure the welfare of the community.

In the Apache society composed of fractious social units that changed over time and integrated new members, all men were equals and each had a heightened sense of self-rule and more than a few boasted massive egos. All military endeavors relied on willing fighters joined together, usually for a short time, to counter enemy advances, to advance a specific personal or community/kin cause, or to join a charismatic leader thirsting for glory and spoil. While the typical Apache fighter detested anything that even hinted at compulsory military service, he felt obligations and responsibilities toward his extended family, but any feeling of connectedness beyond the immediate community could be fleeting.[11]

Lack of compulsion enabled the Apaches to make their own choices. This and the fragmented sociopolitical structure rendered organizing large troop concentrations or long-lasting military extortions next to impossible. During the midcentury, only some influential leaders—men such as Mangas Coloradas and Cochise—managed to momentarily raise as many as one hundred or two hundred fighters. A more typical party of Apache fighters consisted of less than fifty and as few as half a dozen men. Furthermore, had all the Lipan, Jicarilla, Mescalero, Chiricahua, and Western Apache men joined together, which never happened or had even been planned, they could have fielded at the height of their numbers (in the 1800s) a force no larger than approximately two thousand fighters at best. In an age of mass armies and fast population growth in the western world, the Apaches' small population base, marred by high infant and child mortality rate and protracted warfare in their heartlands, posed further limitations on projecting military power.

The Apaches also did not possess (nor could they steal from their neighbors) the transportation facilities (boats, wagons, trains, or even horses) in such quantity that was necessary to move a large army of men and supplies over long distances. While Apaches could make bows, arrows, lances, and other useful weapons, they could not produce anything an army might need on an industrial scale. For obtaining rifles, pistols, and ammunition, as well as horses (the Apaches as a rule did not raise their own herds), trading or raiding remained the only options. Also, they could not raise enough food to feed any sizable military force. Hunting, gathering, and small-scale farming in the borderlands terrain did not support a big population, and Apaches frequently lived in cycles of plenty and near starvation. Habitually Apaches were forced to steal for subsistence, and thus raiding was dictated by hunger as well as being a means for the acquisition of material wealth, status, and social prestige.

Not all Apaches showed great elasticity and durability in their military effort. Often the Apaches engaged on survival mode, raiding outsiders when necessary but most of the time wanting to avoid those thirsting for their destruction. Furthermore, the lion's share of those Apaches who engaged in active military resistance against the Anglos wanted to abandon their endeavor relatively quickly. Numerous war-fatigued and suffering Apaches frequently sought diplomatic overtures. Many chose life on the reservations, or they were recruited into the U.S. Army, as these options were made available by the federal government in the 1870s. Reservations, even with all their suffering and cultural humiliation, constituted a better choice than armed conflict in the eyes of the Apache majority.

Moreover, while seeking to keep the Hispanic, indigenous, and Anglo intruders out of those mountain ranges their homes were situated in, and thus at arm's length, the Apaches did not seek territorial expansion of their own. Even when their raiding emptied hefty sections of rural areas, as happened, for instance, in northern Mexico in the 1840s, it was more an unintended, and unwanted, consequence of escalating violence than a planned outcome of a systematic military policy. Also, direct and/or permanent rule over subject peoples in the shape of administrative and legal apparatuses, occupying armies, or establishment of military bastions and settlements on other people's lands held little or no role in Apache thinking. Subservient villagers, compliant ranchers, and scared citizenry sufficed, as the Apaches had little ambition and equally modest need and incentive to bother themselves with the laborious and potentially volatile administration of subject peoples. Even visits into non-Apache communities carried an increased risk of violence (as amply testified by the massacres Apaches suffered in Mexican villages during some trade meets) and placed families in harm's way (either by relocating them amid the enemy or by leaving Apache homes in the mountains exposed to enemy combatants).

In an ideal world, the Apaches' neighbors would continue to produce the items Apaches coveted. Outsiders would also seek trade but would remain weak enough as to not threaten the Apaches. As one can imagine, finding or keeping this fragile stability in a world where a myriad of different communities competed for resources, markets, and power proved impossible, at least in the long run. Violence tended to spiral out of control and became a survival mechanism in an increasingly cutthroat rivalry. Ultimately, armed conflict wreaked physical and psychological havoc among the Apaches. For some, it nurtured a dangerous overconfidence in their own prowess together with equally risky dependency on the resources of others. The more tempting the rewards offered by raiding got and the more one's freedom as well as status and masculinity became grounded on raiding, the harder it was to stop for a number of Apaches despite mounting casualties, diminishing strength, and excruciating wear and tear.

In general, newcomers to their lands had always posed a complex dilemma for the Apaches. They not only represented a military threat but could deplete game and disturb the annual cycle of gathering of wild plants, both economic pursuits, depending on the Apache group, equally or more necessary as raiding. On the other hand, the coming of new peoples would make available to the Apaches fresh materials to steal, tempting targets to hit, and partners to trade with. Thus, fresh arrivals would occasion not only danger, suffering, and killing but also opportunities. It is this story, the coming of waves of outsiders and the violence and attempts to nationalize the Apaches' space that accompanied their arrival that this book tells.

PART I

CULTURES OF WAR

CHAPTER 1

ETHOS

*The people were poor. . . . Then they found out there were white men living
somewhere. They also discovered that white people had something to live on.
The Indians began to live by stealing. . . . Before this they were poor but now
they lived well. . . . They were happy. They said that stealing from those who
lived on the earth was a grand way to live. . . . They lived by going to war.*

—San Carlos Apache story

*We wint to Arizona
for to fight the Injins there;
We came near being made bald-headed,
but they never got our hair*

—Old army song

"I am the only one living to tell what happened to my people," recalled the adult
Mike Burns, born Hoomothyaa, a Yavapai-Apache. When he was a child, on
December 28, 1872, the family and kin of Burns had been massacred before his
very eyes at Arizona's Salt River, on the north side of the mouth of Fish Creek.
While much time had passed, the haunting tragedy remained fresh in his mind.
The U.S. Army had surprised and blasted a group of Kwevkepayas/Tontos (mixed
assembly of Yavapais and Apaches) who had huddled together for safety in what
they presumed was an impregnable cave protected by sandstone boulders high
above the riverbed. While bloody, the attack, known today as the Skeleton/Salt River
Cave Massacre, was not a random act. In fact, it was part of a meticulously planned
and ruthlessly executed military campaign against Western Apache and Yavapai
homes that lasted for two years. Its purpose was to end the sovereignty of these
Indians and force the survivors to live in reservations under American authority.[1]
     When the battle- and obliteration-hungry white troops, guided and aided by
O'odham auxiliaries, located the Indians at the cave, they, avoiding a frontal charge,
began to fire "bucketsful of led," Burns recounted, from a cliff to the direction of

the entrance. The soldiers actually did not see the Indians, but instead wreaked destruction wholesale. Ricocheting from the walls, the bullets shred to pieces any flesh they hit, whether man, woman, or child. "Not content with the deadly efficacy of bullets," Lt. John Bourke, one of the attackers, noted in his diary, some soldiers took position upon the crest of the overhanging bluff, from where they projected "large masses of rock which thundered down the precipice mangling and destroying whatsoever they encountered." Finishing the ghastly scene, the O'odhams smashed the skulls of the dying. "It was so horrid to look on," as those hit "could not be recognized as humans," Burns recalled of the moment when he faced the remains of his family. Burns had lost his father, grandfather, and two siblings. His aunt, uncle, and five cousins were also among the dead. Many others were slain as well, although no one knows exactly how many. The most commonly accepted number of Indians killed is 76, although estimates range anywhere from 57 to 225. What is certain is that not a single white soldier had died. None was even seriously wounded. The soldiers had also destroyed the indigenous material property, including baskets, hides, skins, and seeds. This was standard practice done so that the survivors could not continue living as independent people.[2]

As representatives of a military culture that favored big battles and tended to measure military success in the volume of carnage produced and in the totality of destruction inflicted on enemy forces, property, society, and environment, Anglo fighters had little doubt in their minds that the clash at Salt River had been a success as great as the generally ignominious borderlands wars could offer. Overlooking the butchery of helpless victims, the troops celebrated a great victory that signaled a bright future for the borderlands. Some of the attackers wrote, for instance, how their achievement represented "an important contribution" toward peace, as it was "the most signal blow ever received by the Apaches in Arizona." In many white minds, the slaughter at the cave stood as a much-needed lesson for the Apaches opposing the benign freedom's empire that the United States saw itself representing. On the other hand, coming from a military culture that linked war with community, individual status, the acquisition of material resources, and the outwitting of rival groups, Burns saw unnecessary and insensible killing of monumental proportions. Even years later, after having lived and been schooled in the Anglo society, he experienced severe difficulties in comprehending and processing the killing that had taken place at Salt River. In fact, Burns felt, "In all history no civilized race has murdered another as the American soldiers did my people in the year 1872. They slaughtered men, women, and children without mercy, as if they were not human."[3]

Freedom's Empire and the Southwest Borderlands

While their government made claims and shed blood over it, masses of white Americans were not drawn to the Southwest borderlands in the mid-1800s. Largely devoid of navigable rivers, water, and rich soil, it instead featured punishing heat, deserts, jagged canyons, and fearsome mountains. The region also lacked industry and infrastructure, such as telegraph lines or railroads, to attract investment. Moreover, the region's Hispanic (and Catholic) culture looked foreign, backward, and inferior, and thus far from ideal for integration in most Anglo eyes. In the view of many Anglos, the Southwest borderlands served only as a grueling passage to California or the terminus of the Santa Fe Trail. Topping the list of less-than-great selling points, however, was the considerable military power of the borderlands' independent Indians.[4]

Settler desires and perceptions deserve attention because demographics had fueled American settler colonialism in the cotton South, the Ohio region, the Kentucky frontier, and most of the places the young republic had coveted and conquered in the past. Aided by contagious diseases that killed Natives lacking immunity, massive movement of peoples and high birthrates, together with technology and market capitalism, thundered American settler colonialism onward. Throughout the 1800s, the continental empire functioned as one of the most massive "supplanting societies," which, according to David Day, is "a society that moves onto the land of another with the intention of making that land its own" in world history.[5]

But the primacy of demographic invasion did not apply in Arizona and New Mexico. Hundreds of thousands of white settlers did not overwhelm the Southwest in a couple of years, like they did in northern California, or even in a generation, as happened on much of the plains. In fact, for most of the U.S.-Apache conflict the borderlands remained mostly unpopulated by whites outside the small, frequently transient mining communities and the handful of predominantly Hispanic villages such as Tucson and Mesilla. Arizona had only 2,421 residents categorized as "white" (including Hispanics) in 1860 and 9,581 in 1870, of whom probably no more than 4,000 were Anglos, most of them U.S. Army soldiers. The number of whites with non-Hispanic parentage in New Mexico stood somewhere between two thousand and eight thousand people during the period between 1850 and 1870. Moreover, the first Anglo-built town of any permanence and a population in the thousands in Arizona had to wait until the mid-1860s with the birth of Prescott, which resulted from a mining boom on the very lands where Mike Burns and his community lived. There, modest growth happened a few years earlier than it did in Silver City (also at the hub of a mining area) and a touch later than it did in Las Cruces, the two principal Anglo-established urban centers in the Apache lands of southern New Mexico.[6]

If settler masses were initially less than tempted by the borderlands, those occupying the halls of government in Washington, D.C., or managing businesses in Boston, Philadelphia, New York, or Chicago did not necessarily find much appeal in the region either. For those who were even aware of the region, it stood for a remote outback, economically and politically irrelevant at least until remade—first, by the potential expansion of cotton agriculture and slavery and, second, after that plan turned sour, by the often prophesized yet generally unrealized mining bonanzas. Prior to the 1880s, it seemed that the borderlands warranted substantial national attention only when episodes of exceptional violence, like the 1871 massacre at Camp Grant or the grimness of Bosque Redondo in the mid-1860s, made a splash on the horizon of the reading public.

If it saw no value in the area, why did the United States invade and fight for four decades to gain control over New Mexico and Arizona? Why did the soldiers slaughter Mike Burns's family at Salt River? One possible answer is that expansion was what made America. The United States was born, manufactured, and maintained through conquest and war. A surging economy with a young and energetic population in the millions was held together and bestowed with social coherence and meaning through an identity built around violence and the taking of other people's lands.

Many Americans, among them Thomas Jefferson, saw that the assertive and relentless activities of white Americans contributed to an "empire for liberty" that extended the sphere of freedom through benign inclusion. Freedom's empire also embraced a vision for America's divine and undivided right to the continent. Made popular in the 1840s, this Manifest Destiny effectively fueled and camouflaged the violent expansion of a race-based regime of settlement, extraction, and exploitation set up on conquered lands. Manifest Destiny also refuted rival claims and stemmed off competition, whether indigenous or European. It additionally proved useful in enforcing a notion of shared destiny in a fractured federation. As pointed out by historian Carroll Smith-Rosenberg, the United States was chronically troubled by a fragile and unstable collective identity in need of constant securing and reaffirming in the face of immigration, the vexed question of slavery, and secessionism. Although competing visions of empire could tear America apart, as happened in the Civil War, empire could be the tool needed to unify diverse interests. Furthermore, together with the just-war ideology, fully developed in the United States during the War of 1812, it was possible to argue that, first, the United States does not commit aggression but only reacts to violent actions of others, and, second, that it does not only suppress the violent and unjust regimes of others (whether indigenous, Mexican, or Confederate) but saves the places it occupies by bringing freedom, civilization, and democracy to the "liberated." Expansion and its justifications proved so intoxicating that the mission to liberate seemed not merely America's right but, often, its duty. For those troubled by the devastation caused by conquest, the solution was to make the Indians clones of whites and thus legitimize empire through the civilizing mission.[7]

In some ways the takeover of the Southwest borderlands represented just the latest stage in a contest for North America that had been brewing for centuries. Precedent was certainly in the United States' favor when only its attempt to take Canada in the War of 1812 could be counted as a major failure.[8] While precedent made conquest a road easier to take and a choice more familiar and fathomable, it still does not adequately explain why U.S. troops marched on the streets of Santa Fe, New Mexico, in August 1846 or why they slaughtered the Burns family twenty-six years later in an effort to make the Southwest theirs. No one explanation actually does.

Gaining nearly half of Mexican territory, some Americans saw in the outcome of the U.S.-Mexican War a shameful exploitation of a weaker neighbor. Many did not expect or demand adding any more lands to the empire at the onset or at the end of the war. But for others the end to the war seemed fair as it brought a lot of land and eliminated Mexican claims to the western lands. Certainly it is difficult to ignore the sympathy for the cause of rebellious Texans and the thirst of southern politicians and plantation owners dreaming of a continent-wide cotton empire and slave economy. Still, equally critical were dreams of Pacific ascendancy, the bounty of "golden" California, and the potency of Asian trade. In part, Apache lands were taken because the needs of Pacific dominance called for a snow-free transcontinental passage, although such a passage would be operated by wagons, mules, and horses rather than by railroads for over thirty years.

And the personal influence and commitment of President James Polk certainly did matter. Imagining himself as a younger copy of Andrew Jackson, whom many saw as the leading expansionist of the realm in the early 1800s, Polk understood expansion as his life's mission. He felt very strongly that it would solve all America's problems, a sizable list that included, but was not limited to, unrestrained immigration, urban unrest, religious friction, slavery, and the supremacy of northeastern business elites. Finding answers to any of these issues in the Southwest borderlands would certainly escape the observation of most contemporaries. Even Polk, who, by obsessively micromanaging the U.S.-Mexican War, worked himself to death, realized that he got New Mexico and what would become Arizona as a bonus alongside the more desirable California and Texas.[9]

That the homelands of Mike Burns had fallen under the umbrella of freedom's empire resulted from a political compromise reached by an expansion-hungry yet internally fragile supplanting society. There had also been those Americans who wanted more or the whole of Mexico, while others had argued that Mexico had too many Mexicans, who, perceived as racially inferior, could potentially poison the white settler empire. While the few thousand Apaches did not threaten the demographic integrity of freedom's empire, they would pose serious questions to its military prowess.

Real War and Real Fighters

If empire corresponded with freedom in nineteenth-century American minds, then the concept of "real war" remained stubbornly linked to battles. For much of the 1800s, American soldiers fought in a succession of unconventional conflicts that transpired with nearly chronic frequency. Typically these engagements, especially in the trans-Mississippi West, included few major set-piece battles, instead blending guerrilla-type conflict with the targeting of societies and their material base. Still, in many minds real war continued to refer to conflicts against and between European powers and their offspring states. War also often meant the same as battles, a series of the latter constituting the former. Battle, in turn, ideally indicated a daylight clash between two armies on an open terrain fought until the other side was destroyed or submitted, surrendering or retreating honorably. Battle was a supposedly legitimate engagement practiced by civilized people. It was governed by rules of warfare that included white flags, respect for bodies of slain foes, and protection of prisoners and noncombatants. Battle represented the singular event where men were measured and things were decided, and where societies overpowered others or fell to oblivion. Napoleon's efforts had represented the contemporary standard of battle-centered warfare in the early century, but later the Civil War and the wars that led to German unification increasingly set the mark in industrial killing.[10]

In part because of their general fixation with battles and European warfare, the upper echelons of American military thinkers routinely failed to take seriously the unconventional wars their armed forces were consistently involved in.[11] Moreover, the War of 1812 had proven the vulnerability of coastal cities on the Atlantic and the Gulf against attack from the sea, and this led American military minds to pay attention to deterring maritime invasion. Shifting the emphasis more toward the offensive, the U.S.-Mexican War and the success of United States in it seemed to reinforce the notion that the nation's greatness would be decided in conventional wars, thus making the study and emulation of European armies ever more vital.

The Civil War brought to the table a new kind of emphasis on total war, a view that the concept covered not merely the destruction of noncombatants or enemy property but also total submission of enemy communities and the grinding down of its collective will by mastery over nature. Still, the Civil War had also made increasingly pervasive the notion that honor in warfare arose almost exclusively from the carnage of the battlefield, from the sound defeat of enemy combatants in the field of glory.[12] This, together with the pervasive belief that battles decide matters efficiently and quickly, ensured that the destruction of enemy's armed force in battle remained representative of American military thinking regardless of the theater of operations or the ethnicity/race of the adversary. This would become evident in the Southwest borderlands as well when officers and soldiers searched in vain for battles when none were forthcoming.

It is plausible that the fascination with battles and the long history of wars that helped and enabled expansion had produced a nationally celebrated military culture in the United States. Certainly the civilian militia, an ad hoc consortium of volunteer everymen defending their lives, families, communities, property, and freedom in the face of danger, was cherished and celebrated by many in the republic across class and political party lines. The citizen-soldier, in many minds, was something profoundly American, and the public image of the American fighting man deferred almost exclusively to the settler abandoning his regular trade temporarily for taking up arms when forced to do so. In contrast, the regular U.S. Army, the professional force unenthusiastically generated in 1784, remained disliked and its survival contested.[13] Many felt that professional soldiers were devoid of loyalties to local communities, while West Point–trained officers constituted an aristocratic elite at odds with the democratic principles of the Jacksonian era.[14]

Nonetheless, during and after the height of "Go-Ahead" (the slogan of the Jacksonian Era) expansion, the army carved out a special role for itself. It became the principal institution representing federal interests as the enforcer and facilitator of

American enlargement, in exploring, aiding emigrants, and constructing telegraph lines, roads, and forts, which often drew settlers and developed into new town sites. It also assisted in civilian law enforcement and later in the near destruction of the buffalo, the building of transcontinental railroads, and the suppression of urban labor unrest.[15]

All these tasks linked to the primary mission of military forces: the search for the monopoly of violence for the federal government in every section of the continental empire. In the trans-Mississippi West, it was more typically the army than the civilian volunteers that ensured that the government had no competition for sovereignty in those lands it claimed.[16] Despite all it did to facilitate expansion, or perhaps just because much of its fighting record stemmed from unsuccessful, irregular, and often controversial showings against independent Indians, the army remained hugely unpopular or irrelevant, depending on one's point of view. Post–Civil War southerners and Democrats saw it as a tool of northern occupation, while Republicans and northerners, trying to forget the horrors of armed conflict or, later, thinking that war was increasingly unlikely and irrational in modern times, tended to ignore the profession in arms. Swelling the army's disapproval ratings, many eastern humanitarians blamed the soldiery for unnecessary acts of brutality against the indigenous peoples, while westerners typically lamented the professionals as soft and ineffective in punishing and/or controlling the Indians.[17]

The army reputation was in such dire straits that enlistment was widely interpreted as an act of desperation by those unable to make it in civil society. Being a soldier not only was a far cry from the ideal of a self-supporting free white man but also presented a low among forms of wage labor. White enlisted men poorly fit in the parameters of independent manhood or those of free labor. Instead they were perceived as a group who had forfeited their birthright as free white men in exchange for small monetary price, dreadful living conditions, excessive manual labor, class tyranny, and life and work on equal terms with indigenous and black recruits. Furthermore, in a time of nativist upsurge, the soldier image was intimately linked with the dangers of urban squalor and immigration. There was no escaping the fact that white enlisted men generally came from two sources: the urban unskilled working class in the East and groups of typically uneducated and poor immigrants from Europe, especially Germans and Irishmen.[18]

More often than not, those who enlisted, usually in the urban centers of New York, Massachusetts, Pennsylvania, and the South (before the Civil War), needed a secure job, a chance to learn the ways of a new country, an escape from their troubled past, or an adventure if feeling alienated and restless in the increasingly urban, market-oriented, and/or industrial environment. To counter their public image, many of these men also assumed the roles of brave and honorable liberators who brought the light of American civilization to the western terrain. They wanted to matter in freedom's empire. In this the soldiers differed very little from their officers, although elsewhere the two groups had little in common. Coming from fairly established, often rural or small-town backgrounds, the majority of officers were native-born, and a good number could introduce themselves as sixth- or seventh-generation Americans. Believing that they embodied not just intelligence and genteel manners but honor and courage, officers, together with their wives, who typically had backgrounds similar to their husbands', aspired to lead the civilizing of the trans-Mississippi area personally by transplanting eastern middle-class lifestyles. Despite this, the reputations of officers were often dubious, giving rise to accusations of elitism, erudition, reclusiveness, incompetence, and even cowardice, drunkenness, and excessive use of violence.[19]

While in many ways it represented a microcosm of U.S. society with its class and race divisions, the army had a foreign feel to it. It was also linked in public to images of societal trash (enlisted men), elitism (officers), danger to democracy, and mishandling (brutality/softness) of indigenous peoples. Fighting in the borderlands would often make the army more familiar with frustration, failure, and misery than with military glory or any sense of accomplishment.

Raiding, Privilege, and Status

In public imagination, Apaches were, and remain, closely associated with war and violence. For instance, Hollywood Westerns usually depict Apaches as a fierce and brutal warrior race with killing and looting in their blood.[20] Rather than Apaches being innately more prone to violence and mayhem than any other group, it was instead a combination of geopolitical context and the cultures of the various Apache communities that shaped their military practices.

Calling themselves Inde or N'de (people), the Apaches originated, according to scholars, from the Arctic regions of modern Canada, arriving to the Southwest borderlands and southern plains sometime before the early 1600s. Most likely their migrations occurred piecemeal in small groups over extensive periods of time and over various routes (Rocky Mountains, Great Plains, Great Basin).[21] Numbering approximately ten thousand people in the mid-1800s the Apaches spread their influence over massive territory. They lived east of the convergence of Salt and Gila Rivers and the White Mountains and the Tonto Basin in the proximity of the Mogollon Rim. They covered both flanks of the Sierra Madre in northern Sonora and Chihuahua from where their impact stretched to Coahuila, West Texas, and northern New Mexico. Their neighbors included the Yavapais, Maricopas, Akimel O'odhams (Pimas), and Tohono O'odhams (Papagos) in the west and Mexican settlements in Tucson and the Santa Cruz Valley, along the Rio Grande, around San Antonio, as well as in Sonora, Chihuahua, and Coahuila. Apaches also shared topography with the Hualapais, Navajos, Utes, and Pueblos, while the empire of the Comanches was on their eastern horizon.

While it is easy to exaggerate the controlled and coordinated aspects of U.S. war making, the fact remains that the United States mainly relied on its federal army, a hierarchical and centralized organization, when it came to armed conflict. The Apaches, on the other hand, did not have a national, or tribal, agency specializing in violence. Nor did they function under centralized leadership, but as splintered and autonomous cells. Even the autonomous cells did not include armies, but various configurations of ad hoc volunteers. While Euro-Americans often wished to see a static group of people, an amalgamated Apache tribe, nation, and race, there in fact existed fragmented and dynamic communities that constantly integrated new members and lost old ones to war, captive raiding, and social dissent. Members of neighboring Apache communities usually, but not always, deferred from raiding each other, recognized certain common bonds, and occasionally joined together for military operations. Each local community and band inhabited its own territory, had its informal, elected leaders, and made its own choices when it came to war and peace. In fact, each man made the decision for himself.[22]

Hammered by the Comanche invasion on the plains and halting the northward advance of New Spain, numerous Apaches had also lived in comparative harmony and in close proximity to the Spanish for a generation in the late 1700s and early 1800s. During this era, many got used to Spanish food, livestock, clothing, and other supplies while adjusting to the idea that the Spanish would pay them in exchange for peaceful coexistence. But after Mexican independence, the Apaches woke up to the gradual realization that peace establishments, appeasement, and free rations and gifts were being substituted with treachery and war, which coexisted with localized peace pacts and vigorous contraband trade. For much of the late-1830s and 1840s, Sonora and Chihuahua shook under pressure from Apache raiders, mainly Chiricahuas, but also Mescaleros and Western Apaches, who in turn dodged soldiers and civilian fighters from different Mexican communities and the multiethnic outfits of scalp hunters and slave raiders the Mexican state authorities supported.[23]

Of all the Apache communities, those identified as Chiricahuas, with a population of fewer than three thousand persons in the mid-1800s, retained their military autonomy the longest and most intensely. The homeland of the eastern band, the Chihennes, stretched from the Rio Grande westward to the Mimbres River and the Black Range. The Bedonkohes, a tiny band, lived west of the Chihennes in the Mogollon Mountains, while the Chokonens saw the country around the Chiricahua Mountains and the Dragoon Mountains in today's southeastern Arizona as theirs. To the south along the northern reaches of the Sierra Madre, on the Mexican side of the international line, lived the fourth band, the Nednhis.[24]

If the Chiricahuas held the southern rim of Apacheria through their active raiding in northern Mexico, the exposed northeast was where the Jicarillas, numbering approximately four hundred to one thousand people in the mid-1800s, resided. They had at that time two bands, the Llaneros (eastern/plains) and Olleros (western/mountains), which drew members from an estimated twelve local groups. Jicarilla territory consisted of northeastern New Mexico, southern Colorado, and the Texas Panhandle, where they surrounded the islands of Hispanic and Pueblo Indian residences between Colorado, and the Arkansas River in the north, Tierra Amarilla and Chama in the west, Las Vegas and Santa Fe in the south, and the Canadian River in the east. Having witnessed the legal evaporation of their land base through Mexican land grants and being hard-pressed on all sides by the Utes, the Mexicans, and especially the Comanches, the Jicarillas proved extremely vulnerable. In the 1830s, Anglo trappers also started operating in the Arkansas River region, arming the Plains Indians in exchange for pelts and depleting the game to such an extent that the Jicarillas faced starvation. Game was in fact nearly gone when the United States annexed the region.[25]

Mescalero Apaches, with their heartlands between the Rio Grande and Pecos River in southern New Mexico and in western sections of Texas near El Paso (Franklin), were comprised of widely scattered people totaling perhaps as few as 700 or as many as 2,500 souls. Some bands resided in the Davis Mountains, raiding on the routes between San Antonio and El Paso; others made the Sierra Blanca and the Guadalupe and Sacramento Mountains their homes. The Mescaleros, like the Jicarillas, also had a long record of incorporating exiled Lipans and other Apaches driven out of Texas and the plains by the Comanches.[26]

Harassed by numerous enemies—a list that included the Comanches, Texas Rangers, U.S. Army, and Mexican soldiers, as well as the Seminoles and Kickapoos removed from points east—the Lipans constituted of a broad assortment of peoples who represented the remainders of a once-powerful Apache consortium. Totaling more than five hundred people in the 1850s, Lipans had fragmented from two main divisions, Ypandes (Plains Lipans) and Ypandes Pelones (Forest Lipans), into ten to fourteen bands and several small factions. They occupied areas on the lower Pecos River, the vicinity of San Antonio, and in northern Coahuila. As a result of their geographical position, long history of conflict with Plains tribes, and incorporating Apache immigrants, Jicarilla, Mescalero, and especially Lipan cultures exhibited clear Plains customs. They, for example, lived not only in dome-shaped brush lodges (wickiups), as did the more western Apaches, but also had teepees. Jicarillas, Mescaleros, and Lipans were also used to regularly traversing to the plains to hunt buffalo and, more than the western Apache groups, relied on horses for transportation. One Mescalero noted how they "were not like the Chiricahuas, who could do without horses. We were accustomed to having them." The Lipans reportedly also counted coup, following a military fashion adopted by many equestrian Plains peoples.[27]

By the time of American occupation, the Western Apaches formed the largest Apache major group, with 4,500 to 6,000 people. The two bands of the White Mountain Apaches, the Eastern and Western, occupied the country from the White Mountains over the Gila Mountains to the Pinaleno Mountains in the south. To the west of them resided the three Cibecue bands, the Carrizo Creek, Cibecue Creek, and Canyon Creek bands, who ranged north of the Salt River beyond the Mogollon Rim and to the Mazatzal Mountains in the west. The third Western Apache group, the San Carlos Apaches, was made up of the Aravaipa, Pinal, Apache Peaks, and San Carlos bands, whose lands were located northward of the Santa Catalina Mountains, in the proximity of Tucson, on both sides of the San Pedro and Gila Rivers.

On the western edge of Apacheria were the Tonto Apaches, also categorized as Western Apaches, who lived from the San Francisco Mountains to the Verde River and from the Tonto Basin to the Salt River. Ethnologist Grenville Goodwin recognized four bands, the Fossil Creek, Bald Mountain, Oak Creek, and Mormon Lake bands, among the Northern Tontos. Among the Southern Tontos he identified seven different bands, all which, except for one, the Mazatzal, Goodwin merely numbered. The Tonto communities drew especially close to the two Yavapai bands closest to them, the Wipukepas and Kwevkepayas, with whom they engaged for raids and reprisals—revolving around captives, food products, and livestock—against their O'odham neighbors.[28] Layered across the basic territorial units, the Western Apaches had clans (other Apaches did not) that formed a cross strata of relationships, a far-flung web that ran through the several local groups, bands, and groups. While there existed no clan government, all members of the same clan were regarded as relatives, and clan members were expected to help each other by military and other means in time of crisis.[29]

In contrast to the U.S. way of war, direct control over subject peoples, possession of new lands, and annihilation of enemy forces were largely irrelevant to the Apaches. Splintered into autonomous localized cells with fluctuating pedigrees of military strength, the Apaches, through demonstrations of violence, sought to make the most of the resources of those around them. By the time of U.S. invasion, their military ethos was shaped by a blend of intimacy and cutthroat competition, especially with the Comanches, Mexicans (including the scalp hunters on their payroll), and O'odhams, and by deeply embedded and tangled linkages between revenge, resource acquisition, and notions of status and manhood inside the Apache communities.

Need initiated much of Apache raiding. Pure subsistence mattered more as the presence of outsiders and their animals hindered the gathering cycle and as civilians and army officers, of whom many harbored a perpetual appetite for game, depleted fauna in various sections of the borderlands. For example, the destitute Jicarillas in the late 1840s and early 1850s and the Chihenne band of the Chiricahuas and many Western Apaches a decade later had little choice but to raid to avoid perishing from hunger. Still, raiding was not driven by need alone.[30]

Significantly, many in the different Apache communities viewed raiding others as their right. This type of mentality is exemplified by Daklugie, the son of Chiricahua leader Juh, who felt that, as the Mexicans had invaded their homes and killed their deer and introduced herds of cattle and horses, the Apaches were entitled to take something back. "Why should they [Chiricahuas] go hungry with abundance of food in their own land," Daklugie argued when interviewed by historian Eve Ball. He also added, "Didn't the Mexicans owe them a livelihood?" Putting their visions into actions, some Apaches did not merely raid but collected toll payments from outsiders traveling through their country. Some also made highly one-sided or exploitative deals, frequently backed by threat of violence, with traveling parties. More commonly, in the words of one Western Apache, they made "a living off" Mexicans and simply took "what we wanted out of them [Mexicans], and used it for ourselves." As for white Americans, they often represented just the latest infringing group expected to pay for their transgressions. When Americans came "into our country . . . we raided" them, "took their horses, and cattle, and drove them back to our homes." Sharing his views, one Mescalero explained, "The Mexicans and others work for us" and largely existed just to satisfy Apache needs.[31]

From the standpoint of many Apaches, their Mexican, indigenous, and Anglo neighbors—the villages, farms, ranches, wagon trains, stagecoaches and stations, mining camps, and even military posts—amounted to something like a vast chain of supply stores. These borderlands supermarkets were open for Apaches to acquire food and other materials from any branch store most convenient for them. They could use the materials for personal consumption or for future trading at one of the other store locations.

In all, Apaches showed much restraint as they sought economic gain from the diverse supply spots that developed on the borderlands. A careful reading of texts written by settlers and travelers, often frightened people who tended to portray the Apaches as fiendish predators, show how much of the Apache focus was on livestock and material property. Of course the Apaches could and did kill people, but that seems often to have been a secondary concern. Some sources suggest that during their raids into Mexico the Apaches allowed those ranchers and communities who cooperated with them to live unharmed and to continue providing supplies in the future. The Apaches did not typically take all the herds but rather took care to leave enough horses or cattle so that the Mexicans could raise more for them. While hardly an advocate for the Apaches, the *Weekly Arizonian*, a Tucson newspaper, in 1869 aptly captured the logic behind the Apache way of war. An Apache, being "quite satisfied with appropriating whatever property we [Anglos and Mexicans] possessed, did not consider it sound policy to destroy a people who so largely ministered to his support."[32]

Scholars usually point out that Apaches regarded raiding and warfare as clearly distinct activities. The former primarily targeted economic gain, and the latter revolved around revenge and taking of lives. While there existed differences in the kind of objectives Apaches set for military operations and while the size of the war and raiding parties frequently varied (war parties were usually bigger), to draw too rigid a boundary between raiding and war does not represent reality. Both activities were often meant to bring the "supply stores," the neighbors, back in line rather than wipe them out and thus secure and boost Apache prestige and reputation. Also, countless times the purposes and methods of raiding and war not only merged but fueled each other. If the opportunity represented itself, war parties could capture property as easily as those on a raid could, if necessary, kill. In the real world raiding easily led into war when outraged Mexicans, O'odhams, or Anglos sought an immediate or postponed payback by launching or sponsoring military expeditions or bounty hunters against the Apaches. The O'odhams, for instance, saw that Apache raiding deprived their power, and they had to reclaim it by killing Apaches. Furthermore, if the Apache raiding party suffered casualties or if their enemies struck back, this usually called for payback in Apache hearts and minds. Avenging the deceased and salvaging the honor of the family, clan, and/or band required action, sometimes in the form of blood vendetta, which did not exclude seizure of enemy property. Retaliatory raids both by and against Apaches often failed to distinguish the specific band or village responsible, the Apaches imparting permanent enemy status to many of their neighbors. Permanent enemy status, however, should not be interpreted too rigidly, for it did not exclude trade, peace talks, alliances, or temporary truces. And it certainly did not diminish the Apache quest for capturing quantifiable goods.[33]

It is true that a sizable part of Apache economy remained grounded on hunting of game, gathering of wild plants, and, with the exception of some Chiricahua bands, farming. Still, there is no denying that, when outsiders introduced new goods and markets within their reach, some of the Apaches developed a growing desire for these things they could not or did not bother to produce themselves but chose instead to obtain from their neighbors either by trading or raiding. The most coveted articles included cattle, mules, horses, clothing, weapons, ammunition/powder, various manufactured items, corn and other food products, and human captives.[34] Raiding, daily life, and military power became interlinked, as the various products obtained from others not only helped to make the everyday function but opened trade possibilities. The Apaches produced few goods of any market value, and the bounty of their raids enabled them to participate in trade networks. This offered another impetus to raiding, aside from its cultural meaning and the need to check the power of rivals.[35]

Beyond their value as commodities, the goods taken in raids were also key symbols of individual success, prosperity, character, and manliness. Oftentimes the minds of ambitious Apache men were preoccupied with, and riddled with mixed feelings of admiration and envy of, each other's stock of horses, selection and quality of clothing, or the newest rifle. Each man yearned to possess equal or superior items to his peers.[36]

But while individual glory and achievement was continuously at stake, service for the community counterbalanced personal accomplishment. More often than not a man went to raid/war not just to bring back material wealth for his own use; as a rule, he was expected to give much of the bounty to his extended family and to also generously distribute goods to those within his community who were in need. While widows received help crucial to them, those fighters who were incompetent, temporarily injured, or permanently disabled could claim a cut in the raided property. Charity, the form of giving to others (even to such extent that one had little left for himself) that fostered group solidary, was one of the most potent trademarks of individual greatness in Apache minds. Appropriated goods were routinely distributed both privately and in elaborate ceremonies in which the givers were praised for their generosity and the receivers showed their gratitude and humility. Still, living on charity was not always acceptable in an Apache society that valued individual skill. If an otherwise fit man lacked in effort or failed routinely in pursuits of war, he was considered no good. However, similar judgment applied if a man was too selfish and failed to adequately distribute his wealth (and in that manner display his wisdom, bigheartedness, and good character).

As the Apaches formed no monolithic political entity, it should come as no surprise that the prevalence and significance of raiding and war varied over time and between distinct Apache communities. For example, for the Chiricahuas, military activity more or less grew to dominate daily life; however, for several Western Apache communities, raiding resembled more a seasonal activity of secondary importance. The reasons for the differences were multiple and varied. Chiricahua residency was closer to Spanish/Mexican settlements in Sonora and Chihuahua, and their proximity to the southern overland routes might account for their proclivity for raiding. Militarization had its impacts on the community. One outsider who worked on the Chiricahua Reservation in the 1870s remarked, "A quite number of them [Chiricahuas] had no remembrance of when their tribe had been at peace."[37]

The Western Apache homes in today's central Arizona as well as those of the Mescaleros in today's southeast New Mexico were stretched thin over expansive territory broken into deep valleys and high timbered ranges with limited rainfall. Both were still relatively rich in diversity. The land with its many streams allowed families sedentary lives, farming corn, pumpkins, squash, and other crops. Also, the abundance of wild plants, especially mescal, acorns, and juniper berries, enabled short-distance subsistence excursions in search of specific food resources in their most optimal locations and seasons. It is estimated that domesticated and wild plants contributed nearly two-thirds of the Western Apache diet, with hunting offering much of the rest. Some bands, such as the Pinals and Aravaipas of the San Carlos group, for example, banked on farming, cultivating plots along streams using ditch irrigation and living at their farms for half the year. Unlike the Chiricahuas, of whom the Chihennes alone lived in areas suitable for planting crops, many of the Western Apaches were largely self-sufficient, at least until miners and soldiers demolished their subsistence base from 1864 onward. Still, most of the Western Apaches intermittently, if not unremittingly, raided the O'odhams and the Mexicans long before this happened.[38]

If there were differences among the Apache communities, it also seems that the Apaches were set apart from their indigenous neighbors. Understandably the peoples who shared the borderlands forged divergent military cultures that reflected varying sociopolitical structures and differing reactions to the dynamic world of violence around them. The valley-dwelling horticultural neighbors and enemies of the mountain-dwelling Apaches—the Akimel O'Odhams and the small community of Maricopas, refugees from the Colorado River area who over time more or less integrated themselves with the Akimel O'odhams—lived in permanent villages along the confluence of the Salt and Gila Rivers. For their part, the Tohono O'odhams, who mixed small farms with hunting and gathering of wild food, occupied the heart of the Sonoran Desert in and around Tucson and Tubac. While the O'odhams were connected by a loose web of kinship and trade, they shared no unified political structure, and many of the Tohono O'odhams lived for much of the year dispersed in small groups organized around the extended family. Thus while the environment and lifestyle set the O'odhams apart from the Apaches, their social organization makes them somewhat similar.

The O'odhams also displayed a keen interest in the metal goods, cattle, and other items the Spanish introduced but never grew dependent on Spanish goods or saw raiding as the most feasible option for obtaining them. Also, while the O'odhams accepted war as a fact of life, favored the surprise attack, served in Spanish presidios, allied with the Anglos, and responded fiercely when Apache raiders charged their homes, fighting was only superfluously connected to material resources while being significant, yet not integral, in defining honorable manliness. Except for trade in captives, all stolen enemy property was often burned. Killing Apaches mercilessly when they had the chance, the O'odhams viewed combat primarily as a contest over spiritual domination or mental supremacy. Carrying strong religious meaning, war was more tightly regulated for O'odhams than it was for Apaches. For instance, those who killed Apaches, or touched an Apache body or belongings, were expected to undergo a purification ritual that, reportedly, could last four days. Only after that could they return to their village, where the others had been celebrating war success with dancing every night. Through the ritual, the O'odham warriors could claim the power of the dead Apache and rise to the status of *siakam*—"Enemy Killer."[39]

Overall, the gradual and uneven militarization of Apache society developed hand in hand with a growing realization (which proved a disillusion) that the Apaches could take from their neighbors what they wanted. Militarization not only led to a mounting casualty rate but also overuse of their Hispanic, indigenous, and Anglo neighbors. As the Mexican population withdrew southward in the 1840s due to Apache (and Comanche) raiding, the Apaches had to make longer and longer trips to get what they wanted.[40] While the Mexican retreat could be interpreted as Apache triumph and while the growing presence of American traders substituted for the weakening Mexican supply, scalp hunters and Mexican efforts to annihilate the Apaches were alarming signs that too big a raiding appetite could prove costly in the long run. Further cause for alarm included the obligation—as stipulated under Article XI of the Treaty of Guadalupe Hidalgo, ending the U.S.-Mexican war in 1848—for the United States to quell cross-border raiding by military force. While Article XI was officially swept aside with the Gadsden Purchase, through which the United States acquired areas south of the Gila River in 1853, the attitude held by the majority of invading Anglos regarding land use and military competition was little impacted. In their minds, Apache raiding constituted a serious threat to the future of the borderlands and was absolutely unacceptable. In fact, freedom's empire would not tolerate any competition or indigenous sovereignty. For white Americans, independent and militarily powerful Indians proved incompatible with the kind of society and economy they sought to establish. Applying various strategies of resistance and accommodation, from 1848 onward different Apache communities struggled in upholding their independence in a world where violence and the machinations of empire gradually engulfed them.

CHAPTER 2

BODY

The men used to be able to run fast like deer.
—Harvey Nash-kin, White Mountain Apache

*After a walk of ten or twelve miles in the sand we experienced
a soreness of feet and pain in the upper legs. Halt was given and
we dropped exhausted under the shade of a tall cottonwood tree.*
—Cpl. Emil A. Bode, U.S. Army

In 1886 Lt. Robert K. Evans published an article in the *Atlantic Monthly* criticizing the United States' performance in the wars against the Apaches. Along with complaints about eastern sentiment's influence on tactics, Evans also noted, "On the warpath, the relative speed of the Indian and the soldier is three to one." Among other things, this implied an unwelcome and potentially embarrassing disclosure: Apaches were in much better physical condition than the white soldiers and thus, as superior athletes, might also constitute superior fighters when pitted man against man. Evans, however, immediately made it clear that this was "no aspersion on the efficiency of our cavalry. They are ready and willing to do all that brave men can do." It was just that, Evans explained, "the task imposed upon them is simply impossible. I do not believe that there is a body of cavalry in the world that can keep in sight of a raiding party of Apaches." Inadvertently or not, Evans skirted the question of how the U.S. Army prepared its men. Nowhere in his detailed article did Evans assess in any detail why exactly the U.S. trooper failed to outdo the Apache raider. Intentionally or not, he declined to acknowledge the relevance of questions pertaining to physical conditioning and exercise.[1]

Men's Bodies: Workers and Gentlemen

When considered from the perspective of training, it seems that not just Evans but practically the whole army was afflicted by disinterest, or what one might call a short institutional memory, a prodigy of its general disinterest toward unconventional warfare. Lessons learned, for instance, in the decades-long Seminole wars in Florida—tactical flexibility, converging columns, attack on enemy food supply, war of attrition, value of good reconnaissance, knowledge of terrain, and the habituation and preparing of men to meet the circumstances—saw the light of day in the borderlands usually only in the often inconsistent trials by individual commanders, but failed, in general, to make the manuals and had no great impact on the education of officers.[2]

Excluding those who started their careers as Civil War volunteers, most officers were graduates of the military academy at West Point. There the curriculum relied on a technical base, infused with liberal arts, French, and drawing (practical for map making). There was also some ordnance and gunnery but very little tactics or strategy. Stunningly, no history of any kind was taught. When it came to the graduates, engineers represented the cream of the crop, while line officers (cavalry, infantry, and artillery) stomached a less esteemed standing. To those expected to fight the independent Indians, the academy offered little of practical value on the theaters of operations, military life, or indigenous warfare. Instead the graduates were imbued with mathematical and mechanical thinking. They also shared a rigid belief in hierarchy among men and an equally stern devotion to the rule of discipline. Machinelike, emotionless, and authoritarian: one could easily see that the ideal graduate did not necessarily occasion the kind of mentality best suited for dynamic, fast-paced, and unpredictable borderlands warfare.[3]

It seems that few people seriously questioned the academy's shortage of preparation. Yet, for a fresh cavalry or infantry officer, who often spent much of his professional life on the outskirts of the expanding continental empire, the realization that he was expected to gain command of Indian fighting in the field must have looked like a daunting proposition. Those heading toward the Southwest borderlands frequently admitted that they based their knowledge of the potential enemy mainly on wild rumors and wilder imaginations. A typical newcomer envisioned the Apaches as racially inferior yet dangerous bloody savages driven by their thirst for white blood.[4]

These novices' knowledge of the area of operations seldom proved any more sophisticated. In fact, many evidenced near complete ignorance of the Southwest, some being unable to locate it on the maps they had. Many also dreaded the region beforehand. For example, upon entering the Southwest in the early 1870s, a young officer and his wife, having heard some turbulent stories of the place, regarded Arizona as "dreaded" and "unknown land." While some young officers could try to gain information from their more experienced peers in advance or en route, for others personal study of published journals and narratives of explorers and travelers was a way to try to fill the gaps left by formal education. Unfortunately, most officers, in order to strengthen their identity as highly cultured people, preferred reading literary classics and European history in place of gaining local knowledge.[5]

While training, together with discipline, constituted the key factors separating enlisted soldiers from armed civilians, the army had no recruit training program in operation until the 1880s. The typical private, who usually held no previous military experience, found his initiation at a recruit depot customarily short, lasting only from a few days to a matter of months. If the private was lucky, he might witness or participate in some basic drills. More typically, if the average regular was taught anything at all, it was instruction in the basic principles of personal cleanliness and military hierarchy, obedience, and subordination. From now on, whether he liked it or not, the fresh enlistee occupied a minor position in the lower rungs of a deeply stratified community. It is indicative that while little attention was paid to physical fitness at the depot, according to historian Don Rickey, "guardhouse sentences and fines were liberally meted out" for any misdemeanor. By and large, this system assured that the recruits arrived to their assigned posts in the empire's outskirts with superficial or no knowledge of their potential indigenous enemies and no more skilled in fighting and in no better shape than they had been on the day of enlistment.[6]

From 1848 to 1886 the army was spread to numerous (175 in 1870) posts averaging from one hundred to four hundred residents each. The post and its immediate vicinity represented not just a temporary home for the men who had signed up for soldier work but also, in theory at least, the place where they would be molded into fit, motivated fighters. However, this was seldom the case. For anyone perusing military texts from this period, the lack of attention given to physical advancement becomes obvious very quickly. When the workout regimen of troopers is discussed, it is customarily for some rare officer or soldier contemplating how most of his peers regard exercise altogether unnecessary. Even those who seemed interested in improving the physique of the troopers were not always really so. For example, in 1884 when the post commander at Fort Bowie, Arizona, suggested that money should be allocated for the construction of a gymnasium, his primary concern was to benefit the enlisted men, but not to make them into fitter fighters. Instead, the post commander sought to provide licit leisure activities to replace the commonplace drinking, gambling, and other vices. The gymnasium was in fact part of a larger construction plan that entailed a bowling alley and an amusement room as well.[7]

It is safe to assume that dress parade, guard duty, and the weekly inspection were unlikely to considerably increase the soldiers' skills in borderlands warfare. Usually, nobody led the foot soldiers on long-distance runs or spent the hours needed to teach cavalrymen who seldom had even seen horses in civilian life to become experts in horsemanship. Also, marred by a shortage of ammunition combined with disinterest, many of the soldiers did not fire their weapons a dozen times a year and thus did not know how to use their tools of trade effectively. Drills were meant for the soldiers as a unit to learn mechanical and synchronized movement on command. Learning to move in line or performing stationary exercises proved inadequate in preparing the individual soldier to physically compete with the Apache fighters. Furthermore, being normally drilled by sergeants and corporals or the greenest and most enthusiastic young lieutenants, soldiers quickly realized that most of their leaders felt indifferent or were in too poor a shape to cope with drills. According to Capt. Charles Morton, it was common knowledge that many of the more senior officers were not fit enough to lead the drills. As a result, according to Morton, those "brave and generous gentlemen and strict disciplinarians turned cantankerous when it came to the subject of drilling." Revealing the sorry state of affairs, the evidence represented in a 1870s hearing before a House subcommittee verified that half of the garrisons in the country had no drills at all.[8] It was not until the 1890s, after the wars against indigenous peoples had ended, that athletics gained wider popularity in the army. Then the reduction in army posts relieved soldiers of much of the labor that occupied their time.[9]

However, what constituted necessary labor often did so because the officers, and their wives, wished their lifestyle, homes, and posts on the western terrain to live up to eastern middle-class standards. Socially somewhat marginal and lacking strong political support in the East, and also forced to fight frustrating and potentially emasculating wars, officers, rather than develop a rigorous training regimen to best the Apaches in guerrilla combat, strived for a sophisticated leisure life, personal avoidance of manual labor, and remodeling of the often rugged forts—public space and domestic realm—into islands of civilization, clones of eastern genteel life. All this served to improve their social standing both in the borderlands and among the eastern middle class. Genteel lifestyle and the gentleman image also functioned as a useful substitute when combat success proved elusive.[10]

Frequently officers and their ladies in the borderlands fell short of the kind of results they had set out to achieve, but this did not mean that enlisted men had it any easier. Instead of schooling in combat skills and working out to improve their muscle strength and endurance, the regulars spent the bulk of their time building and repairing officers' homes and serving as domestic help for officers and their families. They also tended post gardens and constructed various irrigation, landscaping, and other projects. Manual labor proved such a persistent element of enlisted men's lives that it defined their daily routine in the posts. Even in temporary camps that guarded strategic locations along the border, the officers made the soldiers perform all kinds of chores. "The man who enters the United States Army," one soldier who served in the Southwest wrote, "will find that he works as hard as any day laborer who ever lived, and often harder." It is little surprise that enlisted men, of whom many felt cheated, reacted forcefully to their daily lot as laborers and handicapped Apache hunters through widespread desertion, heavy drinking, and reckless gambling.[11]

This labor did not necessarily improve the soldiers' conditioning. Some chores the soldiers had to do, such as putting up and maintaining the regional telegraph system, tending post farms, and constructing buildings, proved hard work that built muscle strength and stamina, especially when drudging long hours in the heat of the Southwest. However, mixed with a poor diet, tight discipline, severe punishment, mental humiliation, as well as the heat, manual labor more typically triggered resentment, emotional anxiety, and physical collapse. Furthermore, tasks like plastering, painting, or shoveling did not exactly hone the skills needed to outdo the Apaches. One worried officer realized, "It is an incontrovertible fact that when soldiers are required to work as common laborers eight hours a day they are in great measure unfitted for their proper duties, and cannot be expected to maintain that military bearing and 'morale' which should characterize the regular soldier." This officer also pointed out that "in drill and discipline . . . there is much room for improvement. This defect cannot be remedied while the labor of troops continues."[12]

If the army had a shortage of formal military training and exercise, then what was the situation during off-duty hours? If motivated enough, both the officers and enlisted soldiers could surely devote much of their free time to playing outdoor games, climbing mountains, and running long distance, in this manner increasing their physical endurance. Certainly the Apaches behaved in this way. With their focus on lifestyle, officers had much more free time on their hands than the regular troopers. They preferred dances, concerts, masquerades, whiskey, cigars, books, horseback riding, or excursions to "ancient" indigenous/ Spanish sites such as the San Xavier del Bac mission church south of Tucson.

Discounting the anomalous baseball or tennis game, the officers failed to find the time for athletics. The officers hunted often to demonstrate their status, while enlisted men did it to expand their diets. In the nineteenth century, hunting was widely considered a sport suitable for gentlemen. While their hunting trips made the officers more accustomed to moving in the borderlands terrain, gunning for an elk, bear, or turkey from afar was vastly different from chasing down or engaging a group of Apache fighters.

Spare time for enlisted men was in shorter supply, but what there existed was spent on drinking, gambling, visiting prostitutes, or organizing the occasional theater plays and dances. It is revealing that even reading, although many in the ranks were illiterate, seemed more popular than sports. Still, especially during the latter years of the U.S.-Apache wars, some borderlands forts organized baseball games and incorporated sporting events to their holiday celebrations. When Lt. John Bigelow, who remarked that his cavalrymen showed no interest in doing any physical exercises on their own, organized Christmas Day athletics in 1885, he could get his men to participate only by offering monetary rewards. The prize for the one-mile walk and two-hundred-yard dash was set at one dollar, as it was for the running straight (long) jump and the running high jump. The winners of the standing straight jump and the standing high jump got fifty cents.[13]

Some might think that it was perhaps the exceedingly hot climate that marred athletics. Certainly, for most officers and enlisted men the Southwest's dry heat, maxing out in the summer well beyond 100 degrees Fahrenheit in the shade, was unlike anything they had ever encountered. There can be little doubt that high temperatures sapped the energies of men who suffocated in their clothing unsuited for any temperature. (The woolen dark blue regulation uniform constituted a private sauna in the summer and served as a personal freezer in the winter.) Still, training did not pick up during the milder months when the weather was more ideal for sports, nor did the heavy clothing and all the sunshine deter manual labor. Neither did the weather keep the Apaches from developing and implementing a sophisticated and rigorous training regimen.

Men's Bodies: Professional Warriors

The military's failure to build a systematic exercise regimen for its troops would prove a serious handicap when pitted against Apache fighters who had been exposed to a demanding, versatile, and systematic workout system from childhood. While young white children learned to sit still in the confined quarters of a school, their Apache peers trained in the outdoors daily, something that their elders encouraged but also expected the boys to do. Boys spent their time running, hunting small game, and playing various games. Hide-and-seek, tag, foot races, tug-of-war, and wrestling were just part of the repertoire. Developing their technical skill set under adult supervision, Apache boys manufactured toy weapons, practiced with bows and arrows, and simulated battles using slings. There was no denying that what a casual observer might have interpreted as play was, when performed systematically, in fact meticulous training meant to hone a perfect fighter. The Apache regimen was more than a fitness program for the individual; it was a community-driven, disciplined, and methodically planned and executed preparation for struggle and conflict today and tomorrow.[14]

While children as young as seven would practice riding horses, running constituted the key element in Apache training. For tactical considerations, Apache raiding parties, in order to avoid detection, moved much of the time on foot using higher elevations. Furthermore, messages in the field between different parties were often carried out by runners who could advance on difficult terrain where horses could not. This would save time and avoid discovery by the enemy. Speed afoot allowed Apaches to ride their horses into the ground and continue by foot, traverse rocky terrain where horses could not easily follow, and sneak up and away from enemy positions.

As boys grew, running not only remained the cornerstone of their practice program but was performed on more difficult terrain and deeper inclines and in harsher weather. There was no slacking off as veteran fighters worked as coaches demanding more and more of their trainees. One common method for a coach was to make the boy carry extra weight, some rocks or weaponry usually, when running. Also popular, the trainees had to fill their mouths with water and not swallow so that they would learn to breathe through their noses when sprinting up and down the hills. This was deemed a crucial skill because the desert climate would quickly dehydrate anyone who inhaled through his mouth.

Most Apache youngsters seemed highly motivated to embrace the challenges of arduous preparation. From a very young age, an Apache boy saw that good physical shape and abilities in combat was how a man commanded respect in the Apache community. Hearing stories of past exploits and encouraged to participate in manly affairs, such as the hoop-and-pole game, young boys grew to admire and mimic their elders. The older generation also shared with the younger generation its cumulative information of water resources, shortcuts, sequestered camps, and other geographical features, thus enabling the youngsters to develop a massive databank of their surroundings.

Apache elders emphasized that nothing less than community survival rested on the shoulders of youngsters honing their talents from a young age. One White Mountain Apache remembered that youngsters had to "do all those things" the older coaches made them do to "get strong," or else as grown men they "will get killed." The logic was brutally simple. "My son, you know no one will help you in this world," a Chiricahua father advised his son. "You must do something. You run to that mountain and come back. That will make you strong." While this Chiricahua father kept on reminding his offspring that "no one is your friend," he also boosted his son's self-confidence by conveying to him that "your legs are your friends; your brain is your friend; your eyesight is your friend; your hair is your friend; your hands are your friends; you must do something with them."[15]

When the boys reached puberty, the training entered a toughening period, a stage of preparation during which an older male who was an established fighter but not necessarily a relative coached the boy more intensively in skills that would benefit him as an adult fighter. At this time, the boy became a *dikohe,* meaning that he entered a novice status that ended after the youngster had satisfactorily participated in four raids. The standards and demands were raised once more as the dikohe hiked, climbed, swam, and rode from dawn until dusk. One man remembered how he was told that he must get up early and run, run, run. Their trainers also made the boys swim and bathe in icy mountain streams as to become numb against cold and pitted the dikohes against each other in rock slinging contests and in wrestling and fighting matches. Cowardice, fault of character, dishonesty, as well as physical weakness would set the dikohe back, often temporarily but sometimes for good. An unreliable and incapable boy could be dropped on his trainer's recommendation or if the adult fighters refused to take him along. The boy would be told to try again in the future if/when he matured.

The intense dikohe period aiming for physical and mental perfection could last for many years, but usually proved shorter. Those communities that demonstrated gaps in their fighter ranks could ill afford a prolonged novice phase. Alongside the physical and mental preparation, the equally important sharing of knowledge continued. Boys were instructed how to survive in the wild on their own, how to conduct themselves during expeditions, and how to manufacture and maintain their weapons. Some of the instructions were very specific, including, for instance, advice on the necessity of keeping one's weapons and moccasins close by when stopping for breaks. Apache youngsters were told that a good fighter arose before sunset and maintained his physique to an old age through running and other exercises. While an Apache boy was not forced to participate in raids or warfare, there were few or no alternatives for warrior training for boys. "The physically fit who wish to enjoy material benefits can hardly choose another course," anthropologist Morris Opler aptly explains.[16]

The warrior training climaxed with the dikohe's first expeditions. This stage involved spiritual preparation, consultation with a shaman, and a set of ritual proscriptions a dikohe had to follow. For example, Western Apache boys had to avoid water. They could not swim, wash, or cross rivers unless necessary during their test raid. The novices also had to drink through cane tubes so that water would not touch their lips and make their muscles weak. If the novices got wet, some believed, a severe storm would arise. They were also forbidden to eat intestines and had to eat meat cold. Novices also could not look back during the first four days, and they had to use a special scratching stick when itchy. If the novices failed to follow these rules, the livestock the party captured would die on the way home, their luck with horses would be gone, or some other disaster would strike the outfit. Furthermore, the dikohes had to master a special vocabulary—a warpath language—which they were obliged to use on their novice expeditions. For example, death was called "that in which one becomes again"; a gun, "that which discharges wind"; a house, "a mass of mud lies"; and cattle, "those who stand facing downward."[17]

On the first raid, the dikohes usually refrained from participating in the actual fighting. Instead, they would observe and study the events unfolding. They would also take care of horses, gather wood, cook, run errands, and do other camp chores. They could also carry extra arms and ammunition and mescal and rawhide for moccasins for the more experienced fighters. Oftentimes the novice boys actually competed for the honor of serving the older fighters, wanting to show their respect, observance, and trustworthiness in everything they did. The novices were also told to never complain or speak unless spoken to. The first raids were training exercises as well as tests. For example, the seasoned fighters instructed the dikohe how to sleep lightly. Some suggested making a pillow of sharp rocks, so that if the novice should fall asleep, his head would roll off it and wake him up. Each morning the dikohes could also have to go for an extra run. During the raiding party's advance, if conducted by running, novices should never slow down the others by stopping or sitting. Apparently a standard advance included at the most two pauses per day, one for lunch (which could be skipped) and the second for camping in the evening. The rest of the time the Apache party kept running or, alternately, riding their horses.[18]

Having successfully completed his trials, the dikohe was considered a man free to do what he wanted and was eligible for marriage. It seems that usually the novices did their four practice expeditions on raids and more rarely did they accompany larger war parties. However, at least in a time of acute crisis this distinction must have blurred. One Chiricahua who reached his youth during tumultuous times in the 1880s had "not done much else" in life than "chased and attacked . . . fought and run . . . [and] ambushed and been ambushed." While he and his peers had not officially reached warrior status yet, they had "received far more training in real fighting than that given in time of peace."[19]

In general, amplified military strain and reservation life made the Apache advance into manhood more difficult. Yet the Apaches adapted as boys trained in warrior skills inside the reservations. For example, at San Carlos in the 1880s Chiricahua youths carried their slingshots at all times and had "battles" against either White Mountain or San Carlos Apache boys. Sometimes the men even participated. "It was no play but our training for battle, but very seldom was anybody seriously hurt. We learned to throw straight and we also learned to dodge stones thrown at us. It was a very necessary part of our education. It trained us for defense in case of attack," one of the Apache boys remembered. Furthermore, modified versions of novice raids were carried out while working as soldiers in the U.S. Army.[20]

Training also did not stop among those Apaches who fought the Anglos and sought refuge in the most inaccessible and remote mountain ranges. In the 1880s, as their fighting numbers declined and they were on the brink of forfeiting their independence, Chiricahua youths were still systematically trained in the Sierra Madre. According to Daklugie, the Chiricahua fighter Geronimo "lined the boys up along a stream, after having them build a fire, and at his command had them jump into the cold water, even when it meant breaking the ice. When we climbed up the bank with our teeth chattering, he let us go to the fire for a short time, but then we had to jump into the water again." All the youngsters, Daklugie added, "wanted to become fighting men" and thus "worked hard" and "obeyed orders." Later, when a student at Carlisle Indian School, Daklugie enjoyed the athletic training he got there, although he felt that the conditioning did not measure up to the Apache training routine.[21]

When they reached adulthood, Apache men had thousands upon thousands of hours of training behind them. But this was just the foundation. Like today's professional athletes, Apache fighters paid meticulous attention to their physique and kept perfecting their skills throughout their careers, which lasted until old age or, more commonly, early retirement caused by injury or violent death. Still, Anglo writings frequently depicted Apache men as lazy loafers. Instead of being physically active, the Apache men purportedly used up their hours gambling or drinking while forcing their women to a life of constant drudgery and toil.[22]

In fairness, several writers did recognize the Apaches' mobility. One white captive of the Lipans wrote that his captors climbed canyon sides "with the alertness and agility of squirrels while I found it extremely difficult and tedious." Lt. William Shipp, who served with the army's Apache recruits in the 1880s, did not consider the Apaches equal to whites in any sport, but still admitted, "They made us feel like babies when it came to mountain work." The Chiricahuas especially, Shipp explained, "were a never-ending source of wonder. Their knowledge of country; their powers of observation and deduction; their watchfulness, endurance, and ability to take care of themselves under all circumstances made them seem at times like superior beings from another world."[23]

Much like his peer Robert Evans, Shipp also surmised that it was "no wonder our [white] soldiers could not catch people like these." Even though Shipp and some of his peers recognized Apache skills and abilities, they brought race to the table when representing Apache stamina, speed, and strength foremost as racial characteristics. Race, not training, was the main reason why the Apaches never complained and seemed unaffected by cold, hunger, or thirst. Still others downplayed Apache training by resorting to practical yet ultimately inadequate reasoning, arguing, for instance, that the Apaches had the ability to move so quickly over long distances in rugged terrain simply because they had next to nothing to carry. It was also common to explain the lean physiques of the Apaches by dehumanizing them as otherworldly or as part animal—for example as tigers of the human species.[24]

Body of Men

As already noted, the Apaches never produced a single cohesive military organization in the European understanding of the concept. The Apache military system rested on the everyman who felt most obligations, responsibilities, and loyalty toward his extended family, which typically comprised five to ten households living together. Although their size varied a great deal, a local group was normally made of three to six extended families, a relatively stable social unit that functioned as a significant economic and military engine. The beginning of military training and the recruiting for leaders and fighters for smaller raids was usually done within the local group, while the more advanced education and larger expeditions might draft volunteers from other communities within the band or clan (among the Western Apaches).

What mattered in making an Apache man join a fighting party in any given time depended on interlinked motivating factors that included the level of outside threat, personal desire for material goods, opportunity for personal distinction, maintenance of kin ties, and concern for the welfare and status of one's family, local group, or even band. What also counted a great deal was charismatic leadership. In the egalitarian and classless Apache society, the position of a military leader was not hereditary, and there existed no specific section of society from which military leadership had to be recruited. In theory, leadership was open to all males, but in reality most men never made it. Still, a man with no family history of leaders or one who exhibited no specific importance or authority in peacetime could take charge of military excursions. And, although an established Apache leader could train a fighter, often his son, to follow him, his success depended on his own aspirations, knowledge, and skills and on whether his compatriots opted to follow him.[25]

One Anglo observer described the Apaches as "pure democrats, each warrior being his own master, and submitting only to the temporary control of a chief elected for the occasion."[26] This observer was not far off. All men were fundamentally equal, the difference between them stemming from fighting spirit and experience. A man whose spirit was broken was considered finished. Also, ambitious but inexperienced hotheads were usually never trusted enough to be chosen for leadership positions. On the contrary, Apaches were often led by seasoned veterans. Of the most famous, feared, and revered Chiricahuas, Cochise, Mangas Coloradas, and Geronimo all directed men into their sixties, while Victorio was most likely over fifty when he died in battle.

An aspiring leader had to prove he was a good talker and a good thinker, while also being a good fighter. Because Apache communities made decisions by reaching a consensus that was preceded by a public discussion, there must have been a great deal of politics at play when leaders were selected. The same held true during the period the leaders held office, especially as the decisions made were rarely expected to have permanence. A group deadlocked could end up dissolving or choosing two or more competing leaders simultaneously. When calling for volunteers, an established or aspiring leader told the men why he had summoned them, why he wanted to fight, what the men should expect, and what was the goal. Other respected men could also make speeches in favor of the candidate, trying to convince the crowd of the soundness of his plans.

But in the end, as any enforced military service was regarded as degrading, men made up their own minds whether they would go. One Apache told Morris Opler that the leaders "didn't tell men that they must go. . . . Chiricahua feel as men on their own. If things like war are going to happen, they themselves have to show they are manly. It is left up to the individual to decide." Shirking raids was seen more as a matter of indolence than cowardice, which nevertheless, as the above quote suggests, could reflect badly on one's masculine reputation.[27]

Leadership styles were as varied as were the individuals. A keen eye for social harmony was crucial for a person in charge at all times, on the road, during engagement with the enemy, when dividing the spoils, and when celebrating victory or recovering from defeat. When choosing the route, setting the pace, assigning lookouts, and handing out other assignments, the leader consulted others and kept his eyes open for dissent, especially from those experienced fighters who held considerable social influence. Still it was the leader who in the end issued orders and orchestrated the moves. It was also he who, typically, had to be able to perform the moves. Thus in combat, an Apache leader frequently led from the front or, at least, took an active part in the fight. After the clash, the party was likely to fragment as fighters quarreled over the spoils. Some might return home immediately with their bounty, while others might continue.[28]

When establishing his following and reputation, the Apache leader was also heavily reliant on his Power, the form of the supernatural he could use to protect and control his fighters. Some Apaches felt that unless the fighters believed their leader had Power he would be out of luck. As a consequence, Apache leaders tended to claim some type of a connection to the spiritual world. Some leaders, such as Geronimo and Juh, reportedly had the gift of premonition, and it was also said that Geronimo had the power to delay the sunrise. As for other Chiricahua leaders, Chihuahua had power over horses, while Nana held power over rattlesnakes and ammunition trains. One Chiricahua told Eve Ball that when no one else could find ammunition, Nana, because of his Power, was able to bring home a good supply.[29]

An Apache military leader was under constant watch, his mandate questioned throughout his career. If he disrespected the fighters, made judgments that proved erroneous, or had little or no success, the leader most likely found it difficult to get any following the next time around. Competition was open and constant. For example, if some other fighter eclipsed the performance of the present leader in combat and showed more initiative, tactical skill, and bravery, then the leadership position could change hands in the middle of a raid. Also, it was not always enough that a leader could bring men together, display bravery, or engage and outsmart the enemy in the field; if needed, he had to be able also to negotiate and trade with the adversary. A wise leader knew when it was time to fight, trade, parley, or run. Of course if a man could not find a following or if he lost one, he could later try to regain the confidence of his peers or even move to another Apache community and see if he eventually would have more success there.

Ultimately, it is easy to conclude that Apache military leadership boiled down to character; a man who was trusted, physically fit, known to be reasonable and fair, in possession of Power, good at persuasion and in social skills, and already proven capable was likely to succeed. Some proved more popular and enduring leaders than others. And a few proved able to draw a following across band lines. According to the daughter of the White Mountain Apache Diablo, "Whenever my father went to war a lot of men always accompanied him, lots of them, just like ants."[30] In a system like the Apaches', drawing and keeping those "ants" was a tough call. There existed no such thing as an unpopular leader; a leader either enjoyed the respect and devotion of his people or he was leader no more.

In the U.S. army, leadership was rigorously hierarchical, and, instead of personal character, consensus, reputation, or kinship, it relied on mechanical chains of command and was made visible in rank grading. Demanding blind obedience from rank inferiors, the army's leadership structure was innately hostile toward personal choice, rational critique, or negotiation. Leadership positions in the army were also isolated from the masses and were never chosen by officers' subordinates or even their peers. And while in theory it was possible to get promoted from the ranks, very few made it because of the massive class gulf—performed, guarded, and enforced daily in military life—separating leaders from followers. As a rule, a leader in the army was a highly educated native-born white man with established middle-class standing and family connections. Even the volunteer officers tended to come from different classes than the enlisted men. If personal achievement was secondary for earning commission, it was not critical afterward, as much of the time promotion went by regimental seniority rather than merit.[31]

While the rank hierarchy of officers appears clear-cut, running from the lowly second lieutenant to the prestigious lieutenant general, it was complicated by the army's intricate structural layout. Gaining extensive experience as a soldier in the U.S. Army, the White Mountain Apache John Rope recognized how soldiers functioned in a manner different from the Apaches: "We kept all our men mixed up together. We never put spear men in one place, bow men in other, [or] club men in other."[32] Certainly the Apaches gave men diverse assignments in combat situations. But they never saw any reason for allotting men permanently into, or making their status depend on, segregated spheres of armament. On the other hand, a soldier and an officer, once assigned into a branch of service (staff bureau or line service in the infantry, cavalry, or artillery) and to a specific regiment and company/troop within it, often stuck with these for his whole military tenure.[33]

In addition to the different branches of service, the army's geographical demarcation added certain bounds. For much of the time, the U.S. forces in the Southwest borderlands stood geographically split, operating (after the Civil War) under two different military divisions, the Pacific and the Missouri, and three military departments, Arizona, Missouri (New Mexico), and Texas. These were often further divided into smaller military districts and subdistricts. Troops crossing department (or district) lines required permission from someone of authority. Reply was often slow, cooperation frequently tardy, and compliance with the request far from given.

Furthermore, the army's geographical configuration proved less than stable. Between 1865 and 1869, Arizona went through no fewer than four different stages as a district (or districts) in the Department of California and the Division of the Pacific headquartered at San Francisco. It all added to one confusing mess, officers being marred and maddened by the constant uncertainty pertaining to the limits of their authority.[34]

While the decision to make Arizona a separate department in 1870 brought more stability, and indicated that the army took the conflict against the Apaches more seriously, the fact remained that New Mexico and Texas were part of a different command chain, being (after 1866), respectively, a district in the Department of the Missouri, and an independent department belonging to the Division of the Missouri. Communicating across administrative boundaries, coordinating operations, devising strategies, and harmonizing military goals proved frequently overtly complicated for those in positions of authority. As for the day-to-day life of troops in the field, they were engaged in operations against a mobile enemy who completely disregarded—or at times knowingly took advantage of—the army's geographical ruptures.

The higher a rank a man had the farther away he usually was from actual operations, field service, and the common soldiers. Whether living in Chicago (Division of the Missouri) or San Francisco (Division of the Pacific), the division commander, typically a major general, answered only to Washington. Far away from the ground—each division controlled numerous states and/or territories—these commanders were responsible for overall logistics. It was the man under the division commander, the department commander—usually a brigadier general but sometimes a lieutenant colonel or a colonel—who was meant to be the most significant man in coordinating and planning operations. He was expected to gain perspective of the overall situation without losing touch of local circumstances. Or at least that was how things should have been, as some of these commanders preferred the comforts of their headquarters over the hardships of the field. All departmental commanders, much to their exasperation, sooner or later arrived at the realization that to lead from the department headquarters in the borderlands was much like leading blind. Difficult logistics, slow communications, and divisions of authority created by the army's own geographical demarcation ensured that. The international border, together with the exceptional mobility and uncertainty of the enemy, did not help. Still, leadership from afar proved the norm.[35]

In the army's system of leadership, post commanders and company officers who lived closer to action carried considerable responsibility in relaying information to their peers, subordinates, and superiors. On their shoulders relied the actual execution of field operations. The ideal leader in the field, who usually "only" held the rank of captain or lieutenant, was strict, decisive, and authoritative, an energetic disciplinarian armed with a sense of justice and courage. His job was to direct and control, and he might lead from the front as an example to his men or he might not fight or carry a weapon at all, instead staying in the background to deploy, instruct, and govern his subordinates.

Even in a rank hegemony, it often benefitted a leader if he was charismatic and skillful, thus gaining the confidence and admiration of his followers. But that was neither necessary nor expected or encouraged. Certainly any type of social fraternization between officers and enlisted men was considered unacceptable among the regulars, if less so among the volunteers. Intermingling with social inferiors would not only be repugnant for many officers but was seen as a danger to discipline and liable to increase sentimentality. The latter, in turn, could cloud the officers' judgment when it came time to order their men in harm's way. Any Apache who grasped this thinking must have been utterly perplexed by the sheer human coldness it necessitated. To officers, the army's mechanical, emotionless philosophy was expected to become something like second nature. Keeping his distance, a typical officer, even a junior officer, did not necessarily know much about his men, perhaps not even their full names.

For a man choosing to live as a soldier, the necessity to heed to the rank hegemony was a fundamental requirement. In private he could and did subject his officers to frequent critique for being, for example, overzealous, tyrannical, petty, impatient, incompetent, overcautious, or negligent. But outside these concealed thoughts, the situation was stunningly straightforward: an enlisted soldier, in the words of an officer, has to "quietly accept the fact that no matter what he thinks about an order, he must unquestionably, unhesitatingly, and promptly obey it."[36] In the regular army, white and black soldiers had, by contracting their work output, forfeited personal freedom in exchange for salary for a period of three or five years. In theory, the same principle of curtailed freedom applied to volunteers, although many liked to think they were still rational, sensitive, and impulsive individuals who could not be expected to obey orders as blindly as the regulars did. Still, in both organizations any attempt to regain full personal freedom prematurely was called desertion, an escape resorted to by scores of disillusioned men.

In many ways, the world of the common American soldier and that of a typical Apache fighter stood miles apart. Devoid of any input in choosing the people who led them, the soldiers likewise could not select who stood by their side when the shooting began. They also had to accept that they enjoyed little influence over their daily lives, whether it was manual labor, military training, or the place, time, and method of combat. Nobody asked their opinion in the matter of who exactly should be fought against. It is also certain that among Apache fighters such social stratification and near complete absence of personal input as prevailed in the army could have never survived but would have resulted in a quick diffusion of the fighting party or swift substitution in leadership.

Then again, the white enlisted ranks, who, unlike the Apaches, came from various regions and countries, felt united with their immediate peers by a common fate. Soldiers shared with each other much more than colleagues in the average workplace do. While most Apache fighters had a spouse and offspring and lived surrounded by their extended families, the mostly unmarried enlisted personnel not only lived far away from relatives but subsisted together in a homosocial setting, with often the whole company being cramped into one building. Until the early 1870s, men actually slept two per bunk. Eating and personal hygiene was taken care of in the company of fellow soldiers, and there was never much room for privacy. When fighting, working, or off-duty, enlisted soldiers stayed close to each other. In this they were in some ways similar to the Apaches. Both the soldiers and the Apaches sweated and cursed in the company of their peers when going to war.

CHAPTER 3

OPERATIONS

If you were careful you lived a long time,
but if you were careless you didn't.
—Barney Tisle, White Mountain Apache

I predict now that we will never see
an Indian [Apache] except [by] accident.
—Lt. John Van Deusen Du Bois, U.S. Army

In 1850, Col. George A. McCall was touring New Mexico and its military posts as a representative of the army's Inspector General's Department. Assessing that the mode of warfare practiced by the area's independent Indians equaled robbery and murder, McCall saw that it was crucial for the independent Indians to be "in the beginning impressed with the ability and settled purpose of the United States." Otherwise, he warned, Navajos, Comanches, and Apaches would "hold us in the contempt with which they now look upon the Mexicans." McCall urged his country to take quick action. "Sooner or later, a war, more or less general, with the surrounding tribes" would represent the "inevitable consequence" of the power the indigenous peoples held. If left for later, the conflict, McCall indicated, could become protracted, messy, and potentially embarrassing for the United States. While he had little doubt that the United States possessed the military capacity to gain quick control of the borderlands if it wanted to, McCall nevertheless felt that the task was "utterly beyond the power of the present military force" in the area. More soldiers and greater commitment would be urgently required.[1]

Getting There

While McCall called for more troops to the borderlands, he and others who came after him had to recognize that no significant increase was likely forthcoming. The national force continued to be spread thin on the ground; the army would have only 18,000 soldiers in 1861, 54,000 in 1867, and 25,000 after 1874.[2] Besides, before the Geronimo campaign, the Southwest borderlands were never the army's priority and the bulk of the troops occupied the Great Plains or the Reconstruction South. In a typical year of the U.S.-Apache conflict, there were some two thousand to five thousand soldiers in New Mexico and Arizona scattered to numerous garrisons.[3]

When the Third Cavalry arrived in New Mexico in 1866, the twelve companies that comprised it were quickly dispersed to posts throughout the territory, a common practice throughout the borderlands. In 1868, for example, there were 2,528 officers and enlisted men stationed at twelve fixed posts in New Mexico, while the 2,249 men in Arizona occupied thirteen others. The situation was much the same in 1885 when 1,308 troopers maintained seven permanent garrisons in New Mexico while 2,235 men were scattered across eleven posts in Arizona. Thus the average garrison strength at the Arizona posts stood at 173 in 1868 and 203 in 1885, while 211 and 187 denote the New Mexico figures for the same years. Both 1868 and 1885 actually represent years when military presence was above average in the borderlands, so, if anything, these figures exaggerate the average fort strength. Furthermore, discharges, desertions, illness, detached duty, and the numerous demands of manual labor kept many of the soldiers from actual military operations. It is actually quite common to locate dispatches and reports in which the garrison strength available for field operations is reported well below fifty men and sometimes even in the teens.[4]

Furthermore, while Apaches were broken into various groups, bands, local groups, and extended families, they at least did not switch places with each other in periodic yet unfixed intervals like the soldiers did. Although the Third Infantry was stationed in New Mexico for the duration of the 1850s and the Sixth Cavalry spent from 1875 to 1884 in Arizona and then up to 1890 in New Mexico, uninterrupted service at one territory did not normally exceed five years. With the army replacing some 25 to 40 percent of its men every year, military traffic to and from the borderlands was continuous. It was also difficult and time-consuming. Those advancing to New Mexico commonly did their whole journey overland, entering the territory either via Fort Union and Santa Fe in the northeast or from the south by way of El Paso. To access Arizona, the soldiers habitually journeyed via California. While sea travel represented the earlier norm, following the building of the transcontinental railroad in 1869, it was common to first go to San Francisco by rail. After sailing southward to Drum Barracks or to San Diego, many took a steamboat around Cape San Lucas, the southern tip of Baja California, to the mouth of the Colorado River. There the army travelers exchanged to smaller river steamers docking at either Fort Yuma, or Fort Mojave, or at the tiny communities of Ehrenberg or La Paz. Overland travel across the Sierra Nevada and the Mojave and Colorado Deserts represented another mode for moving ahead after Los Angeles or San Diego. Forts Yuma and Mojave operated as the main gateways to points farther east in Arizona. For many, the journey signified a passage to a dangerous world outside civilization, a test that assessed their resolve and toughness. But if reaching the borderlands had been hard, fighting the Apaches would prove even harder.[5]

Bases of Operations

Even if reality made them appear more like the government's work houses, or imperfect islands of civilization, military garrisons stood as symbols of power. Never randomly scattered, fort distribution revolved around practical needs and military strategy. Obviously a bastion without some kind of access to water, timber, and grass, or one short of adequate transportation and communication links, could not survive. Still, alongside logistics, it was, in general, the needs relating to Indian policy and Anglo traffic, settlement, and industry that primarily directed post allocation on the borderlands. The army, especially after the Civil War, selected widespread coverage of terrain over concentration of its troops to large garrisons. It hoped that the troops could, from their scattered bases, routinely conduct quick and nimble localized patrols hitting the fragmented enemy and offer protection to settlements and travelers.[6]

In some ways, Apaches lived as scattered as the military, each band and local group having recurrently occupied campsites within their home range. While garrisons were the objects of time-consuming repairs, rebuilding, and removal, the Apaches chose not to spend the bulk of their time fixing their homes. Instead they designed them better suited for mobility, whether caused by the demands of gathering and horticulture or by the more abrupt demands of war. A typical Apache village consisted of a cluster of dwellings built some distance from one another so as to afford privacy but close enough for safety. Usually each dwelling was occupied by a single, more or less nuclear, family. More so than the forts, Apache camps were also defensive entities. Cognizant of impending dangers, the Apaches often built their camps on higher ground with security and quick escape in mind. There preferably was just one path leading into the village, which made guarding the entrance easier. Also, if natural barriers were not enough, Apaches constructed rock breastworks to safeguard their homes from any approaching enemy.[7] Still, the Apaches proved most vulnerable to attacks in their homes.

While many in the army wrote of the vulnerability of the borderlands garrisons to Apache attacks, this concern did not materialize into actual Apache onslaughts. Nor did the fear of Apaches regulate the orchestration of public space in the forts.[8] Outside few exceptions, like Fort Cummings, borderlands posts did not actually constitute "forts" in the strict sense of the word, meaning structures with some type of bastions or high walls. Instead, borderlands posts in general looked more like villages. As a rule, they differed in design and use of building materials, although the commonness of adobe and a general pattern where housing—private homes for officers, barracks for enlisted men, and various administrative and communal buildings, including a guardhouse, a hospital, a storehouse, and possibly a trader's store—centered around a parade ground brought some resemblance of uniformity.[9]

Because the posts lacked defensive postures, from the perspective of soldiers and officers, their military significance should have rested on their being places where the professionals could resupply, recuperate, and hone their military skills between operations. In reality, as we have seen, the soldiers were preoccupied by manual labor, denied military training, and lacking in physical exercise. Several of the forts were also habitually hit by diseases that practically immobilized the garrisons. In the 1850s, Fort Thorn and in the late 1860s the garrisons at Verde, Crittenden, Goodwin, Date Creek, and Grant all had reputations for being particularly unhealthy localities. For example, in July 1856 seventy-eight of the ninety men at Fort Thorn were sick with remittent fever, while two years later not a man at the fort was fit for duty during the warm and wet late summer months. In the late 1850s, the borderlands army, especially in the section between Forts Craig and Fillmore, was tormented by fevers. Statistically, more than two-thirds of soldiers could expect malaria once a year. While the army abandoned or relocated several forts, the immobilizing rates of sickness resurfaced at various locations. For example, menacing fevers troubled the occupants of Fort Thomas in the late 1870s and early 1880s, resulting in several deaths in what one eyewitness, Capt. Anson Mills, called the "most sickly" garrison "in the republic." Augmenting the problems stemming from diseases was not just the lack of exercise and harmful leisure habits, but malnutrition and poor sanitary and housing conditions. When not sleeping in shabby tents exposed to the elements, the enlisted men occupied poorly ventilated and gloomy barracks that had few windows or doors and possibly no floors or ceilings. The quarters were frequently infested with vermin, scorpions, and even snakes, as well as being overcrowded and short on privacy. Adding to the misery, roofs and walls leaked during rain and suffocated all those who ventured inside during the hottest months. In short, the barracks were often totally unlivable. Some were deemed even unfit for animals to occupy.[10]

Tools of Trade

Once the soldiers abandoned their axes and shovels and shook off their fevers, aches, and hangovers, they were expected to take the war to the indigenous home turf: into the deserts, canyons, and mountains the Apaches lived and operated in. Ahead of military operations, the men sorted out their clothing, drew their field rations, prepared their horses if in cavalry, and made sure their weapons functioned. Alongside his physical condition and personal drive, skills, and discipline, a considerable part of any fighter's effectiveness depended on the equipment. Better, but not necessarily technically more developed, tools possibly made better fighters. The extensive resource gap represented a potentially huge asset for the United States. As both the U.S.-Mexican War and especially the Civil War proved, the United States could manufacture lethally effective weapons, raise or buy quality horses, fabricate clothing, grow food, and produce other supplies that would shield the fighter from the elements and make him stronger, as well as transport practically anything in scales unimaginable to the Apaches. But American material superiority that existed on paper did not adequately reflect the borderlands reality.

With high transportation costs and expensive local produce, maintaining the troops in the Southwest cost many times more than it did in the eastern sections of the continent. This caused a constant worry over expenditures in the federal government, which would have preferred decisive results fast and with the least amount of cost.[11] A wealth of animals, weapons, clothing, manufactured goods, and other belongings essential for survival, lifestyle, and war making accompanied the invading U.S. force. With the posts scattered, heat and dust abundant, grass and water sparse, and the roads scarce, long, and in variable condition, the movement of goods proved not just costly, but sluggish and undependable. Posts occasionally ran out of supplies temporarily and had to tightly regulate the supply or rely on aid from other garrisons. And even if enough materials reached the troops, their quality and suitability for borderlands warfare would be another matter entirely.[12]

Always a factor luring young men into service, the uniform was a marker separating officers and soldiers from civilians. But in the borderlands, the uniform, except perhaps on dress parades or during leisure hours, proved more a hindrance and a source of frustration than anything else. According to one military surgeon, "The uniform is totally unfit for . . . our south border," causing "great disadvantage" for the troops. In general, the army gave little thought to climate or terrain as it issued one type of clothing for all troops to wear during all seasons. Furthermore, the quality of clothing was inconsistent (for example, the uniform came in a variety of shades of blue) and so pitiable that it easily deteriorated in active use. Moreover, as late as 1880 soldiers continued to receive Civil War leftovers. Much of the surplus clothing had been stored in warehouses in the East where moths and fungus ravaged the various articles before they even reached their users. Coats, blouses, and pants were also measured in such a peculiar way that they were frequently a poor fit. And, if that were not enough, there were severe difficulties in delivering an adequate supply of various items to the distant borderlands. Considering the kind of clothing offered by the government, transportation difficulties, in this case, could have actually been a good thing.[13]

The standard outfit consisted of a heavy, dark-blue woolen dress coat that kept in all the moisture and drew solar heat like a magnet and of ill-fitting, sky-blue kersey trousers that itched and fell apart quickly. Numerous updates were made over the years, but the basic problems largely persisted. Take, for instance, the headgear. The broad-rimmed fatigue/campaign hat issued after 1872 and the earlier Puritan dress hat were made of black felt. Besides the color, the lack of ventilation, heavy weight, and vulnerability to wind were some of the many problems soldiers came to associate with these hats. The hats also slouched and lost all shape in wet weather and frequently were in pieces after few weeks in the field. Reflecting the barrage of complaints, the 1876 model campaign hat proved stiffer and had ventilation, but remained black instead of a lighter color that would have better reflected the sun's rays. For everyday headgear, the soldiers mostly preferred the dark-blue forage cap. The durable 1872 model of woolen broadcloth with its stiff leather visor, interior lining of glazed brown muslin, and low 2¾ inches height in front proved the men's favorite. Still, the cap offered poor protection from the rain or the sun, and for many it proved rather uncomfortable.[14] In reality, countless soldiers, perhaps the majority, or at least most who could afford it, resorted to buying their own hats, as well as other clothing, from the post traders or civilian outfitters.

The heavy dark-blue dress coat was used mostly in parades and parties. This was perfectly understandable. It was the equally dark-blue flannel sack coat that was the most common outer garment among soldiers. Originally intended only for fatigue duty, it was more comfortable and better fitting than the dress coat—though not unequivocally so. Some models, like that which was issued to mounted soldiers between 1872 and 1874, were unpopular throughout the ranks, who soon discovered these poorly constructed, pleated coats were little more than a haven for bugs while on campaign.[15] The army also issued long-sleeved, gray woolen shirts made of such coarse material that it irritated the soldiers' skin. Luckily, the blue flannel shirt adopted as regulation in 1881 was of better material and was thinner. The boots issued to soldiers were simple and, prior to the Civil War, not manufactured specifically for either the left or right foot.[16] The rocky terrain of the Southwest was bound to destroy the footgear in a relative short time. While at the time of the U.S.-Mexican War something called a "summer uniform," consisting of a white cotton fatigue jacket and trousers worn from May 1 until September 30, had existed, post–Civil War officers did not call for its reintroduction. Instead they recommended that light-colored cotton duck cloth uniforms, similar to the ones used by British colonial soldiers, should be issued to the troops in the Southwest. Several high-ranking officers, among them Gen. William T. Sherman, conscious of tight budgets and wanting to put the massive Civil War surplus into use, were slow in embracing any radical changes in clothing. In 1875, however, the army did experiment with cork helmets by sending one hundred British helmets to troops in Arizona.

As the troopers prepared to go after the Apaches, they selected the least cumbersome articles, such as the durable canteen and the warm blanket, and improvised or, if they could afford to, bought the rest. If permitted by their officers, many disregarded their woolen uniform altogether, wearing instead commercial outfits or the white canvas stable clothing originally issued by the army for use when taking care of horses in the post. The result was a ragtag appearance, a mix of styles that prompted one British visitor to Fort Cummings—who appraised the practicality of U.S. troops in their selection of weapons and clothes—to state, "An English cavalry officer, accustomed to the polish and trimness of his own command, might be excused for standing aghast in horror" at the site of U.S. troops. He felt, "A detachment of American cavalry on march might, to the European conversant with standing armies, bear a suspicious resemblance to banditti." Campaigning against Geronimo, Lt. John Bigelow commented that his cavalry troopers represented "a curious sight" as the men had dispensed their blouses in the warmth of late May in 1886 and instead rode in blue flannel shirts or in their gray knit undershirts. One sergeant wore a bright red shirt, and looked "not unlike a mounted fireman." "There are all sorts of hats worn, of American and Mexican make," Bigelow added. The mixture in trousers was as varied, but most were "badly torn or badly worn, especially in the seat." The "men's feet," Bigelow laconically concluded, "are some in shoes and some in boots."[17]

The Apache raid or war party set to leave their camps also dressed in wide variety of outfits. Over the years Apaches had grown fond of Euro-American clothing and eagerly traded or raided for various items. "We took their shoes and pants and shirts and coats and boots and used them for ourselves, and dressed like Americans we had seen," one Apache recollected. The Apaches dressed in a combination of skins, moccasins of various length, Mexican garments, and Anglo military or civilian pants, vests, and shirts. Although usually much of Apache clothing was of light color, some apparently even put on the woolen dark military jacket, stolen or traded. While the Apaches and the soldiers might have dressed more alike than anyone familiar with Hollywood films would think, Apache clothing tended to be more practical for movement and the weather. When ready for combat, they sometimes dressed very light, sometimes wearing nothing but their breechcloths and moccasins.[18]

Although infantry had its uses in the borderlands wars, it was a reality that the average trooper could seldom catch the average Apache on foot. Thus the cavalry was heavily relied on, and this, in turn, brought the quantity and quality of horses to the pinnacle of war making. According to historian Robert Watt, the twelve companies of the Ninth Cavalry involved in active combat against the Chiricahuas did not enjoy a single month during a period of three years (1879–81) when they would have had a surplus of serviceable horses in relation to available men. On average, the ratio of horses to men in the Ninth Cavalry ran somewhere between 50 percent to 70 percent during the period Watt has investigated.[19]

While the problems of the Ninth Cavalry in 1879–81 presented an extreme scenario, the army repeatedly struggled to provide enough horses. Many also preferred to have "American," or Morgan, thoroughbred horses but had to settle for less distinguished-looking Mexican or California mounts. The latter could not carry the weight the larger horses bore, but they could travel over the rough borderlands country much better, were famed for endurance, and could live on most any type of weed or scrub, even sunflowers and oak brush, much like mules. In short, they were particularly suited for the borderlands operations. For their part, American horses were mighty looking animals, big and strong, but they had to be imported at considerable cost from the East, had problems acclimatizing, and ran on grain. Worse, they would not last. For instance, one officer estimated that most horses from the East did not live three years in the borderlands. On the other hand, these bigger mounts often proved more adept for winter use in (usually mountainous) sections of the Southwest that had cold and snowy winters.[20]

Then there was the conundrum of horsemanship. The recruit, frequently an urban dweller, usually had less concern over the type of horse he got than over the expectation of his riding it. With little or no experience with horses upon assignment to cavalry regiments, many of the new enlistees proved inept even at mounting a horse, let alone controlling it. Anton Mazzanovich, a soldier in Arizona in the early 1880s, remarked how recruits fell off their horses when riding too fast. According to one officer, the situation in the late 1860s had also been such that his "troop was seldom ordered to mount without the air being filled for a few minutes with flying men, carbines, and sabers in inextricable confusion." A 1850s serviceman in turn wrote how he and his comrades, after mounting their horses were occasionally "interrupted by the attraction of gravity." Unable to compete with the Apaches in long-distance running, cavalrymen who had difficulties staying in saddle on the parade ground could be expected to encounter severe problems in challenging the Apache raiders in the canyons, mountains, and sand plains of the borderlands.[21]

While the army relied on long and cumbersome supply transports, or on civilian merchants, what the Apaches could not manufacture or get from nature, they stole or traded. Apaches did not raise large herds, and, while horses had worth as prestige symbols, they never gained the type of economic or cultural value they did among some Plains tribes. Many Apaches, if not some of the more eastern groups, preferred to walk and run. Valuing a practical approach, they had little problems riding horses to their deaths if their own lives depended on it or, if time allowed, even eating the flesh of their mounts before continuing on foot.

The Apaches made lances, clubs, and bows and arrows themselves. It seems that the preferred wood for bows was wild mulberry, while strings were made out of sinew from the back of a deer or from the muscle on the back of the animal's hind legs. For arrows, Apaches used hard wood like wild chokeberry or desert broom; points could be stone, bone, iron, or wood; and feathers were taken from hawks, turkeys, doves, quails, or other birds. Sinew acted as glue and binder. There were plenty of variations in the selection of materials, specifics of manufacture, and coloring. Sometimes Apaches used poison made from deer's blood and plants believed to be toxic on their arrows. Some Apache men became experts in weapon making, and these, usually older, men would teach their relatives and youngsters in the art and also make bows and arrows for order, selling them to those not particularly skilled in the practice.[22]

For much of the 1850s and 1860s at least, clubs, spears, and the bow and arrow, being light, easy to carry, reliable, silent, deadly (in the hands of an expert user), and thus something of an ideal choice for ambush and surprise attacks, constituted the principal Apache weaponry. The customary cavalry weapon of the late 1840s was the muzzle-loading percussion carbine, a shorter and more mobile version of the infantrymen's musket. The foot soldier more typically had to settle for the flintlock, not the percussion, musket, a rather awkward weapon that required twelve separate steps by the user before it was operational. Even a well-trained soldier was expected to fire no more than three rounds per minute. As the percussion musket became the standard infantry weapon during the 1850s, its major improvement did not relate to speed or nimbleness but to better performance in windy and damp weather. Whether carbine or musket, flintlock or percussion, the army's choice proved unsatisfactory in aspects quintessential to unconventional war fought in mountainous and canyon-ridden terrain—namely, in speed, agility, reliability, silence, and accuracy.[23] While the user of a carbine was busily, and often nervously, reloading, an Apache skillful with bow and arrow had plenty of time to make a hit or two, or even three, or a daring sprinter had an ample window to charge and spear or club his enemy.

Significant change happened after the Civil War as the army started converting muzzle-loading to breech-loading rifles and adopted metallic (copper, brass) cartridges. As a cartridge weapon could be loaded from the horizontal position, a soldier no longer had to expose himself as he had done while standing up and reloading the musket. Also, a proficient shooter could fire approximately ten shots per minute using a breechloader. However, officers enjoyed such independence in arming their commands that there was a near complete lack of standardization in weaponry carried by the soldiers. Armed with a mixture of Sharps, Spencers, Springfields, Remingtons, and a smattering of other rifles with divergent caliber of ammunition, the confusion in supply proved often considerable and worrisome as there was many a potentially hazardous situation in the field when the right type of ammunition turned out less than easy to procure. In the late 1870s, the .45-caliber model 1873 single-shot breech-loading Springfield rifle did solidify its position as the army weapon of choice. However, even if the predicament over ammunition size eased, other issues emerged. The copper cartridge of the 1873 Springfield expanded excessively in the breech, and upon firing the rifle easily jammed, which caused considerable concern among the soldiers at least until the cartridge was redesigned with a brass case during the latter years of the borderlands conflict. Even at this time, as weapons manufacturers developed better repeating rifles, the army was slow to catch on, not finding a reliable enough rifle that would fit its budget until the Krag Jorgensen in the 1890s.[24]

As more whites arrived with better weaponry, the Apaches quickly adapted. "They [whites] had rifles, caps, powder, and bullets, and we captured these for ourselves. We kept on fighting the Americans with these," one Apache remarked.[25] While the first repeating rifles had found themselves in Apache hands during the Civil War, it was not until the 1870s that the contest in firepower between the army and the Apaches was turned on its head with the introduction of the Colt "Peacemaker" and the Winchester rifle. The latter's .44 would take the same cartridge as the handgun, which probably pleased the Apaches, whose supply of ammunition was always uncertain. It is ironic that when magazine weapons rapidly developed into weapons of preference for many Apaches, soldiers and officers had to reach into their own pockets to get their hands on rifles such as the Winchester. As a result, during the 1880s the Apaches often fought with more modern and powerful rifles than the army. The Apaches, individual exceptions notwithstanding, had moved from nimble and effective bow and arrow to dominant and effective repeating rifles, largely skipping over the cumbersome and unreliable carbines and breechloaders with which the army remained jammed (quite literally). While Apaches favored the latest models, they also made rifles signifiers of respectable manhood. It is telling that in many of the photographs taken during this era Apache men pose proudly with rifles in hand. Even what is possibly the most famous photo of any Native American—taken at San Carlos in 1884 by A. Frank Randall, a Willcox-based correspondent for *Leslie's Weekly Newspaper*—has a rather solemn-looking Geronimo on one knee clutching his rifle. Rifles in fact grew into such cherished commodities and symbols of prestige that Apache men not only wanted to be photographed with them, or envied each other for the latest model, but joined the army in part just to obtain them (if not receiving the latest models in service).[26]

There is little reason to doubt that the Apaches were skilled in the use of bows and arrows, having trained in the practice intensively. But when it comes to rifles, the question is more complicated. While some sources make the Apaches excellent marksmen with rifles, others report the Apaches as poor shots. The possible lack of proficiency might stem from lack of practice. It was not so much that rifles and pistols were new to them, but their chronic shortage of ammunition made the Apaches careful not to waste any bullets.[27] If the Apaches had little ammunition to waste for practicing, the same went for the soldiers, who seemed to battle something of a lingering ammunition deprivation. While the Apaches always had the bow and arrow to turn to, the soldiers without ammunition were instantly less of a fighting force. Sabers and bayonets, both standard issue, were virtually useless, as the soldiers could rarely force the Apaches into hand-to-hand combat. Some officers kept their sabers as decorative items suitable for parades and when time for field duty approached put them in storage at the posts. Others took their sabers along, claiming it had an effect on the morale of men from a disciplinary point of view.[28]

A soldier was also hindered by all the material the regulations said he ought to carry with him. A cavalry trooper's recommended official field gear included a skillet, eating kit, spare socks and shirt, blanket, canteen, coffee cup, overcoat, saddle tree, two stirrup straps, five coat straps, headstall, pair of reins, saddlecloth, surcingle, side line, lariat, horse brush, carbine loop, carbine socket and strap, hair girth, bit, curb and strap, link, nosebag, picket pin, and currycomb. When personal gear was added to that, keeping up with the Apaches was going to prove hard work. Neither did it help that the trooper did not find much of a boost in his rations. First of all, with the aid offered by pack mules and cook wagons, the soldiers carried their own and their horses' food with them to the field. Second, while no force can fight successfully on empty stomachs, American regulars seemed to attempt it quite frequently. The basic field menu consisted of coffee, flour, bacon or salt pork, and hardtack. At the posts, soldiers fared only slightly better, as their issue also contained beef and beans. Fruits or vegetables were not included in rations. Neither was milk, eggs, butter, or variation in meat. The soldier in search of better nutrition had to resort to hunting or buying. Furthermore, for much of the time in the field, the troops went hungry as their rations ran out or their hardtacks were full of insects, salt pork was alive with worms, and bacon became rancid.[29]

Like the soldiers, the individual Apache fighters made sure their fighting gear was in order, that a sufficient supply of moccasins was at hand, and that their weapons worked. They also made up their buckskin or hide packs for mescal, dried meat, ground corn and berries, or dry cakes made from the fruit of prickly pear. If possible, just enough food was brought to last until the fighters would reach the area they planned to operate in. They could also live by hunting or stealing their food. The Apache fighters typically carried their water in a container made from the intestines of animals. Unlike the troopers, every Apache individual took his own provisions and was ultimately responsible for his own welfare. While they could share provisions in the field or have novices cook or carry for them, in principle an Apache fighter was expected to be self-supporting. He ate what he had and cooked it himself. If he had a horse, he could ride; if not he walked.[30]

Apaches also utilized various ritual proscriptions set to protect their endeavors. Leaders needed Power, and the dikohe observed a plethora of rules when dodging bad luck. The fighters could procure amulets, while some obtained protective caps and jackets, and consulted shamans about the outcome of the expedition. During their endeavor, Apaches should, for instance, eat modestly, never complain loudly, show energy at all phases of operations, be calm under fire, and be reflective during planning and when discussing goals, methods, and outcomes. Also, it seems that among some Apache communities a "warpath language"—a set of special nouns and lengthier phrases that applied to, for instance, horses and Mexicans and that were believed to protect the users from danger—was used by all fighters, not merely the novices, during at least some part of the raids.[31]

Prior to the departure of a war party, those Apache fighters intent on going would participate in a ceremony typically referred to as the "war dance." This convention was meant to ensure success, but it additionally functioned as a powerful public performance of self-confidence and individual competence, thus demonstrating the communal and individual connotations linked to war making, most pertinently manly bravery and the importance of property acquisition. The Western Apache dance consisted of four parts and commenced after sundown, lasting until the next morning. During the first stage, called going to war, the fighters from each clan, carrying their weapons, were called forth to demonstrate by dancing how they would fight the enemy. The second phase, cowhide dance, involved singing descriptions of the acquisition of enemy property. The third segment was a social dance between men and women that lasted all night. The final phase in the morning involved the most experienced fighters, those who in a fight would never hold themselves back in their minds, always think brave, and go right into the fight. These men stood in line and took turns singing about personal success in war. After the last song, the fighters would stage mock battles showing how they would surprise and defeat the enemy. Shortly after this segment concluded, the party was ready for departure and the entire encampment could gather to watch their exit.[32]

Run Silent, Strike Sudden

Because of their physique and endurance, the Apaches were extraordinary runners and did not depend on horses as they got going. Some sources claim that the best of them could run up to 130 miles a day if needed, while more moderate, and reasonable, estimates have the Apaches advancing from 50 to 70 miles per day. The soldiers typically could not ride half of it, often covering less than fifteen miles. Not only the distance covered, but also the tempo of soldier and Apache advance, proved very different. While the soldiers proceeded in an orchestrated manner and stopped to rest, eat, and water their horses several times a day, the Apaches moved more freely and might eat while riding but usually had food only in the mornings and evenings.[33]

Also, each Apache fighter typically possessed detailed knowledge of his surroundings, giving him a distinct advantage when compared to the soldiers, most of whom were novices in the borderlands. However, Apache familiarity with the terrain should not be exaggerated. One Chiricahua told in an interview that "just a few" of the Apaches "were experienced trailers." "Maybe three or four of the band," he estimated. Moreover, the territories of Apache communities were relatively restricted, and although raiding occasionally took Apache fighters to more distant places, they could not be expected, as some in the military presumed, to know every foot of the borderlands. Thus, for example, most of the Western Apaches were operating far from their geographical comfort zone when campaigning in the Sierra Madre on the military payroll in 1883.[34]

For Apache raiders, it was advantageous to march or ride in the mountains, as it allowed keeping a lookout for any possible foe and lucrative spoil. The mountains also offered a myriad of relatively safe resting places for people as well as hideouts for captured property and livestock. Still, travel in the high ranges did not lead to a false sense of security or carelessness. For instance, when Apaches camped for the night, they not only selected the site carefully but usually sent lookouts ahead in all directions to ensure that no enemy were nearby. The same precaution was preferably repeated in the morning. They also endeavored to leave as few traces as possible for anyone interested in their movements. Sometimes the Apaches reportedly walked on their toes or jumped from rock to rock. At other times, they kept a man behind to brush over the tracks with some bushes. When there were no mountains, the Apaches would take cover and conceal their advance in arroyos and canyons. Roads and other heavy-traffic paths were to be avoided. For crossing open terrain, night was the appropriate time. However, Apaches did not like to travel or fight at all during the hours of darkness, when it was difficult to see the enemy, one's own path, or the highly venomous nocturnal snakes (many Apaches dreaded snakes). Usually they could attack, according to one Western Apache, "when it was light enough to see arrows."[35]

Many times Apache raiders sought to avoid contact with other people altogether, pilfering animals and other loot discretely and silently to avoid detection.

While success in Anglo minds was frequently linked to carnage and confronting the enemy face to face, the success of Apache raiding was measured daily, first, in the quantity and quality of captured property that was safely delivered back home and, second, in forestalling anyone of their own getting killed or captured. This partly explains why planning and timing proved so essential. It also suggests that Apaches frequently killed for self-protection. It was also done when it was too risky to let the raiding targets live and give away information on the Apaches' strength and direction of travel. Charlie Smith, a Chiricahua, recounted that if Geronimo's group was seen by a civilian during the heated days of 1885–86, it would mean that their whereabouts would be reported to the military, which would be soon "after us." There "was nothing to do but kill" the civilians, including their families and children. "I do not like to talk of it. I do not like to think of it," Smith confessed. He also stated that the soldiers killed their children as well and that during these years the Chiricahuas frequently felt that they had "no choice."[36]

Killing fulfilled multiple ends. Take, for example, a fight outside Galeana, Chihuahua, in November 1882. By using decoys, the Chiricahuas managed to lure Mexican soldiers out of the town on a chase. At a predesigned spot, the galloping Mexicans ran into a trap. Just one survived, and only because the Apaches wanted him to go back and tell the other Mexicans of the fight and of the Chiricahua might. In this case, a witness served a purpose beneficial to the Apaches. It also did when a group of Apaches in 1866 captured a wagon train outside Tucson. The raiders were satisfied to demonstrate their capacity by aiming arrows at the Anglo teamsters' chests, releasing their bow strings with their right hands, and catching the arrows with their left before letting the startled teamsters depart unharmed but without their property. Both episodes showed how important building and upholding that fierce reputation was to the Apaches. In many ways, reputation, earned over the years, was one of the best weapons they had.[37]

Scalping was one way to sustain that reputation. Scalping, and other forms of bodily mutilation, could also indicate significant martial accomplishments or function as a marker of an exceptional enemy. As a whole, scalping, often connected to Apaches by whites, was atypical to Apache military culture. Copycatted from the Mexicans, Apaches claimed that it was used selectively. One Apache noted how scalping was reserved "as a last resort on a man who has made a great deal of trouble for the Chiricahua. Such a man, when finally caught, would be scalped and 'danced on.'" If it seemed meaningful, scalps, sometimes just one, were taken as tokens and danced on at home so that both the mourners of loved ones killed in combat and the victorious fighters could get rid of their anguish and frustrations. Afterward, the scalp was discarded. It seems that only the Jicarillas kept scalps as trophies.[38]

Banking heavily on surprise tactics, the Apaches excelled as experts in concealment and in arranging elaborate traps. According to Lt. John Cremony, a borderlands veteran from the 1850s and 1860s, the Apaches could, without leaving any tracks or signs, trail a party for days, scanning every movement, observing every act, and taking exact note of the target and all its belongings, in no case incurring the risk of losing life. They waited for an opportunity when their targets, thinking they were safe, became careless and relaxed their watchfulness, to establish a secure ambush. All ambushes, Cremony deemed, were "almost invariably the results of long watching—patient waiting—careful and rigorous observation, and anxious counsel."[39]

While Cremony is quite perceptive, in reality many an ambush were ad hoc events arranged at a moment's notice to combat some imminent threat or hastily orchestrated in response to a sudden appearance of attractive bounty. Delivered from close range, an ambush's goal often included startling the other side and causing them to abandon their belongings and run, preferably without having the sense to shoot or fight back. If possible, the first volley would cripple the enemies' initiative and ability for self-defense or at least paralyze them so that they became incapable of putting up organized resistance and pursuit.

The actual execution had many variables, as Robert Watt has noted. It is apparent that Apaches preferred to strike, fight, and retreat in a specific type of landscape cut by mountains, arroyos, and canyons. Mixing it up, Apache fighters not only met enemy forces and raiding targets at the narrowest point in the canyons or mountains but also could hide in the open flatland. Thus instead of waylaying their objective in a steep canyon that had a rich history of assaults, for instance, Apaches could use arroyos or underbrush as cover for an attack on level ground at either side of the expected ambush site. Or they could dig small holes, where they waited before jumping out with their weapons at the moment their targets passed by. Although typically ambushes relied on complete invisibility for gaining the advantage prior to striking, Apaches could use bogus trails to offset their targets to enter a trap with a false sense of security. One typical method was to pass the actual ambush zone, leaving a clearly visible trail and then double back on the flanks to take up concealed positions. In another variant, a selection of Apache fighters would try to encircle back to the rear of their pursuers. When those in front began shooting, the enemy turned around only to find Apaches to their rear or to the side. Sometimes the Apaches used one or two decoys, who allowed the enemy to detect them. When fired at, the decoys would run and lure their pursuers into an exposed position, usually to the rockiest place available, where an ambush was prepared for the chasers. Furthermore, to fool the adversary, the Apaches could hit at unexpected hours, as many assumed they would not fight in the dark or at sunset.[40]

While Capt. Henry Lawton's troops scouted for the Chiricahuas reported near the Mexican border in June 1885, they left the supply train with eight soldiers at Guadalupe Canyon. On June 8, while eating dinner this outfit was, in one soldier's words, "surprised by a thundering volley." Two men fell dead then and there. Another soldier ran to his tent and commenced frantically praying on his knees before the sergeant in command called him out. Then this terrified soldier escaped with another man to the top of the hills on the opposite side of the little open valley in search of cover. The four remaining men huddled behind the wagons. "I was very much scared and actually thought possible it would be best to surrender," one of them later confessed. There was no such option, as things only got worse. Hit several times, their sergeant fell. Then the wagons caught ablaze. As the ammunition in the wagons exploded to a "mighty roar," the three troopers made it to the hills, from where they shortly escaped to a nearby ranch. One of the soldiers later told that all he could see during the clash had been the smoke from the Apache guns. Meanwhile, the Chiricahuas celebrated. Without losing any of their own, they had routed the soldiers and captured large quantities of food, ammunition, and other materials.[41]

It is obvious that the Apaches did not raid randomly. Not only did topography matter, but so did distance from home. To protect the noncombatants, Apaches as a rule refrained from raiding in the vicinity of their camps. Also, when feeling vulnerable, they could raid in another section of the country in order to lure enemy forces away from the environs of their noncombatants. This is what happened in March 1883. With a large Mexican force threatening their homes in the Sierra Madre foothills, Geronimo's party raided far away in western Sonora and a second party under Chatto operated on U.S. soil, while their families sought cover with an escort in the higher, more remote, reaches of the Sierra Madre.

Exhaustion, Irritation, and Phantoms

After all the ceremony involved in getting the troops off the posts—the loud bugle blowing, band playing (if the post had one in residence), shouting of commands, forming of lines, and synchronized advances in symmetrical formation—which some Apaches found very comical—the soldiers would finally be on the move, taking the war to the indigenous home ground.[42] There were several overlapping types of operations. There were both patrols and direct pursuits resorted to by individual units from a single post. Furthermore, there were campaigns, which were larger enterprises involving troops from several posts, districts, and even departments. As a rule, campaigns relied on meticulous planning, cooperation, and, often, converging commands, while patrols included some planning, as they usually were designed for canvassing a certain area. Direct pursuits in turn involved little or no planning, but instead plenty of reaction. Also, while indigenous soldiers (officially referred as "scouts") had featured on patrols/pursuits and campaigns far earlier, the 1880s saw the implementation of special mobile task forces composed of mixed commands of Apache and white recruits. These units were set to penetrate Apache hideouts (usually in northern Mexico), harassing and striking them relentlessly while living off the land for the most part. Very typical, especially during the 1880s, were also defensive stakeout missions, where a set troop guarded a certain strategic location, hoping to intercept the enemy or, at least, halt their access to the place in question. Ideally, every move in the military playbook culminated in a battle. In reality, this rarely happened. Beside futile chases and skirmishes, assaults on the unsuspecting proved typical.

Boredom also proved typical, at least for those on stakeouts that involved passing irksome and monotonous days on some isolated waterhole, canyon, or mountain pass. Descriptions of these uneventful days reveal that the commitment and interest of the troops were in matters other than in catching Apaches. Most troops actually never saw a glimpse of one. For Capt. Gustavus Doane's men, stationed at the Dragoon Mountains during the 1885–86 Geronimo campaign, alcohol, gambling, and other vices offered by the nearby movable saloons and brothels seemed to present a more enduring fascination than the Chiricahuas. For his part, Doane, rather than keep the men alert and vigilant through field exercises or by having them systematically canvass the country for enemy signs, tried to divert the attention of his troopers from vice by making them perform countless labor assignments. His success in this effort, as in capturing Apaches, turned out to be less than brilliant.[43] To the west of Doane, at Copper Canyon on the western slope of the Huachuca Mountains, Capt. Charles Hatfield's cavalrymen occupied themselves by constructing camp improvements, including a makeshift shower for the officers to enjoy, while their commander pursued his interest in oil painting.[44]

The borderlands war experience was considerably more taxing physically for those officers and soldiers on the move, as they tried to proceed as silently, so as not to alert the enemy; as cautiously, to avoid ambushes and hurting themselves in the rough ground; as and quickly, to catch up the enemy, as possible. With all the materials they carried, and taking into consideration the less-than-superb condition of the men, this was often something of a mission impossible. Many patrols were nothing more than "a sorry march," a term Maj. Clarence Bennett applied to describe his outing from Camp McDowell to Tonto Basin in September 1865. In what was a typical scenario, Bennett's patrol moved at night to avoid the heat and Apache attacks, managing a truly disappointing and equally eye-opening ten miles during their first march. Hindered by cacti, broken hills, steep mountains, as well as deep sand and rocks, their progress, much to the dismay of all involved, did not substantially improve on the following nights. If the advance turned out anything but fast, it was not exactly silent either. The pack mules and the beef cattle Bennett's outfit hauled with them frequently went wild during the hours of darkness. As mules rolled over and packs unfastened, it created much noise, many delays, and plenty of headache and irritation. Still, despite all the commotion, the soldiers attempted, or pretended, to proceed stealthily, as no talk, no fire, and no firing of arms was allowed.

In the end, Bennett's field report became crammed with the words "hard work," as he recounted the march. The troops managed to surprise, capture, and burn an unsuspecting Apache encampment, but they could not muster the strength to pursue the bolting Apaches. Furthermore, because the skirmish occurred on the eighth day of patrolling, and because they only had rations for a total of fifteen days, the troops actually had to halt the whole patrol and turn back in order to reach Camp McDowell alive. On paper, the patrol represented a reasonable military success, as a strike had been inflicted on the enemy, yet Bennett could not escape the feeling that his had in fact been a "sorry march."[45]

As Bennett's march suggests, the violence between the army and the Apaches usually resulted from the former going after the latter, as the Apaches only infrequently sought engagements with the troops, preferring softer targets instead. Apache inclination to attack civilians only fueled the army's tendency to see the Apaches as a universal menace to whose acts of aggression the military only responded. In many white minds, all Apaches deserved severe chastisement in order to learn to respect the power of the United States. According to Bennett, "The killing of Apaches in different parts of the country . . . will have a tendency to make the Apaches understand we are in earnest."[46]

While whites certainly brought violence to the lives of the Apaches, there is no doubt that violence flowed the other direction as well. Apache raids did not only shape the rather venomous tone of military texts but were frequently responsible for triggering the most common form of military operations: the reactive chase, or direct pursuit. This ad hoc activity constituted a pressing effort performed in response to news, or rumor, of some Apache deed perpetrated usually against a third party. For example, the chase that stemmed from the theft of L. A. Stevens's sheep herd a mile outside Fort Whipple in May 1872 had many of the characteristic elements (of which several would fit patrols and campaigns as well)—slow response, arduous movement, exhaustion, surprise attack, heightened antagonism and fury, inability to make the Apaches stand and fight, and the reluctance/inability to keep on pressing the enemy after their escape from the scene of combat.

Hearing the news of the sheep theft as he returned from a picnic, Capt. Azor Nickerson did his best, he wrote, to put together a force from "the ailing" and from those "employed in the care of garrison" in the undermanned Fort Whipple. After examining the scene, the troops, who initially had some difficulties finding signs in the dark, found a trail. It led "directly back into the exceedingly rough and rugged mountains," where the Apaches had hoped to conceal the sheep and make life a nightmare for anyone following. Being already some six to eight hours behind, the soldiers had no choice but to push through all night. Groping their way on a moonless night amid "awful gorges" and "thorny scrubs" in search of a trail, the soldiers were grateful when dawn and open country emerged—as did dead sheep dotting their path. Moving ahead at full speed, at 4:00 P.M. the troops entered a little valley that turned into a watered canyon. "It was a fearfully rough place, obstructed by huge boulders, gnarled old trees, and logs," Nickerson described. They had found the Apaches. A "reckless" charge soon followed, "every man" being "his own commander" in a melee made up of panicky sheep, startled Apaches, and infuriated soldiers, and of shouting, running, and firing. For a short time, intensity seemed to border on madness. Then, according to Nickerson, "most of the Indians slunk away in their usually deft manner, but a few remained long enough to pay the death penalty for their rashness." Gaining possession of the camp and the sheep, soldiers and their horses were too exhausted to continue and had to rest on site. This brought the pursuit to a close, with its limited goal of recapturing stolen property fulfilled. Nickerson, unlike Bennett, seemed content with what he had achieved.[47]

Nickerson most likely knew that an officer in the borderlands was wise to accept even the smallest of achievements, as none were usually forthcoming. Oftentimes direct pursuit led only to exhaustion and bitterness on the part of the soldiers, as there was no enemy to be found or as the Apaches outdistanced the troops. For instance, in the late 1850s, Lt. William Averell's unit at Fort Craig was alerted to news that Apaches had attacked a ranch some two miles up the Rio Grande. After scouting the country up and down for several hours, Averell explained, "Without seeing any trace of the Indians," the irritated troops returned to base. Like Averell himself knew, he was certainly far from being alone with his experience, as dozens and dozens of military efforts played out just like his.[48] Some, however, persisted longer.

During the 1885–86 operations, a small group of Chiricahuas had Lt. Britton Davis and about forty Apache recruits hot on their tail following a fight the Chiricahuas had had with another troop on the Sierra Madre. Keeping up the chase for several weeks, and in the process crossing the most rugged reaches of the Sierra Madre and trekking across the Chihuahua Desert, Davis nevertheless got nowhere close to his target. Reversing directions, scattering, and stealing horses along the way, the Chiricahuas outdistanced their pursuers before crossing over into New Mexico. "On one occasion I marched . . . fifteen and half hours at about three and a half miles per hour," Davis noted, before adding, "It is impossible to keep this up for any length of time." Their physical stamina tested to the limits, Davis and his men, ragged and dirty, many barefoot, suffering from thirst and malnutrition, ended up in El Paso. "We were practically at the end of our rope," Davis remembered. Returning by rail to Arizona, Davis resigned his commission. He had had enough of borderlands warfare.[49]

In many ways, Nickerson's exertion was representative of the army's more successful pursuit, Averell's was something like the exemplary quick chase, and Davis's amounted to the longer version of futile Apache hunting. In all, direct pursuit, giving the Apaches a head start and trying to measure up to the raiders' endurance, determination, and wit man to man, or horse to horse, proved an unsatisfactory tactic for the military and contributed to the need to strike when the opportunity represented itself, while also stimulating the planning and orchestration of multipronged campaigns targeting Apache homes.

Another variant of army operations was the phantom chase. It involved the troops being lured by false gossip spread either by fearful residents or by businessmen seeking an increase to their profits. A false rumor was a way to get the soldiers to come to a certain location, where, once there, troops often had to stay at least overnight because of long distances and poor roads, creating opportunities for people selling hay, food, and water, as well as for those peddling whiskey, sex, or games. Many officers loathed the locals because of this practice, thinking it as a morally corrupt move, a highly disrespectful gesture, and a waste of limited federal resources and time.[50]

When their typical mission involved locating and engaging an enemy who preferred mountainous terrain, the troops could not stay on the roads or follow the easy ground (if there existed such). Making their hardships and sacrifices known, military authors penned plenty of text detailing their ordeals. They wrote how suffering columns traversed amid "volcanic rocks" or "sandy wastes that form the valleys of the Salt and Gila rivers." These were "dreary deserts" of "loose gravel" or "alkali . . . white as snow and, crumbling" into "clouds" of choking dust. Few were also saved from "incredible upward . . . zigzag" trails in the "sterile mountains" that reached "sharp, rocky" ridges. Then "the almost precipitous descent begins" for camp, where rest is "dashed by the prospect of the interminable, heart-breaking, rock-climbing struggle to begin at daybreak." Sharing the tone, and the agony, other military voices scripted how they "for five or six nights climbed the mountains on one side and slid down the other leading our horses, battered and bruised ourselves among the boulders, pricked our flesh with the cactus spines we ran against in the dark, dodged the rolling stones sent crashing down by those above us on the trail, and suffered for want of water which was hardly to be had at all." One officer noted the absurdity of it all, as troops frequently came upon "narrow, tortuous canyons, so deep, so narrow that while it seems possible to hurl your hat across the widest of the lot, you look down into depths unfathomable, and by winding 'goat trails' and hours of dizzy climbing and sliding, sometimes on all fours, you manage to cross."[51]

Excluding the first-timers, the soldiers naturally possessed some rudimentary knowledge of the main roads or the immediate vicinity of their posts if they had traversed in those sections previously. But it was the rare experienced campaigners who had any sort of detailed knowledge or were familiar with the more distant or less-traveled sections of the borderlands. Like Lt. James Parker did, many an officer or soldier was forced, at one point or another during their operations, to recognize that "no one knew anything about the country we were in." Compounding their difficulties, the army had very few maps and even fewer good ones. As late as the early 1880s, Lt. Thomas Cruse remembered that there still existed hundreds of miles of terrain unknown to the army in Arizona and New Mexico. Revealing the slow accumulation of geographical knowledge during the preceding decades, Cruse referred to these sections as "almost *terra incognita* to any but the Indians." Even if intelligence of Apache sightings in the vicinity of some ranch, farm, or mine reached the military, there might have existed no knowledge where such places were located or how the soldiers could get there.[52]

Marred by narrow local knowledge, the army relied on, hopefully, more knowledgeable men, the civilian scouts. These were men of various competences and backgrounds, including local Hispanics, indigenous men, and white hunters, trappers, traders, and others presumed to possess some type of familiarity of the borderlands.[53]

Many pursuits of Apache raiders also came to a halt at the Mexican border. The international line complicated the matters for the army but offered considerable advantage to the Apaches once they realized U.S. troops were forbidden to follow them south and Mexican forces could not reach north. Chiricahuas and Lipans especially used the border to live as independent people. Lipans typically sought refuge from their enemies in Texas amid the Hispanic communities of Coahuila and from the Mexican operations either in the Lone Star State or among the Mescaleros in New Mexico. Until the mid-1870s, three of the four Chiricahua bands who lived mostly on the United States' side of the line embarked on raids deep into Mexico, bringing back contraband for trading on American soil. In the 1880s, the remaining free Chiricahuas made the Sierra Madre their home and base of operations for raids not only across northern Sonora and Chihuahua but also in Arizona and New Mexico.

Barred from entering Mexico, some American troops nevertheless crossed the border. Typically they found more controversy than military success as a result of their efforts. For example, in 1873 Secretary of War William Belknap, Gen. Philip Sheridan, and Col. Ranald MacKenzie, men frustrated by the border raids of Lipans and Kickapoos in Texas and determined to end them by orchestrating a border raid of their own, sent detachments south. While the troops made hits, they were also immersed in intense international polemic and critique due to their illegal crossing.[54] Nearly a decade later, during the Chiricahua escape from San Carlos in spring 1882, American troops clashed twice with the Apaches, first at Horseshoe Canyon on U.S. soil and second in the Sierra de Enmedio in Chihuahua. After the latter clash, the troops kept pushing southward on the tail of the Apaches. Instead they ran into a local Mexican commander who was anxious to know what the U.S. Army was doing in Mexico and demanded their immediate return north of the border. Not wanting to admit that they had been in Mexico, the officers reported that the second clash with the Apaches had taken place at the Hatchet Mountains in southwestern New Mexico. Those who wrote more truthful reports had theirs returned to them by their superiors. An agreement of reciprocal right to cross the boundary in pursuit of "savage Indians" was signed by the United States and Mexico soon afterward in July 1882. Still, this border-crossing episode was not revealed in detail until one of the officers involved, Col. George Forsyth, published his book *Thrilling Days in Army Life* in 1900.[55]

Despite the July 1882 agreement, operating south of the border remained far from trouble-free. When the army's task forces canvassed northern Mexico in search of the Chiricahuas in 1885 and 1886, several incidents took place where Apache soldiers got drunk in Mexican villages or were fired at by locals south of the borderline. American officers also found themselves questioned, detained, and even arrested by Mexican officials. The most damaging encounter, and a cause for bitter diplomatic exchange, was the killing of Capt. Emmett Crawford by Mexican irregulars in January 1886.[56]

Uncivilized War

If the greatest Apache triumphs in the field resulted from stunning the enemy, the army surprise was equally important, for it was in strikes against immobile and unsuspecting enemy camps where most success in all likelihood rested. As one officer put it, "The Apache on the rocky hillside is unapproachable, and to fight him with any chance of success, he has to be attacked with skill and great caution at gray dawn in his bivouac."[57]

There was a certain pattern to the mayhem. In his unpublished memoirs, one prospector provided step-by-step instructions on how to finish Apache hunts with laurels:

1. Travel by night and get as close by as possible to an Indian village before dawn.
2. When bright enough or when Indians begin to rise up, start shooting.
3. Turn loose at what you can see, young and old, big and little.
4. While Indian survivors run, you have "made a good many good Indians" who "will not murder anymore or steal again."
5. March into Indian camp, and if anyone "kicks around" or "has not been well tamed," shoot with pistol.
6. Go through the camp, "count how many good ones there are and what they have got."
7. Look for stuff taken from whites.
8. Set fire to their rags and skins and shanties, but don't burn bodies. Throw them away so Indians can see how many we killed.[58]

While these "instructions" represent one man's views, they provide an accurate enough depiction. The number of enemy dead and wounded, the amount of enemy property ruined, and the psychological impact of striking terror was what mattered the most. All three factors combined would, the Anglos believed, make the Apaches extinct (in the 1860s) or force them to capitulate and throw themselves at the mercy of the federal government.

When hit, the Apaches typically dispersed in various directions. They could abandon or kill their horses, steal new ones, or conceal the mounts some distance away for retrieval once danger passed. To make the matters more difficult for those after them, the scattered Apaches would run on rocks or jump from brush to brush as much as possible so that their tracks could not be seen. Also, dispersing and taking the high ground was a given. "When closely pursued we killed our horses and scaled cliffs no enemy could climb," one Apache explained, before continuing, "Scaling walls was taken for granted," being an integral component of Apache skillset.[59] A willingness to resort to such measures in an effort to avoid capture or death added to the army's already difficult task of tracking the Indians in the field.

The scattered Apaches usually set up a predetermined location for the rendezvous. To make sure the trail was safe, they could leave signs, such as tying pieces of fabric to trees or having stones pointing in a certain direction, as far as whole day's journey apart. Also, mirrors and smoke signals were used to determine whether those in the distance were friends or foes. Typically, the Apache combatants had made agreements on the signs they would use beforehand and thus knew to look for them. Apaches were also taught how to handle the arid environment alone. They knew, for instance, that putting a dry stick or stone in their mouth would release saliva and bring temporary relief. Apaches were also taught to detect the presence of underground water and to distinguish that mescal leafs and particular types of cacti contained water. Furthermore, Apaches also stashed as emergency rations durable items such as dried meat, cactus fruit, baked mescal, acorns, piñon nuts, cooking utensils, calico, weapons, gunnysacks, saddle blankets, fabrics, laces, crochets, and hatchets on their travel routes, in caves, and other hideouts. Decades later, these Apache caches were still discovered by the locals.[60]

For soldiers, being lost without food and water typically posed a more serious matter of life and death. Humiliatingly, some thirsty troops had to buy their water from civilians at high prices. On the other hand, purchases did not seem that bad a choice when some dehydrated columns deprived of this choice came dangerously close to perishing.[61]

It is hardly surprising that a number of military men saw their borderlands assignment as a punishment. There were several officers who just "do not want to live the life of *Indian-trackers*, and accommodate themselves to that kind of service which only can insure success." Many despaired of success or avoided field duty altogether. Then there were those who fumed at their peers and commanders, accusing them of cowardice and incompetence. More than a few resorted to humor and irony when having to cope with chronic frustration. "Our Indian hunters arrived this morning. Saw no Indians, wore out all their clothes and had a good time generally," stated a soldier showing how disappointment could be mitigated with a sense of humor.[62]

Those less amused labeled the borderlands conflict as a completely uncivilized and professionally exasperating experience. One veteran explained how fighting Apaches proved "a wild, vigorous experience—less like soldiering than any service I ever encountered." Another old hand added, "It was not a war to be proud of. Neither officers or men were very happy over it." After just three weeks in Arizona, Lt. John Bigelow wrote in his journal that while he yearned for glory and professional self-improvement through field service, he "also realized that laurels were scarce along Indian [Apache] trails, and that they grew in difficult places."[63]

Rather than blame themselves, many beat-up, bruised, and dehydrated officers and soldiers denounced the borderlands environment. One of them wrote, "Precipitous mountains, jagged and impassable canyons, and scorching deserts all aided the Indians and hampered the troops."[64] When contemplating what spoiled the soldiers' experiences, countless narratives not only referred to the environment but pointed to the Apaches, whom they thought operated beyond the bounds of proper war making. "To rob and not be robbed; to kill and not be killed; to take captive and not be captured, form the sum of an Apache's education and ambition, and he who can perform these acts with the greatest success is the greatest man in the tribe. To be a prominent Apache is to be a prominent scoundrel," one officer wrote. Another soldier claimed that the Apaches preferred to "'fight and run away, live to fight another day.' To fight soldiers merely in defense of his country, he considered height of folly; and he never committed that folly if he could avoid it." In this way, military writers starkly contrasted the Apache way of war, and manhood, with an idealized

American version that revolved around nationalism, land acquisition, battles, and rules of combat.[65]

While many in the army likened the Apaches to robbers and murderers, there existed some officers and soldiers who valued the skills of the Apache fighters. One such man was John Bourke, the aide to Gen. George Crook, and later amateur ethnologist, who took part in the Salt River Cave Massacre. He shared much in common with his peers as he wrote how "in battle he [Apache] is the antithesis of the Caucasian. The Apache has no false ideas about courage; he would prefer to skulk like the coyote for hours, and then kill his enemy, or capture his herd, rather than, by injudicious exposure, received a wound, fatal or otherwise." But, unlike some of his peers, Bourke did not interpret Apache behavior as unmanly. He rather insisted that the Apache "is no coward; on the contrary, he is entitled to rank among the bravest." As "an exceptionally skillful soldier," the Apache's "first duty under fire is to jump for a rock, bush, or hole, from which no enemy can drive him except with loss of life or blood." While the Apache might seem like the wiser fighter, Bourke was quick to point out that the white soldier is often intelligent, brave, disciplined and devoted. But the soldier, and this is where the glitch of evolutionary proportions sits for Bourke, is also "more and more a creature of luxury," who does not possess "the acuteness of the savage races." It is this "acuteness," or lack of it, that in Bourke's mind enables the Apache, but not the civilized soldier, to "follow the trail like a dog on the scent" or "tramp or ride . . . from forty to seventy miles in a day, without water, under a burning sun." For Bourke, the Apache's advantage in the mobile unconventional warfare stems more from inborn racial characteristics than from anything else, such as systematic training. While Bourke praised the Apache fighter, his writings also show that he perceived quintessential differences between a civilized fighter and a savage one.[66]

When representing the Apaches as aggressors or making their methods the antithesis of the American way of war, and when painting the borderlands nature as wild, untamed, and perilous, military writings served several purposes. For one, they represented the borderlands as an obstacle for the civilized troops to overcome and gain possession of. Second, they made it seem that the Apaches did not deserve honorable war in return. In fact, to end their savage reign, severe means would be justified at least within certain parameters. Third, their discourse enabled the military writers to produce a collective self-image of the soldiers as liberators who would bring the light of American civilization to a dark periphery.

Furthermore, a careful reading reveals that the utter hardships and fatigue the soldiers and officers endured made them not merely angry and eager to blame others but doubtful of their own abilities. In many ways, this was only natural. Men from Ohio or New York or from Ireland or Germany hardly were, or felt, ideally suited to conduct military operations in the deserts and mountains of the borderlands. When they were also confronted by a skillful adversary who did not follow "the rules," denied training, overloaded with manual labor, and disadvantaged by cumbersome clothing, among other things, it should be hardly shocking that many were overcome with frustration and resentment on the one hand and sense of desperation, loss, and alienation on the other. It was just that very few of them openly, let alone publicly, acknowledged their shortcomings. Instead, military writings tried to uphold the fragile covers of white superiority and manly honor on which U.S. conquest and rule depended. Diverting their own attention and focus to leisure, and to making military posts islands of civilization, officers as well as soldiers produced discourses that blamed the landscapes and the enemy, and even unscrupulous civilians or stingy government, for their own shortcomings in the field.[67]

It is interesting that some in the army, when seeing the prize unworthy of the effort, went as far as to suggest, in a provocative manner, that the United States would abandon the borderlands. One junior officer who scripted that there existed "the slightest *raison d'être* for any army, no mining, nor manufactures" in the borderlands was far from alone in thinking that the U.S. invasion was a waste of government and civilian time and money. For instance, in 1852, both Col. Edwin V. Sumner, the commander of troops in New Mexico, and Secretary of War Charles M. Conrad recommended, in their yearly reports, that U.S. troops should quit New Mexico. Sumner, apprehensive that all business in New Mexico relied on government money, considered the local Hispanic populace unfit for self-government and painted a gloomy future where raiding and reprisals would continue indefinitely, thus keeping out respectable whites.[68]

Even when doubts of the region's value lingered, the army instituted a notable adjustment for fast-tracking conquest. It hired Apaches. The summary logic was that only Apaches could defeat Apaches in a short space of time. Indeed, much of military success during the grinding campaigns in 1872–74 and again in the 1880s can be linked to the contracting of Apaches.

Not utilizing them like other troops, the army only superfluously integrated the Apaches. They did receive equal pay with other troops, but the enlistment periods of Apache recruits were random. They were typically ostracized by their white peers, who were often jealous that Apaches would steal what little glory there was in the borderlands wars. Apache recruits did not have to do much manual labor or behave and fight like other troops but were expected to use their individual skills and training to the army's advantage. The orders of General Crook, an eccentric chiefly responsible for enlisting (from 1871 onward) and augmenting the role of Apaches as de facto soldiers, to the officers in command of Apache units dated August 14, 1885, state that the Apache soldiers "know best how to do their work. They understand this business better than we do. . . . Only directions that can be given to them is to explain what you expect of them, and let them to do their work in their own way. We cannot expect them to act automatically as drilled soldiers do. Their best quality is their individuality, and as soon as this is destroyed or impaired their efficiency goes with it." As a result, whether operating as individuals attached to other units or organized into racially segregated companies under the command of white officers, the Apaches progressed more or less freely and otherwise functioned much like an Apache raiding party.[69]

Homecomings

When inching back to the fort after some hard times in the field, one officer scripted, "Thirty-six miles on level cow trails and a road. What luxury is a road! What a relief to ride in the cavalry, after pulling your horse up and down for days!" While for this officer, "a merry day it was" to get back to the post, the return to base held multiple significances for most troopers. Yes, it meant a stop to the arduous chasing and shelter from the elements. Perhaps a payday and a payday drunk were also in the program. Yet the soldiers knew that while mountain climbing was temporarily on hold, mountains of manual labor waited them, which definitely dampened the return. For the average trooper, military life was a choice between two evils: toiling in the canyons, sand deserts, or perilous mountains looking for an adversary that did not want to be found, or laboring on the post.[70]

The Apaches' homecoming could also prove a day of mixed feelings. The warriors were often anxiously awaited; lookouts spotted the arrivals miles before home. News of returning fighters could electrify the Apache villages, raising expectations and anxieties. Runners might bring good, or terrible, news beforehand so people could better prepare. If successful, the fighters were celebrated in dance, song, and feasting upon arrival. Thoughts of death were largely kept out of the celebration. Some sources suggest that the names of dead Apaches were announced at the start of the ceremonies once, never to be mentioned again. Others claim that news of casualties were delivered and mourned privately and that dead fighters never made it into the songs. The division of the spoils was an important event, and could occur prior to and during the victory dances. Horses and cattle were usually divided among all those who participated, while weapons could be distributed to the needy. Often each fighter was allowed to keep some of the materials he had personally obtained. However, if the fighters wished, they could share all articles with others in the party or with those who had stayed at home. They could, for instance, place blankets and other captured possessions on the ground free for the taking. Also, some women could convince the fighters to be more generous by dancing naked, although married women and "good girls" refrained from such activity. Generosity was something that was expected, especially from the leaders. Proud of their accomplishments, the Apaches took sweat baths and danced and sang around a big fire, sometimes for days. The accomplishments of the fighters and the ways the spoils had been obtained were recounted in story, song, and play. There were also songs for the different parts of animals butchered for the feast. Also, if someone wanted a captive, he had to sing for the prisoner. After the fighters, the raids, and the livestock had been praised, and captives (if any) allocated, various social dances followed.[71]

Amid the dancing and festiveness, the Apache fighters could pause for a while and reflect what had made their effort a success. They could come up with a list like that looked something like this:

1. Know your enemy.
2. Secure Power for your own party. An outfit without Power is doomed from the get-go.
3. Ensure harmony and group chemistry. Enlist experienced, competent, and trustworthy men; leave out the soloists, the bad-tempered, and the weak.
4. Be prepared. Make sure the men in your party are fit and have working weaponry suitable for the purpose.
5. Know your goals. If you have specific targets, let your men in on it, and direct all focus on fulfilling that objective. If there is no explicit target, make it also known.
6. Keep your eye on timing. Hasty men are often soon dead. Move and attack at the right moment; take no unnecessary risks.

7. Use natural cover at all phases of operations.

8. Be calm, consult often before it is strike time.

9. Shock and awe is the best way to a good result and reputation.

10. Plan ahead. Make sure there is an escape route and a rendezvous site.

11. Arrange for a safe return trip. Obtaining plenty of material bounty is not enough. You need to get the raiders and the newly acquired property back home as well.

In the end, as they ruminated on their triumphs and defeats, past and present, the Apache fighters recognized that, despite success, all too many of their comrades did not make it back over the years. Thus sorrow was also present at the homecoming.

A group of Mescalero Apaches, 1880s.
Photograph by Edwin A. Bass.
Courtesy of Palace of the Governors Photo Archives (NMHM/DCA) (090634)

Jicarilla Apache couple, recently married, 1871.
Photograph by Timothy H. O'Sullivan.
Courtesy of Library of Congress Prints and Photographs Division (LC-DIG-stereo-1s00413)

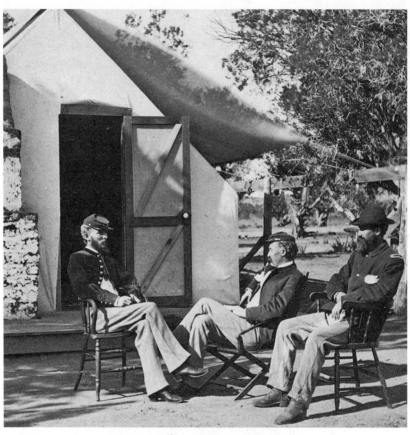

U.S. Army officers in camp, Arizona, 1871.
Photograph by Timothy H. O'Sullivan.
Courtesy of National Archives and Records Administration (523888)

(opposite top)
Apache boy with face and legs painted, n.d.
Courtesy of National Archives and Records Administration (530899)

(opposite bottom)
Sixth U.S. Cavalry troopers in the field near the Mexican border, 1885.
Courtesy of Arizona Historical Society (910)

Troop "A" 6th U.S. Cavalry - Geronimo Campaign - 1885 - Camp on Mexican Border -

Fort Bowie, Arizona.
Courtesy of Arizona Historical Society (19867)

(opposite top)
Geronimo (Goyathlay), a Chiricahua Apache, kneeling with rifle, 1884.
Photograph by A. Frank Randall.
Courtesy of National Archives and Records Administration (530880)

(opposite bottom)
General James H. Carleton, ca. 1860s.
Courtesy of Library of Congress Prints and Photographs Division (LC-DIG-cwpb-07383)

Group of White Mountain Apaches near Camp Apache, Arizona, 1873.
Photograph by Timothy H. O'Sullivan.
Courtesy of National Archives and Records Administration (519786)

(opposite top)
General George Crook, ca. 1870s.
Courtesy of Library of Congress Prints and Photographs Division (LC-DIG-cwpbh-04032)

(opposite bottom)
Rationing Indians at Camp Apache, 1871.
Photograph by Timothy H. O'Sullivan.
Courtesy of National Archives and Records Administration (524211)

Apache recruits used by the U.S. Army, 1881–1885.

Courtesy of National Archives and Records Administration (533091).

Chiricahua Apaches, 1886.

Photograph by C. S. Fly.

Courtesy of Arizona Historical Society (78157)

PART II

SHAPES OF VIOLENCE

CHAPTER 4

CONTAINMENT

When White Eyes began coming in, trouble ensued. . . . They were
greedy and cruel people; they had no respect for the rights of others.
They hunted us through the forests—our own forests—like wild animals.
And they spared nobody. We did not understand why they acted so savagely.
We only knew that they did. . . . These strange people respected nothing or nobody.
—Big Mouth, Mescalero Apache

A savage and uncivilized tribe [Apaches], armed with the bow and lance . . .
hold as tributary powers three fertile and once flourishing states,
Chihuahua, Sonora, and Durango. . . . Such has been the devastation
and alarm spread by these children of the mountains, that they [the states]
are now losing population, commerce and manufactures at a rate which,
if not soon arrested, must leave them uninhabited.
—Lt. Col. William H. Emory, U.S. Army

Poise

Shortly following the May 1846 outbreak of the U.S.-Mexican War in Texas, President James Polk, Gen. Winfield Scott—commanding the U.S. Army—and Secretary of War William L. Marcy organized a force to protect American traders along the Santa Fe Trail, establish U.S. control over New Mexico, and then continue toward California, in the process making an effort to pinpoint a southern all-season route to the Pacific seaports. It was uncertain whether the troops would encounter strong opposition along the way. The officer in charge, Col. Stephen Watts Kearny (soon a general), nevertheless put together a command, dubbed "Army of the West," designed to impress by its sheer size alone. It was comprised of regulars, Missouri Volunteers, and Mormons, altogether 1,458 men plus some 1,000 reinforcements who would follow shortly on the tail of the main force. It also included an artillery battalion together with 1,556 wagons, 459 horses,

3,658 draft mules, and 14,904 cattle and oxen. Like a cumbersome beast, the Army of the West crawled out from Fort Leavenworth and headed toward New Mexico to capture Santa Fe, a borderlands hub whose male population did not exceed two thousand.[1]

It was approximately 820 laborious miles to the New Mexico capital. "Every breeze that swept across the parched and heated plain felt as withering as the breath of Sahara," one military writer, John Hughes, recalled of the summer journey.[2] After stopping at Bent's Fort, a trading station on the Arkansas River, the command pressed south through Raton Pass. The road proved nearly impassable at times, scores of horses died en route, and the bedraggled troops were reduced to half rations or less. Although they obviously had little idea of the prolonged wars awaiting Anglo fighters in the Southwest, the soldiers were receiving a taste of what military campaigning in the borderlands would entail. Suffering, both physical and mental, seemed plentiful. Pain resulted from long marches in grueling, broken, terrain and from the agonizing summer heat, choking dust, and shortage of water, but not yet from chasing the elusive indigenous fighters.

After New Mexico's Hispanic governor fled without offering any resistance, the Army of the West reached Santa Fe on August 18, 1846. The troops confidently paraded through the town and honored the raising of the American flag over the governor's palace, an occasion accompanied by a thirteen-gun salute. Seeking to both awe the locals and reassure them that the invasion would actually prove beneficial to New Mexico residents, Kearny made a series of speeches, including at the nearby Hispanic villages and pueblos. Declaring that New Mexico was now annexed to the United States, he instructed local officials to take an oath of allegiance to their new rulers. Kearny also promised to squash mercilessly all opposition while also vowing to protect religion, persons, and property. Making himself and the occupation known, Kearny attended a local Catholic mass and gave a ball that attracted four hundred or five hundred Hispanics and Anglos. On the surface, it all seemed like liberation, not conquest. Even the majority of those locals who had not run away fearing robbery, rape, and random violence seemed to greet the Americans warmly in most places.[3]

Posing as benevolent conquerors, the newcomers quickly recognized that the country had been scarred by war much older than the U.S.-Mexican conflict. Everywhere they heard stories and witnessed signs of raiding and skirmishes. Kearny assured his audiences that soon both the Navajos and Apaches would cease to exist as independent military powers. "From the Mexican government you have never received protections. . . . The Apaches and Navajos come down from the mountains and carry off your sheep, and even your women, whenever they please," he declared, before adding, "My government will correct all this." Radiating with confidence becoming of the expansionist Jacksonian era, Kearny also brusquely informed a group of Jicarilla Apaches that they "must desist from all robberies, and the committing of all crimes against the laws of the territory; that if they did not he would send his soldiers amongst them and destroy them from the earth." Still, some his officers recognized the potential for another shambolic conflict in the pattern of the Seminole wars. Many local residents who heard Kearny's words also most likely questioned whether the Anglos knew what they were talking about or if they had the capacity and skill to subdue or control the indigenous raiders. Others, suspecting the Indians were in alliance with the Americans, questioned the Anglo motivation to stop the raiding.[4]

Having been ordered to continue his march toward California and keeping an eye on potential Mexican opposition, Kearny and his officers established military government over New Mexico and started building the first U.S. Army post, Fort Marcy, overlooking Santa Fe. Those U.S. troops who would arrive in Kearny's wake would soon confront the independent Indians in diplomacy and violence, and they would come face to face with their own limitations in borderlands warfare.

Years of Containment

By the time Kearny's Army of the West invaded Santa Fe, various Apache groups had been impacted for numerous generations by violent storms of colonial intrusion that had transformed them and the world around them. From the mid-1500s onward, Spanish attempts to impose their authority and culture, their demands for slave labor, and the religion, diseases, crops, horses, livestock, weapons, and manufactured items they introduced had revolutionized indigenous life far beyond the immediate reach of the Spanish. The period of concord attained by Spain and many of the Apaches by the late 1700s and early 1800s gradually dissolved and made way for widespread raiding, captive taking, contraband trade, local and temporary peace pacts, social and cultural mixing, as well as treachery, murder, scalping, and bounties.

While Anglo merchants, trappers, and scalp hunters had preceded the formal U.S. annexation, in 1846 a new player, the U.S. federal government, with exclusive visions of dominance, entered the borderlands. The handful of federal officials in New Mexico experimented with a variety of diplomatic and military approaches when dealing with the indigenous powers. Personal rivalries, contending interests, logistical and financial woes, and bureaucratic matters beyond their control made the actions and policies of government representatives seem often inconsistent and confusing. The Apaches answered this new American challenge with policies ranging from avoidance to diplomacy and from trading to raiding. Some Apaches even hoped the U.S. troops would offer military assistance against Mexico, or they expected the Anglos to pay with rations and gifts for the right to cross or use Apache lands. In western Apacheria, American rule remained at best tentative in the 1850s, more a matter of imperial dreams than anything else. The Chiricahuas, especially the Chokonens, and the different Western Apache communities stood very much as rulers of their homelands. Also, to the east real hegemony on the ground was fleeting at best. Still, here, nearer to the Rio Grande, where the Jicarillas, Lipans, and Mescaleros resided, the Americans attempted to dictate their will on the Apaches and force them to stop combating the Mexicans, relinquish their raiding economy, curb their prevailing modes of survival, submit militarily, and keep their distance from Anglo and Hispanic settlements. For securing a firm grip on the Rio Grande, for enabling the birth of white settler society along its banks, and for keeping the fragile lines of communication open to the Pacific, the United States engaged in a war of containment against the Apaches in the 1850s. It was a somewhat tentative start, and certainly a step removed from the harsher methods that would follow in the 1860s.

Amity-Enmity Networks

In the mid-1700s, the expansionist Comanches overwhelmed the Lipans and demolished much of the Faraones, Natagees, and other Apache groups as they drove the Apaches out of the plains. Some of the Apaches, in turn, pushed their influence in Sonora and Chihuahua, paralyzing much of the mining industry and instigating a decline of commerce and the abandonment of numerous settlements. In northern Sonora, escalating Apache assaults compelled the O'odhams to congregate into larger villages for defense or relocate westward into the deserts and out of Apache reach. Particularly exposed was the eastern O'odham group, the Sobaipuris, who abandoned their villages along the San Pedro River due to Apache pressure. Meanwhile, cultivating friendship, trade, and military alliances, some San Carlos and Tonto Apaches neared their Yavapai neighbors, especially the Kwevkepaya and Wipukepa bands. That Anglos often counted the Yavapais as Apaches speaks not only of Anglo ignorance but of the close intimacy that decades of interaction had resulted in between some communities.[5]

The Western Apache-Yavapai connection, their shared conflict with the O'odhams and the Maricopas, and the O'odham linkages with the Colorado River Quechan-Mohave groups contributed to an amity-enmity network of alliances, trade, intimacy, and lethal conflict in northern Sonora, Adjacent and interwoven was a friendliness-hatred complex made by the different Chiricahua bands in their varied dealings with the communities of Sonora, Chihuahua, and New Mexico. In New Mexico, Texas, and Coahuila, the Hispanics, Pueblos, Navajos, Utes, and Comanches, as well as the Jicarilla, Mescalero, and Lipan Apaches, formed similar amity-enmity networks that also crisscrossed and interlinked with the aforementioned contact zones. They all were made up of intricate, dynamic, and volatile, as well as highly localized, blends of dependency, ethnic mingling, enslavement, trade, raiding, hatred, and vengeance. In these fluid zones, the boundaries between us and them, enemy and friend, were subject to constant negotiation as people, materials, and ideas circulated from one group to the next. Together with many indigenous groups, the Spanish communities produced a massive commodity market in human captives, taking, bartering, selling, and buying human capital with vigor and ruthlessness often associated with slave traders of the cotton South. In fact, owing to extensive trade and slave networks, Apache captives could be found in the households and industries from French Louisiana to as far south as Mexico City. Many Apaches were also sent all the way to Cuba.[6]

In 1786 it was obvious that Spain was still far from breaking the Apaches after years of campaigns and forced deportations of Apache captives. Seeking new options, the viceroy of the Northern Provinces, Bernardo de Gálvez, cemented a policy wherein Spain provided provisions of food, horses, and miscellaneous goods to Apaches who would voluntarily live near Spanish settlements and wage war against those Apaches who did not. The Spanish would take advantage of existing Apache needs and create new ones that could be satisfied only through reliance on the Spanish. Over time, the Spanish expected, the Apaches would become industrious sedentary farmers. In reality, most Apaches used the system to sustain and protect their families without giving up their independence. For many, rations and gifts constituted a payment for peace. Still, some Apaches built close relationships with the Spanish. Some, for instance members of the Compá family (Chiricahuas), lived inside the presidio walls at Janos, attended its school, and became literate in Spanish. Eventually, thousands of Chiricahua, Western (especially San Carlos), Lipan, and Mescalero Apaches, many of whom were tired of war, opted to locate to these "peace establishments" at least for part of the year. Later, this time period in Sonora and Chihuahua was remembered as the provinces' golden era, marked by growing prosperity, birth of new settlements, and the reopening of mines and ranches.[7]

By nurturing the Apache desire for Euro-American materials, the Spanish unintentionally generated the conditions for escalating violence and promoted the growing militarization of Apache culture. When the gift giving and rations withered after Mexican independence, many Apaches, especially the Chiricahuas, increasingly sought to get the materials they had grown accustomed to, and thought they had a right to, by raiding. With its treasury drained by the revolution and subsequent political unrest, the Mexican central government lacked the financial and military resources that had enabled New Spain to confront, if not control, the Apaches. Mexican weaknesses were painfully evident in the decay of the presidio system. During Spanish times, presidios had proven valuable, not only for serving as bases for military campaigns and for providing security to surrounding communities, but also as centers for diplomacy, trade, gift distribution, and the reservations.[8]

As a result, much of the fighting rested on the shoulders of residents. Local farmers and laborers were expected to fight on their own time, often at their own expense, and with minimal support from the government. Unable to defeat the Apaches, individual Mexican towns, ranches, and residents ranging from the upper echelons of society to smugglers made peace pacts with Apache families and communities. In these volatile contracts, the participants pledged not to attack the other and often engaged in mutually beneficial trade arrangements, usually involving goods Apaches had stolen from other Mexican/indigenous communities. Much could, and often did, go wrong.

For instance, during the fall of 1843 many Chiricahuas began to draw rations at Janos. They also left their dependents to the security of Janos while going to raids in Sonora and retreating back to Chihuahua. Shocked Sonorans thirsted for retaliation. In August 1844, Sonoran forces crossed, without permission, to Chihuahua and surrounded Janos. They killed over eighty Apaches. At first they slaughtered a sleeping Apache encampment at Janos using bayonets, and the next day they sacked several unsuspecting Apache camps near Corralitos. For many Mexicans, slaughtering Chiricahuas as they relaxed, traded, or celebrated made sense in times when options for besting the Apaches proved severely limited. Massacre saved one from the often overwhelming expenses involved in building, manning, or maintaining presidios or from the equally unattainable costs of organizing militias and campaigns into the Apache country.

Apache raids and Mexican massacres created a cycle of violence with shifting temporal intensity and no end in sight. Stories of massacres, as well as scalp hunters, enjoyed a vivid afterlife, as Apaches turned the episodes of horror from isolated incidents touching a single Apache family or community or one Mexican village into larger narratives of horror with wider meanings and extensive circulation. When communicating with Anglos, Apaches frequently retold these stories of Mexican treachery to explain their general stance of aggression against Mexicans. Inside Apache communities, the stories gained relevance, first, as cautionary accounts of dangers involved in trusting outsiders, and, second, as a source of motivation for acts of violence against the communities of northern Mexico.[9]

As the 1840s progressed, indigenous raiding started to give the appearance that the whole of northern Mexico was under siege and liable to be emptied of animals and resources. The Hispanic settlements of New Mexico were hampered by raids from the east by Comanches, and their Kiowa allies, and by Jicarilla Apaches and from the west by Navajos, who hit those settlements closest to them, like Jemez and Abiquiú, the hardest. All the Mexican communities in the Santa Cruz Valley except Tucson evacuated due to Chiricahua and Western Apache raids. Even in Tucson, life behind the city walls turned increasingly precarious. Also, the Sonoran state capital had to be removed from the besieged Arizpe south to Ures in 1838. Thousands of tired and shocked people, many of them being reduced to beggary, not only moved to larger towns but left the state altogether in search of safer lives. Some ventured south; others made the trip to the California goldfields. Those who stayed put lived in fear.[10]

White Mountain Apaches recurrently conducted expeditions lasting for as long as seventy or eighty days and covering an immense area, sometimes reaching Hermosillo and Suaqui or the Gulf of California. Chiricahua raids also at times stretched as far as southern Sonora and Chihuahua, occasionally extending even to parts of northern Sinaloa, while Mescaleros and Lipans covered Coahuila and Durango. For their part, Comanches and their allies launched more than thirty campaigns of over one hundred men below the Rio Grande between 1834 and 1846, accessing Durango, Zacatecas, and even San Luis Potosí.[11]

There existed a danger that the raids would prove counterproductive to the Apaches, who desired a hinterland they could use and exploit. Apaches also needed markets close by for trading the part of the stolen property they did not consume themselves. Looking for safer options than Janos, Corralitos, Casas Grandes, or Galeana offered, the Chiricahuas began to cultivate markets in

New Mexico, for example at Santa Rita del Cobre. Moreover, they frequently approached American trappers and traders, who trekked on the Santa Fe Trail and descended on the Gila, Salt, and Colorado Rivers, and supplied guns and ammunition in return for stolen Mexican property.[12]

The Americans rose to prominence in the business not only of contraband but also of scalp hunting. One of the more notorious scalpers was John Johnson, whose mercenaries, after two days of friendly bartering, murdered Chiricahua Juan Jose Compá and his followers without regard to age or gender in April of 1837. At least twenty Apaches died. A prospector, trapper, and trader, James Kirker sold wagonloads of guns and ammunition to the Apaches in the 1830s before the temptation of one hundred pesos for the scalp of an Apache man, fifty for a woman's, and twenty-five for children's eleven years old or younger led him to recalibrate his business focus. In an interview in 1847, Kirker boasted that his outfit had killed 487 Apaches, a figure that certainly seems like a gross exaggeration but may not be.[13]

Two years after Kirker was interviewed, John Joel Glanton, a soldier of fortune and a veteran of the U.S.-Mexican war, and his associates stopped at Chihuahua on their way to California. Tempted by the scalp bounties recorded in a new Chihuahuan state law from May 1849, the gang's operation was widespread, successful, and financially rewarding. Until they could not find any Apaches to scalp. Then the gang started scalping Mexicans, after which it did not take long for them to get thrown out of Chihuahua. Next, Glanton and his men did their killings in Sonora, ending up at Yuma. There, they took control of a ferry crossing the Colorado River. They also killed indiscriminately—Mexicans, Indians, and Anglos—for their goods and money. Fed up, the Yuma Indians massacred the majority of the gang in April 1850. Among the dead was Glanton, who was scalped.[14]

American Rule

As they listened to Kearny's bold promises, encountered his soldiers on a daily basis, or simply heard stories and rumors of the newcomers' activities, many Hispanic New Mexicans must have felt deep ambivalence. The possible end to violence the American officers marketed attracted many, but for those involved in the contraband business with the indigenous peoples the consolidation of national power signaled a danger to their livelihood. Still others had for some time already felt that their troubles resulted from Indian-U.S. collaboration that worked toward future U.S. annexations. Certainly the scheming of Anglo filibusters and the

Anglo involvement in trading stolen goods suggested that such collaboration was not out of the question. On the other hand, the calls for centralism by the Mexican government did not appeal to many New Mexicans. Many were also cognizant of the monumental deficit and foreign debt the national government carried. While present in the hearts and minds of many, Mexican nationalism was lacking in support. Still, resentment toward the occupation was apparent. While the Santa Fe Trail had opened new markets, injected new products into a depressed economy, and encouraged local people, with the cash generated and the capital invested, to begin working for wages, the work they often landed paid poorly and was at the bottom of the emerging Anglo-dominated society. Also, while some Anglos married into, usually prominent, New Mexican families and thus, at least in theory, displayed an interest in integrating themselves into the area's culture, many showed open contempt toward all things Hispanic.[15]

Throughout the 1830s and 1840s, Anglo politicians, journalists, travelers, soldiers, and others—both those who visited New Mexico and/or other Mexican provinces and those who never got within a thousand miles of one—offered broad generalizations on the qualities of Mexicans and their country. They produced a discourse wherein the Mexicans were no longer Spanish but were, in one soldier's words, a "swarthy, copper-colored, half-Indian race," an inherently flawed, superstitious (Catholic), lazy, and intellectually handicapped people. The long list of markers indicating Mexican inferiority included chili-flavored food, crooked streets, dirty adobe mud houses, mutt dogs, weird sports, overcurious, intrusive, and poverty-stricken people, naked and repulsive children, and tobacco-smoking women, who in their dress and behavior crossed the boundaries of decency when, for instance, exposing their arms, necks, and ankles. "As a nation," one observer wrote, Anglo Americans "are brave, honest, and enlightened," while Mexicans "are the reverse." "Perfidy is next of kin to their nature" while "faithlessness characterizes" them.[16]

While the Anglos denigrated Mexican character, they also emphasized how Mexicans dreaded and proved unable to control or crush the independent Indians on their northern border. In Anglo eyes, the local peace pacts between Apaches and Mexicans had resulted in a confusing and revolting mixture of extreme killing and miscegenation. As they wrote of hereditary enemies and unending raiding and war, Anglos painted a picture of European empire building gone terribly wrong. The Spanish had degenerated into Mexicans who were permanently outmatched in a degrading conflict. This vision of a permanent state of uncivilized violence allowed the Anglos to see themselves as liberators who would salvage the region and bring order to chaos. Many Americans made it explicit through their writings and attitudes that they could do a better job than the Mexicans. They would not only save the remnants of the once mighty Spanish empire in North America but would also build a new thriving civilization, making the desert blossom.

This confidence materialized in Article XI of the Treaty of Guadalupe Hidalgo. It bound U.S. authorities to "forcibly restrain" Indian raiding across the border, to rescue Mexican captives held by Indians, and to punish those raiders who managed to slip across the borderline. The article also stipulated that the U.S. government should display "equal diligence and energy" as if the raids from U.S. to Mexico were "meditated or committed within its own territory against its own citizens."[17] This article calmed things little. Besides the continued raiding of independent Indians, there were the questions of slavery, statehood, and New Mexican sovereignty against Texan demands to stir trouble. Having mounted an unsuccessful expedition against Santa Fe in 1841, the land-hungry Texans again grasped for an opportunity to extend their domain and the sphere of slavery to eastern New Mexico. Only after the new chief executive, Zachary Taylor, made it clear that federal troops would repulse any invasion by Texas was a disaster averted. The Compromise of 1850 made New Mexico (including today's Arizona)—being neither English-speaking, nor Protestant, nor "white"—a territory, with an option to decide on slavery in the future. Regardless of what the compromise had actually settled, many Anglos still asked whether it was worth adding massive tracts of desert areas that seemed likely to become a longtime economic burden to the nation. Of the tens of thousands of people who traveled through New Mexico to California, a mere handful stopped and most of them did not wander far from the Rio Grande. Furthermore, New Mexico proved a money pit, as it had the army as its principal—and in many places only—business.[18]

Aside from the Texan threat, in 1847 Hispanic and Pueblo resistance against American occupation expanded from Taos. Before U.S. forces could react, the infuriated inhabitants had killed the first American governor, Charles Bent, and targeted Anglo packtrains and grazing sites. U.S. forces marched north from Santa Fe through the snow and surrounded the resisters, who occupied an adobe church at Taos Pueblo. With the help of howitzers, the troops demolished the church and its inhabitants. The intended message was obvious: anyone who opposed the new regime would be squashed. However, bombing people huddled up in a church was a different matter altogether than catching and defeating mobile cells of knowledgeable Indian raiders.[19] From 1846 onward, the army ran into trouble as it tried to assert its authority by sending expeditions into Navajo lands. The army signed irrelevant treaties and could not make the Navajos fight or prevent their raiding. Also, the campaigns reduced the soldiers and their big mounts to stumbling, starving, and breathless phantoms.[20]

Already in 1846 Kearny had sent detachments into the Apache country in futile searches for stolen property. After Kearny departed, the army's first violent contacts with the Apaches established the pattern for direct pursuits where small detachments of men stormed after Chihenne, Mescalero, or Jicarilla raiders who drove off livestock from the Rio Grande settlements. For instance, in December 1851 and January 1852 alone the Apaches made at least ten raids and captured hundreds of head of livestock in the section of Rio Grande between Doña Ana and El Paso. With the general goal of hitting moving targets and recapturing stolen property, both which would ideally discourage raiding in the future, the troops regularly engaged in futile chases. For example, in February 1850 Maj. Enoch Steen and his soldiers—who operated out of Doña Ana, a farming village set up in 1843 on a Mexican land grant on the east bank of the Rio Grande—caught none of the Mescalero raiders who had struck on February 2. Furthermore, as his men were out chasing the raiders, other Apaches had driven off more livestock from Doña Ana. Reflecting on his failure, Steen called for larger, better organized, and more meticulously planned operations. When Apaches "become so bold" as to steal livestock within "a mile of United States garrison . . . I think it becomes necessary to chastise them and this can only be done by a regularly organized campaign against them."[21]

For the first, but not the last, time in borderlands wars, growing frustration and doubts over the army's abilities in desert combat started to plague Anglo minds. Wanting to appear confident, Kearny, Steen, and the officers and soldiers who followed in their wake felt that it was their task to transform warfare along the border. They wanted raids and chases to make way for battles and all-out war. Writing in 1855, Capt. Joseph Eaton declared, "War with the whole Apache race . . . should be declared, and they should be made to understand that it will never end." Already in 1851, Col. Edwin Summer, commanding New Mexico, voiced the army's prejudices when noting that Indians and Mexicans "steal women and children, and cattle from each other, and in fact carry on the war, in all respects, like two Indian nations. . . . This predatory war has been carried on for two hundred years . . . quite time enough to prove, that unless some change is made the war will be interminable."[22]

In reality the U.S. forces displayed a limited reach. The necessity of securing the Rio Grande base, and also the priority of watching the Hispanic populace,

saw the soldiers initially occupy major urban sites hugging the river: Taos, Santa
Fe, Albuquerque, Socorro, Tome, and Doña Ana. Thinking that indigenous
peoples could not be contained from urban centers, and viewing New Mexico
settlements as nests of vice, Sumner, who also suggested withdrawing U.S.
troops and leaving the Hispanics and Indians to fight it out, moved the troops
to more rural bastions. Still, it was a modest departure for actually challenging
indigenous hegemony, as nearly all posts roughly lined the Rio Grande. With
the exception of Fort Defiance (on Navajo lands), and Fort Buchanan, none of
the more permanent posts in 1850s New Mexico were far off.[23]

As it had been since Kearny's march, the Rio Grande remained ground zero
of U.S. imperial reach for the whole decade. Santa Fe and El Paso represented
not just locales where whites grappled for political and financial power but
settlements that did not have to tremble in the fear of Apaches overrunning
them. In many smaller villages, this was not case. Mesilla and Doña Ana, the
biggest Hispanic communities bordering the river between El Paso and Santa
Fe, were located at the intersection of Chihenne and Mescalero domains. This
was deep in Apacheria, where volatile intermingling in trade and raid defined
community life. Many Anglo observers noted that the countryside was dotted
with deserted buildings and fields emptied by Apache raiding. The first U.S.
troops to inhabit Doña Ana had arrived in 1848, while 1855 saw the U.S. Army
march across the new boundary (Gadsden Purchase) and occupy Mesilla. Many
soldiers felt that they had entered foreign lands, as civilian Anglo presence was
nearly nonexistent.[24]

New Storms Rising

In the early 1850s, it was the Jicarilla Apaches' geographic position in the northeastern New Mexico corridor—where the Santa Fe Trail, with its branches and
cutoffs, continued to function as the main commercial highway linking the
borderlands to the American centers in the East—that placed them at the receiving end of Anglo wrath. The Jicarillas already showed the sufferings resulting
from a long competition against the Comanches, Hispanics, and Anglo trappers
and merchants. Much of their land base in southern Colorado and northeastern
New Mexico had been given away by the Mexican government via eight private
land grants and five town grants, including the 1.7-million-acre area purchased
in 1847 by Lucien B. Maxwell. Bison hunting on the plains was still possible in
theory, but it was a proposition made perilous by Comanche presence. Even
when Maxwell allowed Jicarillas to remain, the hungry Jicarillas, feeling that

they had little choice, frequently stole from the livestock on their lands. This, in turn, gave them a reputation as a group of thieves and vagabonds who must be subdued. The words of New Mexico's first Indian agent and governor, James S. Calhoun, fittingly encapsulate the prevailing mood. Calhoun asserted that the Jicarillas were generally regarded as "bold, daring, and adventurous spirits" who bragged that they had "never encountered the face of a white foe, who did not quail, and attempt to fly from them."[25]

On the other hand, several U.S. officials on the ground, including Calhoun, and his two successors, William Carr Lane and David Meriwether, as well as many local Hispanic and Taos Pueblo residents, recognized the Jicarillas' predicament. They typically suggested that the federal government should give the Apaches some good land for farming. Instead of negotiating a long-term diplomatic solution, the Jicarillas as well as the Mescaleros to the south faced an inexplicably confusing mixture of failed promises and declarations of goodwill intermixed with impulses for annihilation. If the Anglos were attempting to alter the face of warfare on the borderlands, their unreliable diplomacy and propensity for bursts of violence not only left the Apaches anguished and desperate but also reminded many of the Mexican policies that mixed trade, diplomacy, and massacre. No wonder the Jicarillas felt deep uncertainty of tomorrow.

Already in 1849 four separate incidents had demonstrated the likelihood of a major crisis brewing. In May 1849, troops confronted some Jicarillas they suspected of raiding near Abiquiú. The soldiers attacked and killed twenty of the band. In August a party of Jicarillas arrived in Las Vegas, New Mexico, to trade, apparently seeking to buy gunpowder. Unable to get any, they faced independent-minded military officers who felt sure that the gunpowder was meant for killing whites. The officers sought to arrest the Apaches, but a skirmish broke out as the Jicarillas tried exiting the town. When later interviewed, the Indians felt that they had been attacked without any cause.

Two months later the traveling party of James White encountered a group of Jicarillas demanding gifts as toll payment. White refused to pay, ignored the Jicarillas, and hurried onward. An arrow storm killed White and five or six others. His wife, Ann, their daughter, and a servant were taken captive by the Apaches. A few weeks later, the U.S. Army, guided by Christopher "Kit" Carson galloped to the site of the attack. From there they followed the Jicarilla tracks onward to the plains for twelve days with retribution and retrieval of the captives in mind. Near the Texas border the soldiers spotted an occupied Apache camp, eventually charging it after the Jicarillas started hastily packing. Spreading out in all directions, the Jicarillas made good of their escape, while the troops held the field of battle. About two hundred yards from the camp, they found the still-warm body of Ann White. She had possibly been shot while trying to flee. Her daughter and servant were never heard from again. Meanwhile, another group of soldiers from Las Vegas had gone after Ann White with the daughter of Jicarilla leader Lobo Blanco as collateral. En route, the weeping and distraught girl seized a knife and started a commotion at camp, stabbing mules until she was shot by one of the soldiers. That ended that expedition.[26]

While a precious few except the Jicarillas paid attention to the latter shooting, the fate of Ann White was widely reported. It was among the first of such episodes that tarnished what little favorable reputation the Apaches might have garnered in the eyes of Anglo society. While Ann White and her fate became a tale retold in local civilian and military circles, the gossip, public fascination, and news coverage reached altogether grander scales in the case of Olive Oatman. In August 1850, the Oatman family, parents Royce and Mary Ann and seven children, left Missouri as part of a wagon caravan heading for the Colorado River and California. After the O'odham villages, only the Oatmans, fearing Indians and starvation, pushed on. Along the way, they met a group of Indians they thought were Apaches asking for food. As they kept asking for more, Royce Oatman refused, declaring there was none. After a short fight, the Indians took Olive and her sister Mary Ann as captives, leaving the rest of the family to die. While her sister perished, Olive tried to learn to live among the Mohaves, after being traded to the Colorado River group by her captors. After a few years, her presence was discovered by white authorities, who, by threatening to attack the Mohaves, secured Olive's release in 1856.

Next, it was the press that went after Olive. In San Francisco, a local reverend and newsman, Royal Stratton, interviewed her and two years later published *The Captivity of the Oatman Girls*, followed by a publicity tour with Olive in the East. The book became a massive success with about thirty thousand copies sold in two years. (It is still easily available in paperback reprints.) Facing a lifetime of scrutiny in white society, Olive's captivity was made by the press and Stratton to function as a warning to all those Anglos, especially women, who traveled across the Southwest borderlands. The haunting tale embellished fates worse than death awaiting white women caught by the Apaches. In a space of few years, the Oatman saga attained legendary status. Many Anglos who ventured to Arizona referred to Olive's story, fearing and loathing the Apaches in the process. In reality, Olive was most likely captured by Yavapais, probably Tolkepayas, but possibly Kwevkepayas. While Olive herself claimed that it was the Tonto Apaches who had taken her, it was Stratton who used the term "Apache" as a ubiquitous euphemism throughout his work. In doing so, he demonized all the Apaches.[27]

Captivity narratives would continue to erode the Apache image in Anglo eyes. For example, in 1860 new bride Larcena Page was taken by a small Apache party (most likely Tontos, or possibly Pinals) from a lumber camp in the Santa Rita Mountains near Canoa. As she put up heavy resistance, the Apaches quickly grew tired of Larcena. They pierced her with lances and struck her with rocks before abandoning the unconscious woman to die. Gaining her senses, the badly beaten Larcena trekked back to camp, emerging after a two-week absence. It was hardly surprising that the press, with Olive Oatman in peoples' minds, subsequently made Page a heroine who had held her own against the Apaches.[28] Other captivity sagas, used as examples of the predatory nature of Apaches, would become household news across the borderlands and the nation, most notably in the 1880s.

On April 2, 1851, the Jicarillas signed a very lopsided treaty with Calhoun in Santa Fe. If anything, this treaty revealed their desire for peaceful coexistence. The Apaches agreed to submit to the authority of the United States, cease all activities of war, relinquish stolen property, and cultivate the soil. Importantly, they promised to refrain from coming closer than fifty miles to any settlement or major road. The final requirement was meant to contain the Apaches to those regions the Anglos and Hispanics did not use. In practice, it barred all trade and made death by starvation a more likely prospect. In exchange, the Apaches were promised annuities and farming implements from the government. The treaty, however, was never ratified by the budget-stingy and indifferent Congress. With no help from Washington, Calhoun sought to give piecemeal aid to the Jicarillas, who in turn tried to abide to the almost impossible treaty conditions. Calhoun died in June 1852 while en route to the nation's capital to plead the Apache case. Next, it was new governor William Lane, who, being assured by both Jicarilla and Mescalero delegates that they wanted peace, envisioned and tried to put in practice policies of assimilation through farming. Like Calhoun, Lane acted without financial or other support from his superiors, and had to make unauthorized agreements with various Apache communities. Soon after he started issuing rations and farming implements, Lane ran out of funding. Then the reality probably hit him. His government lacked commitment to make his pledges and plans work. Instead, Lane became the subject of criticism from the head of the Office of Indian Affairs for his visionary and unintelligible ideas and was bluntly informed that there was no funding available. While Lane resigned his post, the Jicarillas, insulted by broken promises, once again went hungry.[29]

From 1854 to 1855, the U.S. Army, under the leadership of Gen. John Garland, Sumner's successor, orchestrated a campaign against the Jicarillas and Mescaleros that would prove an illustrative example of the army's strengths and weaknesses. Like many such endeavors in years to come, this was a military offensive camouflaged as retribution and nominally ignited by specific Apache deeds. In August 1853, a group thought to have been Mescaleros sacked an emigrant train bound for California, reportedly taking 150 head of stock. This was an otherwise typical Apache raid targeting material gain except that ten whites were killed after trying to recover their property at Dog Canyon in the Sacramento Mountains.[30] Six months later, and to the north, the beef contractor for Fort Union reported that much of his livestock had been taken by the Jicarillas. This time there were no Anglo casualties, as nobody had challenged the Apaches. In both instances, the army treated indigenous livestock robbery as an act and declaration of war.

The army went after the Apaches by dispatching troops with instructions to retrieve captured property and the guilty perpetrators. If these ultimatums were not met, the troops were ordered to attack the Apaches without hesitation. On the Canadian River on March 5, 1854, the troops encountered some Jicarillas who wanted a parley. Interrogated about the livestock theft, the Jicarillas declared their innocence. Not getting the answer he wanted, and not believing the Apaches, the officer in charge, Lt. David Bell, ordered the Jicarilla leader Lobo Blanco arrested and held until the thieves surrendered. Alerted to foul play, the Jicarillas formed a semicircle around the troops, who, when ordered by Bell, charged. The Apaches sidestepped the rushing formation and hit its rear. The mounted troops turned around and came racing again. Again the Jicarillas got out of the way, shooting arrows at the soldiers while on the move. Having had enough of being the targets of mass armed movement, the Jicarillas, with soldiers on their heels, bolted to the arroyos and ravines that led toward the main branch of the Canadian River. The chase, with the Jicarillas seeking to exploit all the natural cover a difficult terrain could provide, soon ceased as the Anglos feared that they would be taken by surprise. Lobo Blanco and four other Apaches, as well as two soldiers, had lost their lives. The troops, averse to the terrain that seemed to invite ambush, but also exhausted and short on supplies, returned to Fort Union.[31]

Next, on March 30, 1854, troops led by Lt. John Davidson surprised a Jicarilla camp on Embudo Mountain, a steep-sided ridge near the small village of Cienguilla south of Taos. It was not a typical borderlands clash. Although the Jicarillas first fled and the army gained command of the camp, the Apaches returned, charging the soldiers' horses. Now on the retreat, the besieged soldiers rallied off the Jicarilla assaults time and again in desperate fighting, some of which was hand-to-hand. "I was wounded," one army man recounted, continuing that he first "ran about a mile" until he "was not able to walk alone any farther." Then he "got between two horses, seized their stirrups," and the "horses dragged me one half mile when I managed to mount my horse." After this ordeal, he concluded, his "blood flowed freely." Stopping momentarily at Cienguilla, the troops escaped through the night toward the safety of Cantonment Burgwin. Of the sixty soldiers, twenty-two had been killed, and from twenty-three to thirty-six had been wounded. The command also lost most of its horses and arms to the Apaches. When measured in casualties, Davidson's defeat would prove the most serious single rout suffered by regular U.S. troops at the hands of the Apaches.[32]

Opening actions like this where the Apaches were caught off guard were followed mostly by days, weeks, and months of draining pursuits, as the soldiers upped the hunt and as the Jicarillas and Mescaleros spent most of their time—if not making peace overtures and seeking protection from those white authorities not on their tail—eluding the detachments of soldiers sent after them. For example, one weary troop commanded by Lt. Col. Philip St. George Cooke in pursuit of the Jicarillas experienced a thirty-hour snowstorm during and after which their horses ran astray and sank in the thick snowbanks. Alarmingly, their pack mules also bogged down in the heavy snow in the mountains overlooking the Chama Valley. With his outfit in deplorable condition, Cooke had to halt the pursuit despite locating fresh tracks.[33]

Amid all the exhausting marching, the troops destroyed Jicarilla camps on April 8, June 4, and June 30, 1854. The impact: the already-suffering Jicarillas became even more desolate. To the south, one troop led by Lt. Col. Daniel Chandler canvassed the Sierra Blanca and Rio Bonito for three weeks without finding a single Mescalero in January and February of 1854. In the following summer, Chandler's men were abused by the torrid heat and monsoon rains for seven weeks in and around the Sacramento Mountains. This time they managed to have a brief and unproductive parley with one Mescalero group, who had approached the soldiers waving a white flag. Most of the time, however, Chandler's outfit remained clueless of the Apaches' whereabouts. As was becoming customary, the troops limped home exhausted and discouraged. Also, in the summer another group of soldiers, functioning independently of Chandler, canvassed the Capitan Mountains in what also turned out to be an arduous, yet futile, search for the

Mescaleros. The three-week campaign ended as the fatigued men and horses could not continue another step.[34]

Occasionally the troops got what they went after, but then—as with Davidson's experience—it turned out to be more than they could handle. In January 1855, Garland launched a series of detachments in a slightly more coordinated manner than those of the previous year. They investigated the surrounds of the village Anton Chico before heading toward the Capitan Mountains, Rio Ruidoso, and the Sacramento Mountains. On January 17, while most likely trying to ensure the escape of their noncombatants, the Mescaleros pummeled the military column with hit-and-run tactics the entire day. The next day the Apaches ambushed and routed the detachment of Capt. Henry Stanton, who trekked ahead of the main force investigating what appeared, initially, to be an abandoned cluster of Apache lodges. With Stanton dead, the Mescaleros dispersed, having suffered serious casualties (seven to seventeen Apaches had been killed). By now, the soldiers' strength was failing, and their bellies and mounts were in desperate need of nutrition as supplies were running out. Barefoot and starving, the soldiers staggered back to their bases on the Rio Grande.[35]

What followed in the Jicarilla theater after June 1854 was an interlude of diplomacy. Jicarillas dispatched delegates, including one of their leaders, Chacon, who, in a meeting with Governor Meriwether, explained that other Jicarillas had caused the fighting before moving south. Now Congress had also awakened, appropriating funding for Indian management in New Mexico and for nego-tiating treaties. As the wheels of diplomacy slowly turned, and as preparations for more extensive negotiations were planned for the summer or fall of 1855, some Apaches, to avoid starvation, could not refrain from stealing livestock. For example, in the early months of 1855, Jicarilla parties took, according to some inflated reports, some 5,500 head of cattle from the settlers in the San Luis Valley. Judging the threat serious, the army sent a combined force of five hundred regulars and volunteers, called into service by Garland, against the Apaches. Under Lt. Col. Dixon Miles, the soldiers penetrated the Sierra Blanca and the Capitan and Sacramento Mountains. In April 1855, they encountered a sizable group of Mescaleros, who, in turn, had already sent a peace delegation of their own to Fort Thorn on the Rio Grande the previous month. Without firing a shot, the Apaches surrendered to Miles in numbers at Dog Canyon. Now the Mescalero peace initiative found a receptive ear, as Miles proposed a cease-fire under the condition that Mescaleros stop all raiding and set up a future meeting with Meriwether.[36]

Meanwhile, the Jicarillas were chased by Col. Thomas Fauntleroy, who hoped in his 1855 report that the troops would "inflict a final blow of extermination upon" the Apaches. While Fauntleroy's stance reflected a hard-line view, it also showed the level of soldier irritation and disappointment at this stage. Exhausted, the soldiers had to return to Fort Union to rest and resupply after few weeks in the field. Before that, they had managed to surprise an Apache camp at Bear Creek and engage in a two-day fight, during which the Apaches fled toward the Purgatoire River and Raton Pass, having several of their numbers killed and taken prisoner. After resting, the troops were once again on the move in June 1855, this time playing what seemed like a futile game of cat and mouse.[37]

While continuing to hound the Apaches, although with few battlefield accolades to show for it, the federal government also opted for diplomacy. In summer 1855, Meriwether treated with various Apache groups and made treaties whereby the Apaches agreed to surrender specific lands, give up their nomadic way of life, settle on federal reservations, and raise crops and livestock in exchange for government rations and payments. While the Jicarillas put pen to paper on September 12, 1855, the treaty was again not ratified by the unresponsive Congress, and thus did not become effective. With their homelands now under white settlement, the Jicarillas scattered and kept mostly quiet. They had become homeless borderlands refugees. Many battled starvation and sought rations from the Abiquiú, Taos, and Cimarron Agencies. Some drew closer to the Utes in Colorado. Outside of a few isolated raids, the Jicarillas remained hidden from the gaze of the U.S. Army.[38]

The Mescaleros also met with Meriwether and signed a treaty on June 14, 1855. Demonstrating the ongoing trend, this agreement also failed to get ratified. Besides promoting mutual peace, friendship, and goodwill, the agreement, like the others Meriwether made, sought to distance the Mescaleros from other settlements and travel routes. In exchange, it promised rations and specific yearly payments from the federal government. It also pledged the setting up of a reservation in Mescalero homelands where the government was already building a new post, Fort Stanton, on Rio Bonito in the vicinity of the Sierra Blanca and Capitan Mountains. While some Apaches probably intensely disliked this new post, it became a hub for a lively multiethnic society revolving around trade (also contraband), socializing, and various vices—including alcohol, prostitution, and gambling. An officer's wife penned that at Fort Stanton many Mescaleros "came and went as they pleased, walking into our houses and sitting on our porches without the least hesitation." The government, through the U.S. Indian agent for the southern Apaches, Michael Steck, a former military doctor and a man devoted to his underfunded task, also issued rations to the Mescaleros at this post or at Fort Thorn.[39]

Despite the often intimate atmosphere at Fort Stanton, the Mescaleros—who raided wagon trains and small settlements near the Rio Grande, frequently eluding the troops chasing after them—continued to be seen as a military threat by many borderlands residents.[40] Frustrated by the Apache raids and the powerlessness of federal troops, the mostly Hispanic Mesilla residents raised an armed militia in 1857 with the purpose of destroying the Apaches in the vicinity. The outfit, known as the Mesilla Guard, gained fame in February 1858 by attacking a party of Mescaleros who were camped outside Doña Ana for trading. Tensions mounted between the populace of Mesilla and that of Doña Ana, the former accusing the latter of protecting thieving Apaches and the latter charging the former of brutally slaughtering and antagonizing the powerful Apaches. Both communities prepared themselves for the looming Mescalero reprisal. Lieutenant Colonel Miles also felt certain that bloody retribution would follow. Showing the seriousness of the situation, and thinking that the Mescaleros held the upper hand, Miles expected the Apaches to gain revenge "by wiping this town [Mesilla] out." Furious with the turmoil caused by the Mesilla Guard, the army issued a proclamation warning the people of Mesilla that those who perpetrated acts of violence would receive no military protection against the Apaches. The government, through Agent Steck, also informed the Mescaleros that if they sought revenge the army would attack their homes. The Mescaleros did not retaliate. But another crisis loomed just around the corner, as on April 17, 1858, the Mesilla Guard attacked a Mescalero camp, killing seven. This time the target was a group that lived near Fort Thorn and drew rations from Steck, whose agency was at the fort. The army arrested the guard members and put them on trial at Socorro. With the territorial governor on the guard's side, the jury, composed of their peers, wasted little time in acquitting all the accused.[41]

Battle for Survival

Being the most battered of the Apache groups still standing in the 1850s, the Lipans approached the American invasion in terms of survival. They had few notions of regaining the upper hand against their borderlands neighbors. In Texas, it was the state, not the federal government, that controlled public lands. And it was able to conduct quick surveys and quicker sales of vast tracks of real estate. Although allowed at first to remain within the settlement line, the Lipans around San Antonio soon lived in the midst of thousands of fresh newcomers from the French-German borderland province of Alsace-Lorraine and from other German states. Although the Lipans usually got along well enough with the German farmers, white immigrants took control of crucial water, grass, and game resources. A growing number of military rivals also challenged the Lipans. In the 1840s and 1850s, the Mexican government, with the intention of establishing a buffer zone between Mexican settlements and the Comanche and Anglo threat, invited Kickapoos and Seminoles, as well as some Cherokees, Shawnees, and Delawares, to settle in Coahuila. While many Lipans were able to establish trade ties with these eastern transplants, the newcomers also added to the now-long list, which included the Comanches and the state and federal troops from both sides of the international border, of military competition.[42]

Shortly after annexing Texas, the federal government had dispatched commissioners to set up contacts with its indigenous peoples. Meetings held and treaties made at Comanche Peak and Council Springs in 1846, Spring Creek in 1850, and San Saba in 1851 brought little clarity or security for the Apaches. Much like the Jicarillas and Mescaleros did in their treaties in New Mexico, the Lipans placed themselves under U.S. protection, promising to stay away from settlements, stop all raiding on both sides of the border, and deliver all Mexican captives for free. Neither did the Lipan situation change much in 1855 with the short-lived federal reservation experiment on the Brazos River, where the government first wanted Lipans who lived south of San Antonio, north of Austin on the San Gabriel River, and in Coahuila to relocate. The government discussions that followed the experiment at Brazos and calls for the establishment of a Lipan reservation west of the Pecos River proved as protracted as they were unproductive. Meanwhile, in the eyes of the U.S. Army and the Texas Rangers, all Lipans living outside reservations—the Lipans did not have a reservation of their own—were considered hostiles.[43]

Their space eaten up, the starving Lipans, like the Jicarillas, resorted to stealing stock, which, in turn, led to violence. At least three times in 1847–49 a troop of Texas Rangers, who suspected the Apaches of horse thievery, stormed a Lipan encampment. At least fifty Lipans died as a result. The U.S. Army had first engaged a Lipan band suspected of raiding in 1847. Col. Alexander Doniphan's troops killed fifteen Lipans and robbed the band of their captives and material base. To the horror of Lipan survivors, their new enemies took not the scalp but the skull of their leader. It was shipped to Philadelphia for craniological investigation. Another incident in 1848 saw maddened troops, chasing their own horses stolen by the Comanches, to pour down on a Lipan camp that was just unlucky enough to land in their path. Destroying everything, killing indiscriminately, and capturing two hundred horses, the soldiers completely devastated the material foundation and life of the Lipan community in question.[44]

Much as it was with other Apache groups, there existed no monolithic Lipan response to the crisis they now faced. Facing drought, starvation, and military force, some Lipans drew close to the Texas Indian Agency or the army posts, seeking rations and protection. Many hoped to find a stable home and, possibly, start raising corn, but what they found was disappointment in inadequate food supplies or in efforts to assert tight control over their comings and goings. Living close to white military authorities could prove precarious. A handful of Lipans allied with the Tonkawa Indians, who, like the Lipans, represented the remnants of once-powerful Southern Plains indigenous group. They lived near military forts in Texas before being abruptly shipped to the Indian Territory during the Civil War. At their new home, the Lipans and Tonkawas, being perceived as pro-Confederate, endured a massacre at the hands of a pro-Union indigenous alliance. The survivors returned to Texas after the war and settled near Fort Griffin, where they started working for the U.S. Army. Handful of Lipans had also sought shelter in southwestern Oklahoma and the Texas Panhandle. Others fled west and joined the Mescaleros or ventured up the Pecos River out of reach of the forts in Texas. Scattered Lipan settlements were located also across south Texas and near San Antonio. Still, few managed to escape the killing. Witnessing the desperate situation resulting from starvation and repeated attacks, an Anglo observer noted while passing through Texas in 1854–55, "At least half of the Lipans have been exterminated by powder and ball in the open war of the last years."[45]

After 1855, the majority of Lipans resided in Mexico. They built stormy alliances with Mexican communities such as Zaragosa in Coahuila. Many were also hopping back and forth from Texas and Mexico, especially along the border section reaching from Laredo to Brownsville. Many were borderlands refugees constantly on the run, trying to evade pursuers and seek safety when conditions on either side of the borderline called for it. Those Lipans who wanted to, or felt they had to in order to survive, keep the raiding-trading complex alive found plenty of livestock to steal in south Texas. They also found many Mexicans receptive to trading the goods stolen from north of the border. The cleverer raiders wore western-style clothing, thus passing off as Hispanics, or they re-branded cattle. The more daring, or foolhardy, stole livestock from the proximity of forts and then tried to make a quick escape across the Rio Grande to Mexico. Whatever the method, raiding infuriated many borderlands Anglos, who barraged authorities with complaints about the Lipans.[46]

More often than not the Lipans found themselves on the receiving end, as military pressure kept mounting against them in 1856 and afterward. Although some retreated to the Big Bend region of Texas or to the remote mountain reaches of northern Mexico, it was more and more difficult to find sanctuaries from bloodshed and suffering. Seeking to respond to Anglo complaints, and to discourage illegal border crossings by Americans in search of Lipans, Coahuila soldiers demolished two Lipan villages in 1856. Furthermore, small detachments of troops from different Texas posts engaged parties of Lipan raiders on four occasions in March and April 1856 alone. Next, between July 1857 and October 1858, three separate strikes by the U.S. Army hit their Lipans targets with dramatic success. Beside the numerous dead and wounded, many Lipans faced captivity. Additionally, their supplies were lost, camps destroyed, and horses taken. For some Lipans, the devastation they faced was too overwhelming. Tied together and marched onward, one party of captive Lipan women mutinied by cutting the throats of their children. Horrified Coahuilan troops ended up killing forty-four Lipans in the scuffle that ensued.[47]

Campaigns of Clowns

In the mid-1850s, with the Lipans and Jicarillas braving an existence as borderlands refugees and the severely weakened Mescaleros facing an uncertain future, it seemed that the Anglos were gaining momentum in the proximity of the Rio Grande. The lands to the west, however, remained a different matter. Once more experimenting with a variety of diplomatic and military means, the federal government employed policies in western Apacheria that were as inconsistent as they were elsewhere in Apacheria. But the policies were also more cautious. The American government seemed more interested in securing safe passages for Anglos heading for the Pacific than in making the Chiricahuas submit to its will. Furthermore, while the government sporadically targeted the Chihennes and some Western Apaches with military actions, the success of these campaigns pushed by a few aggressive officers remained exceptionally poor. And while it occasionally tried to get some Chihennes to sign treaties and in this manner to gain indigenous acceptance to its proposed dominance and rule, the federal government was more often inclined to contain and appease these powerful Apache communities. In short, the federal government distributed gifts and rations to the Chiricahuas in exchange for peace.

Although the government conducted surveys to get to know the land and to make its presence known to the residents, even in the regional hub of Tucson American influence seemed negligible. Like Mesilla, Tucson fell under nominal U.S. sovereignty with the Gadsden Purchase. U.S. troops did not reach the community until 1856, and in the meantime it had remained garrisoned by Mexican soldiers. While Mesilla represented a new settlement set up by those who after 1848 had preferred Mexico to the United States, Tucson exemplified a regional center built on generations of Hispanic-indigenous mixing. Throughout the 1850s, Tucson's trade continued to flow through Guyamas and Hermosillo in Sonora, immigration was Mexican rather than Anglo, and bells of the Catholic Church set the rhythm of the day and its celebrations marked the year. The few Anglos who settled in the community married into Hispanic families. Those who visited Tucson characterized the settlement as distinctly foreign in its outlook, with crooked, dusty streets and decaying adobe structures dominating the community, where drinking, gambling, and other vices seemed to constitute the principal business and pastime. Until the railroad era, many Anglos saw Tucson as a symbol of the dark and corrupt Southwest, as something they distanced to the realm of the exotic and the inferior.[48]

Some Yavapai and Western Apache groups who lived north of the Gila and Salt Rivers saw little if any change in their lives, while others, such as the O'odhams, witnessed a surge in the demand for their surplus wheat, corn, pumpkins, beans, and other farm produce from Anglo sojourners heading to California. The surviving O'odham calendar sticks mark 1846–48 as "three peaceful years."[49]

Much of the area between Tucson and Mesilla was ruled by different Chiricahua Apache communities that focused on skirting their Mexican enemies and on giving back as good as they got. Take, for example, 1849. During that violent year alone, Chiricahua communities were hit by Mexican troops sixteen times. In addition, various scalp-hunting parties, including Glanton's, clashed with the Apaches at least ten times in 1849.[50] On the other hand, numerous Chiricahua parties, often attributed to the leadership of the Bedonkohe Mangas Coloradas, or the Chokonen Miguel Narbona, laid waste to northern Mexico's ranches and settlements. For example, on March 9, 1849, a party of Chokonens burned and demolished a ranch forty miles south of Arizpe, while on October 11 they raided Janos and its vicinity, procuring dozens of horses and cattle. In the coming years, violence between the Chiricahuas and northern Mexico only intensified. While in the 1840s the Chiricahuas had averaged fifteen military engagements per year, the figure rose to twenty-one actions a year in the 1850s. Importantly, the overwhelming majority of these actions continued to be against Mexicans, not Americans. Other Apache communities could not match the level of military activity that characterized the Chiricahua-Mexican violence.[51]

Ample sections of the Chihenne and Bedonkohe heartlands in the Black Range and Mogollon Mountains were officially on U.S. soil starting 1848, while the Chokonen lands in the Dragoon and Chiricahua Mountains followed suit after the Gadsden Purchase. While the Mescaleros and Lipans shared their raiding zone in Mexico with the powerful Comanches, for the Chiricahuas the situation was different. Except for the intermittent Western Apache raids into Mexico, the Chiricahuas did not have to share. On the other hand, they alone bore much of northern Sonora and Chihuahua's hatred as well. Although confident in their military capabilities, the Chiricahuas welcomed the new international border they could use for evading their enemies and for launching strikes across northern Mexico. They could also welcome Anglo travelers—of whom most were not dangerous or staying—as it meant increased trade. The Apaches provided property taken from Mexico in exchange for Anglo clothing, food, utensils, and weapons. The Chiricahuas also saw opportunities for trade with the U.S. troops traversing their lands. In October 1846, near the ruins of abandoned Santa Rita del Cobre, Kearny's column encountered the Chiricahuas and Mangas Coloradas. The Apaches proved eager traders and promised friendship with the Americans. They also made a powerful impression. When the Mormon Battalion led by Col. Philip St. George Cooke traversed to California in late 1846, it also met Apaches who promised to sell mules to the troops, provide route information, and serve as guides in exchange for compensation, an offer Cooke declined. Like Kearny, Cooke established tough and taxing overland paths that many prospectors followed. Neither party had a violent clash with the Apaches, although the soldiers were badly battered by the environment.[52]

Government-sponsored expeditions in the 1850s charted not only the new international line but the potential passages and topography of the annexed, yet still largely unknown, area.[53] In 1854, Lt. John G. Parke moved from San Diego via Fort Yuma and the Akimel O'odham villages before turning southeast to Tucson and continuing across the San Pedro River to the Apache Pass and the Rio Grande. His maps for the first time officially defined a southern trail across New Mexico Territory. The railroads did not profit from Parke's efforts, as the lines were delayed indefinitely in the mid-1850s by budget complications and slavery debates.[54] However, the overland mail companies utilized Parke's route and spread U.S. influence to western Apacheria. The first mail run operated by James Birch across southern New Mexico left San Antonio in July 1857, reaching San Diego seven weeks later. Birch's "Jackass Mail," which relied on mules, was trumped by the Butterfield Overland Mail Company in September 1858. Butterfield turned the operations large-scale by purchasing some 250 coaches and thousands of head of stock. The company also constructed and staffed 141 stations, 9 of which were located between Mesilla and Tucson. Following the Oxbow Route from Saint Louis via Fort Smith to El Paso, Mesilla, Tucson, and Yuma to Los Angeles and San Francisco, the trip averaging twenty-one days—which was fast traveling for the time—Butterfield coaches crossed the Chiricahua domains regularly, and usually without any trouble from the Apaches.[55]

Well before the stagecoach operations started, the Anglos had made incursions on the Chihenne and Bedonkohe homelands, more specifically to the place where Kearny had met Mangas Coloradas—Santa Rita del Cobre. The area was in fact something of a perennial hot spot of contention and a longtime magnet for daring Hispanics and Anglos. The Hispanics had worked the Santa Rita mines on and off since the early 1800s, sending thousands of mule loads of copper ore to Mexico City via Chihuahua. By the time the first group of American trappers arrived in the mid-1820s, the Apaches had already forced three evacuations of the mines. In the 1830s, the area functioned as a nexus for contraband trade for the livestock the Chiricahuas pilfered from Sonora and Chihuahua and swapped for food, guns, ammunition, and whiskey at Santa Rita, most significantly at the ranch of James Kirker. In 1838, the Mexican government deserted the mines due to extensive Chiricahua pressure. A bigger party of outsiders only reappeared when Kearny stopped by.[56]

In August 1849, and again in March and August of 1850, troops commanded by Maj. Enoch Steen reconnoitered the Santa Rita area. Moving from Doña Ana, the first excursion clashed violently with a group of Chihennes. One soldier and twenty-five Apaches were reported killed or wounded. On the latter outing, Steen held talks with the Chiricahuas and Mangas Coloradas, who again assured the Americans of his friendship. Steen had first advocated that a big campaign be sent against the Chiricahuas and that a post be built at Santa Rita. But after talking with the Apaches, Steen seemed convinced that "an agent with . . . presents can without doubt conclude a lasting peace with this powerful band." Having little money to spare, Santa Fe took no action at this time.[57]

Next, U.S. Boundary Commissioner John Russell Bartlett's boundary survey crew, nearly three hundred men, took temporary residence at the copper mines for several months in 1851. The crew, which made the old Spanish adobes its headquarters and renamed the buildings Cantonment Dawson, was visited by delegations of Chiricahuas who brought food to share and goods for trading. The Chiricahua reaction to Bartlett's crew had been far from uniform. There had been a lot of talk and trade, few disputes, and some pilfering of animals. By the time the boundary crew continued westward, several Chiricahua outfits had already left the mines and were busy in Sonora. They talked armistice, saw nothing concrete coming out of it, and raided. Meanwhile, no more than twenty Anglo miners had started mining operations at Santa Rita. Soon the army, without consulting the Chiricahuas, sent troops to occupy Cantonment Dawson, renaming it Fort Webster.[58]

When the Apaches first approached the post in January 1852 with discussions and trade in their minds, they were snappily told to turn back or they would be shot. After the Chiricahuas left, "they soon showed signs of preparing for a fight so we opened fire on the Apaches first," one soldier recalled. Fired at with muskets and a mountain howitzer, the Chiricahuas scattered, many of them wounded. Interpreted by some Anglos as a show of force, a warning to the Apaches, in reality, the incident was more of a frantic act carried out by soldiers scared out of their minds. Shortly thereafter the Chiricahuas replied. They captured the post herd and ambushed a party sent after them, killing three troopers. One of the troopers was horribly mutilated and scalped by the Apaches. The shock tactics worked. Now the troops at the post dreaded doom at the hands of the Apaches. They worried over an Apache siege and had nightmares of their impending annihilation.[59]

The army was not through yet. If some officers saw Fort Webster as a step in controlling and containing the Chiricahuas, many also believed that building a fort in their midst was not enough. The resolutely independent Chihennes and Bedonkohes deserved "severe chastisement," an officer recorded in his yearly report for 1852. A bigger campaign was needed. In February 1852, Maj. Marshall Howe, under orders from Sumner, led such an effort, hoping to strike a decisive blow. However, after the command of close to two hundred men cautiously limped to the vicinity of Santa Rita and met the terribly frightened soldiers at Fort Webster, Howe, so it seemed to the men in the ranks, began a farcical show wherein the objective was to purposefully avoid the Chiricahuas. Upon discovering fresh signs, Howe and his force, rather than go after their targets, balked and requested reinforcements. After a lackluster aimless trek, the command retraced its steps hastily to Fort Webster and reported that it had been unable to engage the enemy. In truth, Howe had lost his nerve on an expedition one trooper dubbed as "the greatest piece of humbuggery." As for the Chiricahuas, it seems reasonable that some of them had watched the troops wander around and that they had purposefully avoided confronting such a large force.[60]

By May, some Chiricahuas again approached Fort Webster, wanting to trade and make a pact. Trying diplomacy instead of violence, Colonel Sumner invited the Chihennes and Bedonkohes to Acoma for treaty making. Signed by some of their leading men, including Mangas Coloradas, the treaty, dated July 1, 1852, was ratified by Congress. It called for Apaches to acknowledge U.S. authority over them, accept U.S. military posts on their area, stay out of Mexico, and return captives. It made no explicit demands on the Chiricahua lands. Next year, as many Chiricahuas invaded Sonora with devastating force, William Lane negotiated a supplementary treaty that, on the other hand, was never ratified in Washington. In this treaty, the Chihennes and Bedonkohes basically agreed to settle down in permanent campgrounds (reservations) on the Gila River and keep away from the main travel routes used by Anglos. The United States in turn would supply a generous quantity of corn, beef, sheep, cattle, and other goods to the Apaches.[61]

Meanwhile, on September 9, 1852, the army had first relocated Fort Webster to the Mimbres River fourteen miles southeast of the Santa Rita mines. This site, in turn, was vacated on December 20, 1853. The reasons the army gave were many. The fort suffered because of its difficult logistics, expensive maintenance, or danger of being isolated in the middle of Chiricahua country. Some claimed that it served no useful purpose and that it irritated the Chiricahuas. While no major clashes had ensued between the Chiricahuas and the troops at Fort Webster, the post apparently kept losing stock to the Apaches.[62]

Seeing the troops withdraw back to the Rio Grande, the Chiricahuas set the post buildings on fire. Feeling powerful and living as independent as they always had in the country around the Mogollon Mountains and the Black Range, the Chihennes and Bedonkohes had little inclination to take any of the treaty stipulations seriously. They did not recognize U.S. authority over them or accept forts where it did not suit them. Neither could the Anglos tell them what to do or where to go. They would raid whom they liked and when they liked, mostly attacking Mexico but also carrying out minor stock raids near the Rio Grande. By the mid-1850s, Edwin Sweeney writes, there had emerged a clear pattern wherein the raids of many Chiricahua communities in Mexico were followed by retreats to U.S. territory and security. Possibly seeing Anglos as useful allies, or junior partners, Mangas Coloradas, upon meeting Lane and Steen at Fort Webster in May 1853, reportedly asked if the government would build a new post on the Gila River so that it would function as a buffer between his people and the Mexicans.[63]

Most likely the Apaches interpreted the pacts they had made with the Anglos as payments for peace, similar to the ones they were used to in the past with Mexicans and the Spanish. This notion was probably only confirmed when the agents for the southern Apaches started issuing gifts and rations to the Chihennes and Bedonkohes at Fort Thorn. The rations and the government initiatives to increase Apache farming were meant to contain the Apaches' need to raid and make them more sedentary. As they realized that some of the Chiricahuas now expected to get rations and gifts and as they became concerned about the possibility of having to feed as many as one thousand Apaches, the government officials quickly commenced to bickering with each other over financial responsibilities and logistical difficulties. It was soon clear that the federal government was in over its head with the promises it had made to the Apaches. Rations would be forthcoming, but they would be meager and irregular. No reservation was set up for any of the Apaches.

In 1855, Agent Michael Steck and the fresh governor David Meriwether summoned some Chihennes and Bedonkohes to a meeting. Like the Jicarillas and Mescaleros, the Chiricahuas were also made aware that this time the Anglos wanted their land. With over two hundred Apaches present, in the treaty that resulted on June 9, 1855, the Chihennes and Bedonkohes signed away nearly half of their domain in exchange for $72,000 paid over twenty-seven years. They also received promises of rations, healthcare, education, and a reservation on the Mimbres River. Like many other Apache treaties from this era, Congress never ratified the agreement. Ostensibly the reason had something to do with the disinclination of having to pay for land that already had been won in a war with Mexico or with the persistent rumors circulating that the Chihenne and Bedonkohe lands contained massive mineral wealth and that a rush would take care of the Chiricahua problem.[64]

No rush was forthcoming, however. By this time, the mines at Santa Rita were empty of Anglos. Realizing that the Chihennes and the Bedonkohes remained as strong and as independent as ever, some officers orchestrated efforts to display the army's might and to keep the Apaches at arm's length from the Rio Grande. At a time when the federal government was feeding the Apaches and making treaties it did not honor or put into effect, it was also resorting to violence and war with them. In December 1855, Capt. Joseph Eaton, who was a strong advocate of bigger campaigns and even full-scale war against the Apaches, embarked from

Fort Thorn with less than one hundred soldiers. It proved a very exhausting and fruitless expedition. What followed was a two-pronged campaign in February 1856. Led by Lt. Col. Daniel Chandler, another hard-liner, the troops marched out from Forts Craig and Thorn. They first caught a group of Chihennes off guard north of the Gila River in the Mogollon Mountains. They captured the camp and hundreds of animals, killing three Apaches. Next, they stumbled on another camp full of Apaches who frequently drew rations from Steck at Fort Thorn. Chandler ordered the troops to attack. They kept firing for some twenty minutes as the Apaches desperately sought cover. In the aftermath, a livid Steck authored venomous protests against Chandler, hoping to bring charges against the officer, who claimed that he had attacked after discovering stolen stock near the Apache camp. The case reached Secretary of War Jefferson Davis, who took no action against Chandler and thus effectively condoned an attack by government forces against people fed by the same government.[65]

In April 1857, the army tried to build up on its previous efforts. Ostensibly the Gila Expedition was a response to the murder of Navajo agent Henry L. Dodge, a deed the government suspected was done by some Bedonkohes. A large force of regulars accompanied by a company of Mexican and Pueblo scouts, all under the command of Col. Benjamin Bonneville, entered the Chihenne and Bedonkohe lands and stayed for much of the summer. The three-pronged offensive, with troops starting from Forts Buchanan and Thorn as well as the depot at Albuquerque, totaled some nine hundred fighters. Unlike the previous efforts, this campaign was meant to be a killing expedition set to remain in the field until the Apaches no longer existed as a distinct people. Rather than smash the enemy as they believed they would beforehand, Bonneville's men came to realize their own limitations. First, they would recognize the hard way that life on a campaign in the Southwest was no picnic. One young lieutenant, Henry Lazelle, described his dreary and tiresome daily routine in his field journal.

> Arose covered with dirt—washed as people may be imagined to do, under like circumstances,—but without effecting a marked change in my personal appearance. Eat a breakfast consisting of the same variety that characterized our supper the previous evening, except that the order was reversed and, stood—Tallow, coffee, and bacon fried—Marched at the eighth hour. . . . Was . . . highly interested by a strong wind which blew a fine sand into my eyes all day creating, a delicious and refreshing titillating sensation.[66]

As the days got hotter, Lazelle became somewhat less witty, even if not less descriptive. One day in May he characterized as clear and sunny with "heat intense and the dust as suffocating and stifling as the ashes of a burning Vesuvius." He also noticed how poorly the men could cope with the circumstances. During the marching, "the great fatigue consequent from the heat and sandy soil, required frequent halts." Second, the troops saw that instead of challenging a sizable U.S. force, the Apaches rather hid and fled. Most of the Bedonkohes had departed south, and many of the Chihennes soon followed. Many were in fact at Janos trying to hammer out a peace pact.[67] Then the troops had to acknowledge that finding or catching up with those Chiricahuas still in the area was less than likely. Not only were the Apaches faster, in better shape, and familiar with the terrain, but they also scorched the earth as they went to increase the already intense suffering of the soldiers and their horses.

Still, on May 25 one command hit a Chihenne camp on the Black Range, killing seven to nine Apaches, including the noted leader Cuchillo Negro. The soldiers also captured well over one thousand head of sheep and cattle. Then, after several weeks of trying, on June 27 the troops located a camp at Gila River, north of Mount Graham. However, it was not the Chiricahuas' but belonged to White Mountain Apaches, an Apache faction scarcely known by the whites. There was no history of violence between the army and the White Mountain Apaches. The soldiers nevertheless took the unsuspecting camp by storm. They killed twenty-four people and took as many hostages. The lone male captive was, Lt. John van Deusen du Bois wrote, executed "with his hands tied & shot like a dog." This shows how frustrated Bonneville's outfit had become. For du Bois, the attack against the innocent and the execution proved too much to bear. "Humanity, honor, a soldier's pride, every feeling of good in me was and is shocked by this one act," he wrote.[68]

No matter what those in charge explained, Bonneville's outing was nothing if not a disaster, a humiliating failure that scarcely got the attention of most Chihennes and Bedonkohes. And most of the officers and soldiers realized it. The outing became a favorite subject of humor, and one officer accurately described it as "a campaign of clowns." During the expedition, some of the officers and soldiers had been drunk, others overcautious and uninterested, and still others just incompetent and ignorant of the terrain and the enemy. One officer supposedly got all excited when sighting Apaches on a distant hilltop. Then those "keener sighted," Lazelle recounted, notified him that the "Apaches" were in fact "a few straggling antelope." The campaign had also witnessed troops wandering aimlessly, suffering from dust and the heat, or enduring without water and grass. They also had to lie idle in camp when there had been no pack animals or horses for the cavalry. "Ten days of talking and one of action" is how du Bois summarized the operation.[69] Many had also witnessed their clothing coming apart. Troops walking back to the Rio Grande without shoes was a becoming finale for the fiasco. In all, the army's lackluster efforts to control the Chihennes and Bedonkohes by military force had resulted in a succession of "campaigns of clowns" from 1849 onward. And the troops had never even attempted confronting the Chokonen or Nednhi bands of the Chiricahuas.

Apache Rule

In 1858, Steck, who kept advocating a reservation for the Chihennes and Bedonkohes on the Gila River, set U.S. policy as he made the trip from Fort Thorn to the Chokonen domains at Apache Pass. Steck gave assurances to the Chokonen leaders, among them the very influential Cochise, that they could expect semiannual payments from the government. Feeling confident of their military supremacy, the Chiricahuas expected more than the resource-stricken Steck could deliver. However, Steck made no demands on the Chokonens and no treaties were signed. The Apaches could live independent lives at the Dragoon and Chiricahua Mountains and raid Mexico while getting rations from the Americans as a payment for leaving the overland traffic alone. In general, the Chiricahua-Anglo relationship remained amicable. One military man visiting the Butterfield station at Stein's Peak in June 1859 observed that the Chokonens lived "on most friendly" terms with the mail company people.[70]

It can be said that an unofficial understanding developed, a partial "peace pact," along the border by which the Chiricahuas allowed the Anglos the right-of-way (mail route, emigrants) on their lands in exchange for the freedom to raid in Mexico and supplementary payment. This was by and large the case also with the few Anglo mining operations in today's southern Arizona. Take for example Charles Poston, who, with his Ohio associates, started the Sonora Exploring and Mining Company in 1857 and made the abandoned village of Tubac the headquarters of the operations in the proximity of Chokonen lands. While logistical difficulties and labor troubles brought the operation to a halt by the end of the decade, this was not because of the Apaches. Poston is said to have made private treaties with various Apache communities, giving the Apaches gifts and promises not to interfere with their raiding in Mexico in exchange for peace and protection. He also hired some Apaches to work on his mines. This understanding was interrupted only by a few sporadic clashes. While no Apache raids reportedly targeted Poston's operations in 1858, the Apaches took a bite of the company herd three times in 1859 and at least twice in 1860.[71]

Appeasement and nonintervention represented methods of containment suited for the frail American presence on Chiricahua lands. If they had wanted to, the Chiricahuas could have paralyzed the overland travel and driven off the small mining enterprises. While numbers never were their strength, the Chiricahuas in the late 1850s could potentially outnumber the soldiers stationed in the only garrison that remained close to their homes, Fort Buchanan. In all, the inexperienced and poorly acclimatized soldiers present and absent (including the sick, confined, and those on detached service) at Fort Buchanan numbered only 115 men in June 1858, 143 in June 1859, and 139 in June 1860.[72] A major operation, Butterfield, on the other hand, did not muster much armed threat—although the stations contained weaponry for defense—but instead trusted in diplomacy and gifts in its dealings with the Apaches. However, the Chiricahuas did not wish to fight the Anglos. It was not in their interest, especially when raids, massacres, and even poisonings south of the border continued to take a toll. In 1857, Chiricahuas living in Janos believed that the Mexicans had poisoned them by using arsenic. On July 14, 1858, close to forty Chiricahuas were slain at Fronteras after friendly talks, while on December 13, 1858, Mexican soldiers smashed a Chihenne party in Otates Mountains, Sonora, killing eighteen Apaches.[73]

While livestock theft caused minor friction between the Anglos and Chiricahuas, the acrimony was typically handled through diplomatic means. Troops from Fort Buchanan would travel to parley with the principal Chokonen leaders and reach an agreement.[74] By the end of the decade, shortage of food and/or acrimony over U.S. payments led several Chiricahua communities to temporarily relocate to northern Mexico, wishing for relations and possible peace settlements at places such as Fronteras, where their recent history had been bloody. The Chiricahuas would, however, return to U.S. soil when it suited them, seeking rations from Steck and living as independent people on their cherished mountain ranges from the Dragoons to the Black Range. The Chiricahuas, unlike the Jicarillas, the Lipans, or even the Mescaleros, were still very much in control of their lives. And they were a strong military power. As for the Western Apaches, while some groups had encountered soldiers or met with Steck, their contacts with the whites remained limited. They could hardly perceive the level of violence that soon would engulf them. In fact, despite their long history of violence with the Mexicans, few Apaches could prepare for what was coming.

CHAPTER 5

EXTERMINATION

You White People kept coming, and pushing those Indians in front of you.
Finally you reached this country here, and pushed us back in also.
In those first days we fought against you white people,
and took your cattle and horses, and killed you.
Your people killed many of us also.
—John Taylor, Cibecue Apache

We'll whip the Apache
We'll exterminate the race
Of thieves and assassins
Who the human form disgrace
We'll travel over mountain
And through the valley deep,
We'll travel without eating,
We'll travel without sleep.
—Marching song, First California Cavalry

Eradication

In May 1864, Gen. James Carleton, commanding the Union Army of California Volunteers in New Mexico, was busy making plans for another ruthless offensive. His troops had already overpowered the Mescalero Apaches in 1862–63 and the Navajos the following winter by launching merciless military operations that devastated indigenous lives, material property, and food sources. Carleton had also forced the survivors to walk to the desolate camp of Bosque Redondo on the Pecos River. His new objective was the forced removal of Chiricahua and Western Apaches from their homelands to a reservation on the Pecos or their "utter extermination." Linking his plans with the mining booms in the vicinities of Pinos Altos/Santa Rita del Cobre and Prescott, Arizona, Carleton claimed that his goal was to ensure "a lasting peace and security of life to all those who go" to Apache lands "to search for the precious metals." His methods, outlined in the General Orders dated May 1, 1864, pressed for "a serious war; not a little march out and back again"—the latter Carleton saw as typical for borderlands operations—that would bring "lasting results" against the Apache "bands of ruthless murderers." Carleton urged every citizen of the borderlands who had a rifle to take the field to aid the California soldiers. He also wanted to arm and dispatch two hundred O'odhams and Maricopas against the Apaches. Furthermore, he called for the state militia and volunteers from Sonora and Chihuahua to participate, even if it meant Mexican troops crossing the international boundary. "Every effort must be made," Carleton insisted, "to have a general rising of both citizens and soldiers, on both sides of the line, against the Apaches."[1]

Embracing and encouraging extreme forms of violence, Carleton's tactical outline called for Union and Mexican soldiers together with Anglo, Hispanic, and indigenous residents to combine their strength and blanket the borderlands with numerous fast-moving columns whose members would push to the limits of their endurance. The troops would advance in every direction from the new post on the Gila River, Camp Goodwin, which also functioned as the depot for the assault. They would take to the field simultaneously from Tucson and Forts Bowie, Whipple, Wingate, Canby, Craig, and McRae. Thousands of soldiers and residents would start the war on May 25, 1864, and persist in the field for at least sixty days. "Every" unit "must strive to outdo all the others" in "energy, perseverance, resolution, and self-denial," Carleton insisted, so that the Apaches would comprehend that they could not "hold out against us." As in his earlier Mescalero campaign, all Apache men large enough to bear arms would "be slain wherever met," while the enemy food supply and material belongings would be ruthlessly destroyed.[2]

Time to Die

While Carleton's design for a general offensive in 1864 never fully materialized—in part because the enlistment of many Californians expired—the outline of the operation, the intensity and magnitude of destruction it called for, and his choice of words demonstrate the levels of ferocity the borderlands wars had reached in the 1860s. Notwithstanding the momentary withering of troops during the first year of the Civil War, this was a decade when the reach of the United States expanded the Rio Grande toward western Apacheria. The recalibrated military presence (volunteers instead of regulars) and the burgeoning mining concentrations at

Pinos Altos/Santa Rita del Cobre and Prescott, the latter founded and made the capital of the newly created Arizona Territory in 1864, functioned as visible manifestations of the escalation of settler colonialism. As thousands of Anglo prospectors, miners, and volunteer soldiers rushed to the heart of the Chiricahua and Western Apache world, most exertions in diplomacy and appeasement, and their crucial signifiers of goodwill and trust—rations and gifts—as well as the more limited military operations of containment from the previous decade were replaced by extreme forms of violence targeting the annihilation of whole societies.

In 1860, normal Apache life—in western Apacheria—was such that families could usually still sleep their nights peacefully, plan and organize ceremonies, gather wild plants in season, and find game to hunt in their mountain ranges. Despite the occasional dispute or skirmish with the Anglos, the Chiricahuas and Western Apaches, as well as the Yavapais, were still very much masters of their territory. Some of them still lived practically isolated from the whites.[3] Inside a decade or so that would all change. By that time, Western Apaches and Yavapais were nearly routed and the Chiricahuas struggled to hold off the tide of invasion.

Facing a violent maelstrom of extermination and perfidy, various Apache, and also Yavapai, communities were pitted against ruthless outfits comprised of local Hispanic, Anglo, and indigenous men operating on their own or in consortium with the U.S. Army troops, Civil War volunteers, or Confederates. With such miscellaneous crews of fighters and interests coming together and acting separately, and often unrestrained, with the broad general purpose of destroying Apaches and empowering themselves, violence took many forms and bent to many shapes. Carleton's May 1864 plans actually demonstrated how the shapes of extreme killing were constantly debated and negotiated even when the extermination of Apaches gained in momentum and approval in the borderlands. For one, Carleton would not condone the full spectrum of extermination tactics that many civilian outfits at the time used and advocated and which included the intentional slaughter of noncombatants, poisoning of Apache food, chicanery, and massacres during diplomatic meets. While Carleton at times looked the other way when hearing of the bloodbaths initiated by, for instance, King Woolsey and his outfit of miners and ranchers, he made it clear that in his own campaigns different rules applied. He stood firm, for example, in allowing Apache women and children to surrender whenever possible. Still, he refused to acknowledge how his Bosque Redondo experiment turned into a death camp. He also held that the annihilation of independent Apaches should result from all-out war that targeted whole societies and their living space, the land as well as the people.

As different and disparate forces tilted the borderlands warfare toward extermination, they in fact reimagined the boundaries of civilized warfare in multiple ways. Hating and fearing Apaches, and anxious that the Indians stood in the way of their economic opportunity, white newcomers in central Arizona and around Pinos Altos frequently represented their killings as righteous self-protection. They used especially malignant conceptions of race as the basis of differentiation to justify their stance and actions, basically ordering the borderlands around them into hierarchies wherein white civilization connoted unmatched superiority while the Apaches and Yavapais, whom many Anglos mistook as Apaches, were relegated to the lowest tiers as savage predators lacking in any human value.

While it did create recognizable rifts and eventually bigger cracks among the Anglos, extermination as a principal method for the establishment of white settler society temporarily reached such heights and became so socially acceptable in the 1860s that it seemed that settlers believed and talked of nothing else than killing Apaches. Being an outsider from Connecticut, where Indian killing was a memory of generations past, Joseph Pratt Allyn, a newly appointed Arizona judge, felt baffled. His February 1864 letter from the busy Prescott mining district read that it was "difficult to convey an adequate idea of the intensity of this feeling" that was Apache hating. "A miner seems to regard an Indian [Apache] as he would a rattlesnake," he added. Echoing Allyn's perspective of the settler mentality, and testifying to the ongoing negotiation among whites of the parameters of extreme violence, Daniel Conner, a prospector himself, asserted that it "was the rigid rule all over the country to shoot these savages [Apaches] upon sight." Appalled by the level of brutality he witnessed, Conner felt the need to not only distance himself from the slaughter but to denounce its practitioners. He contemplated that, in these borderlands, "savage civilized men are the most monstrous of all monsters."[4]

What made the borderlands wars of the 1860s so extreme was not only the desires, intentions, and methods the parties applied but the shortage of alternatives to killing. Outside the utter failure of Bosque Redondo, a camp better suited for eradication rather than regeneration of its inhabitants, and a few local agencies or military garrisons that at times functioned as feeding stations for the Indians, there was no choice for the Apaches than to fight, run, hide, and try to stay alive. White America could only deliver armed violence but very little in terms of coexistence, diplomacy, rations, gifts, or long-term safety for those Apaches looking to exchange their sovereignty for U.S. control. The establishment of federally managed reservations on Apache homelands would not materialize until the early 1870s, when the U.S.-Apache wars in many ways acquired quite different characteristics. Thereafter the violence of the regular army—by then the civilians and the O'odhams had been largely excluded from Apache fighting—against the Apaches was guided by the general purpose of forcing the Indians to submit to reservation life, not to wipe them all out. That the Apache communities did not simply take off and leave to other regions—like the Nez Perce tried and Sitting Bull's Lakotas managed temporarily when heading for Canada—for good had something to do with their dearth of knowledge regarding distant lands, obviously deep-rooted attachment to their homes, hostility toward northern Mexico, and, among the Chiricahuas, steadfast belief in their own military strength.

Deceptive Illusions

There is little argument that Lt. George Bascom's actions in February 1861 deeply hurt and infuriated Cochise and his people. On February 4, 1861, Bascom, a West Point graduate with little experience, sought Cochise for a consultation near the Apache Pass in the Chiricahua Mountains. His intent was to question Cochise of the whereabouts of a Mexican boy, Feliz Tellez Martinez, who had lived with his mother and her new boyfriend, John Ward, on a ranch at Sonoita Valley before being taken by Apache raiders. Finding Bascom's request for a meeting something of a customary diplomatic practice on the part of the officers from the nearby Fort Buchanan, Cochise, accompanied by his wife and two children, a brother, and two or three nephews, arrived to the parley unsuspicious of any trouble. No crew of Apache fighters escorted him. The reason for the carefree approach is evident. Not only had Cochise established relatively cordial relationships with the Butterfield station employees and cooperated with troops from Fort Buchanan in the past, but the Chokonens did not have young Feliz in their custody. It was Western Apaches, most likely a group of Pinal or Aravaipa Apaches, who had seized the boy. For many Western Apaches, the Sonoita Valley had for decades functioned as a prized thoroughfare to Sonora between the Chiricahua domain in the east and Tohono O'odham lands to the west. But starting in the late 1850s, access to this area had been disturbed by the presence of white ranchers and the troops at Fort Buchanan. The January 21, 1861, attack on Ward's ranch had probably been a reaction to the white occupation of the Sonoita corridor.[5]

While John Ward was out on business, the Apaches pilfered some cattle while also seizing young Feliz. A search by troops and a civilian ensemble commenced but led to minimal results, the Apaches having split and headed north. Ordered by his superiors to demand the immediate restoration of stolen property by force if he thought it proper, Bascom led the latest command in search of the young boy. In a typical borderlands fashion, much was left to the judgment of a junior officer, who seemed to think that the Chokonens were to blame because of their recent raids on the vicinity of Tubac. However, as Cochise's biographer points out, the Chokonens did not abduct any captives during these raids, just livestock. Unaware of this, Bascom demanded the return of the boy as soon as his meeting with the Chokonens got under way. Cochise responded by declaring that neither he nor his band had taken Feliz and promised, if given time, to use his influence to help locate the captive. Next, Bascom, who purportedly stated that he would take Cochise up on his offer, either fell victim to bad (intentional or not) translation on the part of John Ward, who functioned as one of the interpreters in the meeting, or grossly underrated Chiricahua power. Bascom informed Cochise that he and his family would be detained until Feliz was returned. While his family could not, Cochise escaped, most probably by cutting through the tent the meeting was held in. Scrambling past the soldiers, Cochise reached the nearby hills but was evidently wounded in the leg after Bascom directed his soldiers to fire.[6]

In hindsight it is easy to say that Bascom's move was ill-advised. He had a mere fifty-four infantry men at his disposal at the hub of Chokonen lands, an unfamiliar terrain to most of them, including the officer in command. Surely, they could try to hold on, pray, and count on Cochise not risking his family by attacking. They could also send for reinforcements. But there was no hope of attacking the Chiricahua fighters, who held the higher ground. Furthermore, after Cochise's escape Bascom had lost his main trump card as well as the trust of the Apaches but still did very little to rectify the situation.

The next day, Cochise, now accompanied, according to bloated figures given by Bascom, by five hundred Apaches, met with the Anglos. Although Cochise again swore that he did not know of the whereabouts of Feliz, his talk had little impact on Bascom, who was certain that Cochise was holding back something. The negotiations again ended in gunfire. Next, Cochise tried to gain leverage by taking captives (Anglos) of his own. He had already seized a Butterfield station employee, and soon the Chiricahuas would ambush an unsuspecting wagon train crew bound for Mesilla Valley. The Mexican contingent of the wagon train crew was brutally killed by the Chiricahuas, who took three Anglos as prisoners. Still the Apaches got nowhere with the mechanically thinking Bascom, who insisted on getting Feliz back.

Gradually grasping diplomacy's utter failure, Cochise organized an assault on the soldiers' horses as they were watered at Apache Springs. The plan was that, when Bascom would hurry reinforcements to the spring, the Chiricahuas would storm the weakened stage station where the soldiers were holed up with their prisoners. When some Chiricahuas descended on the livestock, others drew near the station, when Bascom spotted them, reacted swiftly, and diverted his men to repel the attack. Apaches, who now judged direct assault as too costly, fell back. At this time, Bascom also received reinforcements (eighty-four soldiers) from Forts Buchanan and Breckinridge. Cochise's men probably realized that diplomacy was useless, Feliz was nowhere near to be found, and to repeat a direct charge had disaster written all over it. The Apaches killed and mutilated their four Anglo captives, left the bodies so that they would surely be found, and absented themselves from the scene.

The soldiers believed that they were bottled up at Apache Pass, and only dared to move a few days later. After some cautious reconnaissance, they finally located what remained of the corpses. Most of them favored an instant hanging of the Chokonen male prisoners in retaliation. On February 19, 1961, Cochise's male family members were hoisted on four oak trees at the western edge of Apache Pass. Pulled so high that wolves could not get them, the executed were, it would seem, left hanging as the soldiers departed back to Forts Buchanan and Breckinridge. Cochise's wife and children were released after reaching Buchanan, while no organized outfit continued to search for Feliz Martinez. The boy, raised from now on in a White Mountain Apache family, next appears on record in 1868 as Mickey Free, a scout at Fort Lowell.

For some time after the Bascom fiasco, many borderlands residents were under the illusion that the Chiricahuas had gained a permanent upper hand. Witnessing the somber atmosphere in Tucson in April 1861 was the newsman Thompson Turner. He explained how the people of Tucson, after having expected military reinforcements from Santa Fe to combat the Chiricahuas in a full-blown war, instead witnessed the abrupt termination of the overland mail as, by an act of Congress, all California-bound overland mail was concentrated on the central route via the Rocky Mountains and the Great Plains. The alarmed citizenry also caught rumors of complete troop withdrawal due to impending Civil War. Any fleeting optimism of better times was gone, and in its place, Turner reported, was a complete stagnation of business and enterprise, as people contemplated whether they would make their escape with the troops. A month later, an even more depressed Turner described a Tucson cut off from civilization, without communications, and at the mercy of Apaches stealing stock and harassing citizens.[7]

The Chokonens and other Chiricahuas made frequent raids on U.S. soil during the spring and summer of 1861. The fighter and shaman Geronimo, who rose to prominence in the 1880s, remembered, "After this trouble [with Bascom] all of the Indians [Chiricahuas] agreed not to be friendly with the white man anymore." He added, "There was no general engagement, but a long struggle followed."[8]

First, the Chokonens cleaned the San Simon stage station of stock, gaining some three hundred sheep. In April, they ambushed several white travelers at Doubtful Canyon near Stein's Peak. Apache fighters killed nine men and, according to a claim made against the government for restitution, apprehended property worth over eight thousand dollars. They also emptied the overland stage stations east of Tucson of livestock and hit again almost as soon as the bases were restocked. On May 3, they attempted to capture a military freight train on its way from Fort Buchanan to the Rio Grande, but had three of their own killed in exchange for mere twenty-three captured mules. Next, they surprised a small contingent of troops outside Fort Buchanan, hit a crew leaving the Patagonia mines, and dashed through Santa Cruz Valley, cleaning the San Pedro station of stock in the process. In mid-July, the Apaches reportedly appropriated four hundred head of livestock at Canoa. They also killed four men and destroyed the ranch. "Sides of the house were broken in and the court was filled with broken tables and doors," an eyewitness recalled.[9]

In August, Tubac, a place of refuge for many of the ranchers and miners, faced a direct attack by a large Apache contingent, who took all the stock, killed one or two men, and forced the abandonment of the community. By this time, both Fort Buchanan and Fort Breckinridge lay abandoned and in ashes, as troops had been sent marching toward the Rio Grande in July. In all, by the end of 1861, only Tucson, whose residents hid inside the walled town and Sylvester Mowry's Patagonia mine, a virtual fortress to the south, remained.[10]

Meanwhile, farther to the east fighters from the Chihenne and Bedonkohe bands of the Chiricahuas targeted the miners around Pinos Altos. In May 1860, a party out of Mesilla had made a discovery that brought a rush of an estimated seven hundred miners and sprang up the village of Pinos Altos near the old Santa Rita del Cobre location. While the newcomers alarmingly depleted the game, they did offer enticing trade/raid targets for the Bedonkohes and Chihennes, whose homes in the Mogollon Mountains and the Black Range flanked the mining areas. Increased contact brought an upswing in whooping cough, tuberculosis, pneumonia, and measles among the Chiricahuas, many of whom flocked to the Southern Apache Agency, whose agent, Michael Steck, was still trying to arrange a reservation for the Bedonkohes and Chihennes on the upper Gila River. Soon contact also brewed conflict. On December 4, 1860, a group of miners liquored up and went after Chihennes suspected of stealing a mule from Pinos Altos to quell their hunger. The only encampment they could find was near Steck's agency and the mining party charged it, killing four Chihennes and taking thirteen others as captives.[11]

Shortly thereafter, the story goes, Mangas Coloradas tried to persuade the miners to leave by offering to show them richer sites elsewhere. Distrusting Mangas, some miners tied him to a tree and whipped him. Regardless of whether this story is a mere legend, as it probably is, in 1861 the Bedonkohes and Chihennes, reinforced at times by Chokonen fighters, pounced on Pinos Altos and its surroundings. They also attacked travelers on their way to the mines, in or near Cooke's Canyon on the southern overland road. With all their activity, the Chiricahuas practically cut off the mines from outside supply. The siege was lifted only when the new Confederate governor of Arizona, Lt. Col. John Baylor, dispatched Arizona Guards (volunteers) to transport provisions to the frazzled miners. Then the Apaches temporarily changed tactics. On September 27, 1861, the Chiricahuas struck simultaneously at the mining camps that spread from the main village of Pinos Altos. Miners were cornered in their diggings, fighting through the morning until the Apaches retreated when facing canon fire of scrap metal.[12]

For many borderlands residents, it seemed that the Chiricahuas had shifted their focus toward utter destruction. Certainly their raiding activity had multiplied, rising from twelve engagements in 1859 and twenty-seven in 1860 to fifty-one in 1861. The Chiricahuas reportedly killed forty-one Anglos and twenty-five Hispanics north of the international line in 1861, a massive increase considering that throughout the late 1850s they had killed few if any people on American soil. Yet, the Chiricahuas were also responsible for the bulk of the 3,000 head of livestock all the Apaches stole in 1861, a staggering increase as well when in 1860 and 1859 the Apaches had taken 552 and 538 head per year. Both the number of Anglos killed and livestock stolen in 1861 would persist as all-time highs in the U.S.-Apache wars, if one accepts the statistics compiled by Berndt Kuhn. What these numbers at least suggest is that, while the Chiricahuas' activity reached new heights, the main focus of their military efforts, regardless of Anglo fears, remained on the acquisition of material property and not on killing and carnage as such. After all, on average the Chiricahuas in 1861 killed just one person (1.3 to be statistically exact) per military engagement.[13]

The Chiricahuas' target selection, with some exceptions, also tells a familiar story. Travelers, stage stations, ranches, and stock herds offered much to steal and relatively little opposition. The Chiricahuas, for instance, did not storm the regular troops when they marched toward the Rio Grande. Nor did they attack Tucson in an full-scale offensive. Instead, they avoided these potentially troublesome targets. The three-day siege on the mail coach on July 21–23 at Cooke's Canyon, which seems atypical for Apaches, can be explained away as a raid gone awry. While the Chiricahuas killed seven people during this strike, they reportedly saw as many as twenty-five to forty men of their ranks killed or wounded. Even the material gains had proven minimal: only a handful of mules. Furthermore, during their uncharacteristic charge against Pinos Altos, the Apaches reportedly stole nearly eighty head of livestock and killed five people. But they also left ten bodies on the ground and presumably carried as many or more with them.

The Apache casualties at Cooke's Canyon and at Pinos Altos functioned as ugly reminders of the cost of exposed combat and of the dangers involved with offensive strikes against targets who knew how to fight back and had the opportunity to do so. In the end, 1861 had witnessed a powerful demonstration of Chiricahua military potency. The Apaches had made the whites aware and respectful of their military muscle. Edwin Sweeney makes a valid point when writing that the charge on the Pinos Altos mines, rather than an attempt to kill all the miners, "had been a show of force, a warning to the whites."[14] After skirmishing with the Confederate volunteers (Arizona Guards) in the aftermath of their attack on Pinos Altos, the Chiricahuas, rather than increase the pressure in an effort to run out all the whites, or risk more casualties, left to recuperate south of the border and in the remote reaches of those mountain ranges they knew best. In late 1861, the Chihennes could still find a refuge from intruders in the Black Range, the Bedonkohes in the Mogollon Mountains, and the Chokonens in the Chiricahua and Dragoon Mountains.

As a consequence of the Apache raids, the mines at Pinos Altos almost died. In 1862, there were twenty or thirty families left, protected by a contingent of California soldiers. However, as a result of new strikes, improved mining techniques, additional labor, and incoming capital, as well as the establishment of new forts (Fort Bayard, for instance) and the community of Silver City, mining gained new momentum and gradually became permanent in the Bedonkohe and Chihenne homeland by the 1870s. The Chihennes, in turn, found less and less room for themselves as the 1860s progressed, while the Bedonkohes ceased to exist as a separate band. The Chokonens would soon witness the erection of a post, Fort Bowie, at the heart of their world. If the Chiricahuas had wanted the whites to become submissive, then their campaigns of 1861 had only partially succeeded, producing deceptive illusions of withdrawal and failure. Already not one but two rival Anglo armies made plans for the invasion of Apache lands, while thousands of Anglos, many of them serving first as volunteer soldiers in the invading forces, desired opportunities to search, claim, and dig the soil for life-changing mineral wealth. And then there were the O'odham and Hispanic residents who spoiled for a chance to challenge the Apaches.

The Confederates

While members of the regular military traveled east to choose sides with the impending civil conflict in mind, federal presence did not altogether disappear from New Mexico. Rather, the federal government had prioritized an anticipated Confederate invasion from Texas over the Chiricahua threat and had assembled to defend its imperial base along the Rio Grande in New Mexico. The first Confederate troops under Lieutenant Colonel Baylor occupied southeastern New Mexico in the summer of 1861, making Mesilla their center of operations. As many Anglo residents between Mesilla and Tucson favored the Southern cause and openly advocated separation from the union, it was initially comparatively easy for Southern soldiers to enter the region. Soon after entering New Mexico, Baylor declared its southern half the Confederate Territory of Arizona. He also made himself its first governor.[15]

As several small Confederate detachments made their way northward from Texas, they proved enticing targets for Apaches raiders. Eating away the already vulnerable, inadequate, and thinly stretched Confederate supply, Apaches turned out to be more formidable adversaries than the Confederate men had anticipated. For example, one unit of fifteen men from Fort Davis, Texas, that charged a Mescalero camp thinking they could rout it comfortably were killed almost to the last man on August 11, 1861. Four months later the Apaches, probably Mescaleros, made two startlingly successful raids right under the noses of Confederate troops. Near Doña Ana they captured some four thousand sheep on December 3, while sixteen days later they made away with fifty to sixty Confederate horses in the vicinity of Mesilla.[16]

Seeing his efforts undermined by the Apache raiders, Baylor realized it was practically impossible to concurrently operate against the Apaches and proceed northward along the Rio Grande to fight the Union troops. His answer was to muster into service a supplementary local force, the Arizona Guards, who exclusively targeted the Apaches and fought several skirmishes between Mesilla and Tucson, most notably at Pinos Altos and at the Florida Mountains, reportedly killing eight Apaches in the latter fight in August 1861. Still, Baylor sensed how the Confederate occupation was stalling and losing its support among the borderlands residents, especially the Hispanic majority, many of whom not only equated the South with the hated Texans, but resisted the occupiers' demands for food and supplies. Trying to win local support, Baylor opted for tougher methods against the Apaches. On February 27, 1862, Baylor's men seized nine Chiricahuas from a private home at Corralitos, Chihuahua, and executed all the adult captives (one man and three women). Then on March 20, Baylor issued orders to the Arizona Guards to "use all means to persuade the Apaches . . . to come in for the purpose of making peace, and when you get them together kill all the grown Indians and take the children prisoners and sell them to defray the cost of killing the Indians. Buy whisky and such other goods as may be necessary . . . and have sufficient number of men around to allow no Indian to escape."[17]

Baylor's instructions were soon made public in Texas newspapers—the leak can be traced to a rival officer, Gen. Henry Hopkins Sibley—which denounced the policies as cruel and barbarous. As Baylor's words reached the office of Confederate president Jefferson Davis, he quickly discovered that the president, with the Confederacy advocating treaty-making policy with Native Americans, did not share his views of exterminating the Apaches. In the eyes of the Confederate government, Baylor had crossed the line of civilized conduct and violated Southern honor by suggesting deception, selling captives, and slaughtering under a white flag. Thus, while trying to please those under his authority in the Southwest, Baylor had grossly misjudged the sentiment in Virginia.

Baylor defended his actions by blaming the Apaches of barbarities beyond conception. He also clarified that his orders excited "no surprise in Arizona," while they "may not be read well in Richmond." Baylor made it seem that he had merely responded to the fierceness of his enemy with equal measure, and, like all good administrators should, listened to the will of the people he was set to convince of the soundness of the regime he represented. Seeing the seriousness of the consequences of his actions, Baylor still refused to rescind his words and instead defiantly attached to his report an Indian warrior's shield with a white woman's scalp tied to it. Most likely he intended to demonstrate the barbarous character of the Apaches by highlighting the vulnerability of white women when faced with such savage masculinity. This package he desired to be forwarded to Davis. Whether the scalp made it to Richmond or not, not only was Baylor instantly ousted from his command but his commission in the Confederate Army was bluntly revoked as well.[18]

As Baylor quarreled with his superiors over the parameters of violence in borderlands warfare, General Sibley tried to finish the Confederate conquest of New Mexico. He intended to take Santa Fe, perhaps annex sections of the Mexican north, at the time in chaotic political state and under French threat, and then proceed toward Colorado goldfields and eventually all the way to California, with its gold and ports the real prize the South yearned for. After a moot victory against Union forces at the Battle of Valverde, near Fort Craig in February, Confederates suffered a pivotal setback when their supplies were destroyed at Glorieta Pass in March 1862. The effort to gain control of the upper Rio Grande dissolved, and Sibley was compelled to withdraw down the river to Texas.

Both Glorieta Pass and especially Valverde were battles in the mold the Anglos preferred. At Valverde, Sibley's men first laid siege on Fort Craig, trying to lure the Union soldiers out for a fight for several days. Running low on supplies, the Southerners then opted to bypass the fort and cut its communication with the Santa Fe headquarters by moving a few miles upstream on the Valverde ford. Union forces rushed to the ford, where the actual battle took place. And this, unlike Apache warfare, was a "real battle" in Anglo eyes. It had skirmish lines, artillery barrages, cavalry charges against infantry positions, and infantry frontal assaults. It even included a temporary truce under a white flag when the Union leader, Gen. Edward Canby, asked for a cessation and Sibley assented for the removal of casualties from the field. Albeit small on Civil War scales, Valverde demonstrates that the Southwest environment did not prevent sizable standing battles. It was the Apaches who did. At Valverde, approximately 3,000 Union men measured their resolve and skills against over 2,500 representatives of the South. After two days of combat, the number of dead and wounded stood at approximately five hundred men.[19]

No clash between Apaches and the United States ever had this many participants, and the typical duration of U.S.-Apache skirmishes, with few exceptions, was measured in hours or even in minutes, not in days. It is a given that the Apaches could never mount armies of this size, but neither would they fight like the Anglos did at Valverde. Even the attacks against Tubac and Pinos Altos had consisted of rapid and unpredictable advances against enemy positions or livestock and of house-to-house fighting.

Still, the Apaches were not as trivial to the Civil War battles in the Southwest as one might think. As noted already, Baylor saw his efforts hindered due to Apache raiding. Sibley also faced severe supply problems, which to a large degree resulted in the Confederates being unable to take New Mexico. Not only had the federal forces, upon their withdrawal, destroyed all the government property they could not haul with them, but the destitute local populace proved utterly incapable of feeding a large occupying force contrary to Sibley's expectations. And the Apaches tapped the meager Confederate supplies even as Sibley's disappointed and demoralized troops traced their steps back to Texas. Sibley, in his report on New Mexico operations, argued that his force was not beaten by any human enemy but by a famished country struggling under indigenous raiders. Sibley advocated the legalization of slavery for Apaches as a method to repress their power.[20]

The California Column

Meanwhile, another military force had entered the borderlands. The forward detachments of the volunteer Union men from California reached Tucson on May 20, 1862. To get there the advance columns had to fight only a few minor skirmishes with the Confederates, the most notable engagement taking place on April 15 at Picacho Peak, a substantial rock formation rising from the Sonoran Desert floor north of Tucson. The task of the California Volunteers was to prevent the junction of Southern sympathizers between Texas and California, and to strike the flank of Sibley's force along the Rio Grande. They were also to revive the southern overland route, and give protection to U.S. citizens living in New Mexico, many of whom were in search of mining treasure. The man in charge, Gen. James H. Carleton, was a seasoned officer with previous Southwest borderlands experience and a reputation as a thorough disciplinarian with an inclination for military minutiae. Entering Tucson in June 1862, he reached the Rio Grande in August, setting up headquarters at Santa Fe.[21]

As he went, Carleton declared the nullification of all Confederate laws, made Arizona a territory in the union, and appointed himself the head of government. Carleton declared martial law, levied taxes on gambling establishments, and confiscated food stores for use by his army. By now, many Hispanic villagers were utterly demoralized, as they witnessed their fragile economy demolished not just by the Apaches but by a second occupying Anglo army. Also, it did not help the popularity of the occupiers when the Californians made the residents swear an oath of allegiance to the Union and forced those who traveled anywhere in the territory to obtain a military pass from a military representative, a potentially maddening and embarrassing process.[22]

It should be pointed out that in some ways Carleton's rigid rule over civilians stood in contrast to the freedom he permitted them in fighting Apaches. If the regular army sought to exclude the civilians from Apache fighting, and was largely successful in the 1870s and 1880s, the Californians, like the Confederates, encouraged civilian initiative. The Californians also looked the other way when news of brutalities surfaced.

Carleton was meticulous when it came to logistics and supply, recognizing that, because the soldiers were not dependent on local game, plants, or crops, well-organized supply could prove to their benefit. When relaying his original column of 2,350 soldiers, augmented by some 6,000 additional men before the Civil War's end, he made the troops advance in small detachments along the old Butterfield Overland Mail route. This way they would have the ability to take advantage of wells, hay, and shelter at the abandoned overland stage stations. The troops also had time for training en route, thus continuing the preparation they had started in California. Officers did not have it any easier. They were expected to set an example, read army manuals, behave irreproachably, and, in the words of their commander, "drill, drill, drill" their troops until the men become perfect as soldiers, as skirmishers, as marksmen. While men sweated their mornings in linear formation exercises at Yuma, in the afternoon they squeezed a few pints more sweat out of their bodies as skirmishers. Later in the garrisons of New Mexico and Arizona, drilling was supposed to continue with regularity, although it seems that dress parades and inspections, and idleness, vice, and manual labor competed for soldiers' time. Still, surgeon James McNulty claimed in his report that the California men in general were in high spirits and in good physical shape.[23]

Some historians have represented the California men as a distinct lot from the much-maligned regulars. Andrew Masich paints the volunteers as intelligent and self-reliant risk takers, who, after experiencing hard lives in the California goldfields, had grown accustomed to working outdoors in demanding conditions.[24] Still, many California men, like their peers in the regular army, lacked previous military experience. Not all were experts, for example, in handling a weapon or riding a horse. Edward Ayer describes an episode where he and three hundred of his comrades, subject to inspection, tried to mount their horses. Only seventy-five of them made it, while the rest fumbled. As a result, their mounts started bucking and running into each other, making a hasty exit to the surrounding valley. It was, according to Ayer's testimony, the first and last mounted inspection his command experienced.[25]

Like those in the regulars, countless officers and soldiers directed their focus on leisure instead of training and war. Many were also averse to the military discipline shoved down their throats by Carleton's inflexible demands and authoritarian orders. During their stint in the Southwest borderlands, California officers faced charges for murder, alcoholism, embezzlement, sexual deviation, desertion, and incompetence. Signs of the class division that so marred the regular army also existed among the Californians. For example, Sgt. George Hand's diary is riddled with contempt targeting his superiors. Short on affection but rich in innovation, Hand dubbed his company commander "Old Toady," "His Majesty," and "High Priest." "They are," Hand surmised the officers he knew, "all in all, a miserable, slovenly set and altogether unfit to command even Indians. That is the whole and nothing but the truth." Hand was not alone in his thoughts. Many a man despised their commanders as tyrants and cowards. Many a soldier also found himself in the guardhouse, dismissed of service, or sentenced to hard labor. Those most unlucky were even shot to death in the field by their officers for disobeying orders.[26]

Fixated, or fully dedicated, to his task, Carleton listed every article—from two handkerchiefs to one towel and from one tin cup to one fork, spoon, and plate—the soldiers would take with them. His attention to detail was higher than average in every way. Like many commanders, he worried over weaponry, its quantity and uniformity—Sharps New Model 1859 carbine being the preferred choice. But he also had his doubts on whether some weapons would prove too heavy to carry and thus requested for his cavalry the lightweight Colt Navy revolver instead of the weighty .44-caliber Dragoon pistol used by the regular troops. Thinking that battles and whole wars could be lost if the cavalry could not function properly, Carleton also gave particularly careful attention to soldiers' footwear and the types of horseshoe nails supplied to the cavalry. In the end, in part due to Carleton's demands, each soldier ought to have carried nearly sixty pounds of clothing, weapons, equipment, and supplies.[27]

In reality, Carleton's standards constituted the ideal, and the California soldiers taking the field against the Apaches preferred fatigue uniforms and used what the quartermaster service had available. Even if he annoyed—and he did—the troops with his ways, among borderlands commanders, Carleton displayed a rare level of devotion and commitment to the task at hand. If it was up to him, his men should be prepared to meet the enemy on a foreign desert terrain. What they ended up confronting were not the Confederates, who, contrary to speculation and expectations, never reemerged from Texas, but the Apaches.

Killing Apaches Carleton-Style

Throughout the summer of 1862, California Volunteers relayed in small units toward the Rio Grande via Fort Yuma and Tucson. They were taking the southern overland route "over a barren desert which we knew nothing about," a soldier in the column recorded.[28] Their first violent contacts with the Chiricahuas, who had bolstered their supplies by raiding Confederate livestock, came in June. First, on June 18 the Chiricahuas hit a small party of Carleton's expressmen east of Apache Pass, killing two of the four men. A week later they met Col. Edward E. Eyre's unit at Apache Pass. The colonel attempted to parley with the Chiricahuas, but in the meantime three of his men who had wandered off from the main assembly were killed and stripped by some Chiricahua fighters. Upon discovery, Eyre, much to the disappointment of his men, did not retaliate. Bound by Carleton's orders not to engage and enrage the Apaches, the troops instead continued onward. The following night, in the San Simon Valley, Eyre's camp was again harassed by some Chiricahuas, whose volley wounded one army surgeon. After that, Eyre's party continued unmolested. His main mission was to proceed eastward quickly and undetected to meet the Confederate forces, who, unbeknownst to him, were no longer at the Rio Grande.[29]

Making it known that Apache Pass was theirs and theirs alone, the Chiricahuas then slew a party of nine civilians two miles east in San Simon Valley on July 13 before setting a massive ambush for the next set of Californians coming their way. This particular command had already split due to the uncertainty of their water supply. Lt. John Cremony with thirty cavalrymen followed in the rear with the wagon train and cattle while Capt. Thomas L. Roberts pushed the advance detachment of ninety-five footmen. The latter marched the whole night across the Sulphur Springs Valley and into the following day before reaching Apache Pass in calamitous want of water on July 15. There the troops faced heavy Apache fire from the hillsides near the abandoned stage station. Barely seeing their enemy, the troops were forced to retreat and regroup.[30]

Again pushing onward, Roberts had his men loaded the howitzers, and he threw out skirmishers over the hills so as to command the main pathway. At this time, the troops had to reach the spring at the pass or perish, as the summer heat of southern Arizona would surely kill them. The Chiricahuas knew this. Keeping up a rapid and scathing fire, Apaches gunned the soldiers from behind breastworks of rock on the two hills near the spring area. Being well below Apache positions limited the effectiveness of the two twelve-pound mountain howitzers the troops had with them. "Under a continuous and galling fire," Cremony scripted, the soldiers penetrated deeper into the pass, driving the Apache "force before them." Managing to relocate the artillery in a more advantageous spot, they launched howitzer shells toward the enemy. The Apaches abandoned their rockworks and fled in all directions when confronted with artillery. After securing water, the soldiers also withdrew for the night to the stone station building. The next morning the combined infantry and cavalry force carefully proceeded toward the spring. They formed, Robert Utley writes, on horseback and on foot and advanced with military precision, firing at the Chiricahuas, who had returned, shelling them with howitzers, and then charging. The Apaches again scattered, this time for good.[31]

Army reports place the number of dead as a result of this battle at two soldiers and anywhere from nine to sixty-six Apaches. Cremony claims that sixty-three of the Apaches died of howitzer shells while only three perished from musket fire. Some Apache sources claim they suffered no casualties. While the truth remains undetermined, it is possible that fatalities proved minimal, as it has been suggested that at least most of the howitzer shells actually flew over the Apache positions, startling them but causing minimal damage.

Still, while it may not rank in the global listings of all-out battles, in the U.S.-Apache wars the Battle of Apache Pass stands out as one of the more pivotal moments. Together, with the show of force in 1861 and the demoralizing and despicable killing of Mangas Coloradas in January 1863, it occupies the intersection between a time when the Chiricahuas stood as masters of their domain between the Dragoon Mountains and the Black Range and the arrival of an era when they started to lose ground to the Americans. The Chiricahuas would rarely expose themselves to any battle of such magnitude in the future if they could avoid it. They would also prefer to have nothing to do with armies carrying artillery. The Battle of Apache Pass had actually been one of the few occasions artillery played any kind of noteworthy role in the U.S.-Apache wars. Furthermore, the Chiricahuas, after seeing more and more troops pass through Apache Pass and witnessing the establishment of Fort Bowie near the site, most likely realized that Anglos, instead of withdrawing, as it had appeared they would in 1861, planned for a more dominant presence in the very core of their world. While the overland mail people had used this strategically important thoroughfare and spring, they had been mere tenants at the Apaches consent. Army forts, on the other hand, signified foreign intrusion, although not yet necessarily permanence. Seeing how posts had come and gone at Santa Rita del Cobre in the 1850s, the Chiricahuas challenged the contemplated regime change at Apache Pass as they would continue to do at Pinos Altos.[32] During the coming months, the Chiricahuas appeared often in the vicinity of the new fort. While they occasionally raided its livestock, they refrained from a head-on assault.[33]

Among the wounded at the Battle of Apache Pass had been Mangas Coloradas. Hurried to Janos for medical treatment in the middle of the battle, he recovered. By now an old man, Mangas sought a return to planting at the Mogollon Mountains. He approached the inhabitants of Pinos Altos. While the first meeting was conducted in a cordial enough spirit, when Mangas with a small entourage walked the streets of the mining village on January 17, 1863, expecting to eat and talk, the residents seized the old fighter as hostage. The next day they turned Mangas over to Col. Joseph West, urged by Carleton for months to strike against the Bedonkohes and the Chihennes.

Held at Fort McLane, a tiny post that had been abandoned at the start of the Civil War, Mangas shivered through the night sleeping on the ground under a single blanket. Soldiers played a cruel game on him, placing their bayonets heated in the fire against Mangas's skin. When the old Bedonkohe protested, two guards raised their muskets and fired. Then they finished the job execution-style by discharging a revolver against his head. The guards had acted as instructed. Thinking Mangas was responsible for all the Chiricahua raiding in New Mexico, West had reportedly told his men, "The old murderer has got away from every soldier command. . . . I want him dead or alive tomorrow morning, do you understand? I want him dead." Still, West was possibly aware of the censure faced by Baylor or perhaps he was uncertain of how Carleton would react when hearing what had happened. He might have also been eager to avoid giving the California troops a bad reputation in the East. Skirting the truth, West noted in his report that the guards had been forced to shoot Mangas on his third attempt to escape.[34]

West fabricated no stories on what happened next. The day after his death Mangas was scalped by one of the Californians and his body dumped into a gully, from which it was dug up a few days later by some soldiers who decapitated the Chiricahua and boiled his head. In 1864, the skull traveled with a military surgeon to Toledo, Ohio, where the surgeon opened a medical practice and offered the cranium for research. It went to a phrenologist in New York City, who discussed the skull in some length and published a picture of it in his 1873 book. Later, the skull possibly ended up at the Smithsonian Institution. Today, its whereabouts remain unknown.[35]

As rumors started to circulate on what exactly had happened to Mangas, Lt. John Cremony, perhaps cognizant of the need to explain it all for the better and to camouflage the doings of his fellow Californians, was among those who actively demonized the Chiricahua leader. In his memoirs, first published in 1868, Cremony wrote that Mangas, although being a wise and respected man among his people, possessed "the ferocity and brutality of the most savage savage." Mangas had "laid waste," "ruined," and "ravished" "large and flourishing towns" and "vast ranchos" "teeming with wealth and immense herds of" livestock throughout the borderlands.[36] Whereas white audiences eagerly ate up representations like these, the Chiricahuas obviously did not. As they learned of the events, many Chiricahuas expressed deep sorrow and fury. It was especially the beheading that seemed exceptional, terrible, and appalling. The Apaches would not forget. For decades, they would think back on what happened to Mangas whenever then pondered whether to trust the military. In the more immediate present, Mangas's fate confirmed suspicions that the recently arrived whites had begun a war of extermination, a killing fest lacking all honor.

The day their dead leader was scalped, Mangas's local group, still unaware of his fate, fell victim to a violent attack by West's men and the people of Pinos Altos, who reportedly killed eleven, among them the wife and son of Mangas. With their sights set on killing more Apaches, the following day another detachment sent by West charged a Chihenne encampment nearby. George Hand proudly noted in his diary that when West's troops returned to Mesilla less than a week later, the "boys brought in scalps." In a few months, the Chiricahuas responded with equal ferocity. Killing Lt. L. A. Bargie and two of his men on a Rio Grande crossing on June 17, the Apaches reportedly decapitated Bargie and carved his heart out. They again ambushed several parties, taking wagonloads of supplies and numerous mules in the vicinity of Cooke's Canyon and emptied more stock near Pinos Altos. On June 21, West, who had evaded censure in the Mangas affair, ordered that the Chihennes "must be exterminated to a man" and that this task should be carried out "at the earliest possible moment." Aiming to wipe out the Chihennes, the California troops also sought to occupy their country. In February 1863, they established Fort West near Pinos Altos, and eight months later they built Fort Cummings at the mouth of Cooke's Canyon.[37]

The killing of Mangas, the subsequent order to exterminate the Chihennes, and the setting up of new forts in the core of the Chiricahua world comprised just one facet of borderlands warfare Carleton-style. When en route toward the Rio Grande in 1862, the Californians had heard stories of the military potency of the Apaches and spotted with their own eyes pillaged wagons, devastated fields, and vacated ranches.[38] Recovering from the disappointment of no Confederates remaining in New Mexico, it did not take long for Carleton to turn his energy against the different Apache communities.

Taking his cues from the latest in industrialized mass warfare, Carleton favored merciless straightforward subjugation of the enemy, pure destruction without chicanery. The first to succumb to Carleton's methodologies of killing were those near the U.S. imperial ground zero on the Rio Grande. While the Jicarillas lived closest to Santa Fe, they appeared militarily too trivial to seriously bother Anglo minds. Thus, Carleton set his sight on the Mescaleros, whom their agent, Lorenzo Labadi, writing on September 25, 1862, described as being in a "continuous state of hostility" and of having committed "heavy depredations." Between September 1861 and September 1862, Mescalero fighters had hit the Confederates several times, skirmished with Mexican forces on more than one occasion, and raided livestock repeatedly from ranches, stage stations, and government wagon trains in the area between Mesilla and Fort Davis. But while their raiding activity had jumped in 1861 as a result of the Confederate invasion and the overall turmoil created by the Civil War on the Rio Grande, 1862 had been a quieter year. Mescaleros had, for instance, clashed just once, on August 31, with the California Volunteers.[39]

This did little to deter Carleton from executing a military offensive. In October 1862, he ordered converging columns consisting of California men and New Mexico Volunteer troops—the latter comprised of local Hispanics from the Rio Grande eager to kill the Mescaleros, pilfer their property, and capture their women and children—to encircle the Mescaleros from three directions—through Dog Canyon and the Sacramento Mountains, south via Hueco Tanks, and from the way of Fort Stanton. The field commanders of the campaign, Colonel West and Col. Kit Carson, were forbidden by Carleton to accept any surrender from the Apache men: "All Indian men of that tribe are to be killed whenever and wherever you can find them. . . . If the Indians [Mescaleros] send in a flag and desire to treat for peace . . . [tell them] you have been sent to punish them for their treachery and their crimes; that you have no power to make peace; that you are there to kill them." Only the women and children could be taken to reopened

Fort Stanton as prisoners to await further orders. As a footnote to his letters, Carleton decreed that if some Mescaleros wanted their lives to be spared they should venture to his headquarters in Santa Fe and beg for peace personally.[40]

Seeing Apaches as "wary" animals who "must be hunted with skill," Carleton initiated tactics that included marching at night, ambushing at desert springs or waterholes, and, most significantly, demolishing all the material property, animals, plants, fields, and crops of the Apaches. He wanted his men to excel as angels of destruction. On the one hand, they were to bring unforeseen levels of systematic destruction to Apache lives, and, on the other, to outdo the enemy on his own terrain. Carleton personally did not feel that he was abandoning the rules of civilized conflict, but only bending them to include scorched-earth tactics and annihilation. News of the massive battles and seemingly unprecedented destruction from the East seemed to confirm the contemporary flexibility of civilized warfare. Furthermore, the federal government's attempt to codify civilized conduct in combat did leave much room for interpretation. Confronted with the occupation of the South, the federal government issued the Lieber Code in 1863. It made a clear distinction between men in arms and the civilian population and denounced cruelty (infliction of suffering for the sake of suffering), revenge, poisoning, perfidy, and wanton devastation of civilian society. But it also differentiated between barbaric and civilized opponents. The code enabled, and in fact practically encouraged, the borderlands Anglos to have a free hand in dealing with the Apaches.[41]

The Mescaleros were totally unprepared for what awaited them. In October 1862, a big Mescalero camp at the mouth of Dog Canyon was overrun by soldiers. The surviving Apaches fled in panic. At least fourteen Apaches had been killed, including their two leaders Manuelito and Jose Largo. Some twenty more suffered wounds. This episode was followed by a relentless and ruthless canvassing and demolishing of Mescalero fields and homes by the Californians and New Mexico Volunteers. The campaigns saw less fighting and skirmishing than destruction of property and constant hounding. As a result, from fall 1862 to spring 1863, some estimates claim, as many as three hundred Mescaleros perished. For West, the campaign of destruction amounted to "vigorous warfare" against the Apaches, "who infest the country." Confronting Carleton at Santa Fe, Cadette, a Mescalero, explained, "We are worn out; we have no more heart, we have no provisions, no means to live. Your troops are everywhere." A younger Mescalero later recalled how he and others learned many horror stories detailing how their people had suffered at the hands of the troops during the winter of 1862–63. In one of the narratives, Apache mothers quieted their children by telling them that soldiers would find and kill them. Then, "even babies dared not cry." By spring 1863, most of those who survived, some four hundred people, found themselves at Bosque Redondo, the only place where the troops would spare their lives.[42]

Shortly after reaching Santa Fe in October 1862, Carleton had ordered the establishment of Fort Sumner on the Pecos River although his officers had reported that the site was unsuitable for a post or reservation. Not only was the broad valley of the Pecos River too remote from forage and roads, thus making supply a massive problem, but the river was alkaline and unhealthy, hindering farming. Nevertheless, Carleton had been a strong advocate of the location since 1852, when he had first witnessed its rich-looking soil, cottonwoods, water, and game, as well as when he realized that the site was far away from any mountain ranges the Indians could escape to. He ignored all objections and drew plans of making Bosque Redondo, adjacent to Fort Sumner, the Indian metropolis of the borderlands.[43]

Driven to their prison camp–like home by the military, the journey itself proved burdensome and mentally discomforting for the Mescaleros. More devastating was the impact that they were forced to leave their densely forested mountain ranges and descend to flatter ground on the edge of the Great Plains. For Navajos, also hit by Carleton's destructive operations, the Long Walk was even more lethal, as hundreds succumbed to sickness, exhaustion, and exposure.[44] The forced relocation was supposed to be guided by Christian kindness but in reality involved rape, hunger, exhaustion, emotional desperation, and overall confusion and chaos. When reaching their destination, the Mescaleros and Navajos, who did not get along, had to begin farming, digging irrigation canals, and constructing buildings.

Carleton's experiment was soon plagued by an immense array of problems, with no end in sight, including prostitution, venereal disease, crop failures, floods, drought, sanitary difficulties, dysentery, and supply problems. After the crop failure in 1864, Carleton tried to rush more food to the reservation, yet refused to budge from his plan of making the Indians civilized farmers at Bosque Redondo. Next, Carleton hinted at the possibility of moving more Apaches, the Chihennes and Jicarillas, to Bosque Redondo. Neither group was forthcoming. To the officers at Fort Sumner and to the civilian agents preparing an inquiry against Carleton for the Department of the Interior, the reality was hauntingly obvious. Bosque Redondo was a death camp.[45]

According to one Mescalero who lived through the ordeal, the "place at Fort Sumner was what is now called a concentration camp. There was nothing there except misery and hunger." Furthermore, not only did the Comanches, Pueblos, and Hispanics threaten to steal the Mescaleros' property and children at Bosque Redondo, but the Rio Grande residents claimed that Mescaleros from Bosque Redondo were responsible for stock raids in the area. Already on April 10, 1863, Carleton instructed one of his subordinates, "Should any of the men of those Mescaleros now at Bosque Redondo attempt to escape, after their promises to remain quietly there, you will be sure to cause them to be shot." Finding life unbearable, it was no wonder that many sought to escape back to their mountains, which were free of sickness, bad water, Navajos, and, they hoped, soldiers. They felt, "Death meant nothing to us if it could be in that good place which Ussen [Apache deity] had given us." Small parties had already left the Pecos River. For example, on May 1, 1864, forty-two Mescaleros escaped back home. One November morning in 1865 all those remaining (except nine) left. Some 350 Mescaleros fled to various directions on stolen Navajo horses in the cover of the night. The carefully planned and meticulously executed escape left the military bewildered.[46]

Shutting his ears to criticism, Carleton had gained the disfavor of many New Mexicans. Steck, since 1863 the superintendent of Indian Affairs for New Mexico Territory, issued complaint after complaint on Carleton's Indian policies. Powerless against Carleton, he exited the Indian management in 1865. In January 1866, the territorial legislature of New Mexico issued a letter to President Andrew Johnson accusing Carleton of his failure in Indian policy and of his implementation of martial law. While Carleton was relieved of his New Mexico command in September, the starvation camp at Pecos lingered for two more years before the government let the surviving Navajos return home. At that time, many of the Mescalero families had not reunited since departing Bosque Redondo. While many scattered across their mountain homes, others ventured farther away. Some lived with the Lipans, and others joined ranks with the Chihennes or the Comanches. Much like the Lipans and the Jicarillas, in the late 1860s many Mescaleros were seriously weakened borderlands refugees enduring diasporic lives of poverty and want, of anger and resentment.[47]

Civilians for Extermination

In April 1863, the word of the mineral discoveries made by Joseph R. Walker's party in the San Francisco Mountains of central Arizona, a Yavapai-Western Apache territory previously relatively free of Anglo residents, spread the news of treasures awaiting. Soon hopes jumped through the roof. "No country [is] richer in gold and silver" than central Arizona, proclaimed one would-be millionaire. By 1864, the area north of Gila River had its share of wild diggers proclaiming, "We wanted nuggets as large as a man's fist." The area would experience a boom groundbreaking for Arizona, the establishment of Prescott as capital for the new territory, and the building of Fort Whipple, yet another post the California soldiers set imposingly at the hub of Apache terrain. In Carleton and the Californians, the news of a fresh goldfield found more than just a sympathetic ear. Carleton personally wanted to find and market fresh discoveries, thinking they would make his job of extinguishing Apache sovereignty easier as a gold boom would accelerate the arrival of white settlers and the railroads. Already, when posting troops at Pinos Altos, Carleton had encouraged his subordinates to use some of their time for prospecting. They needed little encouragement, as California troopers, many of whom were former forty-niners, filed hundreds of claims. Later many stayed or returned to seek for fortunes after being discharged.[48]

As the fortune seekers rushed in, they quickly found their distaste with the resident Western Apaches and Yavapais. What nonviolent accord there existed when first whites arrived evaporated by 1864 as Anglos outnumbered Yavapais and Apaches in the Prescott area. Viewing Apaches as insolent murderers or thieves to whom cordial behavior represented weakness, the newcomers felt under siege, trapped, outnumbered, and vulnerable. In reality, Western Apaches or Yavapais, some of whom were closely aligned with Tonto Apaches, made just two stock raids in the latter half of 1863, during which they killed one Hispanic and no whites. During the first four months of 1864, they executed fourteen raids, killing five civilians.[49]

But at that time, the citizens and volunteers were already hunting the Apaches and Yavapais. Worked up to a frenzy, outfits of civilians went looking for Apaches to kill, calling it self-defense. Of course, the more rational used these murder campaigns for their own ends, hoping slaughter would turn out to be a cost-efficient and effective method for emptying the hypothetically mineral-rich lands of Indians.[50]

As the settlers exposed their deepest fears of a racial war detrimental to the whites, they were not only grossly misjudging the sociopolitical structures of the area's indigenous peoples but were misinterpreting the Apache method of war for the kind of extermination the Anglos themselves advocated. A prospector's January 18, 1864, letter from the Prescott district sheds light on the prevalent Anglo mindset of victimization. On account of livestock robbery, he stated, "We are determined, if possible, to punish the guilty Indians." If the Apaches and Yavapais were not checked, he continued, "We will have to leave this country and let the Indians have it. Many have already left." Obviously, this prospector, and others like him who felt threatened by raiding, did not view themselves as unlawful intruders on Apache and Yavapai homes or consider the Indians rightful owners of Arizona real estate. Interestingly, while the prospector accuses the Apaches of pilfering livestock, the punishment he advocates is the taking of lives. The justification, he rationalizes, is that "the Indians are becoming more bold daily, and as soon as they steal the remnant of stock left, so as not to be followed, *they will commence* murdering small parties of prospectors and miners." That is why, he continued, the Indians "have to be badly whipped." Hence, professing that because the Apaches and Yavapais would ultimately kill the Anglos after the supply of horses, mules, cows, and chickens was exhausted, the whites had to act first.[51]

By depicting the Apaches as a separate and vile race bent on wiping out all whites, the Anglos could justify to themselves the disposing of vestiges of civilized warfare in their conduct. One Anglo journalist, for instance, reasoned that punishing the predatory yet cowardly Apaches "in accordance of the usages of war" was impossible because they would not stand and give fight like civilized people do. Therefore, the citizens had to "do something to spread terror among the savages." In short, and with the risk of simplifying reality, in many white minds they fought for peace, prosperity, and liberation, and to do it successfully against Apaches a civilized person was justified in making not only preemptive strikes but was allowed to temporarily think and act like a beast.[52]

King Woolsey would fit the description. An entrepreneur born in Alabama, he had established a ranch on the Agua Fria River, fifteen miles east of Prescott. His ranch was raided twice in early 1864, once on January 4 and the second time on February 25. On neither occasion did the Indians kill anyone. Altogether they took some sixty head of livestock from Woolsey. By the time of the second raid, Woolsey and his outfit, a mix of Anglo civilians and O'odham-Maricopa Indians, had already claimed many Western Apache/Yavapai lives. On January 24, 1864, Woolsey and his men located a very large winter encampment far away from white settlements in the vicinity of Fish Creek, near the Salt River. Successful in luring some of the cautious Indians, who were possibly Kwevkepayas (Yavapais) and Tonto, or Pinal, Apaches to a meeting and offering them tobacco, clothing, and pinole Woolsey had his men shoot at the seated guests. From nineteen to thirty-three Indians and one white man ended up dead. A white prospector, describing how Woolsey had schemed a masterful trap, professed this butchery as self-defense. The Indians, he wrote, were "fixed to fight," as they had brought knives to the parley and surely "intended to butcher whites" as soon as they had eaten, "for the *Indians* are very treacherous."[53]

Two days later Woolsey killed one Indian when his force of twenty-nine men attacked two hunters near the Agua Fria River. In February, working in conjunction with California Volunteers and local units, Woolsey and fourteen other civilians, among them the new governor of Arizona, John Goodwin, hit a small camp of fifteen Indians on the Verde River, killing five of the residents. In April, Woolsey was again on the hunt for Indians and new areas of mineral bounty. This time his group, according to some sources, was comprised of one hundred miners and ranchers. Accompanied by a handful of California troops, they unleashed their fury on a Pinal (or Tonto) Apache camp at Squaw Canyon between the Agua Fria and Verde Rivers. Depending on the source, somewhere between fourteen to thirty-one Indians lost their lives that day. None of the attackers perished. While Woolsey and his outfit had brought about several slaughters in the first months of 1864, Anglos cheered their heroes onward. Possessing past experience in killing Indians, being "used to mountain travel, cool, courageous, and enduring," and being "eager to chastise the wily foe," Woolsey's men should prove extremely successful in killing Indians on their latest hunt, the *Arizona Miner* acclaimed in its April 6, 1864, editorial. Those already slain at Squaw Canyon, the paper continued, "we trust" would only be "an indication" of what would follow.[54]

As Woolsey was hunting Apaches, so were several other outfits. While their operations would not live up to the full-out offensive Carleton called for in his May 1864 plans, numerous units of California men canvassed central Arizona between May and August 1864. Several of them also hit their targets. Lt. Col. Nelson Davis's command smashed at least five different Western Apaches camps in the vicinity of the San Carlos River between May 25 and 29. His command killed an estimated fifty-two Indians, took numerous captives, and demolished great quantities of precious supplies and camp equipment. Following a barrage of individual strikes by separate commands, Maj. Thomas Blakeley's California and New Mexico Volunteers, augmented by civilians, thumped several Indian camps on or near Pinal Creek in late July and early August. His troops scattered the inhabitants, destroyed much booty, demolished at least 250 acres of fields, and took the lives of approximately ten Indians. Some of his prisoners Blakeley hanged; others he had shot as they tried to escape. It is telling that in their fourteen strikes against the Western Apaches/Yavapais between May and August not one of the California soldiers was killed by Indians.[55]

Meanwhile, Woolsey continued with a succession of expeditions in the summer and fall of 1864, and while massive killings eluded him, they contributed to his reputation as a stalwart defender of the white race.[56] Woolsey's fame had started to grow some three years prior. When working as a hay contractor for the government, he had been attacked by an Apache or Yavapai raiding party on the overland route near Oatman's Flat in 1861. After killing the leader of the raiders himself, Woolsey reportedly had the body dragged to a mesquite tree. Then he hung the dead Indian from the neck, and left the corpse dangling as a warning to the Indians. The corpse allegedly decayed and swayed in the desert heat and wind for several years. One traveler who happened on the site, which for all purposes functioned as a symbolic entrance gate to the borderlands killing fields, wrote of the "strange feelings" he felt when witnessing the "dried and shrunken" corpse with "ghastly but life-like" facial expression slowly turning in the wind. The carcass was missing both hands and one leg on the account of the coyotes. Still, while the observer, a newspaperman, described in detail the horrors he witnessed, he shied away from directly censuring Woolsey and the methods many Arizona fighters used against the Apaches.[57]

In all, 1864 had turned out a life-altering year for many Western Apache and Yavapai communities. In twelve months, they took part in no less than fifty military engagements, being at the receiving end of most of them. In comparison, they had just ten engagements in 1863 and two in 1862, and many of those were raids they themselves had initiated. At least 215 Western Apaches and Yavapais had been slain in combat in 1864, while numerous others had died of hunger and exposure or ended up as captives in Hispanic households. In turn, the Western Apaches and Yavapais had reportedly killed eleven Anglos and six Hispanics during the whole year.[58]

Not only had the Western Apache/Yavapai world caught in flames, but things would continue as bad or worse in the coming years as the civilians, volunteer troops, and the returning regular Army harassed, smashed, and killed the Indian communities struggling to survive. The newcomers would also build roads, cut the earth with their mining endeavors, and set up new ranches, villages, and town sites, including Phoenix in the Salt River valley, between the O'odhams and the San Carlos and Tonto Apaches. White invaders would bring not only their people but their plants, animals, and material goods in an effort to claim the western reaches of Apacheria for themselves.

Undoubtedly one of the more infamous weapons in the arsenal of the settlers was strychnine. The most notorious, but sketchily documented, episode of strychnine poisoning is the event known in Arizona history as the Pinole Treaty, orchestrated by King Woolsey and his men. While meeting with a party of Yavapais or Western Apaches, possibly in 1865, Woolsey placed in plain view a sack of pinole poisoned with strychnine, thinking the Indians could not resist free food. As Woolsey and Indians leaders continued discussions, much of the pinole disappeared into hungry mouths of the onlookers. First one, then another, soon followed by several more victims, wailed and rolled on the ground. Horrified by the events, those Indians unaffected hurriedly made their exit.[59]

Woolsey's Pinole Treaty was not an isolated incident. According to Alonso Davis, a soldier from California, people in Arizona used to place bags of sugar laced with strychnine on known Apache trails or atop large boulders, where the Apaches would be sure to come across them. This "may seem harsh to people who know nothing of conditions" in Arizona, Davis reasoned, but "it was the only way we could get hold of those natives who never would stand and fight."[60] Indeed, Woolsey had many peers in the strychnine business and in championing Apache extermination. And not just among the incoming Anglos. Augmenting and eventually replacing California men whose terms of service expired after 1864 were companies of New Mexico and Arizona Volunteers recruited from the homegrown Hispanic populace and among the O'odham and Maricopa villagers. Frequently longtime inhabitants of the borderlands and oftentimes harboring generations of antagonism, these men were eager to hit back at the Apaches, although they also often shared a level of intimacy with and an understanding of the Apaches unlike any the Californians, Anglo prospectors, or slowly returning regular army troops could ever accomplish.[61]

For the O'odhams and Maricopas, it was a question of retaining their lands and autonomy while adapting to new rulers. They incorporated many trade items the newcomers brought, such as metal tools, cotton cloth, and tobacco. They also quickly suggested the idea of allying with the Anglos against the common Apache foe. Indeed, at first the O'odhams imagined they held the upper hand and would incorporate the incomers to their world, engaging in exchanges that would benefit them. They had every reason to think so on the account of the weak Anglo presence in the 1850s. Anglos, on the other hand, continued to almost unanimously applaud the O'odhams as always friendly and hospitable Indians who proved of great value and assistance to all those traveling through their country. Several Anglos at the time also emphasized the military strength, ability, and vigor the O'odhams and Maricopas had displayed in successfully combating the Apaches.[62]

One borderlands group that usually escaped the Anglo gaze was the people known as *apaches mansos,* or "tame" Apaches. The designation basically refers to Apaches integrated to the Mexican populace on either side of the borderline and stands in contrast to independent Apaches, or *apaches barbaros.* These Apaches were a mixed assortment of people originating from different Apache groups. We know that many Apaches had moved close to Spanish settlements in the past, and while many departed as warfare intensified in the 1830s, others stayed. Some sources suggest that in the 1830s as much as half of Tucson's populace had Apache origins. One would think some of the mansos were former captives holding on to fringes of their Apache identity, while still others had, for one reason or another, more recently deserted their Apache communities. Militarily they proved important because of their intimate knowledge of Apache homelands and their willingness to enlist against other Apaches. Many campaigns in the 1860s had apaches mansos at the forefront of the killings.[63]

When the O'odhams, apaches mansos, and local Hispanics made up the state volunteers, the borderlands wars pitted neighbor against neighbor. For instance, in May 1863 a mixed group that included two companies of California soldiers, ten Anglos, thirty-two Hispanics, twenty O'odhams, and nine mansos stormed an Apache village at Aravaipa Canyon. The expedition's unofficial leader was Jesús María Elías, a man hoping to retrieve his family's captured property from the Apaches. While the Elíases represented Sonora's established classes, they shared a common ground with many of the masses in that their family history was distinguished not just by continuous fighting against the Apaches but also by close intimacy with their nemeses. Apaches had killed several of Jesús's relatives and depleted his family fortunes for decades. On the other hand, Jesús was familiar with the Apache language, band structure, and ways of operation, and he could track them like few Anglos could. Furthermore, for the 1850s and 1860s the Elías household included an Apache captive, José, who was not a slave but a family member. José took the family surname and lived with them until a teenager, when he either died of fever or escaped back to the Apaches.

After Ramón, one of Jesús' brothers, was killed by the Apaches when trying to recapture stolen cattle, the family suffered yet another devastating blow. In early 1863, Apaches reportedly liberated the Elíases of 325 head of cattle, threatening family survival. During the pursuit and skirmish that followed, Jesús and his outfit advanced to Aravaipa Canyon, where another brother, Cornelio, died from an Apache shot. It was after this that Jesús and his brother Juan orchestrated the second campaign to Aravaipa Canyon on May 1863, this time going in with a large force. They orchestrated a surprise attack, killing an estimated sixty Apaches and taking several captives while losing only one of their ranks. The leader of the Californians in this mixed party, Capt. T. T. Tidball, saw his auxiliaries indiscriminately slay men, women, and children. The frenzied outfit also butchered the wounded. Only ten Apaches, who ended up as slaves in homes of well-to-do Hispanics, survived the massacre after Tidball personally intervened to stop the bloody affair. Apparently the ferocity of violence had proven too much for him.[64]

February to September 1866 represented the period of high activity for Arizona Volunteer units. During that time, the Hispanic, O'odham, Maricopa, and manso recruits clashed at least fifteen times with Yavapais and Western Apaches. They proved highly lethal when storming Indian camps. For example, on February 13 the Arizonians killed from fifteen to thirty Western Apaches/Yavapais who had been hiding in caves. Their assault of March 7 slaughtered twenty, and one attack on March 24 took twenty-two more lives. Seven days later another twenty-five Apaches perished, while the smash of April 11 added another sixteen to the tally. August 13 proved a particularly bloody day in the volunteers' offensive. Then a parley turned into bloodbath. At least thirty-three Apaches/Yavapais were eliminated. In the engagements mentioned here, a total of 131 Western Apaches/Yavapais were reported killed. Just two volunteers lost their lives.[65]

For the majority of the approximately four thousand Arizonians, of whom most were newcomers, the deeds of the local volunteers meant a great triumph. The campaigns had also set the new standard in killing Apaches, something the locals would compare to the showing of the regular army in later years, and find the army lacking. The Anglo mouthpiece *Arizona Miner* in Prescott had little qualms about celebrating the Hispanic and O'odham volunteers as enthusiastically as it had the Anglo hero Woolsey, as news of "victories" kept arriving. "Their praises are everywhere shouted," "The soldiers behaved admirably," and "This [the fight of March 31] is another fine feather in the cap of the Arizonians" are some of the commentaries from the April 11, 1866, issue. Also, as the operations started to wane, the paper, in its September 12 issue, noted how "the volunteers have done much toward the subjugation or extermination of the Apaches."[66]

Parameters of Violence

While Arizonians seemed intent on exterminating the Apaches, the parameters of violence were actually constantly renegotiated. Anglos could be quite sensitive, and critical, toward what the society in the East thought of their doings. While some saw little shame in advocating mass murder, others found perfidy or the killing of women and children more troubling. Still others discovered, as Tidball had, that the butchering of the wounded went over their limits.

The Apaches must be "surrounded, starved into coming, surprised, or inveigled—by white flags, or any other method, human or divine—and then put to death," was the outspoken assessment of Sylvester Mowry, a southwestern miner and former military officer, made known to the world in his 1866 book printed in New York. Secure in his belief, Mowry called for Apache extermination. He wrote, for example, "If these ideas shock any weak-minded individual who thinks himself a philanthropist, I can only say that I pity without respecting his mistaken sympathy. A man might as well have sympathy for a rattlesnake or a tiger" than for an Apache. Another prospector, the "heartily sick" Daniel Conner, however, deemed his compatriots most savage monsters. Conner was especially appalled when his fellow Anglos looked on "full of satisfaction" as their O'Odham and Maricopa allies smashed with large rocks "the skull and brains" of wounded Apaches—men, women, and children, even small babies—"to smithereens." Afterward, Conner "mentally resolved never" again to go to war "with this sort of soldierly."[67]

Many California men and most regular army officers, who edged back to the borderlands in 1866 and 1867, portrayed their own killing of Apache women and offspring as unavoidable collateral damage or, more commonly, chose silence as the proper discursive strategy. As a rule, officers' texts, whether private letters, published accounts, or official statistics, either failed to stipulate the gender of those Apaches the army had killed or gave the impression that only men were among the dead. It was also common to briefly note that women and children were taken prisoners by military authorities or were sent to live at the homes of local residents. Silence did not so much result from there being a shortage of women and children among the dead, but for reasons connected with notions of honor and masculinity. Ideally, no U.S. Army officers slew women and children if they could avoid it, and they certainly did not admit to or brag about having done so deliberately. This kind of reporting not only exposes the sensitive boundaries of extreme killing but shows how these boundaries needed to be protected by shielding the often bloody carnage perpetrated on the defenseless.[68]

Different Anglo communities, groups, and individuals diverged in their understanding on what constituted acceptable violence against the Apaches. Still, the borderlands Anglos also shared much common ground. For one, they held fairly similar views of Apache character and war's justifications (a response to savage raiding in the name of peace and self-protection). Also, only rarely did anyone in the 1860s, excluding men like Agent Steck, question the plausibility of extermination as an overall goal. Even the regular army officers in the border-lands, while mulling the dearth of alternatives and the nonexistence of a clearly defined and functional Indian policy, seem to have accepted extermination. For example, in the late 1860s Gen. Edward Ord, commanding the Department of California, viewed annihilation of Apaches to be a plausible option when "every other means fail to protect our people." In Arizona, Maj. John Green expressed something like the prevalent view when stating, "There seems to be no settled policy but a general idea to kill them [Apaches] whenever found. I am also a believer in that if we go for the extermination."[69]

While Baylor found himself censured by his own government, King Woolsey also discovered that his undertakings failed to meet the full approval of General Carleton. In his letter to Carleton, Woolsey acknowledged the gossip and grum-bling his methods had triggered. He was brutally frank about the necessity of massacring Apaches regardless of age or gender, declaring, "I will fight on the broad platform of extermination." He added that it was "next to impossible to prevent killing squaws" in the heated confusion that accompanied attacks on Apache camps. Being, like most regular army officers were, a conservative man with a strict sense of honor, Carleton did not share Woolsey's mentality when it came to deception during negotiations. Nor did he advocate extermination so unequivocally as Woolsey did. For Carleton, who championed wholesale destruction against the Apaches in his military operations, Bosque Redondo represented an alternative to Apache extermination. Carleton certainly did not concur when Woolsey explained that although his outfit had killed mostly Apache men during their latest onslaught, they would have actually preferred killing more women but at the time of the fight most had been away from camp gathering mescal.[70]

While Carleton felt a need to distance himself from some of Woolsey's meth-ods, the rancher was commended by Anglo society in Arizona. According to one Arizona pioneer, Woolsey "was much liked by all who knew him for his bravery and gentlemanly manners." A respected member of Arizona society, Woolsey went on for a career as entrepreneur, member of the territorial legislature, and local politician. Passing away from heart disease in 1879, even mountain peaks were named in his honor.[71] If Woolsey was highly respected, so was John B. Townsend. Proud of the designation "Indian killer," Townsend was a Confeder-ate veteran born in Tennessee, who, at the close of the Civil War, ventured to Arizona, where he worked hard to earn his nickname while becoming a terror to the Yavapais and Western Apaches. From his ranch on the Agua Fria River, "he went out into the country with his two bloodhounds just to shoot Indians," Mike Burns, a Yavapai-Apache whose people Townsend hunted, wrote. Armed with a Winchester and a spyglass, Townsend would follow "the Indians' trails to their camps, using his dogs, and then dash in and kill them while they were asleep. He would keep on shooting whenever he saw an Indian, and kill all the inhabitants, and set fire to the camp so that the Indians would burn up in their" homes. He also served as a scout with the regular army until being dismissed after reportedly scalping fifteen Apache prisoners following a fight at Squaw Peak. Townsend himself was killed when going after one Apache too many. His end reportedly came in the hands of one of the army's recently hired Apache recruits.[72]

In 1871, the citizens of Prescott honored Townsend's "work" by gifting him a thousand rounds of ammunition and a Henry Rifle that had a silver plate engraved with the words "Honor to the Brave." "The more Townsend killed, the more popular he became with his fellow settlers," notes Dan Thrapp. Testifying to his status as a local hero, Townsend's funeral in Prescott developed into a massive social event attended by hundreds of mournful people. The local paper did not hold back any accolades when describing the deceased: "He was the bravest and most dauntless white man that ever trod the soil of Arizona, and had sent 36 Apaches to the happy hunting ground e'er he met his fate." Burns wrote that Townsend had actually claimed of personally killing 98 or 115 Indians.[73]

For Woolsey, Townsend, many of their peers, and the society they represented, it seemed probable that the borderlands wars would end in a complete annihilation of all the Apaches. The years 1862 and 1863 had seen the Mescaleros defeated and the Chiricahuas placed on the defensive, facing a long struggle, later acknowledged by Geronimo. The following year, 1864, had been another turning point, especially for the Western Apaches and Yavapais, who could not match the onslaught they faced. During the 1860s, some 1,671 Apaches had been killed in war. This is quite a figure from a population that probably did not exceed ten thousand people at the start of the decade. And this death toll excludes the Lipans and all those who perished outside actual combat as a result of their habitat, property, and fields being destroyed. It also omits deaths at Bosque Redondo. In contrast, an estimated 108 soldiers (California and local volunteers and regulars) and 244 Anglo civilians died at the hands of Apaches during the whole decade. Having become a race war, the Apache extinction looked like a question of when rather than if. As one California Volunteer put it, the Apache "race is nearly run. Extinction is only a question of time."[74]

CHAPTER 6

INTERNMENT

Indians [Western Apaches and Yavapais] . . . cried to think of their country
deserted by its inhabitants. . . . They were ours, the valleys, gulches, hills, and
mountainsides, the springs, the creeks, the riverlands, where all kinds of green
things grew, filled with wildflowers and game herds and food and herbs.
—Mike Burns, Yavapai-Apache

The Indians mean business this time.
It's a general outbreak and probably the worst we ever had.
—George Whitwell Parsons, Arizona settler

Excitement

For much of summer and fall 1881, the borderlands military reports, news media, and town gossip fumed amid speculation and rumors regarding the military threat the independent Apaches presented. Already in April a few Lipan Apaches had crossed the border, storming an Anglo settlement on the Frio River in Texas and creating anxiety at the local level. Then in the heat of midsummer a handful of Chiricahua fighters led by an able veteran named Nana reportedly covered more than three thousand miles during a two-month operation. They not only captured sizable quantities of plunder in New Mexico but eluded numerous outfits of troops sent to catch or intercept them. Moreover, while the troops hit the Lipans once, on May 3, recapturing much of the stolen property, they engaged the Chiricahuas on seven occasions, with the Apaches coming out on top each time. Saving the army from further embarrassment, in August the Chiricahua raiders retired to their mountain hideouts in northern Mexico. Shortly thereafter, however, Anglo ears caught alarming, almost incredible, rumors from Fort Apache, Arizona. Western Apaches had undergone a powerful spiritual awakening. Aided by "treacherous" Apache soldiers, on August 30 they, allegedly, killed to the last man the detachment of troops sent to question and arrest their priest, after which the Apaches had reportedly also overrun the garrison.

Anxiety and speculation reached unprecedented heights on the borderlands. On September 2, Col. Orlando Willcox, commanding the regular army troops in Arizona, wired his superiors in San Francisco to "hurry forward all the troops you can spare." During the first week of September alone, the army dispatched seven companies from California to Arizona, taking advantage of the new rail connections. As reinforcements rushed to the borderlands, the newspapers fueled the flames on their front pages by asserting that a widespread uprising was in the works. For instance, in its September 9 issue, the *Weekly Arizona Miner* in Prescott argued that Fort Apache had been lost, as "bad Apaches, Navajos, and other Indians have formed a league to wipe out the whites and retake the country." Groundless information reached the highest echelons of the federal government. It contained false intelligences of an Apache attack against Fort Bowie, reports of Apaches pursuing trains along the Southern Pacific rail line, and even a claim that Chiricahua reinforcements had crossed the international border heading north to join the Western Apaches.[1]

Next, some more startling, and this time factual, information emanated from San Carlos. Over seventy Chiricahua fighters had left the reservation on September 30. The conclusion: more soldiers would be desperately needed. Throughout the winter of 1881–82, additional troops poured into the borderlands not only from California but also from Washington, Nevada, and Colorado. Once at the border, the troops marched frantically, as they hunted for Apaches in an immense area spanning from above the Mogollon Rim in central Arizona to the southwestern reaches of Texas. While many feared what a general Apache war would mean for Anglo settlers, others savored that the final confrontation and absolute subjugation of the Apaches was near at last. All-out war had been (over)confidently prophesized by Kearny, eagerly sought after by Carleton and Woolsey, but seemingly refuted by the more recent government policies underlining diplomacy and reservations as a substitute for carnage and extermination.

Era of (More) Diplomatic Killing

In 1881, a decade and a half had passed since Woolsey, Townsend, and many others had seen extermination of Apaches as their goal and imagined it as an outcome for the near future. While the first years of the 1870s still witnessed lethal extermination campaigns, they were also characterized by a fresh wave of diplomacy, alliances, and an energized civilizing mission, with its attempts to impose cultural uniformity. This development was intimately linked to the expanding reach of national power in the region and to a federal peace policy toward the Indians. As alternatives for extermination, and as spaces for forced cultural, social, economic, and political regeneration of the Indians, the federal government had set up permanent reservations for (most) Apache groups in 1871 and 1872. The government envisioned that changes in housing, domesticity, education, religion, and subsistence would recalibrate Apache identities and gender roles to replicate those of the Victorian-era norms. In other words, the federal government operated under the presumption that to survive the Apaches would need to be made into (poor) clones of whites. They would become farmers and/ or wage laborers. Fittingly, the federal government had also started a systematic employment of Apaches in the U.S. Army, partially integrating the indigenous men to the dominant culture as a colonized workforce.[2]

Despite the resurgence of diplomacy, different forms of violence still persisted at the core of U.S.-Apache relations. While the extermination of the Apache population by means of extreme violence was no longer actively pursued, those Apaches outside the reservations were still hunted and killed as "hostiles." The whites also, as in the past, maintained that they acted in self-defense and upheld that the Apaches had brought all the killing on themselves via their murdering and pillaging. Until the federal government made the destruction of Geronimo and his Chiricahuas its primary goal in April 1886, bloodshed functioned foremost as a means toward diplomatic talks and capitulation, and was meant to lead to Apaches accepting reservation life. In short, the termination of Apache autonomy, not their destruction, became the key rationale for the use of violence by U.S. troops.

As the federal government recalibrated the meanings of violence, it also made Apache fighting more and more the monopoly of national troops by excluding civilian Anglo and Hispanic volunteers, as well as the O'odham allies. Regular troops not only often disdained civilian assistance or discouraged the establishment of volunteer units but commonly scoffed at the bravery and efforts of those independent ad hoc civilian outfits that were formed.[3] Furthermore, when the regulars portrayed themselves as gallant, honest, organized, and capable, they typically characterized civilian outfits as deceitful and disorderly gatherings of cowardly and blood-hungry scalp hunters. Recalling much older ruptures between militias and the regular army in U.S. history, the hardening attitude of regular troops was also in some ways a response to the mounting criticism borderlands civilians showed the army for its handling of the Apaches. As newspaper articles drilled the regular troops for incompetence and inaction, and for pampering the Apaches in the reservations, it was inevitable that the soldiers returned the favor. On another level, the army's disdain toward the civilians also hints at the ruptures in the effort to strengthen national control in the Southwest, which was becoming more about managing subordinate populations than of containing them (1850s) or trying to wipe them all out (1860s).[4]

Pushing for greater control, intending to streamline its organization, and judging most Apaches as militarily beaten, the federal government closed down several Apache reservations in the mid-1870s. Unfortunately, this concentration policy forced the Western Apaches and the Chiricahuas, along with the Yavapais, to share a dominantly barren and (to most) unfamiliar section of land near the Gila and Salt Rivers known as San Carlos. This arrangement produced much confusion, misery, and violence. A federal administration that was arrogant, corrupt, and erratic on the ground proved in fact a major trigger for the continuation of the U.S.-Apache wars in the late 1870s. But it was not the sole reason. Oftentimes, many of those Apaches who avoided the reservations and continued raiding were also strongly disinclined to forfeit their autonomy, thinking the whites had no right trying to master them. Some, when infuriated by the contradictions and one-sidedness of Anglo diplomacy, formed a coalition of the distressed and embittered under the leadership of the Chihenne Victorio. They opted to confront their chasers head on, creating much fear and anxiety among the soldiers and settlers.

If violence acquired new characteristics due to emergent nationalization, so did the borderlands society. Throughout the 1870s, diplomacy and reservations vacated plenty of land for Anglo use. While no massive waves of white farmers or ranchers stormed the borderlands, settler colonialism still gained new ground. It was the old recipe repeated. In 1878, news of silver findings on the territory of the Chokonen band of the Chiricahuas ignited an unparalleled mining rush in borderlands history. The boomtown of Tombstone was soon the largest in Arizona, occupied by over ten thousand people and producing silver worth tens of millions of dollars. Transcontinental railroads, a definite sign of whiter futures, also finally extended to the borderlands, reaching Tucson on March 20, 1880, causing the biggest party in the town's history. Some 1,200 people who danced until midnight greeted the rail lines as "the Messiah of civilization," one historian notes. Another marker of nineteenth-century civilization, the telegraph, also made inroads to the borderlands. Step by step, the wires reached various military posts and civilian settlements, linking the borderlands communities in unprecedented fashion by the end of the 1870s. With gains in technology, Anglo residents, and extractive industries, the borderlands were edging closer to full incorporation to the continental empire.[5]

Carnage

"Moving swiftly with their mesquite war clubs loosened the attackers surrounded the sleeping dancers. Striking in every direction they began to smash the skulls of the sleeping Aravaipa"—a number of statements like this testify to a meticulously executed ruthless massacre at Aravaipa Creek on the dawn of April 30, 1871. Putting down the sleeping dancers, the outfit of Anglos, Hispanics, and O'odhams from Tucson next turned their attention to those Apaches, one attacker recounted, who were "sleeping in absolute security." Crushing skulls and cutting throats quickly and quietly, the attackers worked from one Apache home to the next. As screams of the dying finally awoke the camp, complete chaos and mayhem ensued. One of the Apaches who remembered the hellish scene felt that "blood flowed just like a river." Some Apaches managed to get away in the melee, but many never found an opening to defend themselves and their loved ones. Finally, with no more people to kill, the attackers set the dwellings on fire. Then they headed back to Tucson, taking several Apache children as captives. While accounts differ, more than one hundred Apache lives were most likely wiped out that morning. Apparently only eight of the victims were men. This and the fact that the attacking party, some 150 strong, did not suffer a single casualty, speaks volumes of the nature of this butchery.[6]

Following several years of being hunted and killed, these Apaches, who were mostly Aravaipas, had, for a short while, felt moderately optimistic of their future. For much of spring 1871, they believed they were safe under the protection of the U.S. troops from nearby Camp Grant. Feeling festive, they had started preparing for a celebration. Actually, at the time of the onslaught many of the men were most likely out hunting for the upcoming feast, most of the weapons being with them. Although the troops at Camp Grant were not to blame for the massacre, the Apaches paid dearly for their optimism. Instead of being out of harm's way, they met sudden and gruesome death.

Some months earlier, in February 1871, on the intersection of the San Pedro River and Aravaipa Canyon, several Apache women had made their way toward Camp Grant (the former Fort Breckinridge reoccupied in 1862 and renamed in 1865). It was customary for Apaches to employ delegations of women for making initial inquiries about possible diplomatic talks. Women approached enemy settlements, and, based on how they were treated, negotiations were either set for a later date or not. Received cordially at the post by Lt. Royal Whitman, a Civil War veteran from Maine and a fresh (December 1870) arrival to Camp Grant, the women soon made inquiries about the possibility to hold a peace conference. As Whitman was also interested, such a meeting was arranged. Es-him-en-zee (Eskiminzin), representing himself as a leader of Aravaipa Apaches, a band of the San Carlos group, told Whitman how they lived in constant fear of attack and would want to end their exile in the high mountain reaches and return to Aravaipa Canyon, a place they considered home. Whitman, mindful of the new federal peace policy being established by the Grant administration and familiar with its principles of assimilation and reservations for the Indians, but having no authority for establishing a reservation, nevertheless ended up inviting the Apaches to settle near Camp Grant under military protection, provided they stop all raiding at once.[7]

Upon requesting authorization from his superiors, Whitman got none. After six weeks of waiting, even his letter was returned with a remark that it had not followed proper military procedure and was missing a summary report on the outside fold. Puzzled by the tardiness of his superiors, Whitman had a good reason to fear that the whole experiment would lead to a disaster, ruining his career and involving a hefty body count. From Whitman's viewpoint, it would be devastating for the Apaches under his charge to attack anyone or for the settlers to come for the Apaches, who slowly grew to trust Whitman and his soldiers. As Whitman worried, the word of the safety at Camp Grant had already spread. Soon the number of Apaches near the post increased from one hundred to over five hundred with Whitman trying to do his best counting, supervising, and issuing rations to them all. By spring, Whitman was de facto running an improvised reservation for war-fatigued Western Apaches.[8]

In Tucson, townspeople, some of whom yearned for merciless extermination of the Apaches, had organized a series of public meetings in early 1871. Their topic: the "Apache problem." Utter disappointment over the military's reluctance to launch a full-blown offensive and knowledge of the Apaches at Camp Grant proved a volatile mix. Many believed that the recent seizure of cattle near the San Xavier mission and the attack against Anglos on the San Pedro River originated from under Whitman's eyes. Whether this was actually the case seems unlikely, but it all mattered little to Tucsonians, who printed an affidavit from residents wanting to prove the seriousness of their plight.[9] "As faithful citizens," the document read, the citizens sought protection from the federal government "in the name of humanity" against the "savage war" practiced by "hostile" Apaches. After the settlers were convinced that no federal effort was forthcoming, they decided to act on their own. They depicted the April 30, 1871, attack to the Apache village near Camp Grant, historian Karl Jacoby notes, as "an unavoidable response to Apache raiding."[10]

Diplomacy

Carnage had clearly trumped diplomacy on April 30, 1871. Still, times were changing. Aravaipa survivors hesitantly returned to Camp Grant only four months after the massacre to open a new round of negotiations. Making the severity of their sufferings known to the military, they again expressed a strong wish to live at Aravaipa Creek. A conference was set up for May 20, 1872, on the San Pedro River. The O'odhams met with the Apache leaders on the invitation of U.S. officials led by Gen. Oliver O. Howard, a devout Christian with an interest in civilizing African Americans and indigenous peoples. Howard actually represented already the second peace commissary dispatched from Washington in a space of nine months with a mandate from President U. S. Grant. In September 1871, the first government delegate, Vincent Colyer, a Quaker and the secretary of the Board of Indian Commissioners, had met with the Aravaipa leaders, recommending that Camp Grant be set up as their permanent reservation.[11]

Colyer, Howard, Grant, and many eastern humanitarians worried about the spread of bloody, fiscally detrimental, and time- and energy-consuming warfare. Furthermore, they and the eastern press had felt appalled when news in May 1871 had arrived of the ghastly butchering of the Aravaipa Apaches living under army protection. It was not only the actual killing but the fact that the outfit from Tucson had defied federal authority that made the incident appear so provocative in the still tense post–Civil War age. Grant insisted that those responsible be brought to trial instantly. When the indictment of the participants did not happen fast enough, he threatened Arizona with martial law, in which case military officers would handle the trial. While the trial by civilian jury in Tucson eventually proved nothing short of a farce, all the 108 men accused of murder being acquitted in record time, it still functioned as an apt reminder to all borderlands civilians that the federal government was becoming significantly less tolerant of civilian initiative in Apache fighting.[12]

Much of the national approach derived from a new phase of Indian management, dubbed by historians as the "Peace Policy." Under the leadership of Grant, the federal government embraced an ideology where the military threat of the indigenous peoples would be eliminated through their segregation and regeneration. As there no longer existed distant white-free lands to which to remove the indigenous peoples, as had been done in the 1830s, separate spaces had to be set up inside states and territories. There administrators would make the Indians born again as clones of whites. While many white Americans believed that Indians faced extinction through natural selection when confronted by the "superior" white race, the visions of a federal peace policy were energetically implemented across the trans-Mississippi West. To oversee Indian reformation and watch over the proper expenditure of funds allocated to the Indians, the government set up an independent Board of Indian Commissioners composed of renowned humanitarians. To guarantee good tutelage, reservation administration was to be handled by people from religious denominations.[13]

When scrutinizing government motives, it is sobering to keep in mind that separating, feeding, and educating the indigenous peoples would not just appear more humane than slaughtering them indiscriminately but would usually prove less costly. As the commissioner of Indian Affairs put it, for much of the 1860s, "the attempt to exterminate" the Apaches "has been carried on, at a cost of from three to four millions of dollars per annum, with no appreciable progress made in accomplishing their extermination."[14] Furthermore, in case diplomacy and tutelage failed, the government had highlighted the role of the regular army as the agency responsible for forcing and keeping the Apaches in their new homes. Arriving to the borderlands in 1871 was also Lt. Col. George Crook. A highly eccentric man in both looks and behavior with a proven record in the Civil War and against the Pacific Northwest Indians, Crook showed similar determination and seriousness toward fighting Indians as Carleton had. He felt that the Apaches needed a thorough military beating so that they would learn the awesome power of the United States. Only when broken could the survivors be educated and civilized.

During the late 1860s, various Apache groups, overwhelmed by violence, had repeatedly approached the military asking for a truce and the launching of talks. Cautious and alert for treachery and poisoned food, they had very few reasons to trust any whites. They could be met by a hail of bullets or, like one group that approached Camp McDowell in June 1866, they could be told by the officer in command that he had no authority to negotiate. In this case, the officer, Maj. Clarence Bennett, noted in his report, "I was sent here to fight Indians, not to make peace." Bennett suggested that the Apaches go to Camp

Goodwin, designated as a feeding station. If they refused, they would be hunted and killed by the soldiers. Following the ultimatum, the Apache party in question left. Some went to Goodwin, a sickly post on the Gila River, but many returned to their mountain homes, where they faced troops from McDowell as well as civilian outfits from the mining areas. According to Charles Henry Veil, an officer serving at the fort, a "number of Indians were killed" by men who were in the field "almost continuously," as the "mountains and country north of the Gila and Salt rivers . . . were all infested with Apaches," Veil regretted that administrative duties kept him at the post and thus denied him the opportunity "of distinguishing myself by killing Indians."[15]

Life could be exceedingly exasperating for those Apaches trying to break the diplomatic deadlock. Even if they made promising inroads at first, their hopes were often crushed. Prior to Christmas 1866, the post commander at Camp Grant, Capt. Guido Ilges, negotiated on an armistice with several Pinal, Tonto, and Aravaipa Apaches. It was agreed that the Apaches would settle near Camp Grant and receive food assistance and tools for farming, as well as protection. The armistice, however, was quickly nullified by Ilges's superiors, who reprimanded the captain for exceeding his authority. After waiting several months for the promised provisions and seeing more troops reach the post, the Apaches took to the mountains. The division commander, Gen. Henry W. Halleck, expressed the prevalent interpretation in his 1867 report: "It is useless to negotiate with these Apaches," as they honor no treaties or truces. "There is no alternative but active and vigorous war till they are completely destroyed, or forced to surrender as prisoners of war."[16]

Still, the potential for successful diplomacy existed. In the late 1860s, bands of White Mountain and Cibecue Apaches managed what seemed like a breakthrough. After nurturing contacts and receiving from time to time rations at Camp Goodwin, they invited the soldiers to build a new fort in their lands. As a place where the Anglos and Apaches were able to meet on friendly terms, the new post, named Camp Apache in 1871, proved quintessential for developing a close yet frail connection. For instance, these Apaches contributed a steady supply of men from the time the army started enlisting them in 1871.[17]

In August 1871, enraged by the massacre at Camp Grant and adhering to the guidelines of the peace policy, the federal government finally grasped the diplomatic initiative, as the first of its peace negotiators reached the borderlands. In quick succession, from August 25 to October 7, Vincent Colyer sought, with varying success, audience with the Chihennes at Ojo Caliente, New Mexico; the White Mountain and Cibecue Apaches at Camp Apache; the Aravaipas and

Pinals at Camp Grant; the Akimel O'odhams and Maricopas at their villages on the Gila River; the Tontos at Camp McDowell; and the Yavapais at Camp Verde. He favored permanent reservations at Camps Grant, Apache, and Verde, and at the Tularosa Valley (Chihennes). He also proposed the setting up of temporary asylums at Camps McDowell, Beale Springs, and Date Creek. Colyer also authorized a Mescalero reservation at Fort Stanton without consulting the Mescaleros. Next, between March 31 and June 1, 1872, General Howard visited the Colorado River Indians and missed, like Colyer had, the alert Tontos and Yavapais at Camp McDowell, before heading off to Camp Grant. From there, he went on a tour of the O'odham villages, Date Creek, and Prescott, before returning to Grant for the big meeting to settle the Camp Grant Massacre. Howard abolished the Camp Date Creek, Camp Beale Springs, and Camp McDowell feeding posts, as well as the Camp Grant Reservation while extending the White Mountain Reservation (Camp Apache) south to the Gila River.[18]

Although it might be possible to view the arrival of Colyer and Howard as a response from a government receptive to the petitions by local Anglos for more protection, it is hardly surprising that two delegates who sought Apache approval and listened to Apache complaints did not represent the kind of government reaction the borderlands citizens would have preferred. Actually the federal government overlooked the local Anglos and ignored their point of view when making a break from extermination. While Colyer conferred at length with the Apaches, he did not include any Anglo civilians in the talks. And he skipped Tucson altogether. Furthermore, both Colyer and Howard lashed out against the borderlands Anglos and Hispanics. In his report, Colyer painted the Apaches as industrious and inherently peaceful people driven to violence by Mexican and American attacks. He also mocked the borderlands whites as being nothing more than "exterminators." Listing Apache sufferings by using the actions of the scalp hunter John Johnson, Col. Joseph West, and King Woolsey as examples, he lamented the attack near Camp Grant as "massacre . . . which has shocked all Christendom." Concurring, Howard wrote that "under no circumstances whatever can the civilized world justify a deed like" the Camp Grant butchering.[19]

Interestingly, neither Colyer nor Howard had to confer with the army, as the institution had been made their subordinate by presidential orders. As could be expected, the local press attacked Colyer for his "sadly farcical policy" of pampering "murderous chiefs" and "cruel savages." The army brass, with Crook as its headmaster, also showed its disapproval. Crook, for instance, saw "Vincent the good" as an utterly unrealistic man whose efforts "to make peace by the grace of God" would result in absolute failure. Crook's aide, Lt. John Bourke, even dubbed Colyer "that spawn of hell" in his diary.[20]

On the proximity of the San Pedro River in May 1872, both the Aravaipas and the O'odhams appeared willing to reconcile, and the mood of the talks stayed cordial until the question of Apache children stolen during the massacre surfaced. Apaches pointed to the Anglo promises that the children would return and emphasized how deeply they were missed by their relatives. Howard, however, seemed inclined to think that the children were better off in "civilized" Christian homes, even if those homes belonged to those borderlands citizens he held in contempt. Only six children, wrote Howard, were eventually returned to their Apache community. Others, at least twenty-one or perhaps several dozen, never made it back. Some were adopted by Tucsonians, others sold to forced labor in Mexico, and most disappeared from the historical record.[21]

Their children forever lost, prosperous life also eluded the Aravaipas. Few had it more turbulent than Eskiminzin. As Howard closed Camp Grant, Eskiminzin's new surroundings at San Carlos were plagued by sickness, shortage of food, as well as repeated disputes among the Apaches and the white administrators. In 1873, Eskiminzin escaped. Upon returning, he was arrested on New Year's Day 1874 and was sent in chains to the relocated Fort Grant near Mount Graham. Then the new agent at San Carlos, John Clum, had Eskiminzin released and made him a headman on the reservation at San Carlos. Once Clum departed in 1877, Eskiminzin did so also, relocating quietly outside the reservation and to the San Pedro River, where he operated a thriving farm in the late 1870s.

For a while, life seemed decent, although some Anglo ranchers accused Eskiminzin and his family of stealing livestock. In 1887, a sheriff's posse on its way to arrest him, Eskiminzin, probably with memories of 1871 resurfacing, escaped to San Carlos. Taking up farming along the Gila River, Eskiminzin got mixed in the turmoil surrounding his son-in-law, the Indian known as "Apache Kid," a onetime soldier. The Kid had killed the murderer of his grandfather and was sentenced to the territorial prison in Yuma. But he escaped and thus was labeled an outlaw. In 1891, the army, frustrated that its hunt did not pan out, arrested those it saw as aiding the Kid. Eskiminzin, with more than fifty followers, were made prisoners of war and relocated first to Fort Wingate, New Mexico, then to Fort Union, and finally to Mount Vernon, Alabama, to join the Chiricahua Apache prisoners of war. The government returned Eskiminzin and his following to San Carlos in 1894. By then probably thoroughly disillusioned with the Anglo government, Eskiminzin died, reportedly from a stomach ailment, shortly after his return.[22]

Reservations and Military Power

The way the reservations were created (dictated by the federal government or negotiated), their locations, and the way they were run was in some ways related to the relative military power of particular Apache groups. Eskiminzin and the Aravaipas occupied a middling position. They warranted government attention, and both Colyer and Howard heard their views.

For their part, the Jicarillas seemed militarily so unimportant that they hardly registered at the time the peace policy became fashionable. Since their clashes with the army in the 1850s, the Jicarillas had forged a living in northern New Mexico doing odd jobs in the settler economy when such were available or by seeking subsistence from farming when possible. In the 1870s, neither Colyer nor Howard paid any attention to the Jicarillas. They remained a people without a reservation even after inchoate presidential executive orders set up reservations for the Jicarillas on paper first in 1874 and again in 1880. Pushed by the government and escorted by soldiers, the less-than-enthusiastic Jicarillas traveled south to the Mescalero Reservation in 1883. Their stay did not last. In October and November 1886, the unhappy Jicarillas simply left, heading north. Proclaiming that they would rather die than return, the Apaches traveled without resorting to violence. The army, fresh from the exhausting Geronimo campaign, also displayed restraint. Gen. Nelson A. Miles not only ordered rations issued to the Jicarilla sojourners but pleaded in Washington for a separate reservation for this Apache group. If it is difficult to fathom Carleton allowing the Mescaleros to live where they wished, it is equally hard to imagine Miles rationing Geronimo and his Chiricahuas or arguing their case for living space in the Southwest borderlands. President Grover Cleveland, the man who advocated eliminating the Chiricahua military threat by any means possible and who, at one time, wanted Geronimo hanged, agreed to set up the Jicarilla Reservation at Tierra Amarilla in 1887. At that time, close to thirty years had already passed since this Apache group had ceased being a sovereign military power and a threat to U.S. authority.[23]

Much like the Jicarillas, the Lipans did not merit their own reservation in the 1870s. But their experiences differed from the Jicarillas, as the federal government recognized the Lipans as a moderate military menace and therefore targeted them occasionally with inconsistent military and diplomatic measures. For much of the 1860s, Lipans had continued not just to survive but also to gain temporary advantages on some of the border areas. Still, the Lipan military effort was resource raiding at its purest: small groups making quick strikes against soft targets followed by equally swift retreat across the international line. As Lipans raided Texan settlements and withdrew to Mexico with stolen property, the village of Zaragosa in north-central Coahuila was their favorite place for shelter and trading. Santa Rosa, San Carlos, and San Vicente, all in Coahuila, also acted as significant partners in the Lipan contraband economy. Lipans not only traded mules, horses, and cattle for arms, ammunition, alcohol, and food but sought to protect the residents, especially of Zaragosa, from raids by other independent Indians. This, in turn, instigated conflicts.

While the Seminoles had mostly departed to the Indian Territory, the close to eight hundred Kickapoos, who occupied lands near Múzquiz, trading with and protecting that village, represented a superior military force to the approximately 100 to 150 Lipans. The Apaches and Kickapoos had built a fragile equilibrium wherein they joined in gambling, racing, and trading, or cooperated on raids into Texas. But, as elsewhere in the borderlands, peace was delicate and the line between violence, diplomacy, and friendship fleeting. Lipan balance with their neighbors shattered temporarily in the late 1860s. After being bested by a Kickapoo raid and following a violent incident with a rich Mexican rancher, many Lipans sought avenues of escape and shelter in the north. While a few remained in Zaragosa, more or less integrated into the society, others dispersed. As refugees, they joined those Lipans who lived at Fort Griffin. Several also headed toward the Guadalupe Mountains and the Mescalero domains in New Mexico, where in 1871 and 1872 hundreds of Apaches across the region collected around Fort Stanton seeking peace and land of their own. In a few years' time, however, many refugees had trekked back to Coahuila, being unable to carve out lives satisfactorily enough in the north.[24]

Meanwhile, in the United States stronger demands from borderlands residents to oust the Indians from northern Mexico led to a coinciding diplomatic mission and military invasion. Both undertakings had the same objective: induce the Indians to acquiesce to reservation life in the Indian Territory. In May 1873, special commissioners Thomas Williams and Henry Atkinson, authorized by the Department of the Interior, obtained promise of cooperation from the governors of Nuevo León and Coahuila, and sought to visit the Kickapoos, Lipans, and other smaller groups residing along the Rio Grande border. While the commissioners proceeded south, the U.S. Army also launched a campaign of its own, striking Kickapoo, Lipan, and Mescalero camps forty miles from the border west of Remolino at the San Rodrigo headwaters. Theirs would be, in the words of Gen. Philip Sheridan, a campaign of "annihilation, obliteration, and destruction." Sacking the villages and forcing the residents to flight, the white soldiers and the enlisted black Seminoles led by Col. Ranald Mackenzie delivered quick devastation before retreating north of the border. Several smaller detachments continued canvassing both sides of the border for Lipans and Kickapoos during the subsequent summer before outside critique from Mexico and the U.S. State Department on illegal border crossings—along with a military offensive on the Staked Plains and Red River against the Comanches—diverted the army's attention. In the interim, dumbfounded and irritated commissioners Atkinson and Williams met some of the Indians in July. Managing to persuade several Kickapoos to leave Mexico, they found that, after the U.S. Army attacks, Lipans refused to entertain any plans they intended to propose. Diplomacy had been assailed by violence.[25]

In the mid-1870s, the Lipans continued to live in fragmented units seeking places of refuge that would enable survival. For many, MacKenzie's strike had been a life-altering experience. For instance, John Castro, a member of a prominent Lipan family, saw his wife and brother die at the hands of soldiers. Even his infant son was bayoneted to death. Badly wounded, Castro walked for weeks with his son Manuel until finding his other two surviving children. Going into hiding, he advised his people to change their names, stop speaking Lipan, and refuse to admit to anyone that they were Apaches. Thus John Castro became Porfirio Gonzales, and many of his people never regrouped. Instead, they merged into the population of various Mexican settlements. Many of Castro's contemporaries chose a similar path, as had numerous other Lipans ever since their military power began to wane in the 1700s.[26]

Over one hundred Lipans who still identified themselves as Apaches stayed in Coahuila attached to local villages from Remolino to Zaragosa. Being destitute refugees, some Lipans again found sanctuary with the Mescaleros. Others ventured to Fort Sill in the Indian Territory, while a handful once more imposed themselves on Fort Griffin, camping outside the post. Many of the latter soon found occasional work in the army. Ousted from service in 1874, they had no place left to go. Hoping the Apaches would leave, the army forbade issuing rations to Lipans near the post. Performing menial jobs and trying to grow crops, the Apaches nevertheless lingered in the vicinity. When the fort closed in 1881, some Lipans, having still no place to go, continued living in the proximity. With crops failing, several starved to death. In 1884, the government forced the nineteen surviving Lipans, together with seventy-eight Tonkawas, who also still persevered near the old fort, to embark on a grueling journey to the Indian Territory. They reached their new homes on June 30, 1885.[27]

As borderlands refugees, the militarily trivial Jicarillas had difficulties in making the government notice them, whereas the elusive and destitute Lipans engaged in survival mode. In Arizona, the nearly beaten Western Apaches hunted security from a weakened position, but they at least got the government's attention, albeit mostly in the aftermath of a bloody massacre that was denounced in the East. It was the white peace emissaries who granted the Western Apaches, Mescaleros, and Yavapais their reservations. In the end, there really was only one Apache group that was able to dictate its reservation terms: the Chokonens.

The Chiricahuas still had enough will and manpower to function as an independent military might, although they found themselves more frequently on the defensive after 1862. Even the line in the sand that separated their enemies did not offer similar safety in the 1860s, as had been the case during the preceding decade. The Chiricahuas more typically ran and galloped from one country to the next in search of some semblance of refuge from soldiers thirsting for a chance to get at them. Rather than give up and take the doomed trek to Bosque Redondo or, after 1866, the nearly equally uninviting journey to Camp Goodwin, the Chiricahuas upped their efforts, possibly thinking that it would make either the Mexicans or the Americans more receptive for diplomacy. Perhaps they were even so confident as to expect that by organizing overwhelming and fearful displays of their power, a time would come when they could more or less dictate the terms of peace. That day would in fact represent itself in 1872. But they had to first fight hard to get there.

Starting in 1863 much of northern Mexico had grown tired of the intermittent peace treaties and declared concord with the Chiricahua Apaches to be unreachable. Mobilizing local and even some national forces, Mexico had triumphed momentarily, scattering the Chiricahuas to the U.S. side.[28] In 1865, the Chokonens and Nednhis struck back. First, they sent four raiding parties to the Janos, Corralitos, and Casas Grandes sections, taxing its farmers out of their property. Then they took position on the Bavispe–Janos road, executing a series of ambushes, which brought much-needed replenishment in supply. North of the border the Chiricahuas struck east of Tucson, thundering on the Sonoita Valley and the zone in and around Tubac, where Anglos and Hispanics had just restarted mining and ranching. Most residencies in the Santa Cruz Valley, for instance, still remained deserted due to earlier Apache raiding. Tucson itself, an Anglo visitor observed, was "about half in ruins" and thus seemed much like a deserted city.[29]

As the raids continued with force in 1866 and 1867, both sides of the international line undoubtedly got the message that the Chiricahuas were far from beaten. The French invasion, which paid very little attention to the Apaches, had driven Mexico into chaos and war as the central government sought refuge at Paso del Norte. After ousting the French, the Mexicans stormed several Chokonen and Nednhi camps, killing and capturing most occupants. Pushed by the Mexican offensive, the Chiricahuas again hammered the U.S. side until they returned south in August 1867. Numerous skirmishes and raids soon dotted the landscape: in Agua Prieta, Bacoachi, Fronteras, Casas Grandes, Bavispe, the Carcay Mountains, and so on. Some sources estimate that in 1868 the Chokonens lost more than a hundred of their group, while northern Mexico reported massive losses in property and dozens of civilians killed by the Chiricahuas.[30]

If it was apparent that there was little time or place for rest, it was equally obvious that the Chiricahuas still viewed the borderlands as their supply basket. John Smith, a former California soldier, recounted how an Apache theft of some 130 head of livestock from his corral near Tubac in April 1869 represented just one of many occurrences so commonplace that "they hardly merit mention." In other letters, Smith described a life and region paralyzed by Chiricahua raiding. During that summer and the next, the Sonoita Valley was once more trembling under Apache pressure. Receiving news of an Apache sighting during her husband's absence, Phylena Tonge locked herself and her children in their house outside Tucson. The family waited it out for several nervous hours, praying, trembling, clutching a gun, and occasionally peering out through the portholes in the walls of the building. Luckily, her home was not hit that day. Others were less lucky. One July 1869 day was especially bad for John Smith, as a synchronized Chiricahua attack struck several ranches. At that time, it seemed to Smith, the Apaches were "almost making a clean sweep" of the Sonoita.[31]

While the Chokonens spent most of 1869 and 1870 on U.S. soil, they not only raided but searched for ways to open diplomatic communications. Overall, Americans and Mexicans desiring their extermination had shown a singular refusal to sit down with the Chiricahuas. As we have seen, when Mangas Coloradas went looking for a cease-fire, he was arrested, shot, and beheaded. When a group of Chokonens approached Fort Bowie in October 1865 waving white flags, the response they got from post commander Maj. James Gorman was blunt: he had no authority to make peace. Gorman did tell the Chokonens to wait in the vicinity while he contacted his superiors. But instead, he attacked the Chokonen villages. For their part, the Chihennes had also tried to open diplomatic relations at Pinos Altos in late 1865. The result: whites killed three to four Apaches during coffee.[32]

In the late 1860s, the Chihennes did manage to arrange an unofficial truce at Ojo Caliente. On August 30, 1870, Cochise showed up at Camp Apache (Camp Mogollon then), seeking for a truce. Less than two months later he made an appearance at a meeting between the Chihennes and government emissaries from Santa Fe, expressing desire for a joint Chihenne-Chokonen reservation at the Ojo Caliente–Cañada Alamosa area in New Mexico. He had a change of heart after hearing that the government, debating internally over several proposals, wanted to move all Chiricahuas to live with the Mescaleros at Fort Stanton. In June 1871, the government sent a messenger to inform Cochise that Cañada Alamosa was once again acceptable. Three months later over two hundred Chokonens, with more preparing to come, made the trek to their proposed new home only to miss Colyer by four weeks and to find out that he had eschewed Cañada Alamosa in favor of the Tularosa Valley. The Chokonens returned to the Dragoon and Chiricahua Mountains in March 1872.[33]

Meanwhile, preferring a permanent home at their center of the universe— the Ojo Caliente–Cañada Alamosa area—the Chihennes found getting their voice heard an exhausting process. In the late 1860s, suffering from hunger, the Chihennes had sought rations and diplomatic accord from the officials at Fort McRae. As Colyer swept across the borderlands, he met only with one Chihenne leader, Loco, a strong peace advocate. Removed by troops against their will in Spring 1872, many of the Chihennes complained of the Tularosa Valley, its unfamiliarity, unhealthiness, and cold climate. Next, it was Howard who promised the Chihennes that Ojo Caliente was to be the site of the Chiricahua Reservation. However, that glimmer of hope was nullified as the Chokonens got their reservation at the Chiricahua Mountains from Howard. Meanwhile, the disappointed Chihennes found they could do little except to relocate to the Chokonen home while the government continued to argue over what, if any, would be the site of their reservation and seemed to consider Tularosa, which still drew little interest from most Chihennes, as the first choice.[34]

The Chokonen, in turn, tried to break the diplomatic standstill at Janos for much of spring and summer 1872. They failed to get any proper response by August. However, at that time, Howard, back from touring the East Coast with an assortment of Arizona Indians, came looking for Cochise. Howard's small entourage included an assistant, Lt. Joseph Sladen, Cochise's acquaintance, the scout and trader from Cañada Alamosa Tom Jeffords, and two Chiricahua scouts enlisted from Ojo Caliente. The small party located the Chokonens in the Dragoon Mountains. That these talks differed from the previous ones seemed clear early on. The respectful Howard claimed to possess authority handed to him personally by the president and informed the Apaches that he would stay as long as it took to come to an agreement. Cochise in turn summoned to the Dragoons as many Chokonen and Nednhi men of influence as could be reached.

Howard put Cañada Alamosa on the table, while Cochise argued for a home in the Dragoon and Chiricahua Mountains. In the end, Howard was pretty easily convinced to grant Cochise's wishes. It was enough that the Chokonen leader promised to protect overland travel and made a convincing case that his proposal, not Cañada Alamosa, would appeal to the Chokonen majority and even some Nednhis. In exchange for stopping all raiding on the U.S. side, the Chokonens got exclusive rights to their homeland, regular issues of food and other materials from the government, and their choice of agent, which was Jeffords, who favored informal relations and relaxed discipline during his reign. Furthermore, the presence of soldiers, except those at Fort Bowie, was prohibited on the reservation. Unlike the Western Apaches at San Carlos, the Chokonens de facto ruled their reservation. Summoning officers from Fort Bowie as witnesses, the agreement was repeated once more on October 12, 1872, but, to the bafflement of government officials and local settlers, it was apparently not written down.[35]

Killing for Submission

While Howard and the Chokonens talked at the Dragoon Mountains, Crook was preparing for a winter offensive. As the Chiricahuas were now untouchable, Crook targeted the Western Apaches and Yavapais, issuing an ultimatum that all must come to the new reservations or be hunted down by the army. Crook's campaign would prove a highly one-sided killing expedition that resulted in a devastating indigenous body count. Still, in his orders to the troops, Crook shied away from much of the rhetoric and methods of the 1860s. He did not call for the extermination of the enemy. Surrendering was not just acceptable but indeed the ultimate goal of the operations. However, the similarities to Carleton's operations against the Mescaleros were evident. Crook wanted a short, sharp, and decisive campaign that would overwhelm the Western Apaches and Yavapais and make such a devastating statement of U.S. power that the Indians would never again dare to entertain military autonomy. "The enemy," Dan Thrapp writes, "would be starved and frozen as well as fought into submission." The troops would "hunt down" the Apaches, "give them," in Crook's words, "all the fighting they want," as well as burn and destroy their homes and food supplies.[36]

Taking the field from various points across the Western Apache and Yavapai domain, the numerous mobile detachments of white cavalrymen were accompanied by O'odham, Maricopa, Hualapai, Yavapai, and Apache fighters, but not by many Anglo civilians. Supplied by mule packtrains, the detachments were supposed to keep the enemy on the run, strike them at every opportunity, and drive the Indians from their mountain homes toward the Tonto Basin, where more troops would meet them. The army's growing reliance on Apache recruits marked the rupture of its alliance with the O'odhams and Maricopas, who were also soon suffering from the decline of their farming economy and the diversion of the Gila River by Anglo settlers.[37]

The army's onslaught started in September 1872. First, the troops hit Tolkepaya Yavapai camps at the Santa Maria Mountains and smashed a Western Apache-Yavapai village at Squaw Peak. In November and December, the soldiers and Hualapais from Camp Verde devastated numerous Wipukepa Yavapai/Tonto Apache camps near Oak Creek, in "Red Rock Country." Next, it was the detachments from Fort McDowell, accompanied by Akimel O'odham and Maricopa auxiliaries, that stormed Indian homes in the Mazatzal Mountains, while cavalry with Yavapai recruits from Camp Date Creek thundered on encampments near the Agua Fria River. Furthermore, units of white and White Mountain Apache soldiers from Fort Apache engaged the malnourished Apache and Yavapai families north of abandoned Camp Reno on three occasions. The climax of the killing was reached four days before the new year, as a force of 250 men, of whom 100 were O'odham fighters and 30 San Carlos and Tonto Apaches, hit the Kwevkepaya Yavapai/Tonto Apache hiding place on the Salt River Cave. The massacre proved the deadliest attack executed by the regular U.S. forces against people they labeled Apaches. At least fifty-seven Indians met their deaths on the Salt River. In all, the army's statistics show that the first four months of Crook's offensive had produced fourteen clashes and a body count of 177 Yavapais/Western Apache enemies, two Hualapai auxiliaries, and one O'odham ally. No white soldiers died in these exceedingly ill-matched assaults.[38]

Even though the Salt River Cave Massacre represented that long-awaited "decisive victory" in some minds, soldiers had to recognize that strikes that would entirely annihilate some sections of the dynamic Western Apache/Yavapai populace would have limited or no effect on others. Judging that the enemy still needed more hammering, in January 1873 the army's offensive continued, the operations offering a mix of sustained, unrelenting pressure as well as incidents of devastation resulting from attacks on unsuspecting, oftentimes defenseless, villages. For example, in March, as the first phase of the offensive finally peaked, the troops put to death more than fifty Yavapais and Western Apaches at the Tonto Basin and the Mazatzal and Turret Mountains. At the latter place, according to Crook, some of the Indians were so panicky that they "jumped off the precipice and were mashed into a shapeless mass."[39]

While the spring of 1873 witnessed groups of destitute Indians surrendering, the official termination of the campaign, and Crook gaining a rare two-grade promotion from lieutenant colonel to brigadier general, the offensive would continue until all Yavapais and Western Apaches either lived on the reservations or were put to death. Initially, however, surrendering was not an option all Indians necessarily knew even existed. They certainly could not easily draw such conclusions from the slaughter and destruction. Nor did they have much precedence for surrendering, or reservation life, from their earlier experiences. Unaware of Crook's demands, many were caught by surprise as the military's offensive reached them. Those still free in 1873 tried to keep out of sight and avoid all Anglos if possible, making their presence known only occasionally when stealing some livestock. Many also questioned what right the whites had in ordering them to leave their homes, while others proved reluctant to yield because they dreaded perfidy, sickness, poisoned food, and starvation.[40]

The troops launched isolated strikes during the hot summer months until commencing more systematic operations as fall and winter approached. Destroying indigenous camps near the Verde River and in the Sierra Ancha and Mazatzal Mountains in September and October, the troops again pounded the indigenous homes in and around the Mazatzals from December to January. They hit a Yavapai/Western Apache camp at Sycamore Springs on October 29–30, killing an estimated twenty-seven Indians. The focus of the offensive shifted southward in March 1874, hitting the residences of Pinal and Aravaipa bands at the Pinal and Superstition Mountains. One exceptionally deadly assault took place on April 2 against Pinal Apache camps. Army reports claim that this single strike killed at least thirty-one or as many as forty-seven Apaches, while another fifty were taken captive. In all, the troops had engaged the Western Apaches and Yavapais in twenty-three separate strikes between September 1873 and June 1874, killing an estimated 241 people. Again, not one white soldier or officer had perished.[41]

By now even those Apaches and Yavapais who had managed to keep their distance from the troops found the task impossible. After the soldiers stormed their homes and farms, those who survived had to abandon their plots and, often, starve. The army, for its part, felt exalted. The 1872–74 operations were widely seen and promoted as the regular army's greatest borderlands triumph. Officers and soldiers celebrated themselves as heroic peace bringers. Even if the enemy were by now "emaciated, clothes torn in tatters" and some of them "nearly dead from want of food and exposure," they had richly deserved the army's wrath "for their barbarities," one officer wrote. In his unpublished diary of the campaign, Lieutenant Bourke recounted, "By sneaking upon them [Apaches] in the night we can, by good luck, make our attacks at day-dawn and kill their warriors whilst asleep." Elsewhere, he also argued that "not one of the Apaches had been killed except through his own folly; they had refused to . . . come in [to the reservation]; and consequently there had been nothing else to do but to go out and kill them until they changed their minds."[42] While poisonings no longer belonged to the Anglo repertoire, the slaughter of the defenseless still easily fit into parameters of acceptable violence.

Moreover, Crook offered bounties for the delivery of heads of certain Apache and Yavapai leaders. These bounties stemmed from the troubles the army encountered in the management of the recently capitulated Indians. In his orders, Crook made the new setup appear terribly simple and straightforward on paper: "The basis of this peace is simply that these Indians shall cease plundering and murdering, remain upon their several reservations, and comply with the regulations made by the Government, through authorized agents, for them."[43] Reality proved a different matter altogether. Moved from Camp Grant to San Carlos after Howard expanded the White Mountain Reservation to include the Gila River, the Tontos, Pinals, and Aravaipas witnessed five agents (four civilians and one army officer) in a space of ten months (September 1872–June 1873).

While one of the civilian agents was ousted by a scandalous letter scornful of General Howard that later turned out to be a forgery written by a soldier, his interim successor, Dr. R. A. Wilbur of Tucson, allegedly admitted to being a profiteer and a swindler. He made most money by fixing the scales on the agency beef issue, which eventually led to a federal investigation. Unwilling to step down, Wilbur saw the incoming agent Charles Larrabee, a discharged officer from Maine, as a threat to his enterprise. Enhancing his own clout and undermining that of Larrabee, Wilbur apparently fed false information to Tonto leaders Chunz and Cochinay. At this time, the main factions at San Carlos revolved around the bands of Capitan Chiquito and Eskiminzin—mainly Pinals and Aravaipas—on the one hand and those of Chunz and Cochinay—predominantly Tontos—on the other. Some sources claim that Chunz seduced Chiquito's wife and that an Eskiminzin associate avenged the shame brought upon by the infidelity by killing one of Chunz's supporters. Meanwhile, Larrabee, out of his depth and feeling under siege, asked troops to be sent in in early May 1873 to restore order at San Carlos. Deeply troubled by the troop presence, and probably fearing for their lives, Eskiminzin and Capitan Chiquito fled the reservation.[44]

After a dispute with the Canyon Creek Cibecue leader Chan-deisi over ration tickets resulted in the death of Lt. Jacob Almy, Larrabee had had enough and resigned his post, and most of the Apaches returned to San Carlos as things cooled down.[45] However, Chunz, Chan-deisi, and Cochinay, with their following, did not, but instead drew more supporters with their raid on the reservation in January 1874. Meanwhile, a similar type of explosion had taken place at Camp Verde, where the army had assembled many of the Yavapais and some of the Tontos. At Verde, Lt. Walter Schuyler, like many of his military compatriots, felt that civilian agents who favored compromises and conciliation did not act forcefully enough and lacked authority in their behavior, and that the Indians, as well as the soldiers, would interpret this as fear and thus lose all respect for the agent. At San Carlos and Verde, the military started an administration on a prisoner-of-war model that relied on tight surveillance, enforced by the Apache police, composed of ex-Apache enlistees. It also included regular, often daily, roll calls, where the Apaches were identified by tags. Each man was numbered and carried with him, day and night, his metal tag, with the number and designation of his group stamped on it. A corresponding record, including information on the number of family members and description of physical characteristics, was kept by the officer in charge of the reservation.[46]

After the killing of Almy, Crook thundered that not one of their groups would be allowed to surrender until the heads of Chunz, Chan-deisi, Cochinay, and Delshe were delivered to the army. Delshe was a Yavapai-Tonto who had repeatedly sued for peace and a reservation near Camp McDowell in the late 1860s but now led a small independent faction that recurrently left the reservation at Verde to steal livestock and then returned to collect rations. Between May and July 1874, the number of heads brought in exceeded the number of wanted men. Uncertain of the men's identity, Crook nevertheless paid the promised reward for all and placed some of the crania on public display as warnings.

In his *Annual Report*, Crook painted the killed Apaches as criminals who, "after long careers of crime, met the fate they so richly deserved." But in the report, Crook circumvented the beheading, the bounty, and the public display of crania.

He may have thought that his methods would prove unacceptable to the current trends in Indian policy as well as incompatible with the sense of honor among regular army officers. Sixteen years later, in 1890, the issue still seemed a rather touchy one. In an article first published in *Harper's New Monthly Magazine* in April 1890, Wesley Merritt, holding the rank of a lieutenant colonel in the early 1870s, observed rather vaguely that the "Indians themselves punished the outlaws, furnishing satisfactory proof that justice had been done." Although some of the regular army's methods had been grim, its rhetoric represented a clear departure from the open celebration of perfidy and extermination practiced by Woolsey, Townsend, and many others.[47]

As Crook relinquished his command of the Department of Arizona and departed to Nebraska in March 1875, he was the guest of honor at no less than three elegant send-offs.[48] Crook had acquired this level of admiration and eminence by orchestrating a ruthless military operation targeting nearly defenseless Western Apache and Yavapai villages. His confining the Indians to reservations was not what had made him a star in the eyes of borderlands residents, of whom many, like they had done prior to the Camp Grant Massacre, soon would ridicule the military, this time for its alleged "softness" and failure to control the reservation Apaches.

Concentration

The reservations created a sharp distinction between a "friendly" Apache and an "enemy" Apache; all those, regardless of age or gender, not living under U.S. control in the reservations or serving in the U.S. Army, could be killed, while the rest should not. In practice, the division would turn out to be anything but clear. Some Apaches found room to move between reservation and independence, as the borders of the reservations leaked. If the Chokonen Reservation, adjacent to the border, was short of Anglo supervision, San Carlos was marred by near chronic chaos and corruption. Also, the hiring of Apaches into the army (officially as scouts, but as de facto soldiers) and the fact that the army frequently preferred enlisting those most recently capitulated made the task of assigning enemy or friendly/ally status maddeningly confusing. As one officer noted, the "scouts of one year would be turning the Territory topsy-turvy the next, & the officer commanding a company of scouts would be pursuing a party of ex-scouts with an assortment of ex-hostiles."[49] Confounding the matters even more was the new concentration policy, a government initiative by which all Arizona Apaches and the Chihennes from New Mexico would move to San Carlos. Although this policy created strong antipathy and plenty of misery and violence, it was followed through.

Much as it had in the 1850s, mail and other traffic again proceeded without Chiricahua intervention. Still, the army saw the Chokonen Reservation as a constant irritation and an international embarrassment. Highly critical of Howard's accomplishment, Crook issued a barrage of private and official objections. For example, he complained that he never got to see any sort of written verification on what Cochise and Howard had actually agreed upon. Most problematic for the military, however, was the location of the reservation, as it hugged the international line. The lure of raiding, security from both U.S. and Mexican retaliation, and the word of relaxed management quickly spread, and hundreds of Chihennes from Tularosa, many Nednhis from farther south, and also some White Mountain Apaches ventured to this promised land along the border. Not only did the reservation function as a jumping-off place for raiding expeditions into Sonora and Chihuahua and as a place of refuge, but also—as in the 1850s—an active contraband trade developed on the roads crossing it, as Apaches exchanged stolen horses and mules for guns, ammunition, and booze from Anglo and Hispanic traders.[50]

While the search for status or the fancy for contraband trade caused raiding, so did hunger. Although steadily increasing its appropriation since the start of the multiple reservation era in 1872, Congress failed to deliver enough food to the all the borderlands reservations and actually tightened the belt in 1876, directing agents to reduce expenditures by all means. Strict budget discipline hampered the efforts of the agents, as they could not obtain all the farming implements or seed needed. Together with the soaring prices of beef and flour, tight fiscal rule led to a critical supply shortage. As Jeffords made urgent pleas for more supplies, the Department of the Interior attempted to direct food to the Chokonen and San Carlos Reservations from the Colorado River Reservations, judging the Indians there to be less of a danger than the Apaches even if on half rations. But this effort failed and the Chiricahuas were expected to hunt their own food, which proved a mission impossible for the swelling reservation population, while rations were increasingly reserved for the elderly, for the sick, and for children.[51]

Already by October 1873, a year after Howard's conference with the Chokonens, the Chiricahua raiding in Mexico had placed such a strain on the chronically fragile diplomatic relations between United States and Mexico that Jeffords was instructed to tell the Chokonens that if the raiding did not stop immediately the reservation would be in danger of closure. Cochise, in a meeting with the army in early 1873, made it certain that he would not personally send any raiders south but also could not prevent others from going. Cochise acknowledged, "Young men are liable to go down . . . and do a little damage to the Mexicans" because their relatives had been killed by Mexicans. Besides, he explained, the Chokonens had "made peace with the Americans, but the Mexicans *did not come to ask peace from me* as the Americans have done."[52] While making it clear how he saw the Chokonens as an equal or as a dominant power in the region, Cochise nevertheless tried to use his exceptional influence to stop the southbound raiding. Rather than bow to his wishes, many took their exit from the reservation. The influential Juh and the up-and-coming Geronimo with their supporters moved to Mexico, while many of the Chihennes departed to Cañada Alamosa, where the unpredictable federal government also relocated its agent from the Tularosa Valley in September 1874.

While the federal executive once again entertained ideas of gathering all the Chiricahuas to the Cañada Alamosa–Ojo Caliente area, internal division and power struggle erupted among the Chokonens in the aftermath of Cochise's death from what was probably stomach cancer in June 1874. The main factions revolved around Taza and Naiche, Cochise's sons, who leaned toward reservation life, and Skinya and Pionsenay, also brothers, whose backers preferred life as free raiders. Killings between the two main blocs generated ample disorder. In April 1876, Pionsenay, after obtaining spirits from the station keeper at Sulphur Springs, got into a quarrel with Skinya and killed two of their sisters in the melee. Next, Pionsenay murdered the station keeper and his partner as they refused to supply more whiskey. Ransacking the station, Pionsenay's party withdrew to the Dragoon Mountains, where the army, with Taza, made a futile effort to break their defenses. In early June, Skinya and Pionsenay reappeared to pressure Taza and his devotees to go on raids once more. Results of the firefight that broke out included Skinya killed, Pionsenay wounded and on the run, and Taza brought to safety at Apache Pass by troops and Jeffords. With meticulous (unintentional) timing, on the day following this fight the agent from San Carlos arrived to the scene to terminate the Chokonen Reservation. On June 12, 1876, over three hundred Chokonens, among them Taza, Naiche, and forty other men, started under military escort for the reservation at San Carlos. Others, perhaps as many as five hundred Chiricahuas, bolted to the mountains or crossed the international border instead.[53]

The shutting down of the Chokonen Reservation was part of a larger plan executed by the government and the new civilian agent at San Carlos, John Clum. Besides the international tension and the dreaded revival of Chiricahua war, rationale for the concentration of the Apaches rested on the notion that, with the Apaches kept in one place, management would be more efficient, thus preventing any outbreaks. It was also meant to prove less costly. After the termination of the Chokonen sanctuary, the Chihennes at Ojo Caliente would follow in May 1877. The Apaches and Yavapais from Camp Verde had been moved to San Carlos already in March 1875. Next to go, after midsummer 1875, had been those Apaches in the proximity of Fort Apache. Only Hashkee-yànilti-dn (Pedro) and his group were saved by their close alliance with the military. As for the others, Diablo, a Cibecue Apache and an army sergeant, pleaded their case. He assured the army that his Apaches would need no assistance from the whites but would continue to provide men for the military if left alone. Discharged and ordered to move his people, the disillusioned Diablo acted defiantly, but the bulk of the White Mountain and Cibecue Apaches reluctantly relocated to San Carlos.[54]

Ever since Congress had moved Indian administration from the military to the Department of the Interior in 1849, the army had yearned for total control of Indian affairs. Many an officer believed that the army was the one section of white society that treated the Indians firmly and fairly, whereas civilians wanted to steal land or otherwise profit at the Indians' expense. An often intense hatred developed between civilian agents and army officers. A genteel lady and an officer's wife with plenty of borderlands experience, Martha Summerhays described an Indian agent in an excessively harsh manner. "Of all unkempt, unshorn, disagreeable-looking personages who had ever stepped foot into our quarters, this [Indian agent] was the worst," she wrote.[55]

With Clum, the Arizona officers confronted an ambitious and energetic agent who not only wanted all power on the reservation for himself but was openly antagonistic toward the military. He not only concentrated the Apaches at San Carlos but reorganized a vigorous farming program and assumed personal control of an Apache police force and an Apache court. He was effectively running the show and seeking to civilize the Apaches without help from the army. Highly jealous of his authority, Clum verbally attacked the new Arizona commander, Col. August Kautz. While Washington curtailed his effort to have Fort Apache removed outside the reservation borders, Clum suggested to his superiors that with a few more companies of Apache police the army could be withdrawn from the borderlands, a stunning proposition for Washington, the army, and those local businesses dependent on military contracts and consumption. Kautz retaliated. Clum had twice reduced the reservation for the benefit of miners, and Kautz insisted that Clum's management was corrupt and that the agent was engaged in fraud for his own and Tucson merchants' benefit. With permission from Washington, Kautz sent an inspector to examine agency issues at San Carlos in May 1877. Feeling his mandate undermined, Clum shunned the inspector, refused cooperation, wrote livid protests, and asked for an increase in authority and wages. Not getting his way, on July 1, 1877, Clum resigned, leaving a brewing chaos in his wake.[56]

With Clum or without him, living in the Gila River valley on the parched southern edge of forested ridges rising to the White Mountains and a few miles below deserted Camp Goodwin proved a testing ordeal for the Chiricahuas. For people used to life in the mountains, the summers on the lowlands were excruciating. Beside the plethora of spiders, scorpions, and snakes, there was too little water for farming. Fever had made the soldiers bolt Camp Goodwin in 1871, and now the dreaded prospect of malaria threatened the Apaches. That Taza died under uncertain circumstances (most likely of pneumonia) in September 1876 when touring faraway eastern cities on the initiative of government officials did little to ease the Chokonen transition. Neither did the death of some fifty to sixty shaking Chokonens from malaria in early 1878 help.[57]

Furthermore, all the quarrels with other Apaches and the drinking and violence that went with it—not to mention the constant uncertainty over their next meal—exasperated the Chiricahuas. San Carlos, one Chiricahua voiced, "is a place of death. Few people can endure a summer there.... There was nothing but cactus, rattlesnakes, heat, rocks, and insects. No game; no edible plants. Many, many of our people died of starvation." Indeed, more often than not the rations did not arrive on time, and, to prevent wholesale starvation, the army was forced to distribute emergency rations or the civilian agents had to make purchases on the open market. At dire times, the Chiricahuas received temporary hunting passes and were told to get their food themselves from the nearby mountains. Often there was precious little to hunt. Furthermore, Clum's successor as agent for the over 4,600 indigenous residents of San Carlos, Henry L. Hart, proved an excessively corrupt man. He swindled the agency beef issue and launched mining ventures and sold mining claims on (inside) the reservation borders. Following an investigation, Hart was promptly dismissed by the secretary of the Interior in summer 1879.[58]

Border Campaigns

San Carlos was proving a massive failure with violent consequences. The majority of the Chihennes departed the reservation in September 1877, and in the same month Pionsenay lured several Chokonen families to come with him. Eleven months later Geronimo with his close following thought it was time to go. They and those Chiricahuas who never entered San Carlos now faced life on the run. If life in San Carlos was arduous and potentially life-threatening, it was not much better outside, at least not for the long haul. Their lands would soon be swarming with prospectors on their way to the booming Tombstone. Hiding out in the various mountain ranges on both sides of the border, making quick strikes against vulnerable targets, and occasionally showing up at towns to barter and on the reservation to meet their friends and obtain food became the new routine. So did constant worry and stress.

In January 1877, a Chokonen winter camp in the Animas Mountains was surprised by the troops. A two-hour stalemate was broken as the Chokonens, facing attacks from two directions, deserted their belongings and fled, fighting a rearguard action, which kept the soldiers at arm's length. What made this clash different was the Chokonens encountering a new enemy for the first time—U.S. Army Apache recruits.[59] While the impact of the White Mountain Apaches was not overwhelming, realizing that from now on Apaches would be sent against them increased not merely the caginess the Chokonens felt toward U.S. troops but their general anguish and uncertainty of life.

More often than not the Chiricahuas kept hitting soft civilian targets. In fact, the army's January 1877 attack originated as a response to settler outcry created by Chokonen raiding in the Sonoita and Santa Cruz Valleys in late 1876 and was meant to deter any such desires from rising among the Chokonens for some time. The Apaches, showing that the army's harrying tactics had been fruitless, once again hit the two valleys in February 1877, killing nine men and taking as many as one hundred horses and many mules and cattle before exiting rapidly south of the border. After witnessing their reservation terminated, the desire for a piece of land free from Anglo or Hispanic intrusion grew strong in Chiricahua minds. In late 1877, they sought trade at Janos, only to be attacked by Sonoran troops. Although the Chiricahuas had been alert enough to avoid a general disaster, Pionsenay was killed in the battle. The next year the negotiations for a reservation at Chihuahua continued, but the terms—Nednhi relocation to a remote Rio Grande hamlet called Ojinaga—seemed insulting. Hoping that Chihuahuan authorities would take their peace efforts more seriously, the Nednhis made their case by slaughtering a wagon train southeast of Casas Grandes, killing twenty-five people. Then they split, the majority hiding in various locations in the Sierra Madre and one group, directed by a man called Nolgee, venturing back to Janos to see if peace would now be possible. It was not. The infuriated

Mexicans got the Nednhis gloriously drunk, before wiping out two-thirds of the group, including Nolgee. Sonorans also hit one of those groups hiding in the mountains, killing ten to twelve Chiricahua fighters.[60]

Then the U.S. government offered a lifeline. The new Arizona commander, Col. Orlando Willcox, assigned Lt. Harry Haskell the task of seeking out the Chiricahuas and convincing them that it was in their best interest to come back to the "new" San Carlos, now, after Hart's exit, again temporarily under military control. Haskell enlisted the help of Tom Jeffords and sought the services of five influential Chokonens still at the Gila River. The Chokonen delegation located Juh and Geronimo's camp in the Carcay Mountains, an offshoot of the Sierra Madre, but most of the fighters were away. Still, the word was now out that the Americans were open to a diplomatic solution. On December 12, 1879, Haskell received a message that Nednhi leaders wanted to meet him, but that he should come without troops to their camp in the Guadalupe Mountains. The first meeting was followed by a bigger parley at Fort Bowie. In the end, over one hundred Chiricahuas, among them Juh and Geronimo, found the will and the trust to follow Haskell to San Carlos, where they arrived on January 7, 1880, just at the time when violence was about to engulf Victorio's hybrid Apache group, united by, among other things, their distaste for San Carlos.[61]

As the Chokonens assessed the risks involved with San Carlos, on the Texas-Coahuila border outfits of Lipan raiders, in ever-smaller groups, reached as far inland as the vicinity of San Antonio, infuriating U.S. authorities. Sensitive to the expanding newspaper coverage the persistent border conflicts had received in eastern cities, and basically ignoring international complications, U.S. troops orchestrated several expeditions deep into Mexico. Between April 1876 and November 1877, they made nine cross-border offensives going after the remaining Lipans. Typically, the Americans rode several days, but found nothing, as the Apaches were broken up in small clusters that kept no villages. Still, the troops collected some victories, striking camps and seizing Lipan property, including horses. Between that and a large Mexican force sent to destroy all Apaches in Coahuila, by 1879 the combined attack was proving too much for any Lipan to bear.[62]

Like many of the Chokonens who declined to enter San Carlos, those Lipans opting to fight on joined the hybrid conglomeration identified through its principal man, the Chihenne Victorio. Now, some three decades after the Treaty of Guadalupe Hidalgo, the Apaches were organizing an army of sorts. It would be a cluster of the disappointed, indignant, and aggrieved men from different Apache groups thoroughly embittered by U.S. actions and determined to fight, even if recognizing the futility of their effort. For the United States and Mexico, these kind of Apaches were the most dangerous of them all. Unlike the events during the Jicarilla and Mescalero campaigns of the 1850s—with Carleton's ruthless efforts or the genocidal onslaughts by the civilians, or with Crook's cold and sharp assaults on Western Apache homes—the sacking of sleeping villages of unsuspecting Apache children, women, and men would not be the case with Victorio. He would lead the Apaches on the offensive, attacking the troops and settlements with force.

Victorio's "army" started to materialize after the reservation at Ojo Caliente faced closure in spring 1877. Clum, assisted by his Western Apache policemen, surrounded the Chihennes assembled for a talk, placed their leaders—among them Geronimo who had joined the agency in search of food—in shackles, and threw them in jail. The experience turned out to be a deeply traumatic one. An Apache boy later recollected, "Until I was about ten years old I did not know that people died except by violence. That is because I am an Apache . . . whose first vivid memories are of being driven from our reservation near Ojo Caliente with fire and sword."[63]

For Victorio, a man who emerged, in the eyes of white officials and historians, as a superb tactician, three summer months was all he could take of San Carlos. Hunger caused by shortage of rations, disease (malaria), and strife with other Apache groups, but most of all, deep affection for home, the Ojo Caliente–Cañada Alamosa area, drove him off. Most of the Chihennes who fled surrendered at Fort Wingate, on the southern edge of Navajo land, making it clear that they would not venture back to San Carlos but, if allowed to settle at Ojo Caliente, would bother no one and want nothing from the government. The government, after mulling things over for such a long time that most Chihennes had actually settled once more at Ojo Caliente, eventually rejected the Chihennes' offer. After months of further deliberating, and after airing thoughts of moving the Chihennes to the Indian Territory, the government acted not only against the wishes of the Chihennes but contrary to the recommendations of local authorities by sending the Apaches back to San Carlos in October 1878. Now most of the Chihennes fled to the hills before the soldiers arrived, and it was mainly dismayed and angry women and children who found themselves driven back to San Carlos.[64]

Probably thinking that the erratic and hesitant government would eventually give in, the Chihennes upped the diplomatic pressure. Two more times they sought to negotiate. If Ojo Caliente would not do, they could live at the mountainous Mescalero Reservation. But the barren lowlands of San Carlos were out of the question. In February and March of 1879 at Ojo Caliente, the Chihennes, fearful of arrest or slaughter, fled before any government answer was delivered. Also, at the Mescalero Reservation in July and August, Victorio and his following, now doubting everything the government did, took off as troops approached. Next, the Apaches returned to Ojo Caliente to wait. They lived in constant preparedness for attack, concealed their horses, checked emergency rations each morning, and kept their equipment ready for flight. From time to time, they struck, stealing livestock and eluding the cavalry troops chasing them. In late September on the Black Range, Maj. A. P. Morrow's troopers attacked, only to see, according to Lt. Charles Gatewood, the Apaches escape "into the high and rocky fastness that seemed to swallow them." Next, the Apaches pounced on the troops at breakfast, skillfully using the thick underbrush, rocks, and timber to their advantage. In the course of the pandemonium that followed, the soldiers had to withdraw, being precariously short on water.[65]

Arduous searches, constant movement, quick strikes launched by both sides, and steadily more panicky settlers resulted. The Apaches evaded the troops, chose when and where to fight, and retreated to Mexico when necessary. Armed with Winchesters acquired through trade, Victorio's army grew in size, witnessing an influx of Mescaleros and Lipans until it numbered perhaps as many as 150 to 250 fighters.

At the Mescalero Reservation, as in San Carlos, fraudulent agents had dealt in stolen cattle, falsified vouchers, misrepresented beef weights, and issued irregular and insufficient rations and little or no clothing. Agent F. C. Godfroy was suspended from office in 1878 after he sold government property for his own gain. Adding to the misery had been the Lincoln County War, a violent conflict between rival Anglo business factions in the area, which brought increased insecurity and lawlessness. Destitute Apaches ventured to the Staked Plains, by now free of Comanches; the Guadalupe Mountains; the Monahans Sandhills; and other hidden corners of West Texas and northern Chihuahua and Coahuila—a vast expanse of mountains, desert, and plains, much of it unsettled and untraveled by Anglos or Mexicans. Many could only find hunger and misery, or alternately Colonel MacKenzie and his men, and thus opted to link with Victorio.[66]

Camped in the Candelaria Mountains, Victorio's Apaches ambushed and virtually demolished two groups of Mexican citizens from the town of Carrizal, who had invited the Apaches to a fiesta with plans of getting the Indians drunk and massacring them. Next, the Apaches moved deeper into Chihuahua, producing substantial demolition. In the meantime, Col. Edward Hatch, the commander of the District of New Mexico, had positioned numerous cavalry troopers on the international line from Arizona to Texas to intercept and entrap the Apaches as they crossed the border. With Mexican forces closing in, the Apaches hopped north using a decoy strategy that enabled their women to reach the Mescalero Reservation in safety while the men lured Major Morrow's cavalry troops on a futile and exhausting chase on the Black Range. Skirmishing on several occasions, Victorio's men eluded the cavalry, which by late February was too exhausted, short on rations, and beaten to continue. As he outfought the troops, Victorio still tried to keep the diplomatic channels open, sending word—twice in fact—to the Mescalero Reservation and to Cañada Alamosa that he was willing to talk. Nothing came of it.[67]

Next, Victorio's men raided the settlements in the Rio Grande Valley in March 1880. That month alone they made as many as twenty-four or twenty-five raids, plundering hundreds of horses, cattle, and sheep, while also killing at least forty people, most of them civilians.[68] Hatch, feeling the mounting pressure from terrified and irritated settlers and superiors, reorganized the troops on a complicated, basically three-pronged, offensive in an attempt to catch the Apaches at the San Andres Mountains. Troops from Arizona closed in from the west, whereas Hatch moved cavalrymen from the east. Additional troops blocked escape routes and water resources to the northeast and northwest, while Col. Benjamin Grierson's cavalrymen from Texas were to cut off any escape routes to the southeast. By now, the army was chasing the Chihennes with the black Ninth and Tenth Cavalries, detachments of the white Sixth Cavalry, as well as with companies of Apache and Navajo recruits. Owing to problems in communications and logistics, including water shortage, the operation failed to trap Victorio. It was the Apaches who seized the initiative. As the troops under Capt. Henry Carroll approached the San Andres, they drank from a polluted spring of gypsum water. Helpless and suffering, Carroll's outfit began a desperate search for good water, the feeble and vomiting men reaching the spring at Hembrillo Canyon on April 6, where they were ambushed and outfought by the Apaches. The day before another troop, unbeknownst to Carroll and commanded by Lt. John Conline, had been nearly overrun by the Apaches in another section of the canyon.[69]

As Hatch was rushing in, the Apaches rushed out. This plunder made the colonel, in the words of James Haley, "the fool of the year" in the eyes of local settlers and newspapers. For example, the *Weekly Arizona Citizen*, with some very dry humor, printed how the people of Silver City, gathering to a mass meeting on June 7, were "after Hatch's scalp" due to his mismanagement of the campaign.

Reacting to the accusations, Hatch claimed that the "troops had worked hard" and "certainly do not deserve the abuse so lavishly expended upon them." It was obvious that the campaign, wherein the Apaches held the initiative and attacked the troops when it suited them, had deeply humiliated the army. Hatch vented his frustrations, making few friends by accusing locals of being apathetic and cowardly people who willingly furnished as well as traded arms, ammunition, horses, food, shelter, and military information to the Apaches. "Victorio himself," Hatch fumed in his report, "lived with a Mexican ten days," and, although it was common knowledge, no one had reported it to the military. Furthermore, locals, according to Hatch, occupied most of the springs and waterholes, making the soldiers on many occasions to "pay exorbitant prices" for water and grain.[70]

Angry and spoiling for some type of results, and suspecting that the Mescaleros were aiding and supplying Victorio's Apaches, Hatch, ignoring the protests of the Mescalero agent, led some one thousand soldiers to the reservation in April. Bullying troops disarmed as many Apaches as they could and took some two hundred Mescalero horses and mules. They also impounded many Mescaleros at the agency corral, where manure was several inches thick, for five days. The soldiers also mistook Mescalero stock herders for thieves and attacked them. Many angered and alarmed Mescaleros escaped. They had vivid memories of Carleton. Many feared such large numbers of soldiers and the prospect of being forced to go to San Carlos. Several joined Victorio's Apaches, while some raided independently of them. On the other hand, many also aided the army and enlisted.[71]

Dodging the troops, Victorio moved his raiding focus to the ranchers and miners in the Mogollon and San Francisco Mountains. His men also struck the Western Apaches in the reservation in response for their army service. Marred by the withdrawal of Arizona troops to their department and denied by his superiors of enlisting more Apache soldiers, Hatch again sent the cavalry in search of the raiders, who yet again evaded the troops. By mid-May, weeks of chasing had drained the cavalrymen to such extent that they were unfit to continue. Furthermore, their horses and mules were also heavily reduced and those still standing so worn out by want of grass and water that Hatch, in a May 14 dispatch, had to acknowledge that he could not overtake the enemy, who were at least a full twenty-four hours ahead of the soldiers. Nevertheless, on May 24 a company of Apache recruits managed to surprise Victorio's camp on the Palomas River. Running short on ammunition after a daylong fight, the troops were forced to retreat, opening a way for Victorio to escape. Reportedly as many thirty to fifty-five of Victorio's followers had been killed.[72]

Palomas River represented a turning point, a first defeat in what would turn into a series of disasters. Before that, from September 1879 to the fight at Hembrillo Canyon, the army had not only been humbled but had suffered many more casualties than the Apaches. Twenty-three soldiers had been killed compared to five Apaches, a remarkably different ratio when compared, for instance, to Crook's campaigns in 1872–74 or the slaughter of Apaches and Yavapais in the 1860s.[73] After Palomas River, Victorio himself was wounded, and many of his followers also began to abandon his outfit, seeking refuge in the remote mountain ranges or in the reservations. The main force, an estimated 100 to 150 fighters, headed south with Morrow's persistent cavalry troops again in pursuit. Unable to destroy or hold the Apaches, the cavalry engaged in several skirmishes, tormenting their targets and killing Victorio's son.

Back in Mexico trading and raiding, the Apache options were running out. Crammed between Hatch's troops and Mexican forces, the Apaches went toward West Texas in late July, where Colonel Grierson's cavalry repelled them. Returning to Mexico, the Apaches tried again to reach Texas in August, but were pushed back. Finding their efforts increasingly futile, dissent took over the Apache fighters, evidently short of an escape plan. Next, they confronted the American and Chihuahuan state troops working in concert to entrap them. Sensitive to border crossings, and with uncertain federal sanction, Chihuahuan officials allowed U.S. troops under Col. George P. Buell to link up with Col. Joaquin Terrazas's citizen army. They orchestrated a major operation, sweeping through the Candelaria Mountains where the Apaches hid. Eluding the first attempt, Victorio's men, running short on ammunition, demoralized, and drained, found themselves permanently on the run.[74]

Their luck ran out when trapped by Terrazas's troops on a remote, low, and island-like outcropping of volcanic rocks in the Chihuahuan Desert known as Tres Castillos on October 14. Upon cornering Victorio's Apaches, Terrazas ordered U.S. troops to leave Mexico. In the following onslaught by Mexican troops, some seventy-eight Apaches perished, sixty-two of them being men. Among the deceased was Victorio. Some sixty-eight Apaches were also taken captive and rushed south in the direction of Mexico City. The Apache army was annihilated and the borderlands wars finished, or so many at that time liked to believe. Others wondered whether the violence spurred by the concentration policies had only just started.[75]

General Uprising, or Not?

While many Anglos had for years hungered for the decisive battle and yearned the borderlands guerrilla clashes to mutate into a more conventional all-out war, and while they had radiated with confidence, there also had always existed a deep underlying uneasiness over being isolated, outnumbered, and under siege in a rising Apache storm. For example, one officer touring the borderlands in 1871 considered most forts to be in harm's way. The condition looked particularly grave at Camp Grant, where, the officer recorded, "one small company" of infantry was surrounded by nine hundred Indians "full of treachery" and liable to "massacre the garrison at any moment."[76] While this officer could not have been more mistaken with his take on Camp Grant, excited rumors of a universal Apache revolt never waned but rather intensified as Victorio drew followers from multiple Apache groups. The fact that Victorio's influence, although exceptional, had still been severely limited seemed to go unnoticed for many settlers and even for those in the government hierarchy. Not even all the Chihennes or most of the Chokonens or Mescaleros, let alone members of the various Western Apache communities, had linked up with Victorio. Indeed, the vast majority of Apache fighters never even considered the option, and many had fought against Victorio on the army payroll. Still, less than a year after Victorio's death a general war seemed imminent in many feverish minds.

Shortly after a raid by seven Lipan fighters on April 14, 1881, had killed a boy and a woman on the Frio River in Texas, the remnants of Victorio's outfit led by Nana went on a forceful raid during which they made close to forty different hits, attacking at least a dozen ranches and causing the death of perhaps thirty civilians. They also captured hundreds of head of livestock. Much of the bounty they hauled securely to the Sierra Madre by late August. Officers chasing the raiders reported wounds inflicted on the Chiricahuas, but not one dead or wounded was found. In all likelihood, there were none. Meanwhile, the troops from Texas forts once again took to the border. They found, and sacked, one Lipan camp in the process. Mexican forces, infuriated by the U.S. callousness, were also pursuing the Lipans, once again determined to eradicate them as a military force. After narrowly avoiding an ambush and engaging in two small skirmishes, their success was also far from overwhelming.[77]

Nana's hit-and-run extravaganza was closely followed by the press and readers in several states and territories ranging from Louisiana to Minnesota and from California to Washington, D.C. While the press was confused by what was going on, so, for much of the time, seemed to be the military. Still much maligned in the local press, Colonel Hatch, in his yearly report, not only recounted the succession of failures against Nana. He also deliberated on the identity of the raiders as "probably Mescaleros from Mexico," "others under Nana," and "renegade Navajoes and others," thus revealing both the army's dearth of knowledge and an inclination to see a pending general confrontation in the works. In all, the phantom-like advance had provoked disbelief, shock, and fury as well as great anxiety, despair, and feelings of helplessness among the military and borderlands residents. It had also showcased unrelenting Apache prowess while painfully exposing the limitations of the fighting Anglo and black troops.[78]

Next, the soldiers and settlers received alarming news from Fort Apache. Refusing to live at San Carlos, some of Diablo's Apaches had escaped back home within a year after the removal in the mid-1870s. Bitterness between Diablo's and Pedro's people, who had been allowed to live near Fort Apache all along, led to a violent outburst on August 30, 1880, which resulted in Diablo's death. This in turn contributed to a vicious cycle of murders and retributions the following months. It also saw the birth of a revivalist movement. Although white authorities expressed such a concern, the Cibecue preacher Noch-ay-del-klinne, an ex-soldier with a good service record in the U.S. Army, was not encouraging the Apaches to take up arms. Instead, his spiritual movement, expressed in powerfully emotional singing and dancing, was more concerned in reasserting damaged self-confidence. He was seeking advice from the otherworldly for the current cultural crises and the sense of loss and alienation and was prophesizing the return of past leaders and more bountiful times. Still, the new agent, New Yorker Joseph C. Tiffany—who, in by now established San Carlos pattern, initiated irrigation projects, sought to launch a school, and relied on the Apache police for strict discipline, but was also suspected, and later charged, of fraud and mismanagement—called the troops for help.[79]

Col. Eugene A. Carr, the commander of Fort Apache, was sent to bring in Noch-ay-del-klinne for questioning. Concern over violence seemed limited by the fact that many of Noch-ay-del-klinne's followers were Cibecue Apaches, some of the army's loyal allies from the past decade. On the other hand, many were worried. Victorio's actions had shown how a ruthless internment policy and abysmal diplomacy could ignite violence.

After the mixed column of white and Apache troops got Noch-ay-del-klinne to accompany them from his village on Cibecue Creek, a violent explosion erupted en route back to Fort Apache on August 30. Accounts differ on who actually started the shooting—some Apaches suggesting it was Carr's cook; many white soldiers were convinced it was the Apaches—revealing much about the confusion those present felt. Some Apache sources also suggest that Noch-ay-del-klinne was trying to prevent violence to the last moment. While suffering a number of casualties and seeing the Apache recruits run away, the stunned white troops held the Apaches at bay, killing the shaman in the melee. Next, they made a daunting trip back to Fort Apache. Two days after the first fight, some enraged followers of the revivalist movement attacked the post, but their charge was thwarted. After that, some sporadic raiding against white ranchers, ferry operators, and travelers more or less concluded all there was to this Apache uprising.[80]

For some days in August and September, it seemed as if the borderlands whites believed that the "entire Apache nation" would rampage across the rural areas and pour down on Prescott, Tucson, Tombstone, Silver City, and Mesilla, destroying and killing everything in their path. Fearing the complete annihilation of Carr's command, those left at Fort Apache had prepared for the worst. "We put everything in the best shape for defense. Surplus arms and ammunition were removed to the commissary storehouse; water, barrels, tools, etc., etc., were placed in this building ready for use, if needed. There we intended to collect the women and children, and if compelled to do so, make the final stand," the temporary post commander, Maj. Augustus Cochran, recounted.[81]

As Carr and his command limped back to the fort, it brought a sense of relief, but the outside world—meaning both the chain of command and various newspapers across the country—still ran with the disaster story. The *Arizona Weekly Citizen* in Tucson cried, "Massacre at Apache" and "not one" soldier "is supposed to have escaped." The Associated Press placed on wider circulation the stunning news that Carr's men "have all been massacred by the White Mountain Apaches." Reminiscent of Custer's demise at Little Bighorn in 1876, the *New York Times* printed a shocking Sunday headline sure to catch the readers' attention on September 4: "Shot Down by Indians; Gen. Carr and His Command Murdered."[82]

That the telegraph line to Fort Apache was down for several days curtailed the news flow and did little to prevent the spread of panic. After military couriers delivered the update that most of Carr's command had survived, the press revised its stories accordingly, but the word on Carr's safety did little to calm down those most suspicious. One Tombstone miner, for instance, wrote in his journal how people were afraid of the Apaches, as "thousands" were "reported on war path and a general outbreak" was "imminent." People flocked to Tombstone for safety, and armed squads were formed to repel the expected Apache attacks.[83]

Wild rumors made it seem that all the Chiricahuas still in Mexico were joining the fight. In reality, of course, they were not. As the Cibecue fervor reached its climax, most Chiricahuas at San Carlos also sought to stay clear of the turmoil. However, mistrust resulting from past wrongs, confusion, and the mounting presence of troops—there had been no white troops stationed permanently in the reservation since Clum removed them in 1875—made for a potentially volatile situation. As the military sought to arrest two Chiricahuas who had involved themselves at Cibecue, namely Bonito, a White Mountain Apache married to a Bedonkohe woman, and George, a Chokonen married to a White Mountain woman, the scared men fled to the Chiricahua camps. There they told wild stories that the soldiers were coming to murder them all, deport them far away, or arrest and place shackles on Geronimo and other leading men. After talks where past pains, including what happened to Mangas Coloradas in 1863 and to Cochise in 1861, as well as Clum's incarceration of Geronimo in 1877, resurfaced, approximately 375 Chiricahuas, of whom 74 were men, opted to leave the reservation on September 30, 1881. Close to three hundred Chiricahuas chose to remain put. The decision to leave was done in the heat of the moment and was anything but clear-cut. For his part, Naiche, by now an emerging leader of some repute—following the death of his older brother Taza—later deeply regretted their choice: "I have always been sorry that I left for [we] suffered a great deal."[84]

While the 375 Chiricahuas represented only a small fraction of the estimated 5,500 Indians on the reservation, they still signaled big trouble in the eyes of the U.S. and Mexican regimes. None of them probably thought of joining the Cibecue Apaches. The Dragoon or Chiricahua Mountains were out of the question, and so were the Mogollons and the Black Range, all teeming with miners. Also, with the aid of Apache soldiers the army would most likely find them there. The Chiricahuas made a decision to head for the Sierra Madre. With close to three hundred women and children, the Apaches needed to keep away from the soldiers sent after them but had to engage in subsistence raiding to procure enough food. Avoiding the bulk of U.S. troops, who were on Cibecue alert scouting the country northeast of the San Carlos Agency, the Chiricahuas chose a more direct and less mountainous course southward than they otherwise might have done. Off to a good start, they soon hit the jackpot by overtaking a packtrain.[85]

Armed and supplied, the Apaches continued in the direction of Fort Grant. They ambushed four soldiers repairing the telegraph line and killed a lonely freighter so that word of their presence would not spread. While most troops were farther north, four companies of cavalry led by Capt. Reuben F. Bernard inspected the corpses of the four dead soldiers near Mount Graham when the Chiricahuas opened fire. During this fight, known as Battle of K-H Butte, Chiricahuas fought a delaying action, holding off the cavalry while their women and children headed in the direction of the border. Apparently they had no casualties, whereas Bernard's soldiers limped to Fort Grant with one dead and three wounded.

Reaching the Sulphur Springs Valley, the Apaches had few settlements and no garrisons between them and the border. Unknown to them, the army was by now busy transporting troops to Dragoon Springs by rail, from which a combined force of seven cavalry troops led by Capt. Henry Carroll and Captain Bernard chased the Chiricahuas and surprised them just as they were in the process of butchering stolen steers. Caught off guard, the Chiricahuas abandon hundreds of horses and cattle and fled south along the eastern foothills of the Dragoon Mountains. After a running fight of several hours, the Apaches had to make a stand against the pursuing troopers. Unable to break the Apache defenses, soldiers lost the momentum. Only one Chiricahua was killed, while three soldiers were wounded. At night while the soldiers rested, the Chiricahuas ran. Crossing the border either at Guadalupe Canyon or San Luis Pass, they made good their escape. The hammered yet successful group reached Nana's fighters in the Sierra Madre with a good supply of horses, mules, and cattle. Importantly, they had suffered just three casualties along the way.[86]

As the Chiricahuas disappeared to the Sierra Madre, Lipans vanished to the remotest reaches of Coahuila and Texas, or integrated into the Mexican communities. And as Western Apaches took cover in their mountains or flocked to the San Carlos Agency for safety, it became quickly obvious that no matter how much the Anglos dreaded or clamored for it, no general war was forthcoming. No such thing was in the cards even if the army had not made a visible statement of its power by hurrying in reinforcements or by arresting, sentencing, and publicly hanging three of the "mutinous" Apache troopers from Cibecue.[87]

Only a small group of Western Apaches took up arms. When in July 1882 they killed the chief of reservation police and headed off the reservation with stolen ammunition and weapons, the troops from Forts Apache, McDowell, and Thomas, and from Whipple Barracks, chased down the outfit in a matter of weeks. Locating the Apaches at Chevlon's Fork, the troops forced a stand in which they destroyed much of the group. They reported some fourteen to twenty-two Apaches killed and six captured of the fifty-strong enemy outfit. Many of the survivors fled to the reservation. This Battle of Big Dry Wash was an isolated incident. That and the lack of general support for these Western Apache raiders even among their relatives, of who some reportedly participated in the fight as U.S. soldiers, speaks volumes of the infeasibility and unpopularity of violence, let alone a general war among the Western Apaches.[88]

In sum, no plans, social cohesion, or will for an full-blown war existed among the Apaches in 1881 or at any other time. Extensive revolution remained a potential reality only in worried Anglo minds. It would remain so until the wars concluded in 1886 and beyond. What then did Nana's raid, the incident at Cibecue Creek, the Chiricahua escape, Victorio's war, Lipan raiding, and Chevlon's Fork share in common? All were the acts of a militarily proficient people driven to desperate measures by the one-sided and confusing policies of an imperial power. The Apaches who took part were not only sick of reservation poverty and oppression but also maddened by the feverously vacillating and contradicting ultimatums, dictates, and demands of the government. Although Apache groups had entered a "new" era of diplomacy in 1871 from diverse positions of power, revealed disparate goals, and used various methods to draw government attention, they sooner or later found that attempts at concord and alliance were countered by mistrust and dishonesty. They negotiated a new world where a fickle U.S. government, rather than resort to diplomacy between equals, often tried to dictate its maddeningly inconsistent and arrogant will to the Apaches.

While Victorio's campaign stood for a futile effort to gain a permanent home in their preferred location at Ojo Caliente/Cañada Alamosa, Nana did not merely keep up the cause he knew was at that time extremely unlikely to materialize. Preferring freedom, and even death, over San Carlos, many Chiricahuas desperately hung on to their military independence in a clash that turned increasingly desperate. So did those few Mescaleros who still rode with them. Most of the Mescaleros tried adapting to reservation life and to cling on to their homes in the vicinity of the Rio Grande rather than face the prospect of being forced to San Carlos where more raiding could potentially lead them. The Lipans, in turn, simply battled starvation and sought escape options from violence the best way they knew how. For much of the 1870s, they kept running away from their enemies, hiding in the mountains, or seeking diplomatic accord and personal integration with various borderlands communities. Survival had become the key, or even sole, military policy of these borderlands refugees. The Apaches at Cibecue, like so many peoples throughout world history, sought solace from religion for their everyday misery and emotional confusion resulting from the sweeping changes forced upon them by colonial policies. These people turned to religious revivalism in search of hope of a better tomorrow. As things turned ominous upon Carr's arrival, they, remembering days past, feared treachery and the slaying of their spiritual savior in the hands of the occupying force who had captured him. Those who ended up at Chevlon's Fork were most likely both afraid and irritated by the troop presence on the reservation as well as the hangings that had taken place. Short on plausible options, they vented their anger.

If the Western Apaches were no longer militarily autonomous, the same applied for the Lipans. The raid on April 24, 1881, had been their last. Although the Lipans never capitulated in a single battle or campaign, their resources, manpower, and will had been smashed over a long period of time. In military terms, the Lipans had turned into borderlands ghosts, while their surviving members dispersed as refugees from Arizona to Texas and from Coahuila to Indian Territory. Many individuals and families assimilated into the Hispanic world of northern Mexico and Texas, quickly passing as Mexicans.[89]

CHAPTER 7

INSURGENCY

Since Tres Castillos our people had known the outcome. . . .
[The] little band had fled so often, starved so much, slept so little,
and suffered so long that death had no terrors.
—James Kaywaykla, Chiricahua Apache

It is a question in my mind how long these savages will stand being hunted.
—Gen. Nelson A. Miles, U.S. Army

Exasperation

None of the Anglo soldiers probably wanted to be there. Crammed into stockcars at Deming Station in New Mexico, they waited and sweated while telegrams reporting possible Chiricahua sightings arrived all day. It was May 1885 and the army was once again frantically organizing operations against the Apaches, this time targeting parties of Chiricahuas who had left San Carlos and were presumably on their way toward Mexico. After a detachment of Apache troops arrived on the westbound train, all the troops, commanded by Capt. Emmett Crawford, started off in the direction of the international border. The command consisted of nearly one hundred Apaches, whom, with few exceptions, were afoot, and a troop of white cavalry on horseback. Not a massive force in the annals of combat, this mobile task force still outnumbered enemy combatants four to one. Furthermore, the lineup acutely indicated the army's mounting dependency on Apache recruits. Not only did the Apache troopers, of whom many at this time were Chiricahuas, comprise the majority, but they would prove indispensable for locating the enemy, who had separated into several tiny clusters. They would also do all of the actual fighting.

Leaving Lang's Ranch at the southwest corner of New Mexico, the command traveled through the San Louis Pass and turned south, crossing into Mexico along the eastern base of the Sierra Madre. Advancing south, the task force moved much like an Apache raiding party. There was "no attempt at any regular order of march," Lt. Robert Hanna pointed out. Instead, each Apache followed "his own inclination, all keeping the same general direction." Unlike the situation at Deming Station, in the Sierra Madre it was the Apache footmen who waited for the white cavalrymen to catch up. Lt. Charles Elliott noted that the troops were "subject to every possible hardship," including shortage of water and poor rations, as well as an abundance of mosquitoes, ants, and centipedes. The marching was also impeded by "frightful" heat and summer rainstorms. The latter not only soaked everybody and everything but wiped out signs of the enemy. Discipline and spirit sank, and much of the command got drunk from the "firewater" sold by the Mexican villagers they encountered along the way. It "was not a pleasant feeling," Hanna remarked, to be in a "not overly friendly" foreign land "with a small force . . . of such irresponsible beings," of whom some "had been raiding this country only a short time before and might be tempted to try it again."[1]

On Bavispe River above Oputo, the Apaches proved their value and discovered a fresh trail left by the Chokonen leader Chihuahua and his following. White cavalrymen stayed behind as a chosen group of Apaches under Sergeant Chatto, a Chokonen himself, advanced on foot and on June 23 stormed Chihuahua's camp. The fight, like so many before and after it, proved brief and chaotic. It was also indecisive and, as such, disappointing for the army, hoping to paralyze even this small bloc of Chiricahuas. Hanna recorded that the enemy "made but little fight, but fled as fast as they could, leaving one dead upon the ground, all their camp equipage, and horses." In addition, the army captured from eleven to fifteen women and children, or approximately half of the camp residents. Their raggedy appearance displayed the impacts that the grueling escape from San Carlos had had on the independent Chiricahuas. Nevertheless, by the time the troops were ready to continue their pursuit, the Chiricahuas were already far away.[2]

Age of Speed

Following all the calamities of 1879–81, the borderlands conflict acquired new characteristics. It was foremost the military objectives and expectations as well as the pace of operations that got tuned. The wars also began to involve fewer and fewer Apaches fighting against a growing numbers of U.S. soldiers. By May 1885, more than seven out of ten Chiricahua men resided at San Carlos. Some of them were neutral, but many worked for the U.S. Army. One year later nine out of ten Chiricahuas were nonaligned. At that time, those who still raided, a tiny cluster consisting of fifteen Chiricahua fighters and their families, had close to five thousand U.S. Army soldiers on their tail, a record number of troops for the U.S.-Apache wars.[3]

Why did the manpower imbalance between the Chiricahuas and the U.S. Army border on the absurd in 1886? Why did the federal government send so many against so few? Did it again, like in 1881, worry that all the Apaches would join in a general revolt? And why in 1886 did the San Carlos homecoming no longer stand as a viable alternative for the independent Chiricahuas, even though the Apaches themselves would have liked to keep that option available? After all, since the early 1870s the federal government's practice had been to force the Apaches to become permanent residents of the Southwest reservations. But in 1886 the government ousted Gen. George Crook—who, by then, favored diplomacy, San Carlos (with military control), and the use of Apache troops—and brought in Gen. Nelson A. Miles as his replacement. Known for his swagger, boundless ambition, and dynamic effectiveness, Miles received orders from Washington to discharge most of the Apaches, highlight the role of white soldiers, and organize a vigorous military offensive that would destroy or capture the remaining independent Chiricahuas. It seems as if the exasperated federal government reacted to what is saw as a crisis. These adjustments in methods and goals in 1886 not only stemmed from the fresh directions the conflict had taken on the ground, although that was the case as well, but also revealed the new level of significance the Southwest borderlands had in the continental empire.

In years past, the gaze of the federal government and the nation had been on matters elsewhere, but in the 1880s the borderlands got more attention. One obvious contributing factor was that the U.S.-Indigenous wars had practically ended in other sections of the trans-Mississippi West. Even the (in)famous Lakota Sitting Bull, who epitomized indigenous resistance and ferocity in many white minds, had returned from exile in Canada in 1881 and would soon be touring with Buffalo Bill's Wild West Show. With the rest of the continent under the federal government's control, the continual fighting in the Southwest began to look more important and more embarrassing. What made this concern more pressing was the demographic and market transformation taking place in the borderlands itself, a process with the potential to reshape a distant corner of the continental empire into a valuable site of commerce and settler communities where neither distance nor the international line would be a limit to trade, investment, or labor migration.

While the Tombstone silver boom that had brought thousands of whites to Chiricahua lands would bust in a matter of years, in the wake of the exponential global surge in copper demand, Arizona mining would soon reach unprecedented heights in Clifton, Morenci, Jerome, Bisbee, Globe, and Miami, all locations that stood on or near Chiricahua Apache heartlands. Millions of pounds of copper would be the result every year, as well as employment for thousands of workers, many of them newcomers from Mexico and Europe. Also, when finally stretching to the borderlands, it did not take long for three major rail lines, and many smaller arteries, to cut Arizona and New Mexico, and to link with Sonora. In 1881, the Southern Pacific Railroad crossed both Arizona and New Mexico, while the Atchison, Topeka & Santa Fe Railroad, penetrating New Mexico from the north, reached the western corner of Texas, where it attached to the Southern Pacific and Texas & Pacific near El Paso. The third major operation, the Atlantic & Pacific Railroad, branched from the Atchison, Topeka & Santa Fe, was constructed west from Albuquerque, and linked with the Southern Pacific on the Colorado River in the vicinity of Fort Mojave in 1883. In the preceding October, the Sonoran Railway had joined the Arizona lines at Nogales Pass, opening a new era of cross-border operations for U.S. businesses and investors. Furthermore, drawn by rail links and driven by the violent decline caused by drought, blizzards, and overgrazing that hit the plains, Anglo ranchers, backed by outsider investments, took control of New Mexico's plains and Arizona's ranges. The number of cattle and sheep in the borderlands grew exponentially, totaling in the millions by the end of the 1880s. In all, the thousands of newcomers, the rail lines, and the increased presence of industries linked the borderlands to the eastern industrial revolution and the capitalistic world economy with unprecedented intensity and volume. Soon even the old Spanish-built urban centers like Santa Fe and Tucson acquired a more Americanized outlook.[4]

At first glance, it seems that the railroads and the surging white presence tilted the resource advantage decidedly in favor of the army, now able to move troops, animals, and supplies with greater speed and in surging quantities. Many the transport problems of years past when oxen, mules, and wagons had reigned became the subject of tall tales and bad dreams. The growth in civilian enterprises also rapidly closed up the space used previously by the Chiricahuas. Their favorite hunting, gathering, and raiding areas between the Sonoita Valley and the Rio Grande were now more firmly under permanent white occupation. As a result, the Chiricahuas found less to hunt or gather, and fewer opportunities to do so without disturbance. However, for daring and skillful raiders, the growing number of whites meant that there was more to steal than previously. Also, one did not have to worry about indigenous competition, as most of the potential Apache raiders (even most of the Chiricahuas after 1883) were confined to reservations. Consequently, the escalating white presence and the subsequent growth in material resources opened unintended possibilities for active Chiricahua raiders. And active they were.

The borderlands wars that had often been fought with breakneck pace in the past gained in tempo when the independent Chiricahuas made speed their lifeline. Once more using the U.S.-Mexico borderline and the borderlands topography to their advantage, the Chiricahuas turned the remote reaches of the Sierra Madre into their sole refuge. They also used the mountains as a launching pad for strikes to a geographically scattered selection of targets in Sonora and Chihuahua as well as Arizona and New Mexico. According to a new study, the Chiricahuas took part in 104 documented engagements in 1882. They tied this record in 1883, only to top it with 139 actions in 1885. In 1886, the tiny Chiricahua parties still contributed to 103 encounters. Most of these actions did not involve the U.S. or Mexican military, but consisted of raids against miners, travelers, freighters, merchants, ranches, and farms, a selection of vulnerable, exposed, and resource-rich victims. In comparison, the number of engagements the U.S. Army was involved in against the Chiricahuas was a mere two in 1883, eleven in 1885, and seven in 1886.[5]

Setting new highs, the Chiricahuas raided more frequently between 1883 and 1886 (except in 1884 when practically all Chiricahuas resided at San Carlos), surpassing what they had accomplished during the Victorio wars. Yet these more recent raids were the work of substantially fewer raiders. The record is all the more impressive when compared to the late 1860s and the early 1870s, when the number of Chiricahua engagements averaged from thirty to forty per year, and in some years numbered many fewer than that. Even in 1861, a year of exceptionally high Chiricahua activity, they managed a "mere" fifty-one engagements. That being said, raiding frequency in this case does not convey so much Chiricahua dominance over the borderlands in the mid-1880s as it suggests an increasingly frantic attempt by the independent Apaches to check fading fortunes, declining resources, and deteriorating military clout.

Their sheer speed as well as the scarcity of Apache fighters made finding, fighting, and defeating the enemy extremely difficult for the American troops, who remained poorly equipped and trained for their task. On one level, the army's demolition of Apache goods and encampments, calculated to break the enemy's spirit and capacity for armed resistance, started to matter less than before because the Chiricahuas could now resupply with more ease by raiding.

Trying to counter the activity and pace of the Chiricahuas, both Crook and Miles created special mobile task force units. The idea was to defeat the Chiricahuas by applying uninterrupted pressure, by penetrating their most impenetrable hideouts, and in Crook's case by using their own people. The command that Lieutenants Hanna and Elliott were assigned to in 1885 represented just such an attempt. Still, as Hanna's and Elliott's experiences testify, success remained very limited if one measures it the way white settlers and government officials tended to do—in the frequency the enemy was forced to fight, in victories achieved in the battlefield, and in the number of casualties.

In 1883, the federal government listed nine, in 1885 eleven, and in 1886 two Chiricahuas killed as a result of army actions. Even these modest figures are likely to be slightly inflated, as some of the Chiricahuas listed as dead could not be confirmed and were probably merely wounded. In contrast, there might have been as many as 142 Anglos and Hispanics killed in the borderlands by the Chiricahuas in 1883, 114 in 1885, and 109 in 1886. Of these deaths, thirty in 1883, sixty in 1885, and twenty-seven in 1886 were American civilians, and many of the rest Mexican noncombatants. If we compare the casualty figures with those from the 1860s and early 1870s, when whites slaughtered scores of Apaches, it is easy to think that something had profoundly changed in the borderlands wars. In fact, non-Apache deaths outnumbered Apache fatalities already in 1879 during Victorio's wars. However, with so many raids in 1883, 1885, and 1886, the average death ratio per Chiricahua strike was still very low, just one person per each Chiricahua engagement. This in turn suggests that some things had not changed—the Chiricahuas still did not prioritize killing but instead continued to focus on the acquisition of material goods. The small Chiricahua outfits stole, for example, at least 500 head of livestock during the seven months after they left San Carlos 1885, while the even tinier Chiricahua cells pilfered over 450 head in 1886 before surrendering in September.[6]

Whether cognizant of its poor statistical showing or not, in the army a growing sense of disappointment and humiliation prevailed among men who knew they were expected to defeat and control the Chiricahuas, but seemed to be doing a poor job at it. Regardless of their numerical superiority, white soldiers seemed nearly helpless in preventing the small Chiricahua cells from raiding at will. And the troops seemed to suffer a further blow when Crook, who did not believe that white troops were up for the task, highlighted the role of Apache recruits in the most visible offensive operations. Vocally articulating their frustrations and protecting their wounded manliness, soldiers and officers wrote scores of bitter commentaries of the conflict, the environment, and the enemy.[7] As for the white civilians, their role in combat remained as minimal as it had been since the Camp Grant Massacre. But they were perhaps more vocal than ever in proclaiming a failure of massive proportions when subjecting the army to heavy-handed criticism.

As settler petitions for help reached the White House with increasing velocity, even President Grover Cleveland grew interested in the borderlands wars. He promised, for instance, the Arizona delegate to Congress that the federal government would gain full control of the border area even if took the whole army to accomplish it.[8] Seeing the growth of white settlements and industries and witnessing how prominent papers such as the *New York Herald, New York Times,* and *Washington Post* followed the borderlands events more closely than before, or, like the *Los Angeles Times,* sent a correspondent to the field to get more exclusive coverage, Crook recognized the changes in the air.[9] Already in 1883, he warned his superiors, "With all the interests at stake we cannot afford to fight" the Chiricahuas anymore. By "all the interests," Crook referred not only to increased population and business activities or to the heightened public attention the borderlands events got in the East, but conceivably he also indicated the army's tarnished reputation. Two years later, when a new war with the Chiricahuas had started, Crook again warned his superiors in Washington that a prolonged war would be disastrous for the settlers and for the army, which could not control, quickly defeat, or ignore the independent Chiricahuas.[10]

Then how much power did the Chiricahuas actually muster? Even if they enjoyed a rewarding selection of raiding opportunities, hit many targets and with great frequency, and usually outran and outfoxed the tired and exasperated troops, there was another, much grimmer, side to their story. The rise of settler colonialism and increase of troops made normal life unattainable, every day precarious, and future uncertain for the independent Chiricahuas, who were losing ground fast. Even the skillfully executed lightning raids by Geronimo, Chatto, and Josanie that so terrified and infuriated the borderlands residents represented attempts by anxious people to secure resources vital for survival and for maintaining military autonomy. The Chiricahuas were no longer the fighting force they had been in Cochise's or even Victorio's times. They had lost the bulk of their fighting men, and many of their women and children had been either killed or taken captive. In the early 1880s, the Chiricahuas also made more than their share of bad choices due to carelessness, drunkenness, or egoistic behavior on the part of their leaders. In fact, more than one hundred Chiricahuas were killed in

1882 alone.[11]According to one military source, in 1883 the Chiricahuas could still muster approximately 120 men and boys old enough to fight, while another text puts their fighting strength in 1885 as high as 140 warriors.[12] The latter estimate surely included all the boys from aged twelve and up. But more importantly, by 1885, and to a somewhat lesser extent, in 1883, most of the Chiricahuas did not want to fight anymore. The majority sensed that continued warfare would bring their destruction.

Those Chiricahuas who resolutely tried to live outside white control saw their effort develop into war of avoidance, resource raiding where casualties could not be tolerated. Any notions they might have had of retaking their lost homelands on the U.S. side of the border were nothing more than fantasies. There was but a single place left that offered even a fleeting sense of security, the Sierra Madre. In American minds, these mountains represented a formidable barrier to penetrate and wrestle from Chiricahua control.

A Not-So-Great Escape

While the winter of 1881–82 in Mexico brought nothing dramatic in military fortunes for the Chiricahuas, neither did it take them out of harm's way. Seeking to gain some advantages, the various Chiricahuas assemblies led by Juh, Geronimo, Naiche, Nana, Chihuahua, and others mixed diplomatic overtures and trade, mostly in the proximity of Casas Grandes and Janos, with raiding, mainly in northwestern Sonora, but also in Chihuahua. Illustrative of their mixed fortunes, Juh's bloc managed to capture hundreds of horses in Sonora and trade the animals for ammunition in Chihuahua, while Nana's Chihennes, with some Mescalero allies, who sought to negotiate and gain information on Apaches captured at Tres Castillos, were attacked by Chihuahuan forces near El Paso.[13]

In April 1882, the Chiricahuas once again set their sights on Arizona, aiming to repeat their escape from 1881 by liberating the Chihennes still at San Carlos. Many of the reservation Chiricahuas followed Loco, a headman who not only worried about Chiricahua prospects or was receptive to changes in their lifestyle, but who rather persistently looked to avoid fighting and bloodshed. It was a peculiar yet bold move oozing with confidence, but more likely motivated by military weakness. One plausible explanation, although downplayed by some historians, was that the Chiricahuas needed the additional fifty fighters at San Carlos to bolster their strength. Still, it was uncharacteristic for the badly fractured Chiricahua community to force any Apache to take up arms. As messages from the Sierra Madre reached Loco, he, after making it clear that going to war was not an option, forwarded the dispatches to reservation authorities. Still, on April 19, 1882, the reservation residents were awakened to shouts and confusion, as mounted Chiricahua fighters led by Geronimo and Naiche approached their homes with guns in hands. "The suddenness of this attack, its surprise effect, and the inhuman order . . . calling for the shooting of [us if we did not obey] . . . threw us all into a tremendous flurry of excitement and fear," Jason Betzinez, one of the reservation dwellers, recalled. His people had little choice but to obey.[14]

Killing the chief of the reservation police, the escapees continued up the Gila River toward Clifton, changing course several times to evade any forces sent to get them. With women and children to take care of, the party wanted nothing to do with the army, but, hurrying onward, sent small detachments to steal horses from local ranches to keep up a swift pace. Still, demonstrating the importance of rituals, the Chiricahuas apparently paused to arrange a puberty ceremony for one of the girls along the way. Being on the run, they only managed a shortened version of the four-day-long ceremonials that mark this singular event in a Chiricahua woman's life. After the ritual, the people were off again. Betzinez recollected how they made tiresome night marches in nearly zero visibility. Besides cactus, yucca, and other thorny plants, the Chiricahua column had to watch out for knife-sharp rocks, holes, and crevices on the ground and precipitous cliffs.[15]

Worn out by rapid marching, the Chiricahuas saw their luck ran out near Stein's Peak, when Col. George Forsyth's six cavalry troops from New Mexico intercepted their run at Horseshoe Canyon. Like many of his compatriots, Forsyth regarded Apaches as "cruel" and "crafty" slayers of lone miners and freighters. He also viewed the Apaches as "tireless when pursued." At first, as so often happened, a reconnaissance party of soldiers ran smack into a Chiricahua ambush. When Forsyth's main command reached the site, the colonel found the Chiricahuas "strongly entrenched" in the canyon. Next, Betzinez recalled, "the soldiers fired ferocious volleys," so that "those of us who were watching were shivering with excitement as our men slowly withdrew under this fire." Forsyth saw things his way: "We had forced them up the canyon, and I regarded the affair about over as we could no longer reach them." He also added that the "air was suffocatingly hot in the canyon, and we were weary and very thirsty." Until sunset, the Chiricahua fighters kept the troops at bay while allowing their women and children time to escape.[16]

Crossing the border, the Apaches eased their guard and rested and relaxed for two days, thinking no U.S. troops could pursue them. They were wrong. Capt. William Rafferty and Capt. Tullius Tupper, with two companies of cavalry and two companies of indigenous troopers, also crossed the border, unauthorized. About twenty miles south of the border in the Sierra de Enmedio, the soldiers located their target. Excited by the prospect of a decisive battle, the officers planned to encircle the enemy camp and subject the Chiricahuas to a murderous cross fire. Unfortunately for Tupper, his Apache soldiers opened fire prematurely, thus alarming the camp. Showing their enthusiasm, the cavalrymen went on a furious charge. The soldiers shot hundreds of rounds in a matter of few minutes, recklessly wasting their ammunition. Managing to drive off a considerable portion of Loco's horses, the soldiers in turn had to take cover and withdraw due to ammunition shortage and exhaustion. Meanwhile, a group of Chiricahua fighters made a flanking move to the high ground behind the Apache recruits, this way diverting their attention and allowing the main body to reach the foothills of the nearby mountains. While U.S. casualties totaled one dead and two wounded, the Chiricahuas reportedly lost from five to fourteen warriors. Whereas Anglo troops had surprised the Apaches from the north, another determined force was closing in from the south.[17]

Putting distance between themselves and Tupper, the Chiricahuas, perplexed by American presence on Mexican soil, marched the night in a column a half-mile long, their fighting men mainly deployed in the rear in case the U.S. forces showed up. In one sense, the fleeing Chiricahuas were right to remain watchful. Some eight hours after the fight, Forsyth had appeared in Tupper's camp, and after Tupper's exhausted soldiers got a little rest, the combined command of some 450 soldiers, hungry for that decisive battle, pushed deeper into Mexico. They still had no authorization to be there. Of course they knew the risks involved and had heard of the kind of censure those who crossed into Mexico from Texas had faced from their superiors. Evidently the possibility of an all-out battle against the already exposed Chiricahuas proved too tempting.

Little did the U.S. troops or the Chiricahuas know that a Mexican force—possibly informed of the Chiricahua route by two Apache captives—was waiting for the Apaches at Alisos Creek on April 29. From their concealed positions, Col. Lorenzo Garcia's men opened a deadly fire against mainly women and children. The Chiricahua women turned back, scattering as they went, while their men from the rear tried frantically to reach the battle and protect their dependents. "Almost immediately Mexicans were right among us all, shooting down women and children right and left. . . . A few warriors tried to protect us while the rest of the band were running in all directions," Betzinez remembered. He added, "It was a dreadful, pitiful sight. . . . Whole families were slaughtered on the spot, wholly unable to defend themselves."[18]

Caught in a dreaded pitched battle, with their women and children in the firing line, the Chiricahuas were in a terrible spot. According to some sources, Geronimo suggested that the warriors make a break for freedom without the women and children, whereas a man called Fun threatened to shoot Geronimo for that kind of talk. Forcing the Mexicans into a stalemate, the Chiricahuas used the cover of darkness to run off to the neighboring mountains. In the end, Garcia had killed as many as seventy-eight Chiricahuas, many of them women and children. He also had taken over thirty captives.[19]

Refugee Life

Compared to their escape from San Carlos the previous fall, when only three Chiricahuas had perished en route, the story this time around was very different. At least twenty to twenty-five fighters had been killed. Not only were their deaths irreplaceable, but so too were the losses of numerous women and children who had also been killed or taken captive. Understandably, the Chiricahuas were deeply divided and demoralized when finally reaching the Sierra Madre. Feeling they were not welcome, Betzinez found many of Juh's Nednhis "hard to deal with on friendly terms." Perhaps some of the Nednhis saw Loco's Chihennes as intruders or somehow blamed the Chihennes for the recent disasters. On the other hand, some Chihennes had happier reunions with relatives, who, Betzinez continued, "gave us food and blankets" and "tried to take our minds off our losses." Nevertheless, the abduction of Loco's people left permanent marks on the Chiricahua community.[20]

Still, they tried to make ordinary work in their new home. People went about their daily business of housekeeping and cooking; some engaged in sports and relaxed by gambling and socializing, telling stories, and cracking jokes. The lofty Sierra Madre consists of two north-south ranges enclosing a central plateau: the Sierra Madre Oriental faces Chihuahua and parallels the Gulf of Mexico, while the Sierra Madre Occidental curves through Sonora facing the Pacific Ocean. The mountains include plunging, steep-sided canyons, oak and pine forests above five thousand feet, humid and thickly vegetated outer slopes, and nearly barren inner slopes. Winters are mild and summers are rainy. The Chiricahua stronghold of Bugatseka at the head of the Bavispe River was a perfect natural fortress. A zigzag trail as its only access, this level top of a mountain had game, tall grasses, edible plants, and perennial streams.[21]

As so many Apaches now lived in the Sierra Madre, food resources were quickly exhausted. This was the largest number of Chiricahuas together, some five hundred to seven hundred people in all, since the termination of the Chokonen Reservation. They included also an assortment of Mescaleros and White Mountain and other Apaches in addition to a few Navajos—fighters tired of reservation poverty and eager to fight and raid as a way of life. There being little mescal, the Chiricahuas lived mainly on meat, although even game was getting harder to find. The men had to venture ever-greater distances on their hunting expeditions or were forced to steal Mexican cattle and thus risk retaliation. Resource depletion and general alertness resulted in nervousness, and in frequent changes of campsites. While life in the Sierra Madre could be joyous and free, more often it was by now troubled by the dark clouds of uncertainty and violence.[22]

While Chiricahua raids in 1882 and 1883 were certainly efforts to respond to a growing resource shortage, they can also be interpreted otherwise. Perhaps they signified denial in the face of waning military might, the Chiricahuas wanting to live as in years past when much of northern Mexico functioned as their supermarket. Although several Chiricahuas questioned the soundness of war, theirs was also developing into a society that was geared more and more exclusively toward combat. In the spring of 1882, approximately one-third of the Chiricahuas journeyed to Casas Grandes for trading and diplomacy. For two days, they engaged in friendly bartering as well as drinking and dancing late into the night just outside the town walls. Sleeping off their hangovers, Chiricahuas proved easy victims for the Mexicans, who assailed them on the third morning. Few of those who had accepted the hospitality escaped the slaughter.[23]

After the devastation at Casas Grandes, the Chiricahuas enjoyed success raiding Sonora and the United States. It was primarily necessity that drove them north of the border, not enough ammunition being available in Mexico for their American-made weapons. Short on supplies once more, the Chiricahuas went on December raids in Sonora. Operating around Baviácora and Cumpas, Geronimo and his party captured mule trains, hundreds of rounds of ammunition, and food supplies, whereas Juh was active in the proximity of Trinidad and Sahuaripa. Upon the party's return to Bugatseka, Geronimo enjoyed festive celebrations that were suddenly disrupted by anguished relatives who brought news of a disaster from Juh's camp farther south. On the cold winter morning of January 24, 1883, Chihuahua volunteers struck Juh's people. According to Mexican accounts, they killed, wounded, and captured at least eighty Apaches during a fierce fight. They also robbed and burned the village and captured all of its stock. The defeat had been devastating, and, according to some accounts, Juh had been too drunk to lead during the fight. Discredited, his shattered group plagued by quarrels, Juh and his family abandoned the others shortly thereafter. By September 1883, the ostracized Nednhi leader enduring a reclusive existence would be dead. The stories of how Juh perished differ in their details. The most common version recounts that, while riding along a trail overlooking Casas Grandes or the Aros River, Juh fell off his horse and plummeted to the river. Perhaps intoxicated—or not—Juh perished either due to the fall or because he drowned.[24]

To The Sierra Madre

In March 1883, after first slipping past the approaching Mexican troops, approximately eighty warriors led by Geronimo and Chihuahua targeted food and livestock hundreds of miles away near Ures, while twenty-six men with the relatively unknown fighter Chatto at the helm crossed into Arizona and New Mexico to acquire weapons and ammunition. Unleashing practically all they had, the Chiricahuas once again thrived temporarily.

If General Crook, who had returned to Arizona in September 1882, was expecting a Chiricahua strike across the border, as he suggested in his correspondence when claiming that the independent Chiricahuas on Mexican soil constituted a constant risk to U.S. security, his troops were far from ready to meet it. It seems that Crook had also suspected the unprepared state of his men. During the winter, he dispatched some Chiricahua women and Apache troops across the border to open communications with the Chiricahuas concerning surrender. Their attempts proved futile, as no Chiricahuas were found. Possibly the Chiricahuas were simply unaware of Crook's envoys, or perhaps they had lost faith in the sincerity of American diplomacy. Excluding Loco and his following, they made no effort to reach out to the army.[25]

Crossing the border near Fort Huachuca on March 21, Chatto's men immediately struck a coal camp, killing four men. Continuing north, they attacked mining parties and dispersed into smaller units in search of ammunition. Despite the telegraph lines connecting the posts, information of the raids did not arrive to Crook's headquarters at Whipple Barracks in the first days. Also, at first the garrisons at Forts Huachuca, Grant, and Bowie remained passive. Next, for many days they were unsure whether there were Chiricahua parties in the country. The army's next confusion centered on whether the raiders originated from Sierra Madre or from San Carlos. Meanwhile, the Chiricahuas struck, cut the telegraph wire, took cover in the mountain ranges, and kept moving. On March 28, the raiders spotted the traveling party of Judge H. C. McComas, his wife Juanita, and son Charlie riding a buckboard on their way to Lordsburg from Silver City. Ambushing and slaying both parents, the Apaches took the six-year-old Charlie captive and stole everything, from the driving whip to raincoats, they could transport. By now the troops had become active, but the Chiricahuas split into several parties and, transporting a supply of ammunition, guns, and other provisions, headed south of the border. During the nine-day-long raid, the raiders, according to historian Marc Simmons, covered, in their zigzag advance, somewhere between two hundred to four hundred miles.[26]

While Chatto's raid in general generated much uproar in the press, it was the McComas incident on the Lordsburg road that raised the level of criticism of the army to new heights nationwide. The local press raged, among other things, how the soldiers would "follow at a safe distance," felt more comfortable fighting Indians "in railroad cars," or were too busy "sucking sutler whiskey" to fight the Apaches.[27] Capt. John Bourke explained, "To attempt to catch such a band of Apaches by *direct* pursuit would be about as hopeless a piece of business as that of catching so many fleas." Crook agreed: "To ensure success campaigning against them [Chiricahuas] must be incessant." Still, cutting their advance or setting an ambush for the raiders had proven no more doable for the army than success in direct chase. In fact, according to Crook' report, "not an Indian was seen by any of the various parties [troops] at different times on their [Chatto's men] trail."[28]

In the meantime, Geronimo's men had boldly raided in the proximity of northern Sonora's industrial and demographic centers. Both nations now fumed with anger. Determined to take the war to the Chiricahua sanctuary, Crook firmly believed that "in operating against them [Chiricahuas] the only hope of success lies in using their own methods, and their own people." To make sure those in Washington comprehended that the military situation demanded the use of Apache recruits instead of white troops in offensive operations, Crook was not shy at making his views known in his correspondence.[29]

Crook made the Apache soldiers the cornerstone of his strategy, in which offensive operations constituted a requisite for success. One of the first things Crook did when reentering Arizona in 1882 was to request from his superiors that the number of Indian scouts be doubled to 250. Then he personally went on a recruiting tour in San Carlos, hearing a barrage of complaints about poverty, injustice, and thievery, many of them pointing to agent Tiffany and his entourage. While Crook assured his Apache audiences that things would improve and urged the Apaches to remain calm, he used recruitment as a bargaining chip. Except for some Cibecue Apaches near Fort Apache, most people at San Carlos depended on government annuities, and thus approached enlistment as a means to provide for their families. Additionally, recruitment offered something they could identify with and make suit their notions of manliness.

As for those Apaches who hesitated, Crook narrowed their options. During a meeting at San Carlos in October 1882, he informed the Western Apache headmen, "You can't have any rest here until those Chiricahuas are brought in, and you must bring them in. You must do this at once." Not getting the response he wanted, Crook suggested that the Western Apaches would be blamed for the Chiricahuas' deeds and warned that they would be counted daily as well as prohibited from departing to their homes near Fort Apache until the Chiricahuas were brought back. The result: scores of Western Apaches enlisted.[30]

To invade the Sierra Madre, getting Apaches to enlist was not enough. According to Dan Thrapp, troops first required a specific reason for launching operations; second, troops must know where to look for the Chiricahuas and have somebody from the inside to guide them; third, permission to cross the international line was necessary; fourth, cooperation or at least consent from Mexican officials for the American troops to cross the border was also needed.[31] Chatto's raid satisfied the first requirement. While the pursuit by Forsyth, Tupper, and Rafferty in 1882 had, following the Mexican victory at Alisos Creek, ended in a cordial yet tense meeting during which Garcia's forces had ordered the U.S. troops back north, a few months later the two countries signed an agreement that enabled troops from either country to cross the international border when in close pursuit of Apaches.[32] Recognizing that his offensive did not exactly fit the terms, Crook personally met with officials in Sonora and Chihuahua to discuss his plans. Drawing a favorable response from his meetings and receiving orders from his own superiors to pursue the Chiricahuas regardless of national lines, Crook completed his diplomatic maneuvers and started to assemble his troops at the San Bernardino Ranch near the border.

Guiding the operation would be four Apaches familiar with the Chiricahua hideouts in the Sierra Madre. The best known of them was called Tso-ay, named "Peaches" by the whites due to his light complexion. A Cibecue Apache married to a Chiricahua woman, he had lost his wife shortly before abandoning Chatto's raiding party to rejoin his relatives at the reservation from where Crook enlisted his services. On May 1, 1883, the force that consisted of 42 white cavalrymen and 193 Apache soldiers crossed the international line. Accompanied by a sizable packtrain, the soldiers and officers were allowed only one blanket, forty cartridges, and the clothing on their backs. In addition, Crook placed eleven companies of white cavalry to watch over various points of the border and to ensure that no Chiricahuas slipped past him.[33]

As Crook prepared for the field, Colonel Garcia had followed the trail left by fifteen Chiricahuas after they raided for stock at Oputo. He ran into an ambush in the Sierra Madre on April 24. As many as one hundred Chiricahua fighters fought together, and they were well-armed following Chatto's raid. Blasting the Mexicans approaching the mesa from their cover, the first Apache contingent drove the intruders back while another Apache force pounded the Mexicans' right flank below them. A third outfit of Chiricahuas rolled rocks from the crest down on the Mexican troops in the lower positions. The Mexican command was badly shattered, but managed to regroup and avoid annihilation. The young Betzinez was impressed. "Our sharpshooters . . . were just a little too much for" the Mexicans, he observed. The Chiricahuas had successfully repelled the invaders. But unknown to them, as in April 1882, another army was fast approaching.[34]

On May 15, 1883, Crook made contact in the Sierra Madre when Apache troops stormed a Chiricahua camp. They took possession of the village, killing nine people, seizing most of its materials, and capturing one woman and four children.[35] While warriors were largely absent from the camp, Crook's attack did test the combat motivation of many Chiricahuas. Years later Geronimo explained that the numbers of troops sent against them in the Sierra Madre "were so much greater than ours that we could not hope to fight them successfully, and we were tired of being chased about from place to place." In fact, already before Crook's attack, some Chiricahuas had contemplated going back to the reservation. They had dispatched two men, who reached Fort Thomas, Arizona, on April 29, 1883, to scout the prevailing mood regarding their possible return. Also in late April, twenty-one Chihennes, mainly relatives of Loco, had enough and left the Sierra Madre. They reached San Carlos a month later, surrendering to the military.[36]

Meanwhile, the situation at the Sierra Madre remained tense. As Chiricahua fighters gradually returned, soldiers not only switched campsites repeatedly for the sake of forage and to avoid possible Apache assault but mulled over the best plan of attack, if that would become necessary. According to Bourke, the Chiricahuas were armed with Winchesters and pistols of the latest model. They also mostly kept to the high ground and could potentially try a siege or the use of sharpshooters against the troops. On the other hand, Bourke also noted that the Chiricahuas seemed to have little ammunition to spare.[37] Probably they had exhausted their cartridges against Garcia and had yet to resupply. Soldiers also outnumbered the Chiricahua fighters and most of the troops were Apaches.

Yet the situation for the Chiricahuas was still far from hopeless. Crook and his command stood in a precarious spot, as they now fed those Chiricahua women and children who in small parties surrendered. By May 19, one hundred Chiricahuas already camped with the army, and more followed in the days to come. Geronimo returned on May 20 and felt he still had enough leverage to enter negotiations and demand terms. While Crook and Bourke fail to mention it, Apache recruit John Rope noted that the general went hunting that day and was caught by Geronimo and his men. Scholars have pondered whether Crook let himself be captured so as to get the talks going, but remain conflicted on what exactly happened. Nevertheless, the Chiricahuas and Crook apparently talked for few hours and then came to the military camp to continue discussions.[38] The records of these meetings display a taciturn and confident Crook who acted as if he had nothing to offer, stood ready to exterminate the Chiricahuas at any moment, and could not care less of their ideas of surrendering. Crook, like many officers, believed that if they showed any fear to the Apaches, the game was lost. He did not disarm the Chiricahuas and made it appear that it was a personal favor if he agreed to take them back to San Carlos.[39]

In reality, Crook faced narrow options. The surprise factor was long gone, and Crook could expect little success if the Chiricahuas opted to bolt. Crook also held a general understanding on what had happened to Garcia's troops just few weeks before, and thus he realized that a fight against all Chiricahuas on their home terrain could prove very costly, even with Western Apaches on his side.[40] It has to be remembered that the Sierra Madre represented an unfamiliar territory for most Western Apaches, many of who came from communities that had last actively raided in Mexico in the 1860s and whose homelands were in central Arizona. Chase in the rugged mountains would most likely prove futile, only scattering the Chiricahuas. If the Chiricahuas would escape, the press would make Crook look like a blundering fool while his superiors would question his dependence on Apache troops. Furthermore, he knew that the situation could potentially explode at any moment. For example, on May 22 or 23, the Chiricahuas wanted to hold a dance and invited the Western Apache soldiers to dance with their women. The plan apparently was to gun down the Apache soldiers as they danced and thus gain the upper hand. Probably oblivious to the plot, Al Sieber, the white chief of scouts, refused permission for the Apache troops to participate in the dance on the account that one of them had died that day.[41]

Rather than demand an unconditional surrender, Crook offered amnesty for past crimes and return to the reservation. In his reports, Crook claimed that the thoroughly demoralized Chiricahuas gave themselves up at his mercy. He added, "It is now too late to punish them for past atrocities . . . without sacrificing the interests of the present." To "fight" all the Chiricahua combatants "would be to endanger the life of every" rancher and miner and "would ruin many important interests" in the borderlands, Crook also explained. It was almost as if he was apologizing for his "soft" goals. Being in a hurry to depart before some unfortunate clash of violence might undo everything, Crook indicated that his troops were running short on rations and could not wait for the Chiricahuas to gather all their people, who, the Chiricahuas claimed, had dispersed after the May 15 fight. In reality, Thrapp observes, "Crook had no means, except psychological pressure, to force the Apaches to return to the United States." He had to merely accept the Chiricahua headmen's word that they would return to Arizona at their own pace. This proved acceptable for the Chiricahuas. They still could imagine they were their own bosses.[42]

Returning to Arizona on June with his 325 Chiricahua prisoners, mainly women and children but also Loco and Nana, Crook triumphantly declared victory. "This was one of the boldest and most successful strokes ever achieved by an officer of the United States Army," Bourke claimed. Although Tucson hosted a banquet in Crook's honor, substantial criticism also surfaced at once. Many saw Crook's invasion as not the superior success he and Bourke painted it to be. With Crook arrived armed, undefeated, Apaches. Worst, Geronimo, Chatto, Naiche, and Chihuahua, indeed most of the first-class fighters, remained absent. Their word as given to Crook did not have much value for many borderlands whites. Obviously the icy reaction infuriated Crook and his entourage. Crook was "made the target of every sort of malignant and mendacious assault," Bourke fumed, claiming that Arizona business interests could not stand the possible reduction of troops or Chiricahuas becoming self-supporting, as that would kill their profits.[43] But it seems that the critique centered on the absence of Chiricahua leaders or on Crook's decision to bring the Chiricahuas back to U.S. soil in the first place. The borderlands citizens had expected that Crook would at least hit the Chiricahuas hard before bringing back the survivors. As months went by with no signs of Geronimo or Chatto, it became obvious to all that the Chiricahuas remained an independent military power, raiding in Mexico, and free to show up in Arizona when they wanted to.

Crook was also blamed for failing to ascertain the fate of Charlie McComas, which remained the subject of gossip and speculation in the borderlands and beyond. Eager to learn the fate of Charlie, Crook and his men had made inquiries after the May 15 fight but had failed to get a definite answer from the Chiricahuas, who told him that the boy had run away after the clash. To confuse the matter,

Mexican intelligence variously claimed that Charlie was alive but far away, slaughtered in a fight against Mexican forces, or killed in a retreat after the May 15 fight. Years after the search for Charlie had died down, one Apache told that a Chiricahua whose mother had been killed in the May 15 attack had taken revenge by killing Charlie on the same day.[44]

Civilizing Mission

During winter and spring 1883–84, small Chiricahua groups, one by one, arrived at the border, from which point U.S. troops escorted the newcomers to the reservation. Kept first at the San Carlos Agency, the Chiricahuas settled in their new homes at Turkey Creek, a tributary of the Black River forty miles northeast of San Carlos, in May 1884. Entrusted with the police control of the reservation as well as full authority over the Chiricahuas, the army again played a visible role at San Carlos. Reservation management obviously called for different kind of force than operations in the field. Disarmament of the Chiricahuas and posting a large body of soldiers led by several seasoned officers in or near Turkey Creek would sound like a potential way for the army to claim authority. But it was not Crook's way, who felt that the Apaches must be shown at all times that the army exercised absolute power. "Authority," "control," "subordination," "regeneration," and "advancement" were the keywords in Crook's thinking. In his words, the Chiricahuas were unruly "children in ignorance, not in innocence," who needed a strict yet fair parent to maintain firm discipline.[45]

Daily management at Turkey Creek was entrusted to Lt. Britton Davis, whose familiarity with the Chiricahuas consisted of escorting some of the recent arrivals, including Geronimo, from the Mexican border to the reservation. With his Apache recruits, most of them Chiricahuas, and two interpreters, Sam Bowman and Mickey Free, Davis did not enjoy much freedom in policy implementation.[46] He was to follow Crook's plan of making the Chiricahuas individual farmers who could participate in the market with their produce and have opportunities to spend their earnings. For many whites, farming was quintessential to civilization, a step upward in evolution from nomadic barbarism. Farming also entailed the reordering of Chiricahua gender roles and division of labor by placing men into farm work and women into the domestic sphere. This was a tough sell in a time when the cornerstones of Chiricahua masculine identity—war, raiding, and hunting—had been recently obstructed. Further eroding its popularity, Crook's policy did not include listening or respecting the views of Chiricahua men.[47]

Turkey Creek, being in high altitude, with pleasant climate, cool running water, grass, and some tall pines, was a healthier location than the agency of San Carlos. It had no mosquitoes, few rattlesnakes, and, importantly, Apaches pointed out, no cavalry. Still, life for the Chiricahuas coming to terms with their loss of sovereignty proved challenging. For one, Turkey Creek had less-than-ideal surroundings for farming, although eventually the Chiricahuas got to planting and tilling fields of barley and corn on the east fork of the White River.[48] Moreover, not only was Davis steadfast in making the Apaches farmers, but, following Crook's guidelines, he launched a temperance campaign. He outlawed the manufacture and consumption of the Apaches' brew, tiswin. Also, to recast the Apache gender roles successfully, Davis felt that the Apache women needed to be rescued from their "tyrannical" husbands, whose practice of cutting the noses of cheating wives had to stop. Thus, rather than appease the proud Chiricahua men or hear their side of the story, Davis sought to curtail male authority over unfaithful spouses by listening and recording Apache women's complaints. He also launched investigations on his own, apprehended suspects, questioning them publicly, and handed out punishment on his own authority. In Chiricahua understanding, the relation between a husband and a wife was a deeply private matter in which the army had no business interfering. What Davis was doing not only offended the Apache husbands' sense of fairness and justice but emasculated them. As for Davis's tiswin hunts, while the Chiricahuas naturally recognized that excessive use of alcohol caused many problems, they obviously knew that soldiers and others in the borderlands drank and wondered why they should bow to different rules.[49]

What the Chiricahuas faced at Turkey Creek represented quite a different reality than the negotiations in the Sierra Madre had implied. At Turkey Creek, Geronimo felt betrayed and insulted upon arrival, as the army took away the cattle he had stolen and driven from Mexico. "These were not white men's cattle, but belonged to us. . . . We did not intend to kill these animals, but . . . wished to keep them and raise stock," he later remembered, adding that the military "would not listen to me, but took the stock." Furthermore, when the Chiricahua leaders almost unanimously voiced their opposition to the rules concerning domestic intrusions and the tiswin ban, Davis felt that the dissatisfaction of the Chiricahuas grew "out of their own worthlessness" and determination "not to be punished for offenses committed on the reservation."[50]

Davis also organized a network of spies to unearth any opposition and made Mickey Free, the boy (now grown) whose kidnapping had brought trouble to the

Chokonens in 1861, and Chatto, whom Geronimo and others saw as a power-hungry upstart, his confidants. This move further galvanized a relatively small, yet militarily potent, section of the Chiricahua community, who already felt affronted. Also, it did not take long for the spies to become open knowledge. Davis, with the help of four troops of cavalry from Fort Apache, also arrested the Chihenne Kaytennae, describing him as openly antagonistic and surly. He was sentenced in absentia to three years of imprisonment for starting an uprising. In the trial, Capt. Emmett Crawford, the army representative at San Carlos, had acted as prosecutor and judge and a group of San Carlos Apaches, eager to please Crawford, served as the jury. It seems that Kaytennae did not have an opportunity to defend himself before being sent to Alcatraz Island on San Francisco Bay, a location beyond the known world of the Apaches. For a people who for generations had been painfully familiar with captive deportation to unknown reaches in central Mexico and beyond, this must have been very alarming. Rumors of Kaytennae's death were circulated, according to James Kaywaykla, the stepson of Kaytennae, by Chatto, who also reportedly made claims that the army would return to kill or imprison Geronimo, Nana, and Chihuahua. It was little wonder that the three experienced fighters kept, in Kaywaykla's words, "expecting trouble all the time."[51]

Haunted by past memories and sensing the intense hatred that prevailed among borderlands residents toward the Chiricahuas, Geronimo especially was concerned that he would be handed over to trial in civil courts. In that case, he would be publicly humiliated, rendered symbolically impotent and helpless, and hanged. Then, he dreaded, his body would be placed on public display by the whites or, worse, decapitated like that of Mangas Coloradas. In neither case would he have peace in the afterlife. He was determined to do almost anything to avoid such a fate.[52]

Fed up, Geronimo, Chihuahua, and approximately thirty Chiricahua men started a tiswin drunk on May 13, 1885. For much of the night, they discussed how they could not submit to all demanded of them. The next morning this tired but determined group represented their case to Davis, testing once more if the young lieutenant would hear their side of the story. "We agreed on a peace with Americans, Mexicans, and other Indian tribes; [we said] nothing about [our] conduct among [ourselves]," they argued. The Chiricahuas had a point. Nothing had been said about private lives in the Sierra Madre negotiations. But from past experience, the Chiricahuas already knew that the army usually did what it saw fit when it came to orchestrating Apache lives. Still, this party challenged Davis by claiming that they all had been drunk during the night and by asking if the lieutenant had a cell large enough for them all. Davis was taken aback, telling his audience that he would inform Crook and ask his advice on the matter.[53]

As they later explained what had gone wrong, many in the army emphasized the restless nature of the Chiricahuas and the problems resulting from divided authority and the interference of civilian Indian agents in reservation management. Yet, the Chiricahuas battled much more pressing concerns. Shortage of farming enthusiasm and success; intrusions reaching the most private and personal areas of their lives; distrust—even hatred—toward Davis, Chatto, and Free and their unjust rule; rumors of impending trial in the hands of local civilians; as well as fear of retribution due to tiswin drinking all poisoned the atmosphere and made some opt for a departure.

Geronimo Campaign

With Mangas, the son of Mangas Coloradas and a minor leader, whispering rumors of soldiers drawing closer, Geronimo was among the most eager to go. He in turn convinced Naiche and Chihuahua. When dictating his memoirs twenty years later, Geronimo said he had thought it "more manly to die on the warpath than to be killed in prison." He also added, "I firmly believe that he [Crook] did issue the orders for me to be put in prison, or to be killed in case I offered resistance."[54] Despite intense lobbying, Geronimo had trouble selling the idea of escape to his fellow Chiricahuas. Bitter, he threatened to return to the reservation later and kill those who would not instantly join him. For those with fresh memories of the abduction of Loco's Chihennes in 1882, this must have seemed like valid threat. Geronimo reportedly also told them that the plan for the assassination of Davis was already in the works. Fear of retaliation from the army made some of those still hesitant to bolt. Nevertheless, on May 17, only an estimated thirty-five to forty-two men and ninety-two women and children of the more than five hundred Chiricahuas left the reservation. More than fifty Chiricahua men soon enlisted in the army, while, of those who had at first stayed on the reservation, approximately half enlisted during the later phases of the 1885–86 campaign.[55]

The army response was probably quicker than ever before but still awfully cumbersome when compared to the speed and skill of the fleeing Chiricahuas. Although the Chiricahuas had cut the telegraph wire connecting to the department headquarters, the army discovered the break during the first twenty-four hours and news got out fast. In two days, the whole nation knew of the event. By that time, cavalry outfits guarded the usual Chiricahua routes across the border: Fort Grant troops at San Simon Valley, Fort Bowie taking watch at Doubtful Canyon and Stein's Pass, and Fort Huachuca men patrolling Guadalupe and Skeleton Canyons. Several cavalry units from Forts Bayard and Wingate also traversed the upper Gila River, Mogollon and Mimbres Mountains, and the Black Range, while one company watched Cooke's Canyon. Even troops as east as Fort Stanton were ordered to patrol the banks of the Rio Grande in case the Chiricahuas would head in that direction. At least twenty troops of cavalry, one thousand soldiers, and between one hundred and two hundred Apache recruits were active in the field following the Chiricahua escape.[56]

The pursuing units still fell behind from the start. When Davis heard of Geronimo's departure at 4 P.M. on May 17, he sent a telegram to Lt. Charles Gatewood to bring the Western Apache soldiers from Fort Apache. Gatewood, as well as two companies of the Fourth Cavalry commanded by Capt. Allen Smith and Lt. James Parker, departed at 7 P.M. and found Davis still at Turkey Creek. Davis apparently had hesitated to start the pursuit on his own, possibly feeling unsure about the loyalty of his Chiricahua recruits. By now, the fleeing Chiricahuas were at least fifteen or twenty miles away. Careful not to land in an ambush, the troops advanced gingerly during the difficult descent and ascent at Bonito Canyon. The result: a soldier with a broken leg and several horses unfit to continue. After halting for one hour to reassemble the command, the pursuit was on again. Later that night scouts reported that they had seen the Chiricahuas crossing the Black River. The troops decided to wait and cross the river in the morning. With morning came more delays as more horses had to be left behind. When the command finally reached the river in broad daylight, scouts again told them to hurry up, as they had sighted the Chiricahuas just a few miles away crossing the fourteen-mile-long Prieto Plateau. Slowing their pace was the fact that the troops could not run their animals into the ground, whereas the fleeing Chiricahuas changed mounts frequently by stealing new ones along the way. Moving hard, the Chiricahuas traveled an estimated ninety-five miles that first night and full day, while the army managed a respectable, and unusual, sixty to sixty-five miles.

As the pursued reached the Mogollon Mountains, they climbed up into them and hid for a rest. With Chiricahua sentries watching their pursuers from up the mountain walls, the soldiers in turn were able, with their field glasses, to eye the mountaineering Chiricahuas in the far distance. The distance separating the two parties was just eight to ten miles. It was as close as the army got during the initial pursuit. But rather than push on, the soldiers camped. Failing to catch the Chiricahuas, the exhausted and hungry troops had nevertheless outdistanced their packtrain and now had to wait for their food to catch up. The chase commenced afresh in the mountains the following morning. By May 20, the escaping Chiricahuas were already perhaps fifty miles ahead.[57]

In the Mogollons, the Chiricahuas divided into several smaller groups and scattered over the roughest country. The split was not just a strategic one but reflected disharmony, as Chihuahua and Naiche were furious with Geronimo for bullying them into leaving the reservation.[58] The troops under Smith, Parker, and Gatewood continued their chase, discovering en route the bodies of four ranchers and prospectors killed by the rapidly moving Chiricahuas. "All these men were buried and we became very expert in the business," Parker recollected. He continued, "There was no opportunity to dig graves, but there were plenty of loose rocks and so at the command . . . 'bury this man' . . . each dismounted man, picking up a heavy stone, placed it on the corpse until it was hidden from sight. Then we mounted and marched on."[59]

Fearful of ambush, the soldiers nevertheless soon ran into Apaches unsuspectedly in a narrow canyon on the banks of Devil's Creek as the pursuers and the pursued accidentally camped in close proximity to each other. Detecting the soldiers first, the Chiricahuas faced a choice: retreat quietly and abandon the large quantities of meat they were drying or launch a strike against a much larger force following them. Perhaps they felt constrained, thinking their women and children needed time to escape. It is also possible that the Chiricahuas could not resist the temptation of striking the unready foe camped in a disadvantageous position. In his memoirs, Parker, who felt that the situation and their position invited attack, blamed his superior, Captain Smith. When gunshots broke out from the adjacent heights, Smith, together with another officer, were some distance away taking baths. Other officers and the troopers in turn rested carelessly on opposite banks of the creek. After initial confusion, advancing troops running the steep slopes to the top drove back the Chiricahuas, who scattered in every direction. The troops also took the Chiricahua camp, seizing clothing, meat, and other belongings. On Smith's order, the troops then stopped pursuit. The next day Apache signs led toward the Black Range. Much to Parker's dismay, Smith reasoned that their supplies would not suffice to continue the hunt, which now led into such a "wild country." The troops instead turned toward Fort Bayard.[60]

Soon thereafter it became apparent that most of the Chiricahua contingent had reached Mexico. Crook, who had moved his headquarters to Fort Bowie in order to be closer to the action, posted troops along the border to intercept the Apaches should they try to return. In New Mexico, several companies of the Sixth and Eighth Cavalries and the Tenth Infantry and in Arizona troopers of the Fourth Cavalry made up the first line, being stationed at water holes and passes along the border. To make sure that the enemy would not slip through, each detachment included five indigenous soldiers for reconnaissance purposes. The African American soldiers of the Tenth Cavalry formed the second line farther north. A third line of infantrymen were positioned on the Southern Pacific Railroad line, while the troops at Forts Thomas, Grant, and Bayard effectively constituted a fourth line.[61]

Simply waiting in defensive positions was not enough. Instead, a vigorous, initiative-grabbing offensive that snubbed the international border was needed to appease the press and the superiors in distant Washington. Also, sick of Apache raiding, Mexico seemed to tolerate such a temporary Anglo invasion, although the use of Apache troops did strain the diplomatic goodwill. The army's hunt for the Chiricahuas was spearheaded by two mobile and independent task forces that consisted of a troop of white cavalry and approximately one hundred Apache soldiers each. These columns, led by Crawford, reassigned from Texas on Crook's request, and Capt. Wirt Davis were set to make Chiricahua life hell wherever they went in northern Mexico.

For most white and black soldiers, the daily life of the campaign proved less than life-threatening, thrilling, or motivating. Guarding water holes, mountain passes, and other strategic locations, they endured irksome and monotonous days. For instance, Lt. John Bigelow and his Tenth Cavalry troopers spent the latter half of 1885 mainly on the lookout at the Tempest and Mowry Mines. For much of the time, Bigelow, in his words, stayed inside his tent "sitting or lying" and oftentimes reading. On August 15, a rare thing happened and Bigelow's soldiers rode out toward the village of Lochiel to find reported Apache signs. Not only did they miss the mark when it came to the Apaches, but Bigelow finished his day in a local Mexican baile. The festivities, the lieutenant noted, deprived him of all but three hours of sleep.[62]

Those troops on the move found their daily life not as relaxed as Bigelow's but perhaps even less interesting. For instance, from June 16 to July 2, 1885, Lieutenant Gatewood and his Western Apaches still scouted the upper Gila River. They were in search of Mangas. "Up one hill and down another would sum up the whole thing," Gatewood scripted to his wife. He found no Apaches but plenty of white civilians, who were either wild with fear, eager to make a buck at soldiers' expense, or thirsting for revenge and wanting to kill the Apache troops. "Few are friendly toward the troops," Gatewood ruminated, "unless they can sell things."[63]

The experience was considerably more taxing physically for the officers and soldiers in the two mobiles columns canvassing northern Mexico. Sweating under the broiling sun, drenching under thundering summer rainstorms, and negotiating rugged canyons and steep mountains as well as choking sand deserts, noteworthy fighting triumphs evaded them. Between June and October, the two strike teams clashed with Chiricahua cells on five occasions. While not suffering significant losses in manpower, the Chiricahua summer was one of running, riding, and raiding. After Crawford's and Chatto's Apache soldiers hit on Chihuahua's camp on the Bavispe River in June, the second major skirmish took place on August 7, as a detachment of Apache soldiers from Wirt Davis's command decimated Geronimo's camp at Bugatseka and captured fifteen women and children, including Geronimo's family. Losing their family members as captives was of course nothing new, but still it caused a significant blow and threatened the functionality of daily lives, which depended on the organizational and labor skills of women.[64]

It is of little surprise that Geronimo focused on retrieving his family. Assuming he would find them at San Carlos, with four to six Chiricahua fighters Geronimo headed for the reservation. While the army knew that the Chiricahuas had crossed the border, it speculated that they might seek new recruits among the Mescaleros or even among the Navajos. Geronimo outwitted the military, at first advancing quietly. When he realized that avoiding whites in the mining country around the Mimbres River was impossible, he started to loot and kill isolated targets, before disappearing in the Mogollon Mountains in reaches inaccessible to whites. Meanwhile, the reservation was put on high alert in the case of a pending attack. Reservation Chiricahuas moved closer to Fort Apache, while White Mountain Apache camps resembled armed fortresses. Geronimo nevertheless slipped past the Apache soldiers patrolling the boundaries, caught one of his several wives, stole horses from the White Mountains Apaches, and left as silently as he had arrived.[65]

During the summer, reports that inflated Apache losses filtered back to Crook from officers in Mexico, who, Angie Debo observes, were either too eager for promotion or uncertain about what actually took place among the canyons and rocks. For example, Nana and Geronimo were erroneously reported killed after the August 7 clash. Angered by the inaccurate information and lack of decisive results, Crook and some of his officers vocally criticized the regular soldiers for being unable to find the enemy trails or keep up with the Apaches. While Crook's official reports commended the Apache recruits, his unpublished correspondence also blamed the White Mountain and Cibecue soldiers for apathy and lack of commitment. It was as if Crook took their failure to catch Geronimo's party during its excursion into Fort Apache as a personal insult. From now on he would more openly favor the Chiricahuas in recruitment.[66]

Crook also remained active on other fronts during the pressing situation. He recognized that much had changed in the borderlands since the Victorio campaign and especially since the early 1870s, and that a prolonged war could prove disastrous for the army and the borderlands citizens. The commanding general of the army, Philip Sheridan, also acknowledged the changing circumstances and the increased gravity of the situation in his dispatches, "Previously to three years ago the scene of these Apache raids was sparsely settled, and the loss of life and property was, consequently, much less than during the present outbreak.... Now the Indians obtain all they desire in the way of animals without difficulty, as large herds are located at every spring and water-hole, and every few miles mounts of fresh horses are at their service," he wrote. Crook also kept open diplomatic lines with Sonora's governor Luis Torres, initiated a bounty of one hundred dollars for the head of any "hostile" Chiricahuas, and got full authority in the reservation after threatening to withdraw his troops if divided control would not be abolished. He also wrested the military command of the District of New Mexico, which had belonged to the Department of the Missouri since the Civil War, for himself.[67]

Meanwhile, the task force under Wirt Davis had continued the chase and struck a Chiricahua encampment at Teres Mountains, Sonora, on September 22. Next, a party of Chiricahuas led by Naiche and Chihuahua trekked north of the border in search of supplies. With Apache soldiers on their tail and several cavalry companies placed in spots where the army believed it could ambush the raiders, the Chiricahuas stole fresh mounts and escaped without injury. Crook did his best to cast the latest episode in a favorable light: the Chiricahuas found "that it was impossible to get north of the railroad" due to army pressure and "returned to Mexico," he wrote.[68]

Still, it was evident to all that even then the army's mobile units were too clumsy and ineffective against the Chiricahua fighters to achieve crucial results quickly. The conflict was taking new forms. The Chiricahuas dispersed to ever-tinier factions not only when actively pursued by their enemies. Crook noticed how the Chiricahuas "act differently than ever before, are split up in small bands and constantly on the watch. The trails are so scattered that it is almost impossible to follow them." He also asserted, "Unless aided by some stroke of good fortune, it will take years to kill all these hostiles situated as they are. . . . It is believed they could be induced to surrender after a little more hammering, if they are assured their lives would not be forfeited and that they would simply be transported [from the Southwest]."[69]

While Wirt Davis and Crawford returned to U.S. soil to rest, resupply, and recruit new Apache soldiers, Chihuahua's party of Apaches emptied the ranches of southern New Mexico of livestock while Josanie (Ulzana), accompanied by ten warriors, slipped past the troops and moved toward Fort Apache in search of ammunition and revenge. Their specific target was Chatto and his family, who, expecting danger, had relocated to the post. After having one of their combatants killed, Josanie's party took the lives of twenty-one White Mountain Apaches. They also stole a herd of reservation horses. Facing two Chiricahua scares in a matter of months, the furious White Mountain Apaches wanted to wipe out the reservation Chiricahuas. Sensing this, Loco secretly met Gatewood, who was in charge of the Indians around Fort Apache, and asked permission to move to the fort for protection. Worried that violence might break out between the different Apache groups under his management, Gatewood, who was also confronted by the angry White Mountain men questioning why he protected the Chiricahuas, was deeply concerned. Resorting to a compromise, Gatewood told the Chiricahuas to move to a safe zone in the proximity of the post outside of which the White Mountain Apaches were free to kill any Chiricahua they met.[70] This, apparently, eased the tensions.

While Chihuahua's raiders returned south of the border, Josanie's fighters used the safe reaches of the Mogollon Mountains for a series of strikes against ranches north of Silver City. On December 9, they suffered a rare setback, losing their recently acquired material wealth to Lt. Samuel Fountain's cavalry troop. Ten days later, however, Fountain's command, in turn, lost much property and the lives of four soldiers when ambushed by the Chiricahuas, who had in the meantime already resupplied themselves by thumping a ranch near the road at Little Dry Creek. As Josanie's party headed toward Mexico later that month, army reports summed its exploits: in eight weeks the Chiricahua raiders had traversed approximately 1,200 miles, killed thirty-eight people, and stolen nearly 250 horses—all with the loss of only one man killed by the White Mountain Apaches in the reservation.[71]

Bitter and outraged, many borderlands residents felt that these types of lighting raids could continue indefinitely. Representatives of Cochise County in southeastern Arizona filed official petitions to government officials, and letters from startled citizens filled the mailboxes at the White House and Congress. Most demanded tougher actions against the Chiricahuas. Many Arizona papers, displaying little sympathy toward the operational problems the military faced, directed their anger equally toward the Apaches and the soldiers. For example, in its May 30, 1885, issue the *Arizona Weekly Citizen* speculated that "people should rise up and forever wipe out that fester upon the fair face of our land of sunshine, the Apaches on the White Mountain reservation." The paper also ridiculed the "incompetent and impotent force of lazy soldiery." Seven days earlier the *Arizona Silver Belt* had pointed out somewhat sarcastically, "The Chiricahuas, notwithstanding General Crook's oft-repeated published assurance that they were blissfully happy and resting contentedly under his wing, have again turned their back upon Uncle Sam's flesh pots."[72]

In late November, General Sheridan arrived at Fort Bowie to confer with Crook. It was highly exceptional that the commanding general traveled to Arizona field headquarters in the midst of active operations. Naturally, better transportation facilities made the visit more feasible than in years past, but still the appearance of Sheridan speaks to the amounting anxiety felt by the federal executive. The inability to catch Geronimo and others right at the start in May, the ambushes at Devil's Creek and Guadalupe Canyon (see chapter 3), and all the futile chases and inconclusive strikes in Mexico during the summer months, not to mention Geronimo's and Josanie's bold incursions right through Crook's leaky defenses, made for a heightened crisis.[73]

Already in October Sheridan and Secretary of War William C. Endicott, following Crook's suggestions, had established the government's policy toward the independent Chiricahuas. They should be allowed to surrender unconditionally as prisoners of war to be transmitted to some distant point. At Fort Bowie, Sheridan, doubting their loyalty, not merely critiqued Crook's dependence on Apache soldiers but suggested that removal of all Chiricahuas would be needed to end the conflict.[74] Despite their red headbands, which functioned as marks of identification, Apache soldiers had been mistaken as hostiles by the Mexicans. Accidental shootings, exchange of fire between Mexicans and Apache soldiers, arrests of not only Apache soldiers but of Anglo officers by Mexican authorities, individual disobedience, drunkenness, and disputes over captured booty had taken place during the summer campaign in Mexico.[75] Then there surfaced arguments that the Western Apache soldiers feared the Chiricahuas or that the Chiricahua soldiers in turn did not want to kill their tribesmen. The times when Apache soldiers attacked prematurely seems to support at least the latter interpretation, as do the remarks made by some Apaches on the military payroll. On the other hand, the intense factions within the Chiricahua community suggest how sensitive a subject working for the military had become. Geronimo and others hated Chatto and saw him and others as traitors and regarded the red headband as a symbol of servitude, while some of those Chiricahuas who stayed on the reservation and/or enlisted viewed Geronimo and others as irresponsible bandits who caused Apaches to fight Apaches and who brought all sorts of troubles on their own people.[76]

Even if the Apache recruits did not aim to kill their brethren, it is possible that this was less consequential for Crook, who sought Apache surrender rather than a war of extermination and the greater casualties it would have brought to both sides. During their talks at Fort Bowie, Crook and Crawford both assured Sheridan that Apache soldiers were essential for success and that any removal would badly sap their morale and compromise their efficiency. Sheridan decided to backtrack on the matter and support Crook, for the time being.[77] Resupplied and rested, the two columns under Wirt Davis and Crawford returned to Mexico by year's end to continue the search for the Chiricahuas. Meanwhile, the Mexican response continued to be marred, as it had been since May. Disputes between some of its leading generals and the demands of the ongoing Yaqui conflict had led to problems in force allocation. Thus the Mexican pressure on the Apaches was significantly weaker than it had been in 1883 or during the Victorio wars. The American effort also seemed to fumble. Canvassing the eastern base of the Sierra Madre, Davis broke down his men, his packtrains, and his own health. In January, he had to return to Fort Bowie for medical treatment. This left Crawford, whose force at this time consisted exclusively of Apache recruits, many of them Chiricahuas. In January, Crawford's men not only struck a Chiricahua camp at Aros River, capturing horses, food, and camp equipment, but managed to open communications with Geronimo and Chihuahua. While a subsequent clash between Mexican irregulars and the Apache soldiers led to Crawford's death, the Chiricahuas managed to get a message to Crook that they wished to talk.[78]

The meeting at Canyon de Los Embudos took place in March. Crook applied his familiar taciturn tactics, vowing that he would keep after the Chiricahuas "and kill the last one, if it takes fifty years." He also discredited Geronimo's explanations and grievances of life at Turkey Creek as lies, which deeply offended the Chiricahua, who upheld, "I am a man of my word. I am telling the truth."

On the third day of the meeting, Crook largely ignored Geronimo and sought to influence Chihuahua and Naiche instead. He also had the Apache soldiers going around the camps trying to persuade the Chiricahuas to give up. Still, it was the Chiricahuas, not Crook, who held the upper hand. They had insisted that no white or black troops accompany Crook to the meeting in northern Mexico, and thus none did. Also, they would not give up their weapons, and they would camp where it suited them, a place which turned out to be atop a small rocky hill amid a lava bed surrounded by deep ravines—in other words, a perfect natural fortification. Nor could the soldiers prevent the independent Apaches from drinking more than enough mescal. Importantly, the Chiricahuas also categorically refused Crook's proposition of unconditional surrender. They would keep fighting or return to the reservation.

Needing results, Crook proposed that the Chiricahuas would go east for two years imprisonment (with their families), after which they would return to San Carlos. As all agreed, Crook, who had exceeded his authority, hurried ahead to Fort Bowie to get Sheridan's views via telegraph. His terms were firmly rejected by Washington. Crook was urged to renegotiate and press for unconditional surrender. Meanwhile, en route to the fort the still-cagey Chiricahuas, rather than march as body, scattered. They also camped at a distance from the Apache soldiers and had some of their men at all times off camp keeping watch. Geronimo, always one of the more alert ones and also offended by Crook's attitude and unforgiving words, evidently got drunk from mescal sold to him by a border peddler, had a change of heart, and escaped with eighteen fighters and sixteen women and children.[79]

Hearing that Geronimo had ran away once more, Sheridan again questioned Crook's use of Apache troops and in no uncertain terms told Crook to make more use of the thousands of white and black soldiers he commanded. His chosen strategy censured, Crook assured his superiors that his methods would finally prove effective. He also selected to test his mandate by asking to be relieved of his command if his methods were judged improper. Crook's request was granted without delay. The general felt both stunned and humiliated, especially after he realized that his successor in Arizona would be one his staunchest rivals and critics, Gen. Nelson A. Miles. As for the seventy-six Chiricahuas, including Chihuahua, who did surrender, they never learned that the terms of their peace had been rejected. They bid farewell to Arizona on April 7, 1886, and climbed aboard a train heading to Florida. They were prisoners of war.[80]

Race War

A decade had passed since the national embarrassment at Little Bighorn. It was crucial that the summer of 1886 not replicate that of 1876 as a massive army failure. This time there was little possibility of a massive massacre, but not getting Geronimo and his tiny Chiricahua bunch could prove just as upsetting to a continental powerhouse that stretched from ocean to ocean. Washington not only emphasized to Miles how "the greatest care [is to] be taken to prevent the spread of hostilities among friendly Indians in your command, and . . . the most vigorous operations looking to the destruction or capture of the hostiles [are to] be ceaselessly carried on." Just to make sure he realized why exactly Crook was gone, Miles was also reminded of the "necessity of making active and prominent use of the regular troops of your command."[81] Although the orders left the details for Miles to contemplate, they made absolutely certain that regular—white (preferably) and black—troops must recapture the spotlight and victory must be accomplished quickly through their efforts, while the role of the Apache recruits was to be reduced to mere reconnaissance. Miles was also supposed to shun Crook's "softer" goals by destroying the enemy, while being on guard against any general Apache outbreak. Raising the stakes, the federal government turned the borderlands wars into a race war.

On the one hand, Miles was delighted to upstage his contender, Crook. For an officer wanting military glory and personal advancement through success in Indians wars—and Miles certainly fit the description—the Apache conflict represented one of the last chances there was in an empire built on Indian wars.[82] Still, in private Miles acknowledged the weight placed on him. "In many respects this is the most difficult task I have ever undertaken, on account of the extensive country, the natural difficulties and the fact that the hostiles are so few in number and yet so active," he wrote to his wife. Shortly after his arrival to Fort Bowie, he exploded at the local press, claiming that its inflated and unsubstantiated reports made it seem that the whole area was bursting of Chiricahuas gunning for whites. Writing home, he admitted that the troops were very much discouraged and thoroughly disheartened, even so much so that they had very little hope of ultimate success. Thus, battling low morale, baffled by a skillful adversary, preyed upon by a sensationalist press, constrained by his orders to rely on white soldiers, and tormented by his own career ambitions, which included notions of grandeur reaching all the way to the White House, Miles dreaded the prospect of an embarrassing failure.[83]

Wanting to convey an appearance of dynamism and activity, Miles quickly subdivided the borderlands into twenty-seven districts of observation. He assigned the infantrymen to important mountain passes, ranches, and other strategic locations as well as guarding the supplies. He also organized white cavalry into light scouting parties expected to be in constant readiness. He also tried to make the white troops better respond to Chiricahua mobility by instructing those commands in close pursuit to dismount as much as one-half of their soldiers so that the best riders could make chase until all the animals in the command were exhausted. Officers were also told to continue pursuit until capture or until assured that another command was on the trail. However, it is uncertain if Miles had enough horses to implement this method of pursuit. Miles also covered his districts with a network of heliographic stations. In the land of intense sunshine, clear air, and soaring mountain ranges surrounded by level plains, heliographic observation points were thought to cater to the military's advantage by effectively detecting and communicating Chiricahua movements to fast-moving units patrolling the borderland.[84] How efficient the heliographs were the army never found out, as the last Chiricahua raids north of the border took place before the stations were in full operation in the summer. Furthermore, at this time Chiricahua parties usually traveled by night when on U.S. soil to avoid detection.

On the ground it was the familiar cat-and-mouse warfare. Scattered in small parties, the Chiricahuas struck the Santa Cruz Valley in late April. They made headlines by ransacking the home of Artisan Peck, killing his wife and baby daughter, and taking captive his ten-year-old niece Trinidad Verdin. The raiders also beat and robbed Peck, but left him alive to face the devastation. In pursuit, Capt. Thomas Lebo and his cavalrymen tracked the Chiricahuas, reportedly for two hundred miles. In the process, the Chiricahuas rode thirty horses to death, while Lebo's efforts brought about a single skirmish on May 3 in the Pinito Mountains, Sonora, with the soldiers capturing Apache supplies. After Lebo's strike, Mexican troops clashed twice with the Chiricahuas, who, after having set an ambush, sent their pursuers on retreat. But just a few days later, on May 15, 1886, troops under Capt. Charles Hatfield surprised the Chiricahuas at the Sierra Azul in Sonora, capturing their camp equipment and horses, only to lose them and the lives of two soldiers shortly thereafter in a Chiricahua ambush. One day later Lt. Robert Brown's cavalrymen stormed a Chiricahua camp in the Cananea Mountains, seized the camp, and recaptured some of Hatfield's horses.[85]

 In late May, Naiche and a small party of Chiricahuas went on what proved to be the last Apache raid of the Geronimo campaign on U.S. soil. Hiding the women and children in the Rincon Mountains, from where they soon crossed the border, Naiche thrust down the Santa Cruz River, wended his way among the mountain chains grossing the Gila and Black Rivers until he reached Fort Apache. Next, he went into the lodge of his mother only to discover that his family was not present. Heading back south, Naiche raided mines and captured horses but avoided the troops until losing some horses when attacked on May 27. Next, on June 6 another cavalry troop surprised Naiche's party near the Mowry Mine. Abandoning everything they owned, the Chiricahuas scattered and ran.[86]

To an outsider, it might seem that Miles's efforts were off to a fair start. Yet the capture or destruction of the enemy failed to materialize. Miles had also dispatched a special force of picked white troops to Mexico. The command, led by Capt. Henry Lawton, consisted of thirty-five white cavalrymen and twenty white infantry soldiers. It also included twenty White Mountain and San Carlos Apaches. The latter were to function solely as trackers, not as combat forces. No Chiricahuas were recruited. In addition, there were one hundred pack mules and thirty packers. Crossing the border on May 5, Lawton's men pursued the Chiricahuas through the summer. In their subsequent writings, Miles, Lawton, and army surgeon Leonard Wood, also with the command, gunned for glory and tried to paint the men of the task force as heroes of the white race who triumphed in extreme conditions. "The endurance of the men," Lawton, for example, argued, "was tried to the utmost limit," as only one-third of the picked soldiers made it to the end, the others having to be replaced. Other officers, not belonging to Miles's devotees, argued that no soldiers became so exhausted that they were ordered back to garrison for this reason and that neither was the command without water or supplies, as implied by Lawton and Wood, at any time. What Lawton and his critics agree on is that only once did the troops strike the Chiricahuas.[87]

As the summer wore on, Miles became more and more alarmed that military success could avoid him indefinitely while the Chiricahuas still raided just across the border and could potentially turn north anytime. Sensing that his time was running out, Miles pushed forward the removal of all Chiricahuas from the borderlands and opted for peace emissaries to open talks with Geronimo and Naiche's party. All the while he also kept Lawton trekking across northern Mexico. Miles asked George Noche, a former sergeant of Apache troops, to make contact with Naiche and Geronimo. Noche introduced the general to Kayitah, a Chokonen, and Martine, a Nednhi, two men capable of locating the free Chiricahuas. "We got relatives up there. . . . We want to take our people back so they won't suffer. . . . We got to do something to help our people," Martine later explained on why he accepted Miles's offer. Some sources say that for his efforts Miles promised Martine, and probably Kayitah as well, money and a new dwelling on the reservation. After successfully accomplishing their mission in September 1886, both ended up as prisoners of war in Florida with Naiche and Geronimo. Escorted by the reluctant Lt. Charles Gatewood, who had little faith in the plan and suffered from an old bladder inflammation that made riding painful, the two peace emissaries entered Mexico, joining first Lt. James Parker's and later Lawton's command. The latter still insisted that he would fight, not parley, with the Chiricahuas if he could only find them.[88]

Gaining intelligence that the Chiricahuas were worn down and hungry near Fronteras, a town filled with Mexican troops, Kayitah and Martine located their targets atop a steep ridge in the Teras Mountains near the big bend of the Bavispe River. Not only did the efforts of these two Apache soldiers get the famous negotiations—of which much has been written by historians—under way, but, before the Chiricahuas met any white officers, Martine and Kayitah persuaded Geronimo and others to consider surrendering. Next, Geronimo parlayed with Gatewood. Geronimo at first sought the upper hand and insisted that they return to San Carlos, get exemption from punishment, receive rations, and get their farms back. The only thing the very diplomatic Gatewood had to offer was confinement in Florida. It was not until after he made the shocking announcement that reservation Chiricahuas were being moved to Florida as they spoke that Geronimo and Naiche realized their options were finally running out. They decided to meet Miles.[89]

Escorted by Captain Lawton's troops as well as Gatewood and the two emissaries, the Chiricahuas, still armed and free, marched to the border, surrendering to a nervous Miles in person at Skeleton Canyon, Arizona, on September 4, 1886. Prior to escorting Geronimo to Fort Bowie, pressure had almost gotten the better of the general, who—seeking at all cost to avoid the public humiliation and potential career suicide that another last-minute escape by the Chiricahuas would bring—had stalled on his arrival and delivered confusing messages to Lawton. Miles had even suggested the securing and disarming of the Chiricahuas by force. Only when Lawton replied that such move would spark new wars and that the Chiricahuas appeared sincere on their intent to give up did Miles arrive on the scene.[90]

Meanwhile, Miles had been busy executing the removal of reservation Chiricahuas. In his reports, Miles painted gloomy and threatening images of the reservation as a time bomb of drunken indolent savages bound to explode at any time. Neatly ignoring that no reservation Chiricahuas had joined Geronimo's group and that most Chiricahua men had served in the army during Crook's administration, Miles pressed for the removal, arguing that it was necessary for the peace and prosperity of the border area. He found much sympathy in Washington. To discuss their future, Miles also sent a Chiricahua delegation under Chatto to Washington, where they uniformly stood against removal. While the executive branch deliberated, the main question was not whether the plan for Chiricahua exile was humane or just, or whether it should happen at all, but when and where the Chiricahuas should go and how their seizure and shipment could be conducted without sparking off another war. Government officials appeared more apprehensive on whether the removal of such "bad element" would raise protests among whites in the East, than of the possible impacts it would have on the Chiricahuas. Miles argued that the reservations could not contain the Chiricahuas, and that if reservation Chiricahuas were sent away, then their independent kinsmen would have no place to return to and no linkage left to the borderlands. In short, for the army the only way to guarantee an end to the U.S.-Apache struggle was the removal of all Chiricahuas as far away from Arizona as possible. It was the president who decided for Florida. By sending them there, the government eliminated the Chiricahuas—desert and mountain fighters—as a military power and thus made sure that they never again troubled the United States empire.[91]

EPILOGUE

In early June 1887, the Chiricahuas were again busy preparing for a war dance. For most of the evening, the painted men wearing breechclouts moved to the beat of the drums and chanted wildly. This time, however, the Chiricahuas performed for an audience on the Gulf coast of Florida eager to catch a glimpse of "wild savages" and their customs. Ever since boarding the train in Arizona on September 8, 1886, Geronimo's group had been a must-see attraction, first at San Antonio and then at Fort Pickens, outside Pensacola, Florida. Thousands of enthusiastic people, many of them in all sorts of small boats, swarmed the garrison, located on a sandy island at the mouth of a large bay. It had been much the same with Chihuahua and the others who surrendered in March. En route to Fort Marion, near Saint Augustine, Florida, "people were wild" in New Orleans, one soldier escorting these Apaches recalled. "Most had never seen an Indian. . . . Our money was no good [as] they treated us . . . royally." Also in Jacksonville, Florida, the frantic crowd eager to witness the furious Apaches almost "swamped the ferry that took us across the river." The Chiricahuas not only tolerated the sightseers, but some danced for them and sold craftworks and signed photographs.[1]

This all may seem a bit absurd and peculiar, as Geronimo and company had barely missed swinging in the gallows and as other Chiricahuas had suffered and feared for their lives when made to board trains heading east. At San Carlos, on August 20, 1886, the army had lured the close to four hundred reservation Chiricahuas into the agency and lined them up. Surrounded by white soldiers, the Apaches were disarmed and the men placed under guard. Chiricahua lives fell apart. "They thought they were all at home at Fort Apache," the Chiricahua Samuel Kenoi later recollected. "After these Indians had gone through all these hardships for the good of the people of these two states, they did this to them." He also confessed, "We didn't know where we were to be taken. . . . Some thought we were going to be taken to the ocean and thrown in. Some thought we were going to be killed in some other way." Transported to the railroad station at Holbrook, they were put in stockcars and sent east as prisoners of war. They, together with Chatto's delegation, which had been rerouted on its return from Washington, arrived at Fort Marion on September 20, joining there those that had surrendered in March.[2]

Meanwhile, there was much confusion on whether Geronimo had been captured or if he had surrendered, and if any terms had been given. At first, all—including General Oliver O. Howard, commanding the Division of the Pacific, Commanding General Philip Sheridan, Adjutant General R. C. Drum, Secretary of War William Endicott, and President Grover Cleveland—were under the impression that an unconditional capture had taken place. On August 23, Cleveland had telegraphed the Department of War, saying, "I hope nothing will be done with Geronimo, which will prevent our treating him as a prisoner of war, if we cannot hang him, which I would much prefer." On September 7, he ordered Geronimo's party to be sent to the nearest prison for confinement.[3]

Thinking that handing Geronimo and his fighters over to local civil authorities for trial would be a mockery of justice and refusing to go back on his word to Geronimo, Miles shipped the prisoners by train to Florida. Miles did this without authorization and in fact against the explicit wishes of the president and Sheridan's orders. The excuse he gave was that there had been interruptions in the telegram communications between Arizona and Washington, and that Arizona had no facilities secure enough for holding the prisoners. Miles obviously dreaded the possibility of the Chiricahuas escaping, leaving his reputation in tatters and the distasteful war continuing indefinitely. Not getting the answers he wanted from the purposefully evasive Miles, the president ordered Geronimo's train stopped at San Antonio.

For weeks, Miles held out under the barrage of telegraphs from Washington, failing to provide a clear answer to what actually had been said at Skeleton Canyon. From the accumulating correspondence, Washington was able to gather that Geronimo had never been captured but had instead surrendered and the surrender was "contrary to expectations here," in the words of Drum, then the acting secretary of war, "accompanied with conditions and promises." On September 29, failing to obtain the information he wanted from Miles, the annoyed Cleveland decided to ask the Chiricahuas at San Antonio. After interviewing Geronimo, the local commander, Gen. D. S. Stanley, reported that, according to Geronimo, Miles had assured the Chiricahuas that no one would hurt them, that past deeds were now wiped out, and that they would begin a new life united with their relatives in Florida in four or five days. In short, Miles had promised amnesty from all past crimes and removal in exchange for surrender. Approved by the less-than-happy Cleveland, Stanley shipped Geronimo's Chiricahuas to Florida on October 22. The men would go to Fort Pickens and the women and children to Fort Marion.[4] A few weeks later, the men would be joined by Mangas and one other warrior who had separated from the rest soon after the 1885 outbreak and had lain low until captured by the military on October 18, 1886, near the Black River. The women and children of Mangas's party went to Fort Marion.[5]

Despite the controversy, Miles had gained favor in reputation and was treated to a grand party in Tucson on November 8, 1887. There, the future commanding general of the army witnessed a parade that included four hundred O'odhams, schoolchildren, and town club and society members. Reviewing the parade, the hero of the hour was greeted by a canon salute and ceremonies at Levin's Park, which included telegrams from the country's notables read out loud, an array of speeches, and the presentation of a ceremonial sword to the conqueror of the Apaches, who was commended for having brought peace and security to the people of the borderlands. Miles felt jubilant for having defeated the Chiricahuas, whom he saw as "the remnant of a once powerful and warlike tribe that has contented against civilization for three hundred years."[6]

Miles still could not ignore how the treatment of reservation Chiricahuas caused an outcry with Crook and his followers and with several Indian reform groups in the East as the overcrowding at Fort Marion quickly took its toll. In May 1887, the army sent the Chiricahuas from Fort Marion to Mount Vernon Barracks in Alabama, another damp, hot, and unsuitable environment for the Apaches, while eligible children were delivered to boarding schools, where alienation and disease soon struck. The families of Geronimo and his men also finally made it to Fort Pickens. A year later Geronimo's following departed to Mount Vernon. Now the Chiricahuas at least were together again. They would go to Fort Sill, Oklahoma, in 1894 and remain as prisoners of war until 1913. Geronimo would die in 1909.[7]

Had the army triumphed in the end? After all, the war had ended, and the Apache communities were no longer independent military powers. However, it was an ending achieved partially by lies and deceit. At best, it was a victory by attrition, the American military effort grinding down Apache freedom and, together with the influx of settler society and extractive industries, taking away the Apaches' space. As for military triumphs—as understood in the tradition of the western way of war—there were few if any, especially during the latter stages of the war. Whites had killed only one Chiricahua during the 1885–86 operations. While raiding a ranch in Sonora, a Chiricahua named Chin-che was shot by the rancher John Hohstadt.[8] It is safe to say that while regular troops did not usually lack in effort—although their motivation oscillated considerably—their success in borderlands wars proved unspectacular to the end. In fact, if anything the regulars became less effective toward the end of the wars. Placing them in the spotlight after April 1886 had failed miserably. This was demonstrated by the whole removal scheme as well as by the invaluable part played by Martine and Kayitah in making the final surrender happen. The thousands of white soldiers failed to fulfill their mission to either destroy or capture Geronimo's tiny group. Nor could the troops stop the Chiricahuas from raiding. It was Geronimo and his group who chose to negotiate, meet with Miles, and surrender. They did not go in chains because of their own free will, judging surrendering to the Americans as the most feasible choice at a time when their choices were indeed running out. While Lawton's task force attacked a Chiricahua camp only once during the whole summer, it is notable that the Chiricahuas never charged Lawton's men.

That more Apaches did not continue fighting speaks not merely of the strong will to resist the lure of raiding but of the determination to find a diplomatic solution to their crisis. While the Jicarillas and Lipans probably realized it as early as the 1850s and the Mescaleros and Western Apaches did in the 1860s and early 1870s, by 1880, many Chiricahuas also recognized that they would be fighting a losing war. The majority chose to try to adapt to the new order. The actions of Victorio's Apaches, as well as those of the remaining Lipans, Nana's raiders, and Cibecue Apaches in 1881, had already been desperate acts by desperate men reacting to an acute crisis. What awaited the U.S. troops in the 1880s had been even more mobile and ruptured guerrilla fighting against progressively desperate and smaller but exceptionally able and potent Chiricahua fighters, who garnered the attention of the nation, and later the admiration of the world. They were top-class fighters, some with massive egos, who answered primarily to themselves and to their immediate following. Raiding had become their way of life. According to his son, the Nednhi leader Juh had recognized two choices: death from degradation, toil, and heat at San Carlos or a wild and free, but probably short, life fighting. Juh had pursued the latter.[9]

As a whole, the U.S.-Apache wars enabled and secured profound socio-economic change on the borderlands. It involved federal, state, and civilian actors, gradations of perpetrators and victims, and diverse shapes of violence and management ranging from unorganized killing, murder by deception, systematic slaughter, relentless hounding, material destruction, famine, cultural onslaught, and physical segregation and relocation. Negotiating the parameters of violence, and balancing the slippery slope of genocide, the distance from wars of containment to one-sided killing fests to civilizing mission and more limited killing was a short one indeed. The survivors of the people who once dominated the Southwest borderlands either gave up their Apache identity and integrated to Hispanic communities or found themselves restricted to reservations in Arizona and New Mexico or banished to Florida and later Alabama and Oklahoma. As people they adapted, persevered, and survived, but as independent military powers they succumbed to the U.S. empire after contesting it for decades.

NOTES

Abbreviations

AHS   Arizona Historical Society, Tucson
ARCIA   U.S. Commissioner of Indian Affairs, Annual Reports
ARSW   U.S. Secretary of War, Annual Reports
CSR   Center for Southwest Research, Albuquerque, New Mexico
FDNHS   Fort Davis National Historic Site, Fort Davis, Texas
GP, ASM   Grenville Goodwin Papers, Arizona State Museum, Tucson
HL   Henry E. Huntington Library, San Marino, California
NARA   National Archives and Records Administration, Washington, D.C.
UASC   University of Arizona Special Collections, Tucson

Introduction

Epigraph 1: Ball, *Indeh*, 104.
Epigraph 2: Letter no. 4, Feb. 6, 1864, Fort Whipple, Ariz., in Nicholson, *Arizona*, 68.

1. On the intergroup competition in the Southwest borderlands, see, for example, Brooks, *Captives*; DeLay, *War*; Spicer, *Cycles of Conquest*; Moorhead, *Apache Frontier*; Braatz, *Surviving*; Jacoby, *Shadows*; Blyth, *Chiricahua and Janos*; Griffen, *Apaches at War*; Alonso, *Thread*; and Radding, *Wandering*.

2. On borderlands and rule over imperial space, see Adelman and Aron, "From Borderlands"; St. John, *Line in the Sand*, esp. 1–11; Truett, *Fugitive Landscapes*; and Truett and Young, *Continental Crossroads*. The idea of empire has been a contested one in U.S. history as its national identity has been shaped by a strong sense of exceptionalism. Still, a growing number of scholars treat the United States as an empire among many others in world history. See Burbank and Cooper, *Empires*; Kramer, *Blood*; Kramer, "Power"; Go, *Patterns*; Stoler, *Haunted by Empire*; Nugent, *Habits*; Kaplan, *Anarchy*; Bender, *Nation*; Porter, *Empire*; Maier, *Among Empires*; and Smith-Rosenberg, *Violent Empire*. Williams, *Empire as a Way of Life*, represents an influential older classic.

3. Even after 1886, individual Apaches who hid in the Sierra Madre of northern Mexico made occasional raids in the borderlands. The last of them were recorded in the late 1930s. See Meed, *They Never*; Goodwin and Goodwin, *Apache Diaries*; and Kuhn, *Chronicles*, 292–309.

4. On settler colonialism and its demands on people and the environment, see Veracini, *Settler Colonialism*; Ostler, *Plains Sioux*; Jacobs, *White Mother*; White, *It's Your Misfortune*; Hixson, *American*; Wolfe "Settler Colonialism"; and Belich, *Replenishing the Earth*.

5. On indigenous power and Euro-American empires in North America, see, for example, Ostler, *Plains Sioux*; DuVal, *Native Ground*; White, *Middle Ground*; Richter, *Facing East*; Mapp, *Elusive West*; and Hämäläinen, *Comanche Empire*.

6. For the mentalities and aspirations of the regular army officers and soldiers in the Southwest borderlands, see Lahti, *Cultural Construction*.

7. On borderlands and shapes of violence, see Blackhawk, *Violence*; Brooks, *Captives*; Barr, *Peace*; Hämäläinen, *Comanche Empire*; DeLay, *War*; Anderson, *Conquest*; Blyth, *Chiricahua and Janos*; and Santiago, *Jar*.

8. Paraphrased from Keegan, *History*, 12. Today's military historians can be divided into three (overlapping) categories: the operational historians, the war and society scholars, and those who emphasize culture and the history of memory. See Citino, "Military Histories." Military culture can be divided into different levels such as societal, strategic, organizational, military, and "soldiers." I use "military culture" in a broader sense to refer to all these levels and to indicate how certain societies/groups of people comprehend and encounter war and violence. On military history and military culture, see Lee, "Warfare," esp. 3, 7, 11; Lee, "Mind"; Lynn, *Battle*, esp. xx; Wilson, "Defining Military Culture"; Moyar, "Current State"; Morillo and Pavkovic, *What Is Military History?*; Black, *Rethinking*; and Keegan, *Face*, 22–78.

9. On the broader inclusion of non-European military history, see, among others, Peers, *Warfare*; Black, *Rethinking*; and Vandervort, *Wars of Imperial Conquest*.

10. Historian Victor Hanson argues that there exists a western way of war that centers a single collision of armies on the open field, a clash aimed toward the absolute destruction of enemy forces originated by ancient Greeks. Besides the decisive battle, for Hanson the western way of war entails civic freedom and militarism, rationalism, technology, discipline, dissent, free critique, and vibrant markets. Hanson also hints that linking the purpose of war to the acquisition of real estate is a uniquely western idea. Hanson, *Carnage*, esp. 168, 213, 443; Hanson, *Western Way*, esp. 9–18.

11. On Apache social relations, see, for instance, Opler, *Apache Life-Way*; Opler, "Summary of Jicarilla Apache Culture," Goodwin, *Social Organization*; and Basehart, "Mescalero."

Chapter 1

Epigraph 1: Goddard, "Myths," 47–48.
Epigraph 2: Rickey, *Forty Miles*, 189–90.

1. Rockwell, "Autobiography of Mike Burns," 72 (see also 68–73).

2. Burns, *Only One*, 4, 6; Bourke, *Diaries*, 51. One O'odham had died in the attack. Eighteen Yavapai-Apache women and children, all wounded, were taken captive by

the military. They had apparently been saved by hiding under the dead bodies of their kin and friends.

3. Nickerson, "Major General," 17–18, Henry E. Huntington Library, San Marino, California (HL); Burns, *Only One*, 6. See also "Early Days in Arizona," 144–46; Price, *Across the Continent*, 148–52; Braatz, *Surviving*, 2–3, 138–39; Porter, *Paper Medicine Man*, 17–19; and Thrapp, *Conquest*, 127–31. Mike Burns was adopted by a military officer after the massacre. He worked for the military, was schooled at Carlisle, and lived a very colorful life until returning to Arizona. Later, Burns wrote his memoirs but could not get them published during his lifetime. He died in 1934.

4. On white settlement, perceptions, and the Southwest, see Sheridan, *Arizona*; Holtby, *Forty-Seventh Star*; Benton-Cohen, *Borderline*; Truett, *Fugitive Landscapes*; and González, *Refusing the Favor*.

5. Day, *Conquest*, 5–6. On market economy and U.S. expansion, see Robbins, *Colony*; and Cronon, *Nature's Metropolis*.

6. In 1860, California had a population of 370,000 people and Texas had over 600,000, while the number of residents in New Mexico was 93,000 and was 6,400 in Arizona only. U.S. Census Office, *Statistics*, 3–4, 12, 50, 299, 334–35, 340–41.

7. Smith-Rosenberg, *Violent Empire*; Anderson and Cayton, *Dominion*. On Manifest Destiny, see Stephenson, *Manifest Destiny*; Greenberg, *Manifest Manhood*; and Horsman, *Race*.

8. On the contest for North America, see Mapp, *Elusive West*; Black, *Fighting*; White, *Middle Ground*; Nugent, *Habits*; Cumings, *Dominion*; and Anderson and Cayton, *Dominion*.

9. On the ideological and practical underpinnings of the U.S.-Mexican War, see, for example, Foos, *Short*; Greenberg, *Wicked War*; DeLay, *War*; and Johannsen, *To the Halls*.

10. On the American way of war, see Weigley, *American Way*; Weigley, *History*; Linn, "American Way"; Linn, *Echo*; and Vandervort, *Indian Wars*.

11. For nineteenth century American military thinkers, see Mahan, *Influence*; Upton, *Armies of Asia and Europe*; and Upton, *Military Policy*. Even the latter study, an overall assessment of American military policy, is heavy on Civil War, the War of 1812, and the campaigns of the 1770s, but includes little on fighting independent Indians.

12. Linn, "American *Way*," 507–9; Weigley, *American Way*, esp. xxii, 3–17, 128–52; Waghelstein, "Preparing," 6–7, 11–13. On total war, and its many shapes and definitions, see also Black, *Age*; Brady, *War*; and Janda, "Shutting."

13. On the citizen-soldiers, see Winders, *Mr. Polk's Army*, 12–14, 66–87; Bellesiles, *Arming*; Herrera, "Self-Governance"; and Cooper, *Rise of the National Guard*.

14. Wooster, *American Military Frontiers*, esp. 4–8, 23–27; Weigley, *History*, 97–116; Skelton, *American Profession*; Prucha, *Sword of the Republic*.

15. Tate, *Frontier*; Smits, "Frontier Army"; Goetzmann, *Army Exploration*; Cooper, *Army and Civil Disorder*; Ball, *Army Regulars*.

16. In the Southwest, the army and the volunteers took turns. The mix of regulars and volunteers of the U.S.-Mexican War made way for a smaller force of regular soldiers,

As professionals left to fight the Civil War in 1861, California and local volunteers replaced them. After the Union victory, the regulars again returned.

17. Coffman, *Old Army*; Wooster, *American Military Frontiers*; Wooster, *Military*; Utley, *Frontier Regulars*.

18. In 1886, for instance, 11,377 enlisted men reported being native-born and 10,163 were foreign-born whites. Of the latter, 3,640 originated from Germany and 3,518 had left Ireland. U.S. Secretary of War, *Annual Report Secretary of War* (*ARSW*), 1886, 594.

19. Adams, *Class*; Lahti, *Cultural Construction*; Lahti, *Soldiers*; Coffman, *Old Army*; Hutton, *Phil Sheridan*; Smith, *View*.

20. This image not only applies to older silver screen representations but also stunningly, and disappointingly, retains value with more current productions like *The Missing* (2003) or *Cowboys and Aliens* (2011). Lahti, "Silver Screen."

21. Estimates of the arrivals of Athapaskan-speaking Apachean peoples to the Southwest vary from sometime after the year 1000 to the early 1600s. The term "Apache" possibly stems from Zuni or Yuman languages. Haskell, *Southern Athapaskan*; Perry, "Apachean Transition"; Walde, "Avonlea." Apaches have several versions of their own creation story. See Goddard, *San Carlos Apache*; Goddard, *Jicarilla Apache*; Opler, *Myths and Tales of the Jicarilla*; and Opler, *Myths and Tales of the Chiricahua*.

22. On Apache sociopolitical system, see Goodwin, *Social Organization*; Opler, *Apache Life-Way*; Basehart, "Mescalero"; and Record, *Big Sycamore*.

23. Griffen, *Apaches at War*; Babcock, "Turning Apaches into Spaniards"; Jastrzembski, "Enemy's Ethnography."

24. Opler, *Apache Life-Way*, esp. 67, 140–86, 462–72; Ball, *Indeh*; Ball, *In the Days of Victorio*; Geronimo, *His Own Story*, 54–57; Sweeney, *Mangas Coloradas*, 7; DeLay, *War*, 374.

25. Opler, "Summary of Jicarilla Apache Culture"; Opler, "Jicarilla Apache Territory"; Tiller, *Jicarilla Apache Tribe*, 12–30, 41; Gunnerson, *Jicarilla Apaches*, 294–95; Wilson, *Jicarilla Apache*, 301–5, 313–14, 324–39.

26. Ball, *Indeh*, 200–15, 281–85; Basehart, "Mescalero"; Sonnichsen, *Mescalero Apaches*.

27. Ball, *Indeh*, 281. See also Britten, *Lipan Apaches*, esp. 3, 21–24, 32, 76, 196, 210, 214, 226; Minor, *Turning*, esp. 2–6, 161–62; Sjoberg, "Lipan Apache Culture"; Opler, "Summary of Jicarilla Apache Culture"; and Tiller, *Jicarilla Apache Tribe*, 21–22.

28. The preconquest Yavapais were four different peoples: (from west to east) the Tolkepayas, Yavapés, Wipukepas, and Kwevkepayas. They spoke mutually intelligible Upland Yuman dialects, practiced similar lifestyles of hunting and gathering, and occupied contiguous, overlapping territories. Ties of kinship, friendship, and economic collaboration formed the basis of social cohesion, although relations among the different Yavapai people were not always friendly or cooperative. Braatz, *Surviving*.

29. Goodwin, *Social Organization*; Goodwin, "Social Divisions," 55–60; Goodwin, "Characteristics and Function of Clan"; Opler, *Grenville Goodwin*, esp. 53; Record, *Big Sycamore*, 43–54; Kaut, "Clan System." See also Harvey Nash-kin interview, 8–15, Folder 32, Box 2, Walter Hooke interview, 1–10, and James Nolan interview, 70–75, all in Folder 34, Box 3, Grenville Goodwin Papers, Arizona State Museum (GP, ASM).

30. Opler, *Apache Life-Way*, 332–35. On hunting and the army, see Lahti, *Cultural Construction*, 211–12.

31. Ball, *Indeh*, 34; Gila Moses interview, 220–21, Folder 34, Box 3, GP, ASM; Goodwin, *Western Apache*, 43, 45–46; Sonnichsen, *Mescalero Apaches*, 8. See also Weber, *Mexican Frontier*, 87; Emory, *Notes*, 578–79, 586, 588–90; Clarke, *Original Journals of Henry Smith Turner*, 84–86; Baylor, *Into the Far, Wild Country*, 129–31; and Wallace and Hevly, *From Texas to San Diego*, 60, 102.

32. *Tucson Weekly Arizonian*, May 15, 1869, http://chroniclingamerica.loc.gov/lccn/sn84024829/1869-05-15/ed-1/seq-2/ (accessed Oct. 17, 2012). See also Ball, *In the Days of Victorio*, 12; Ball, *Indeh*, 212–13; DeLay, *War*; and Britten, *Lipan Apaches*, 13–14; as well as Barney Tisle interview, 63–66, Folder 33, Box 3, Nosey interview, 181–85, Folder 35, Box 3, and Weapons, Raids, and Warfare, 5–11, Folder 44, Box 4, all in GP, ASM; William M. Breckenridge, "Trailing Geronimo," Folder 4, Box 1, and Petra Etchless, "A Brave Woman," Folder 6, Box 2, both in Wood Papers, Arizona Historical Society, Tucson (AHS); and Mary Bailey interview, Folder 1, Box 1, Wood Manuscripts, AHS.

33. Opler, *Apache Life-Way*, esp. 334–36; Jacoby, *Shadows*, 23–24, 41, 151; John Rope interview, 81, Folder 33, Box 3, and Nosey interview, Folder 35, Box 3, both in GP, ASM; Emory, *Notes*, esp. 60, 580; Bartlett, *Personal Narrative*, 1:301, 2:388.

34. For Apache economy, see Record, *Big Sycamore*; Opler, *Apache Life-Way*; Castetter and Opler, *Ethnobiology*; and Goodwin, *Social Organization*.

35. Goodwin, *Western Apache*, 43, 262; Barney Tisle interview, 65, Folder 33, Box 3, GP, ASM.

36. The discussion in this and the following two paragraphs is rooted on Harvey Nash-kin interview, 10–13, Folder 32, Box 2, and John Rope interview, 45, Folder 33, Box 3, both in GP, ASM; Britten, *Lipan Apaches*, 13–14; Opler, *Apache Life-Way*; and Goodwin, *Social Organization*.

37. "A Short Indian History," 33, Folder 7, Box 1, Hughes Papers, AHS.

38. The Western Apache sustenance cycle followed a seasonal pattern: all seasons when possible—hunting; early spring—gathering of mescal; April–May—planting crops; summer—gathering of acorns; fall—harvesting, processing, and storing crops as well as gathering of juniper berries; winter—raiding. Still, raiding could be practiced during all seasons, depending on circumstances. Record, *Big Sycamore*, 38–43, 69, 224–27; Opler, *Grenville Goodwin*, 44–45, 52, 55; John Sippi interview, 76–78, Folder 34, Box 3, GP, ASM; Perry, *Apache Reservation*, 47–48; Boyer and Gayton, *Apache Mothers*, 16–22.

39. Jacoby, *Shadows*, 13–14, 20–24, 40–41; Underhill, *Social Organization*, esp. 131–38; "Interview with Papago historian," Folder 7, Box 1, Wood Manuscripts, AHS; Dobyns, "Military Transculturation"; "Early Days in Arizona," 146; Carr, "Days of the Empire," 33; Carmony, *Civil War*, 86.

40. Apache sources recount raids when they visited the Pacific coast and the land of jungles and of tropical fruit. Ball, *In the Days of Victorio*, 45; Barney Tisle interview, 64, and Palmer Valor interview, 151, both in Folder 33, Box 3, GP, ASM.

Chapter 2

Epigraph 1: Harvey Nash-kin interview, 6, Folder 32, Box 2, GP, ASM.
Epigraph 2: Bode, *Dose*, 145.

1. Evans, "Indian Question," 608.
2. See, for example, Mahon, *History*; and Missall and Missall, *Seminole Wars*.
3. Of course, training leaders for borderlands warfare or Indian fighting was never the academy's goal. Smith, "West Point," 32–33, 43; Weigley, *History*, 272–73; Mort, *Wrath*, 68–80; Waghelstein, "Preparing," 8–11.
4. See, for example, Reeve, "Frederick E. Phelps"; King, "On Campaign"; Splitter, "Tour in Arizona"; and Carr, "Days of the Empire."
5. Summerhayes, *Vanished Arizona*, 19, 46. See also Reeve, "Frederick E. Phelps," 40; Averell, *Ten Years*, 107; Cruse, "From Hembrillo Canyon," 262; Schreier, "For This," 185–88; and Boyd, *Cavalry Life*, 95.
6. Rickey, *Forty Miles*, 44 (see also 33–49). See also Coffman, *Old Army*, 336–37; Averell, *Ten Years*, 53–61; and Walker, "Reluctant Corporal."
7. Letter, June 30, 1884, Fort Bowie, Ariz., Folder 1, Series 1, Beaumont Forsyth Papers, AHS; Walker, "Reluctant Corporal"; Henry, "Cavalry Life."
8. "Historical Sketch of the Third U.S. Cavalry," 7, Folder 5, Box 1, Morton Papers, AHS. See also Henry, "Cavalry Life," 99–100; Rickey, *Forty Miles*, 101–2; Vandervort, *Indian Wars*, 94–95; U.S. Congress. House, *Reorganization of the Army*, 246; and Bigelow, *On the Bloody Trail*, 63, 90, 104–5 (see also 88 for a rare field exercise).
9. Coffman, *Old Army*, 282–83; Weigley, *History*, 290.
10. Lahti, *Cultural Construction*.
11. Barnes, "In the Apache Country," 622.
12. *ARSW, 1880*, 212.
13. Bigelow, *On the Bloody Trail*, 99–100.
14. My discussion of Apache training is based on Harvey Nash-kin interview, 10–12, Folder 32, Box 2, and John Taylor interview, 30, Folder 35, Box 3, both in GP, ASM; Opler and Hoijer, "Raid," 618; Cole, *Chiricahua Apache*, 13–27; Ball, *In the Days of Victorio*, esp.113; Goodwin, *Social Organization*; Opler, *Childhood*; Opler, *Apache Life-Way*; Boyer and Gayton, *Apache Mothers*, 16–22; Tiller, *Jicarilla Apache Tribe*, 23–25; and Robinson, *I Fought*, 2.
15. Harvey Nash-kin interview, 12, Folder 32, Box 2, 32–33, Folder 33, Box 3, GP, ASM; Opler, *Apache Life-Way*, 67 (see also 45–53, 65–69). See also Ball, *Indeh*, 14, 45.
16. Opler and Hoijer, "Raid," 618–19; Opler, *Apache Life-Way*, 69–74, 134–39; Chamberlain, *Victorio*, 41–45.
17. Goodwin, *Western Apache*, 290–98; Harvey Nash-kin interview, 12–13, Folder 32, Box 2; Weapons, Raids, and Warfare—Addendum, 121–29, 132–36, Folder 45, Box 4, GP, ASM; Opler, *Apache Life-Way*, 137–38; Opler and Hoijer, "Raid," 620–34. In their essay, Opler and Hoijer note that they learned of seventy-eight special words the dikohes used.

18. Goodwin, *Western Apache*, 290–98; Ball, *Indeh*, 3–4,105; Ball, *In the Days of Victorio*, 29; Opler, *Apache Life-Way*, 134–39; Weapons, Raids, and Warfare, 172–76, Folder 43, Box 4, GP, ASM.

19. Ball, *Indeh*, 47. See also Goodwin, *Western Apache*, 297–98.

20. Robinson, *Apache Voices*, 188. See also Goodwin, *Western Apache*, 108.

21. Ball, *Indeh*, 86–87 (see also 103, 146–47).

22. Howard, *My Life*, 190; Loring, "Report," 186–89; Platten, *Ten Years*, 30; Barnes, *Apaches and Longhorns*, 47.

23. Buckelew, *Life of F. M. Buckelew*, 12 (see also 13–91); Shipp, "Captain Crawford's Last Expedition," 519.

24. Shipp, "Captain Crawford's Last Expedition," 519. See also Wood, "On Campaign," 547–49; Merritt, "Incidents," 156; Bode, *Dose*, 157–58; Forsyth, *Thrilling Days*, 80; Loring, "Report," 182–84; and Bourke, *Apache Campaign*.

25. My discussion on Apache leadership relies on Weapons, Raids, and Warfare, 108–111, Folder 45, Box 4, GP, ASM; Opler, *Apache Life-Way*; Goodwin, *Social Organization*; Goodwin, *Western Apache*; Basehart, "Mescalero," 98–103; Tiller, *Jicarilla Apache Tribe*; Sjoberg, "Lipan Apache Culture," 94.

26. Cremony, *Life among the Apaches*, 21–22.

27. Opler, *Apache Life-Way*, 333–34. See also Goodwin, *Western Apache*, 75–80, 254; Ball, *Indeh*, 22–23, 40, 45, 89; and Walter Hooke interview, 7–8, Folder 34, Box 3, and John Taylor interview, 38, Folder 35, Box 3, both in GP, ASM.

28. Goodwin, *Western Apache*, 47, 49–51, 69, 253–55, 257–59; Opler, *Apache Life-Way*, 342, 344–45; Ball, *Indeh*, 45.

29. Power was understood by the Apaches as a personal gift, something that represented itself to a person, or, more rarely, as something a person might seek alone via prayer, fasting, meditation, and tests. Power was bestowed on the individual for virtue and courage. Power did not necessarily relate to war; it might be a healing art or some other form of special talent. Ball, *In the Days of Victorio*, 11, 16; Ball, *Indeh*, 9, 25, 61–65, 87, 111, 173, 206–7.

30. Goodwin, *Western Apache*, 35.

31. In 1886, for example, just 176 of the 2,140 officers had their place of birth listed abroad. *ARSW*, 1886, 594.

32. Weapons, Raids and Warfare, 65, Folder 44, Box 4, GP, ASM.

33. The number of regiments and companies varied according to army size. See, for instance, *ARSW*, 1846, 63–64, and *ARSW*, 1874, 5–20.

34. Altshuler, *Chains*, 39–46, 61–69, 129–33, 162–66.

35. Col. George Stoneman, the last commander of the District of Arizona and first commander of the new Department of Arizona, was notorious for actively avoiding Arizona. Opting to live at Drum Barracks, near Los Angeles, he managed to keep away for much of his tenure while earning the criticism of the Arizona residents. See Altshuler, *Chains*, 162–66, 184–90; and *Tucson Weekly Arizonian*, Jan. 28, 1871, http://chroniclingamerica.loc.gov/lccn/sn84024829/1871-01-28/ed-1/seq-2/ (accessed Sept. 3, 2013).

36. Forsyth, *Story*, 88. On the officer-soldier schism, see Bennett, *Forts*; Hammond, *Campaigns*; Carmony, *Civil War*; Gustafson, *John Spring's Arizona*; Bode, *Dose*; and Walker, "Reluctant Corporal."

Chapter 3

Epigraph 1: Weapons, Raids and Warfare—Addendum, 2, Folder 45, Box 4, GP, ASM.
Epigraph 2: Hammond, *Campaigns*, 6.

1. McCall, *New Mexico*, 98.
2. The actual army strength was never the same as the authorized one was, as desertion, discharges, illness, transportation difficulties, and problems in recruiting took their toll. Also, many soldiers and officers served in the army's staff bureaus such as the Quartermaster's Department, responsible for food, clothing, and shelter; the Ordnance Department, with authority over armament; and the Adjutant General's Office, the administrative center link. In 1875, for instance, the gap between the actual line and authorized total strength was nearly four thousand men. *ARSW*, 1875, 34, 49.
3. For the variation in troop numbers, see, for example, *ARSW*, 1855, 138–39; *ARSW*, 1859, 606–7; *ARSW*, 1868, 737–38, 744–45; *ARSW*, 1871, 90–91, 104–5; and *ARSW*, 1886, 92–95.
4. "Historical Sketch of the Third U.S. Cavalry," 25, Folder 5, Box 1, Morton Papers, AHS; *ARSW*, 1868, 736–37, 744–45; *ARSW*, 1885, 84–85, 88–89. A useful source for tracking garrison strength is the monthly posts returns. See, for example, Roll 33 for Fort Apache, Rolls 129–30 for Fort Bowie, Rolls 414–15 for Fort Grant, Roll 1265 for Fort Thomas, and Roll 1325 for Fort Verde in Arizona; and Rolls 87–88 for Fort Bayard, Roll 156 for Fort Buchanan, Roll 261 for Fort Craig, and Rolls 1216–18 for Fort Stanton in New Mexico. All in Returns from U.S. Military Posts, M617, National Archives and Records Administration, Washington, D.C. (NARA).
5. Lahti, "Journey," 354–56.
6. There existed constant calls for concentrating troops to bigger garrisons. *ARSW*, 1854, 51; *ARSW*, 1876, 452–53; *ARSW*, 1880, 92–93; Utley, "Captain John Pope's Plan."
7. Opler, *Apache Life-Way*, 22–25; Ball, *In the Days of Victorio*, 75; Hammond, *Campaigns*, 11.
8. For fears of Apache attacks against posts, see Upham, "Incidents," 90–91; Splitter, "Tour in Arizona," 78, 80, 83–84; and Carr, "Days of the Empire," 26.
9. Lahti, *Cultural Construction*, 157–67.
10. Mills, *My Story*, 189–90. See also *Statistical Report*, 210–18, 222–27; U.S. Surgeon General's Office, *Circular No. 8*, 528, 534, 536; Kraemer, "Sickliest Post," esp. 227; Letter, Nov. 20, 1867, File 15, Box 2, Widney Letters, AHS; Letter, July 1, 1879, Fort Lowell Records, AHS; and Boyd, *Cavalry Life*, 121.
11. U.S. Congress decided the army budget through annual allotments. At worst the army went without funding for several months as the deadlocked Congress debated the budget. Frazer, *Forts and Supplies*; Miller, *Soldiers*; Walker, "Freighting"; Wooster, *American Military Frontiers*, 216–17, 237.

12. Lahti, *Cultural Construction*.

13. Wood, "On Campaign," 549. My discussion of military clothing relies on McChristian, *U.S. Army*, esp. 3–21, 45–51, 53–64, 67–69, 72–75, 147–49, 160–62, 165–66, 170, 230–31, 247; Rickey, *Forty Miles*, 122–26; Coffman, *Old Army*, 342–44; and Winders, *Mr. Polk's Army*, 103–6.

14. McChristian, *U.S. Army*, 14; Hook and Pegler, *To Live and Die*, 18.

15. Hook and Pegler, *To Live and Die*, 19.

16. McChristian, *U.S. Army*, 67, 21.

17. Forbes, "United States Army," 144–45; Bigelow, *On the Bloody Trail*, 197–98. See also King, "On Campaign," 169; McChristian, *U.S. Army*, 72–73; and Winders, *Mr. Polk's Army*, 106–12.

18. Goodwin, *Western Apache*, 262. On Apache clothing styles, see Sweeney, *Making Peace*, 91, 100–101; Betzinez, *I Fought*, 27; and John Rope interview, 94–97, and Barney Tisle interview, 65, both in Folder 33, Box 3, GP, ASM.

19. Watt, "Apaches," 155–56; Rolls 88–89, Ninth Cavalry, Returns from Regular Cavalry Regiments, M744, NARA; *ARSW*, 1880, 86–89, 93–110. On horse scarcity, see also Hammond, *Campaigns*, 33–35; Pettit, "Apache Campaign Notes," 533; Henry, "Cavalry Life," 99; and *ARSW*, 1871, 78, 208–9. In the 1850s, the army also experimented with camels, thinking the animals from the deserts of Africa and the Middle East suitable for the southwestern terrain. By the time of the Civil War, the experiment was forgotten. Many camels were sold to private owners while others escaped to the desert, where some were still sighted decades later.

20. Masich, *Civil War*, 25; "Historical Sketch of the Third U.S. Cavalry," 35, Folder 5, Box 1, Morton Papers, AHS; Cruse, *Apache Days*, 57–58; Carter, *From Yorktown to Santiago*, 175; Carr, "Days of the Empire," 20, 25; Barnes, "In the Apache Country," 615; McCall, *New Mexico*, 126, 140, 148–49, 164, 168–69, 186–87; *ARSW*, 1876, 272, 340–41; Vandervort, *Indian Wars*, 56–57.

21. Carr, "Days of the Empire," 20; Bennett, *Forts*, 17 (see also 11). See also "Trailing Geronimo," 22, 89, 100, Folder 5, Box 1, Mazzanovich Papers, AHS; "Reminiscences," 17–20, Folder 1, Box 1, Ayer Papers, AHS; and Tevis, *Arizona*, 64–65.

22. On Apache weaponry, see Goodwin, *Western Apache*, 223–45; Robinson, *Apache Voices*, 187–89; Opler, *Apache Life-Way*, 340–41; Britten, *Lipan Apaches*, 13; and Harvey Nashkin interview, 36–42, Folder 33, Box 3, and Weapons, Raids and Warfare, 12–29, Folder 42, Box 4, both in GP, ASM.

23. The commands for the flintlock musket were as follows: 1. load, 2. open-pan, 3. handle-cartridge, 4. tear-cartridge, 5. prime, 6. shut-pan, 7. cast-about, 8. charge-cartridge, 9. draw-rammer, 10. ram-cartridge, 11. return-rammer, and 12. shoulder-arms. With the percussion musket, open-pan and shut-pan were eliminated. Winders, *Mr. Polk's Army*, 92–100; Bruhl, "Primacy of Method," 37–67; Vandervort, *Indian Wars*, 98–101; *ARSW*, 1874, xvii–xx, 256–57, 267–99; McCall, *New Mexico*, 120–21, 126, 133, 139–40, 148, 155, 160, 164, 168, 172.

24. McChristian, *U.S. Army*; Brinckerhoff and Chamberlin, "Army's Search"; Weigley, *History*, 268–69, 290–91.

25. Goodwin, *Western Apache*, 262. See also Gila Moses interview, 220, Folder 34, Box 3, GP, ASM; Ball, *Indeh*, 201; Betzinez, *I Fought*, 6; and Opler, *Apache Life-Way*, 341.

26. Ball, *In the Days of Victorio*, 18, 80; Ball, *Indeh*, 95; Betzinez, *I Fought*, 85; Robinson, *Apache Voices*, 189–91; Cremony, *Life among the Apaches*, 188–89, 194; Dinges, "New York Private," 62.

27. On Apache marksmanship, see General Crook's interview in the *New York Herald*, July 9, 1883, reprinted in Cozzens, *Eyewitnesses*, 404; "Reminiscences of Early Days," 15, file 8, box 1, Fourr Papers, AHS; Betzinez, *I Fought*, 107; and Watt, *Apache Tactics*, 24.

28. See, for example, Winders, *Mr. Polk's Army*, 95, 100–103; Bigelow, *On the Bloody Trail*, esp. 14, 63, 90–94, 101, 104; "Gashuntz," "On the March," 55; and Coffman, *Old Army*, 278–80.

29. With varying success, soldiers raised gardens and pooled their money for a company fund to purchase variety to their diets.

30. Apaches could also use various markers, styles, and colors of war paint. Opler, *Apache Life-Way*, 340–44; Goodwin, *Western Apache*, 256–57, 260–61; Robinson, *Apache Voices*, 194; John Rope interview, 85, and Barney Tisle interview, 73, both in Folder 33, Box 3; Weapons, Raids and Warfare, 163–65, Folder 43, Box 4; 4–6, Folder 44, Box 4; 8–9, Folder 45, Box 4, GP, ASM.

31. Opler and Hoijer, "Raid," esp. 623–24; Goodwin, *Western Apache*, 264–66.

32. There existed variations in the context and length of the dances. See, for example, Goodwin, *Western Apache*, 75, 86–87, 116–18, 246–52, 260; Palmer Valor interview, 183–89, Folder 33, Box 3, GP, ASM; and Opler, *Apache Life-Way*, 336–40. For the calling together of a raid or war party, see Goodwin, *Western Apache*, 32–33, 75, 77–87; and Opler, "Summary of Jicarilla Apache Culture," 208–11.

33. Ball, *In the Days of Victorio*, 82; Robinson, *Apache Voices*, 192; Daly, "Geronimo Campaign," 448. For soldiers, see Bigelow, *On the Bloody Trail*, 30, 41, 50; Bourke, *Diaries*; Frank West, Journal, University of Arizona Special Collections (UASC); Notebook, 1881–85, Finley Papers, UASC; and Field Diary, Folder 1, Box 1, Howard Papers, AHS.

34. Robinson, *Apache Voices*, 101. See also Goodwin, *Western Apache*, 154–72; Charlie Norman interview, 269, Folder 34, Box 3, GP, ASM; Ball, *Indeh*, 48; Cruse, *Apache Days*, 186–87; and Crook, *His Autobiography*, 213.

35. Nosey interview, 184, Folder 35, Box 3, GP, ASM. For firsthand accounts of Apache raiding, see Ball, *Indeh*, 4–12, 32, 249–50; John Rope interview, 52, and Barney Tisle interview, 63–64, both in Folder 33, Box 3; Walter Hooke interview, esp. 79, Folder 34, Box 3, and Weapons, Raids and Warfare, 5–11, Folder 44, Box 4; 31–35, 52–71, Folder 45, Box 4, all in GP, ASM; Goodwin, *Western Apache*, 31–39, 43–71, 257–58; Opler, *Apache Life-Way*, 343; and Ball, *In the Days of Victorio*, 19–20, 75–76, 110–11.

36. Ball, *Indeh*, 104.

37. Jacoby, "Broad Platform," 262; Betzinez, *I Fought*, 82–96.

38. Opler, *Apache Life-Way*, 349. On scalping among the Apaches, see also Goodwin, *Western Apache*, 76; Ball, *Indeh*, 4, 35, 83; Ball, *In the Days of Victorio*, 13; and Weapons,

Raids and Warfare—Addendum, 96–97, Folder 45, Box 4, GP, ASM. Scalp dances were arranged at least among the Jicarillas, Western Apaches, and Chihennes. Opler, "Summary of Jicarilla Apache Culture," 211–13; Tiller, *Jicarilla Apache Tribe*, 24–25.

39. Cremony, *Life among the Apaches*, 180 (see also 87, 140–41, 195).

40. Goodwin, *Western Apache*, 262; Opler, *Apache Life-Way*, 345–46; Watt, *Apache Tactics*, 24–43 (see also 18–23 for evasion and 44–52 for attack).

41. Jett, "Engagement," 495–96. See also Walker, "Reluctant Corporal," 32–36; Wright, "In the Days of Geronimo," 500–501; Rice, "Across Apache Land," 506–7; and Elliott, "Geronimo Campaign," 432.

42. Clarke, "Hot Trail," 630; Goodwin, *Western Apache*, 183, 314.

43. Scott, "'Whiskey,'" 31–52. For stakeout duty, see also Diary, Chrisman Papers, AHS; Bode, *Dose*; Bigelow, *On the Bloody Trail*; Elliott, "Camp at Richmond on the Gila," Folder 4, Series 1, Beaumont Forsyth Papers, AHS; and Corson Reminiscences, UASC.

44. Bigelow, *On the Bloody Trail*, 30–33; Gale, "Hatfield," 449–50.

45. Report, Oct. 3, 1865, Camp McDowell, Ariz., Folder 5, Box 1, Bennett Papers, AHS. See also Chance, *My Life*, 132; and Dinges, "New York Private," 59–61.

46. Letter, Oct. 16, 1865, Camp McDowell, Ariz., Folder 16, Box 1, Bennett Papers, AHS.

47. Nickerson, "Apache Raid," 107–12. See also *Prescott Weekly Arizona Miner*, May 25, 1872, http://chroniclingamerica.loc.gov/lccn/sn82014899/1872-05-25/ed-1/seq-3/ (accessed Nov. 22, 2013).

48. Averell, *Ten Years*, 130.

49. Davis, "Difficulties," 493; Davis, *Truth*, 189 (for the whole episode, see 176–95).

50. Pettit, "Apache Campaign Notes," 533; Elliott, "Geronimo Campaign," 431; *ARSW*, 1868, 46–48; *ARSW*, 1880, 97–98; Gatewood, "Campaigning," 218. It has to be remembered that pre-railroad Arizona and southern New Mexico were dependent on government spending. It was in businessmen's interest to have as many soldiers as possible nearby.

51. Reeve, "Frederick E. Phelps," 122–24, 218; Merritt, "Incidents," 155–56; Carr, "Days of the Empire," 29; King, "On Campaign," 162; Bowman Diary, esp. 13, 17, 68, 82, UASC.

52. Parker, *Old Army*, 161; Cruse, *Apache Days*, 71 (see also 48–50, 91).

53. On civilian scouts, see Radbourne, *Mickey Free*; Smith, "White Eyes"; Thrapp, *Al Sieber*; and Sweeney, *Merejildo Grijalva*.

54. Carter, *On the Border with MacKenzie*, 422–65; Wallace, *Ranald S. MacKenzie's Official Correspondence*, 161–62; U.S. Congress. House, *Texas Border Troubles*, 187–204; Wooster, "Army," 154–57; Robinson, *Bad Hand*.

55. Frelinghuysen, "Mexico: Reciprocal Right"; Sweeney, *From Cochise to Geronimo*, 222; Thrapp, *Conquest*, 249; Kraft, *Gatewood and Geronimo*, 11; *ARSW*, 1882, 148–50; Forsyth, *Thrilling Days*, 116–21.

56. On the killing of Crawford, see *ARSW*, 1886, 152–53, 155–64; Utley, *Geronimo*, 177–81; and Bowen-Hatfield, *Chasing Shadows*, 89–99.

57. Merritt, "Incidents," 156.

58. "A Young Man's Life in the West," 226, File 5, Box 1, Fourr Papers, AHS.
59. Opler, *Apache Life-Way*, 346; Ball, *In the Days of Victorio*, 75–76. See also "My Life in the West," 26, 31, Folder 1, Box 1, Glover Papers, AHS.
60. Opler, *Apache Life-Way*, 347–48; Ball, *In the Days of Victorio*, 74; Robinson, *Apache Voices*, 31; Chamberlain, *Victorio*, 70.
61. On troops and water, see Eaton, "String for the Bow," 179–80; Crook, *His Autobiography*, 166–67; Parker, *Annals*, 17; Reeve, "Frederick E. Phelps," 122–28; Gressley, "Soldier," 42; and Bowman Diary, UASC.
62. *ARSW*, 1867, 95; Carmony, *Civil War*, 160. See also Letters, May 24, 1880, and May 28, 1880, both in Folder 1, Box 1, Worthington Letters, AHS; Bennett, *Forts*, 34–36; Parker, *Old Army*; and Hammond, *Campaigns*.
63. King, "On Campaign," 163; Bigelow, *On the Bloody Trail*, 1–2; Barnes, *Apaches and Longhorns*, 87.
64. King, "On Campaign," 162, 171; Henry, "Cavalry Life," 104.
65. Cremony, *Life among the Apaches*, 86; Davis, *Truth*, 74. See also Carter, *From Yorktown to Santiago*, 252–53.
66. Bourke, *Apache Campaign*, 34–36.
67. For more detailed discussion, see Lahti, *Cultural Construction*. On colonizer identity and its fragility, see Stoler, *Carnal Knowledge*; Stoler, *Haunted by Empire*; and Cooper and Stoler, *Tensions of Empire*.
68. For Sumner and Conrad, see *ARSW*, 1852, 5–6, 23–26. For others, see Averell, *Ten Years*, 133; and Gressley, "Soldier," 36, 39.
69. Crook's orders are reprinted in Bigelow, *On the Bloody Trail*, 43–44. On Apache recruits, see Lahti, "Colonized Labor"; Lahti, *Cultural Construction*; Dunlay, *Wolves*; and Smits, "Fighting Fire."
70. Clarke, "Hot Trail," 641.
71. Opler, *Apache Life-Way*, 334–36, 352–54; Ball, *Indeh*, 6–12; Goodwin, *Western Apache*, 34, 63, 76, 90–91, 279–83; John Rope interview, 81–83, Folder 33, Box 3; Nosey interview, 183–85, Folder 35, Box 3; Weapons, Raids and Warfare—Addendum, 91, 93,116–20, 138, Folder 45, Box 4, all in GP, ASM. Some of the captives, usually women and children were raised as equals, while others, especially adult men, could be given to fresh widows to exact their revenge. Weapons, Raids and Warfare, 139–40, Folder 43, Box 4, GP, ASM.

Chapter 4

Epigraph 1: Ball, *Indeh*, 200.
Epigraph 2: Emory, *Notes*, 76.

1. Cutts, *Conquest*, 68–74; Bauer, *Mexican War*, 127–131; Emory, *Notes*, esp. 14; González, *Refusing the Favor*, 40, 135.
2. Hughes, *Doniphan's Expedition*, 25.
3. Ibid., 33–40; Edwards, *Campaign*, 45–57; Bauer, *Mexican War*, 134–35; Cutts, *Conquest*, 52–55; Magoffin, *Down the Santa Fe Trail*, 102–45; Richardson, *Journal*, 22; Bieber, *Journal*, 195, 205–25; Clarke, *Original Journals of Henry Smith Turner*, 71–74.

4. For quotes, see Hughes, *Doniphan's Expedition*, 25, 51 (see also 33–40, 60–61, 78–82); and DeLay, "Independent Indians," 59. See also Clarke, *Original Journals of Henry Smith Turner*, 71–74, 78–80, 103; Edwards, *Campaign*, 45–57, 65–66, 94–96; Cutts, *Conquest*, 52–58, 68–74; Magoffin, *Down the Santa Fe Trail*, 102–45; Richardson, *Journal*, 22; Bieber, *Journal*, 195, 205–25; Bauer, *Mexican War*, 127–35; Emory, *Notes*, esp. 14; and González, *Refusing the Favor*, 40, 76, 135. Kearny also issued the famed Kearny Code, officially known as the Organic Act, a "new constitution" for New Mexico that promised to respect its legal and religious traditions. The code was not accepted by the U.S. Congress, which accused Kearny of exceeding his authority. Chávez, *New Mexico*, 115–16.

5. Braatz, *Surviving*, esp. 37–40, 43–50, 78; Record, *Big Sycamore*, 86–94; Jacoby, *Shadows*, 30, 50–51.

6. On cultural and ethnic mixing, see Blyth, *Chiricahua and Janos*; Brooks, *Captives*; John, *Storms*; Radding, *Wandering*; Anderson, *Indian Southwest*; Griffen, *Apaches at War*; Weber, *Spanish Frontier*; Kessell, *Friars*; Kessell, *Spain*; Barr, *Peace*; Forbes, *Apache*; Spicer, *Cycles of Conquest*; Moorhead, *Apache Frontier*; and Santiago, *Jar*.

7. Gálvez, *Instructions*; Griffen, *Apaches at War*, 53–118; Jacoby, *Shadows*, 55–57, 157–60; Britten, *Lipan Apaches*, 138–63; John, *Storms*, esp. 503–35, 629–43, 697–705; Weber, *Barbaros*, 151–61; Blyth, *Chiricahua and Janos*, 87–119; Babcock, "Turning Apaches into Spaniards," esp. 152–80, 214–44.

8. Weber, *Mexican Frontier*, 108–15; Moorhead, *Presidio*.

9. Jastrzembski, "Treacherous Towns"; Jastrzembski, "Enemy's Ethnography."

10. Bartlett, *Personal Narrative*, 1:272–76, 283–85; Velasco, *Sonora*, 85–86, 132–46; Voss, *On the Periphery*, 105–6, 111; Weber, *Mexican Frontier*, 89, 183–84; DeLay, *War*, 194–96, 384; Sheridan, *Arizona*, 46–49; Kessell, *Friars*, 284–89; Foos, *Short*, 151.

11. Goodwin, *Social Organization*, 93; DeLay, *War*; Weber, *Mexican Frontier*, 92.

12. Braatz, *Surviving*, 69–73; Cooke, *Conquest*, 179–81; Emory, *Notes*, 86; Weber, *Taos Trappers*; Griffen, *Apaches at War*, 120–21, 131–35; DeLay, *War*, 198–99, 384–85.

13. On Johnson, see Strickland, "Birth and Death." On Kirker, see Smith, *Borderlander*, esp. 71, 170.

14. Smith, "John Joel Glanton." See also Smith, "Scalp Hunt."

15. González, *Refusing the Favor*, esp. 41; Resendez, *Changing National Identities*; Mora, *Border Dilemmas*.

16. Bieber, *Journal*, 195, 205 (see also 193–94, 204, 215–16); Reid, *Reid's Tramp*, 225 (see also 145). For Anglo views, see also Reeve, "Puritan," esp. 21; Magoffin, *Down the Santa Fe Trail*; Averell, *Ten Years*, 111–15; and Bennett, *Forts*, 14–20.

17. Griswold del Castillo, *Treaty*, 190–91; Miller, *Treaties*, 5:219–22. American negotiator Nicolas Trist was certain that Mexico's northern states would never have approved the treaty without Article XI. DeLay, "Independent Indians," 65–66.

18. Frazer, *Forts and Supplies*; Lamar, *Far Southwest*; Holtby, *Forty-Seventh Star*.

19. It is estimated that during the 1847 unrest, 102 Americans and their sympathizers along with 318 Hispanic and Indian resisters were killed or wounded. Brooks, *Captives*; Sides, *Blood*; González, *Refusing the Favor*, 75.

20. Ball, *Army Regulars*, 20–21, 35–36; Averell, *Ten Years*, 145–227; Utley, *Frontiersmen*.
21. *ARSW*, 1850, 69 (see 68–70 for Steen's report, dated Feb. 5, 1850). See also Thompson, "With the Third Infantry," 355–57; Kiser, *Dragoons*, 63–71; Kuhn, *Chronicles*, esp. 49–50; Bauer, *Mexican War*, 136–37; and Cutts, *Conquest*, 76.
22. Eaton quoted from Kiser, *Dragoons*, 168. Sumner quoted from Ball, *Army Regulars*, 21, 31. See also *ARSW*, 1851, 106–9, 125–28.
23. Ball, "Fort Craig," 153–54; Ball, *Army Regulars*, esp. 4; Winders, *Mr. Polk's Army*, 11; *ARSW*, 1851, 238–39; *ARSW*, 1852, 23–26.
24. Bartlett, *Personal Narrative*, 2:391; Bennett, *Forts*, 74.
25. Abel, *Official Correspondence*, 69. See also Tiller, *Jicarilla Apache Tribe*, 10–11, 31–33; McCall, *New Mexico*, 33–34; Wilson, *Jicarilla Apache*, 302, 339; and Gunnerson, *Jicarilla Apaches*, 294–95.
26. *ARSW*, 1849, 108–9; Abel, *Official Correspondence*, 63–73, 88, 94–95, 151–52, 166–72; Bennett, *Forts*, 23–25; Tiller, *Jicarilla Apache Tribe*, 34–36; Sides, *Blood*, 247–48, 252–59.
27. Smith, *Captive Arizona*, 1–35; McGinty, *Oatman Massacre*; Mifflin, *Blue Tattoo*; Braatz, *Surviving*, 74–76, 253–54; Thompson, *Civil War*, 43–45; Stratton, *Captivity*. On Anglo travelers, see Browne, *Adventures*; Summerhayes, *Vanished Arizona*; and "Reminiscences," 10–12, Folder 1, Box 1, Tonge Papers, AHS.
28. Smith, *Captive Arizona*, 43–54; Letters no. 13–19, March–May, 1860, Tubac, Ariz., in Altshuler, *Latest from Arizona*, 46–71; Viola, *Memoirs of Charles Henry Veil*, 101; Tevis, *Arizona*, 69–73.
29. U.S. Commissioner of Indian Affairs, *Annual Report Commissioner of Indian Affairs (ARCIA)*, 1853, 432–41; Tiller, *Jicarilla Apache Tribe*, 37–42; Hays, "General Garland's War," 255; Taylor, "Campaigns . . . 1854," 269–70; Bieber, "Letters." See also Carson, "William Carr Lane Diary."
30. Kuhn, *Chronicles*, 47; Hays, "General Garland's War," 256.
31. Taylor, "Campaigns . . . 1854," 271–72; Tiller, *Jicarilla Apache Tribe*, 43–45; *ARSW*, 1854, 33; Bennett, *Forts*, 48; Webb, *Chronological List of Engagements*, 11.
32. Bennett, *Forts*, 54. See also Wetherington and Levine, *Battles and Massacres*, 15–26, 51–75; Tiller, *Jicarilla Apache Tribe*, 46–47; Webb, *Chronological List of Engagements*, 11–12; *ARSW*, 1854, 33–34; and Taylor, "Campaigns . . . 1854," 275–76.
33. Tiller, *Jicarilla Apache Tribe*, 47–51; Webb, *Chronological List of Engagements*, 12: Hays, "General Garland's War," 263–64; *ARSW*, 1854, 34–37; *ARSW*, 1855, 57–58.
34. Hays, "General Garland's War," 256–59.
35. *ARSW*, 1855, 57–61; Hays, "General Garland's War," 260–62; Bennett, *Forts*, 60–61, 69; Webb, *Chronological List of Engagements*, 12; Sonnichsen, *Mescalero Apaches*, 74–79; Kuhn, *Chronicles*, 54; Utley, *Frontiersmen*, 149–51; Kiser, *Dragoons*, 244–45.
36. Letter, Apr. 3, 1855, Folder 4, Box 1, Steck Papers, Center for Southwest Research (CSR); Kiser, *Dragoons*, 252–53.
37. *ARSW*, 1855, 69 (see also 62–68, 70–72). See also *ARCIA*, 1855, 506–7; Hays, "General Garland's War," 265–67; Tiller, *Jicarilla Apache Tribe*, 52–53; Taylor, "Campaigns . . . 1855"; and Webb, *Chronological List of Engagements*, 13.

38. *ARCIA*, 1855, 507–8, 526–28; Tiller, *Jicarilla Apache Tribe*, 53–60; Ball, *Army Regulars*, 16; Kiser, *Dragoons*, 164–66. See also Arny, *Indian Agent*; and Letters, Apr. 28, May 3, May 15, and August 28, 1855, Folder 4, Box 1, Steck Papers, CSR.

39. Lane, *I Married*, 65 (see also 66–67). See also Ryan, *Fort Stanton*, 1–32; Kiser, *Dragoons*, 251, 254–55; and Sonnichsen, *Mescalero Apaches*.

40. Kuhn, *Chronicles*, 54–69; Kiser, *Dragoons*, 269–70.

41. Kiser, *Dragoons*, 262–68 (quote on 263); Kiser, *Turmoil*, 118–25; *Santa Fe Weekly Gazette*, Feb. 20, Mar. 6, Apr. 24, July 24, 1858; Kuhn, *Chronicles*, 64–65; Averell, *Ten Years*, 139–42.

42. Smith, *From Dominance*, 161; Britten, *Lipan Apaches*, 207–9, 216–17, 220; Minor, *Turning*, 157; Anderson, *Conquest*, 211, 261–63.

43. Britten, *Lipan Apaches*, 202–13, 218–19; Opler and Ray, "Lipan," 72; Minor, *Turning*, 152–53, 157–60; Robinson, *I Fought*, 215–21; Anderson, *Conquest*, 218–19; Hicks, "Journal." For the treaty texts, see Winfrey and Day, *Texas Indian Papers*, vol. 3.

44. Wislizenus, *Memoir*, 69–72; Duval, *Adventures*, 150–62 (see also 103–10, 163–66); Opler and Ray, "Lipan," 74–75; Anderson, *Conquest*, 220–23; Britten, *Lipan Apaches*, 206–8; Robinson, *I Fought*, 226–27.

45. Olmstead, *Journey*, 296. See also Britten, *Lipan Apaches*, 212–16; 218–19; Smith, *Fort Inge*; Chance, *My Life*, 179; Minor, *Turning*, 176–77; and Sjoberg, "Lipan Apache Culture," 80.

46. Robinson, *I Fought*, 239–50.

47. Minor, *Turning*, 162–63, 169–72, 174–76; Britten, *Lipan Apaches*, 217; Robinson, *I Fought*, 249–50, 252–57.

48. Jacoby, *Shadows*, 68–78, 98; Lahti, *Cultural Construction*, 77–79; Sheridan, *Los Tucsonenses*.

49. Underhill, *Papago Calendar*, 19–23; Emory, *Notes*, 82–89; Clarke, *Original Journals of Henry Smith Turner*, 107–10; *ARCIA*, 1859, 719; De Jong, "'Good Samaritans'"; Turner, "Pima and Maricopa Villages."

50. Kuhn, *Chronicles*, 25–33; Smith, "John Joel Glanton," 9–10; Smith, *Borderlander*, 292–93.

51. Kuhn, *Chronicles*, 25–33, 330–31; Sweeney, *Mangas Coloradas*, 159–77; Chamberlain, *Victorio*, esp. 71.

52. On Kearny and Cooke's encounters with the Apaches, see Clarke, *Original Journals of Henry Smith Turner*, 58–124; Emory, *Notes*, 59–75; Cooke, *Journal*; and Cooke, *Conquest*, esp. 132–41.

53. Bartlett, *Personal Narrative*, vols. 1–2; Emory, *Report*, vols. 1–2.

54. Parke and Emory, *Report of Explorations*.

55. McChristian, *Fort Bowie*, 7–13.

56. On Apaches and Santa Rita, see Chamberlain, *Victorio*, 46–47, 52, 73–76, 84; Sweeney, *Cochise*, 20–21, 40–41; Huggard and Humble, *Santa Rita*, 1–58; Pattie, *Personal Narrative*; and Smith, *Borderlander*, 42–65.

57. Kiser, *Dragoons*, 71, 79–85 (quote on 81); Sweeney, *Mangas Coloradas*, 176–78; Kuhn, *Chronicles*, 30.

58. Bartlett, *Personal Narrative*, 1:300–354; Cremony, *Life among the Apaches*, 23–30, 47–72, 80–88; Sweeney, *Mangas Coloradas*, 227–40.

59. Thompson, "With the Third Infantry," 360–65 (quote on 363); Sweeney, *Mangas Coloradas*, 240–47; Kiser, *Dragoons*, 112–14; Kuhn, *Chronicles*, 40–41.

60. *ARSW*, 1852, 80; Thompson, "With the Third Infantry," 366–68. See also Bennett, *Forts*, 33–37; Sweeney, *Mangas Coloradas*, 249–50; and Kiser, *Dragoons*, 115–19.

61. Kappler, *Indian Affairs*, 598–600; "Articles of the Treaty between Apaches and Colonel E. V. Sumner," Folder 1, Box 3, Steck Papers, CSR; Carson, "William Carr Lane Diary," 191–96, 218–29; Bieber, "Letters," 193–94; Sweeney, *Mangas Coloradas*, 255–61, 273–75; Kiser, *Dragoons*, 126–48.

62. Post Returns, Fort Webster, N.Mex., Roll 1407, M617, NARA; Frazer, *Mansfield*, 25–26; Kiser, *Dragoons*, 158–59.

63. Sweeney, *Mangas Coloradas*, 280; Sweeney, *Cochise*, 94.

64. *ARCIA*, 1855, 507; *ARCIA*, 1856, 731–32; Sweeney, *Mangas Coloradas*, 281–92, 303–14; Kiser, *Dragoons*, 153–67.

65. Webb, *Chronological List of Engagements*, 14–15; Kuhn, *Chronicles*, 57; Kiser, *Dragoons*, 170–79; Sweeney, *Mangas Coloradas*, 321–27. On Steck's protests, see Letters, Apr. 10, June 16, and June 29, 1856, Folder 5, Box 1; July 9, Oct. 18, 1856, Folder 6, Box 1, all in Steck Papers, CSR; and Thrapp, *Victorio*, 48–50.

66. Reeve, "Puritan," 277.

67. Reeve, "Puritan," 296. On the Chiricahua retreat to Mexico, see Sweeney, *Cochise*, 102–5; and Letters, Mar. 5, Mar. 14, Mar. 18, and Mar. 19, 1857, Folder 7, Box 1, Steck Papers, CSR.

68. Hammond, *Campaigns*, 29–30 (see also 3–35). For the Gila Expedition, see also Reeve, "Puritan," 274–301, 12–50; *ARSW*, 1857, 55–56, 135–41; *ARCIA*, 1857, 563–64, 580–84; Kiser, *Dragoons*, 203–31; and Kuhn, *Chronicles*, 63.

69. Thrapp, *Victorio*, 55; Reeve, "Puritan," 12; Hammond, *Campaigns*, 25.

70. *ARSW*, 1859, 300. See also Tevis, *Arizona*, 93–94, 110–14, 146–47, 168–69; *ARCIA*, 1859, 713–14; Letter, Feb. 1, 1859, Folder 9, Box 1, Steck Papers, CSR; Gustafson, *John Spring's Arizona*, 52; and Sweeney, "Cochise and the Prelude."

71. Poston, *Building*, 67–68, 93–99; Cozzens, *Marvelous Country*, 83–97, 164–65, 175–77; Thompson, *Civil War*, 67–78, 135; Kuhn, *Chronicles*, 65–75; Reid, *Reid's Tramp*, 190–93; Tevis, *Arizona*, 97–101, 154–60; Voss, *On the Periphery*, 110. See also Poston, *Apache-Land*; Diary, Folder 2, Box 1, Poston Collection, Arizona State Library, Phoenix; and Storms, *Reconnaissance in Sonora*.

72. Fort Buchanan, N.Mex., Roll 156, Returns from U.S. Military Posts, M617, NARA.

73. Sweeney, *Cochise*, 108–13; Kuhn, *Chronicles*, 66–67.

74. Sweeney, "Cochise and the Prelude," 441–46.

Chapter 5

Epigraph 1: John Taylor interview, 26, Folder 35, Box 3, GP, ASM.
Epigraph 2: Santa Fe Gazette, Dec. 17, 1864, quoted in Masich, *Civil War*, 63–64.

1. *War of the Rebellion: A Compilation of the Official Records* (*OR*), series 1, vol. 34, pt. 3, 387–89; *Indian Tribes*, 172 (see also 173–81).

2. *OR*, series 1, vol. 34, pt. 3, 389. For Carleton's plan, see also *Prescott Arizona Miner*, May 25, 1864, http://chroniclingamerica.loc.gov/lccn/sn82016242/1864-05-25/ed-1/seq-2/ (accessed Oct. 23, 2012); and Haley, *Apaches*, 248.

3. John Rope, a White Mountain Apache, claimed that his people first interacted with white Americans when California Volunteers set up Camp Goodwin in 1864. Goodwin, *Western Apache*, 98–101.

4. Letter no. 4, Feb. 6, 1864, Fort Whipple, Ariz., in Nicholson, *Arizona*, 70; Conner, *Joseph Reddeford Walker*, 188, 221. The goals and methods of the 1860s borderlands wars might fit the parameters of genocide. On settler colonialism and genocide, see Moses, *Empire, Colony, Genocide*; and Wolfe, "Settler Colonialism." For genocide and ethnic cleansing in the American West, see Madley, "Reexamining"; Anderson, *Conquest*; Anderson, *Ethnic Cleansing*; and Lindsay, *Murder State*.

5. Smith, *Captive Arizona*, 56–58; Sweeney, *Cochise*, 144–50; Utley, *Geronimo*, 42. On Feliz Tellez Martinez, see Radbourne, *Mickey Free*; Smith, "White Eyes"; Smith, *Captive Arizona*, 58–60, 70, 74; and Lahti, *Soldiers*.

6. Cochise was allegedly wounded by John Ward. A detailed and authoritative account of the February 1861 events at Apache Pass is Sweeney, *Cochise*, 146–65. See also Utley, *Geronimo*, 38–43; Haley, *Apaches*, 225–28; Worcester, *Apaches*, 75–80; Roberts, *Once They Moved*, 21–29; and Kuhn, *Chronicles*, 79–81.

7. Letters no. 60, 62–63, and 65, Mar. 20, Apr. 1 and 2, and May [?], 1861, Tucson, Ariz., in Altshuler, *Latest from Arizona*, 189–98 (see also 212–26).

8. Geronimo, *His Own Story*, 117.

9. Pumpelly, *Travels*, 168. See also Kuhn, *Chronicles*, 81–86; and Sweeney, *Cochise*, 169–76.

10. The attack against Tubac was possibly the work of Western Apaches. Kuhn, *Chronicles*, 87–88; Sweeney, *Cochise*, 177–78; Wilson, *From Western Deserts*, 56–58; Altshuler, *Latest from Arizona*, 225–26.

11. Utley, *Geronimo*, 36–37; Chamberlain, *Victorio*, 85, 86–88, 94–95; Tevis, *Arizona*, 206–16. A personal account of the gold boom at Pinos Altos is in Anderson, "Mining," esp. 85–94, 111–15.

12. Kuhn, *Chronicles*, 84–90; Sweeney, *Mangas Coloradas*, 400–406, 445; Sweeney, *Cochise*, 178–88; Utley, *Geronimo*, 46, 51; *OR*, series 1, vol. 50, pt. 1, 105; Tevis, *Arizona*, 206–14; Anderson, "Mining," 95–100. The whipping of Mangas Coloradas was a story circulated by Lt. John Cremony of the California Volunteers in his *Life among the Apaches*, 172–73.

13. Kuhn, *Chronicles*, 67–92, 315, 323, 331.

14. Sweeney, *Cochise*, 188 (see also 177).

15. Baylor's report and declaration is in *OR*, series 1, vol. 4, 17–22.

16. Kuhn, *Chronicles*, 88, 91–92; Mangum, "Mays Fight"; Geldard, "The Lost Patrol," Fort Davis National Historic Site (FDNHS); Hall, *Confederate Army*, 327 (see also 306–8); Haas, "Diary," 54.

17. For Baylor's instructions, see *OR*, series 1, vol. 50, pt. 1, 942. On Baylor, the Confederates, and the Apaches, see also *OR*, series 1, vol. 4, 25–26, 60–61; and vol. 15, 914–19; Sonnichsen, *Mescalero Apaches*, 90–94; Hall, "Thomas J. Mastin's 'Arizona Guards'"; Anderson, "Mining," esp. 102–5; Wilson, *When the Texans Came*, 229–35; Thompson, *Westward the Texans*, esp. 19; and Kuhn, *Chronicles*, 89, 92.

18. *OR*, series 1, vol. 15, 857, 914–19 (quotes on 918). Seeking to vindicate his career, by March 1865, Baylor had managed to get a colonel's commission and permission to raise a regiment of volunteers to retake Arizona. At that time, this plan was as unrealistic as the Confederate collapse was imminent.

19. For the Confederate plans and the Battle of Valverde, see, for example, Taylor, *Bloody Valverde*, esp. 136, 142; Frazier, *Blood*, esp. 150–82; and Thompson, *Confederate General*, esp. 216–18, 244–68.

20. On Confederate skirmishes with the Apaches, see Alberts, *Rebels*, esp. 107–29; Thompson, *Westward the Texans*; Thompson, "Is This to Be the Glory"; and Haas, "Diary." On Sibley's views, see Josephy, *Civil War*, 85; and *OR*, series 1, vol. 9, 506–12.

21. On Carleton, see Hunt, *Major General*; Kane, "James H. Carleton"; and Sides, *Blood*, 308–26.

22. Cremony, *Life among the Apaches*, 197. See also Carmony, *Civil War*, 33, 42, 44, 70, 81; Miller, *California Column*, 13–15; Kiser, *Turmoil*, 194–99, 202–7; Masich, *Civil War*, 48–50; Pettis, *California Column*; and *OR*, series 1, vol. 50, pt. 1, 773–80; and pt. 2, 303, 405–6. One Civil War military pass and written oath of allegiance is found in "Oath of Allegiance to U.S.," Folder 11, Box 1, Fourr Papers, AHS.

23. The report of surgeon James M. McNulty is in *OR*, series 1, vol. 50, pt. 1, 136–45. See also Masich, *Civil War*, 14–17, 28–29, 37–38, 42–45; and Utley, *Geronimo*, 49–50. On the size and composition of the California Column, see Pettis, *California Column*, 8; and Masich, *Civil War*, 13–14. On Carleton's instructions to his men, see, for instance, *OR*, series 1, vol. 50, pt. 1, 699–700 (quote), 869–70. For training and the stay at Yuma, see also Carmony, *Civil War*, 18–26, 30–45; Apr. 4, 1862–Apr. 18, 1862, Akers Diary, UASC; Tidball Diary, HL; "Pioneering in the Southwest," Folder 2, Box 2; and "Letters to Sister, 1862–1865," Folder 3, Box 2, both in Tuttle Papers, UASC; and Bowman Diary, UASC.

24. Masich, *Civil War*, 14–17.

25. "Reminiscences," 19–20, Folder 1, Box 1, Ayer Papers, AHS.

26. Carmony, *Civil War*, 23, 36–43, 58, 70, 78–79, 82–83, 85–87, 95–99, 116–18, 157 (long quote on 39). See also Kelly, *Navajo Roundup*, 15; "A Young Man's Life in the West," 96–101, Folder 4, Box 1, Fourr Papers, AHS; Bowman Diary, UASC; Tidball Diary, HL; and Miller, *California Column*, 32–33.

27. Masich, *Civil War*, 18–27.

28. Letter no. 1, Feb. 2, 1863, Fort Craig, N.Mex., in Ryan, *News from Fort Craig*, 34.

29. Masich, *Civil War*, 51–52; *San Francisco Daily Alta California*, Aug. 10, 1862; Cremony, *Life among the Apaches*, 169: *OR*, series 1, vol. 50, pt. 1, 89, 100, 120–22; Sweeney, *Cochise*, 194–98; Kuhn, *Chronicles*, 92–95.

30. For the march from Tucson to Apache Pass, see *OR*, series 1, vol. 50, pt. 1, 130–32.

31. Army reports concerning the battle are in *OR*, series 1, vol. 50, pt. 1, 128–29, 132–34. See also Radbourne, *Battle*, esp. 23, 29; Ball, *Indeh*, 19–20; Ball, *In the Days of Victorio*, 47; Sweeney, *Mangas Coloradas*, 430–40, 531–32; Sweeney, *Cochise*, 198–202; Utley, *Geronimo*, 47–49; McChristian, *Fort Bowie*, 48–63; Letter no. 1, Feb. 2, 1863, Fort Craig, in Ryan, *News from Fort Craig*, 34–36; Walker, "Soldier," esp. 40–41; *Las Cruces Rio Grande Republican*, Jan. 2, 1891; *San Francisco Daily Alta California*, Aug. 16, 1862; Schrier, "California Column"; and Cremony, *Life among the Apaches*, 155–69. On page 169, Cremony gives the number of troops as 129.

32. U.S. army posts in the vicinity of Pinos Altos and Santa Rita del Cobre included the following: 1. Cantonment Dawson, instituted by the boundary commission on January 23, 1851, which occupied the buildings of an old Mexican fort at the abandoned Santa Rita mines. 2. Fort Webster I, set up after the boundary commission left in October 1851 and the army took its place, renaming Cantonment Dawson. 3. Fort Webster II. On September 9, 1852, the camp at the mines was abandoned and a new post was erected at the Mimbres River fourteen miles northeast. This site, in turn, was vacated on December 20, 1853, due to Apache pressure. 4. Fort Webster III. In June 1859, the army ordered troops to safeguard the growing numbers of prospectors at the mines with the intent of setting up a permanent bastion. This, however, was not done due to troop shortage. 5. Fort McLane, first called Fort Floyd, was established by the army on September 16, 1860, fifteen miles south of the Santa Rita mines. The post was abandoned July 3, 1861, due to the Civil War. 6. Fort West, founded by the California Column on February 24, 1863, at the Pinos Altos Mountains, north of present-day Silver City. It was abandoned on January 8, 1864. 7. Fort Bayard, located ten miles east of Silver City, was launched on August 21, 1866, by the army and abandoned after the U.S.-Apache conflicts ended in 1900. Frazer, *Forts of the West*, 95–96, 100, 106–8.

33. *OR*, series 1, vol. 15, 230; and vol. 50, pt. 1, 233–34; Kuhn, *Chronicles*, 96–99, 102; Sweeney, *Cochise*, 202, 208, 210, 214–15; Carmony, *Civil War*, 92.

34. Conner, *Joseph Reddeford Walker*, 35–40; Sweeney, *Mangas Coloradas*, 445–63, (West quote on 455); *OR*, series 1, vol. 50, pt. 2, 296–97; Utley, *Geronimo*, 52–54; Utley, *Frontiersmen*, 249–56.

35. Conner, *Joseph Reddeford Walker*, 40–41; Sweeney, *Mangas Coloradas*, 534–35. The publication that has a photo of the skull is Fowler, *Human Science*, 1195–97.

36. Cremony, *Life among the Apaches*, 176–78 (see also 194–95).

37. Carmony, *Civil War*, 101; *OR*, series 1, vol. 50, pt. 2, 490. See also Sweeney, *Cochise*, 213–14; and Kuhn, *Chronicles*, 97–103.

38. On the journey and observations California soldiers made from Tucson to Mesilla, see Akers Diary, UASC; Aug. 4, 1862–Aug. 20, 1862, Folder 5, Box 1, Bennett Papers, AHS; Carmony, *Civil War*, 89–95; and Walker, "Soldier."

39. *ARCIA*, 1862, 392; Kuhn, *Chronicles*, 89–96, 331.

40. For Carleton's orders, see *OR*, series 1, vol. 15, 579–81; *Indian Tribes*, 99–100 (quote on 100); and Sonnichsen, *Mescalero Apaches*, 98–100.

41. Carleton quoted from Ball, "Fort Craig," 162–63. The Lieber Code, approved by President Abraham Lincoln on April 24, 1863, relied on the thinking of former Prussian military man turned law professor, Francis Lieber. See Jacoby, "Broad Platform," 260; and *OR*, series 3, vol. 2, 301–9; and vol. 3, 148–64.

42. *OR*, series 1, vol. 50, pt. 2, 299; Robinson, *Apache Voices*, 116 (see also 122); Ball, *Indeh*, 200–201. See also *Indians Tribe*, 105–7; Sonnichsen, *Mescalero Apaches*, 100–101; Kuhn, *Chronicles*, 96; and Thompson, *Desert Tiger*, 49–54.

43. *Indian Tribes*, 101–2, 133–34; Sides, *Blood*, 318–19, 326–27; Henry B. Davidson, "Journal of an Expedition to the Bosque Redondo, 1854," Reeve Papers, CSR.

44. On U.S.-Navajo wars, see Kelly, *Navajo Roundup*, esp. 42; Dunlay, *Kit Carson*; Sides, *Blood*, 266–75, 307–8, 336–59; and Thompson, *Army and the Navajo*.

45. On life at Bosque Redondo and Carleton's policies, see Robinson, *Apache Voices*, 122–23; Cremony, *Life among the Apaches*, 198–202; "Reminiscences," 41, Folder 1, Box 1, Ayer Papers, AHS; Sonnichsen, *Mescalero Apaches*, 103–19; Thompson, *Army and the Navajo*, 46–68; Sides, *Blood*, 363–69, 380–88, 400–402; *ARCIA*, 1863, 544–47; *ARCIA*, 1864, 163–65, 327–31, 347–60; *ARCIA*, 1865, 188–91, 345–47, 357–60; *ARCIA*, 1867, 198–203; and *Indian Tribes*, for instance, 197–201, 207–212. On Carleton's ultimatum to the Chihennes, see *OR*, series 1, vol. 48, pt. 1, 1195.

46. Ball, *Indeh*, 201–3; *Indian Tribes*, 107 (see also 108–9, 261). See also Robinson, *Apache Voices*, 116–17, 122–24; and *ARCIA*, 1866, 32, 138–41, 145.

47. On Steck and Carleton, see, for example, Steck's letters for Jan. 25, 1864, May 28, 1864, and June 18, 1864, in Folder 15, Box 1, Steck Papers, CSR; *Indian Tribes*, for example, 155–56, 192–93, 212. See also Sonnichsen, *Mescalero Apaches*, 112–19; *ARCIA*, 1867, 11–13, 190–93; and *ARCIA*, 1868, 464, 620–26, 634.

48. May 23, 1863 letter, Folder 2, Box 1, Benedict Papers, AHS; "A Young Man's Life in the West," 124, Folder 4, Box 1, Fourr Papers, AHS. See also *OR*, series 1, vol. 34, pt. 3, 204–6; and vol. 50, pt. 2, 653–54; *Indian Tribes*, 110, 115, 121–22, 135–36; "A Short Indian Story," esp. 13–18, Folder 7, Box 1, Hughes Papers, AHS; *San Francisco Daily Alta California*, Jan. 26, 1864, and May 14, 1864.

49. Kuhn, *Chronicles*, 100–107.

50. On white settler mentality in the Prescott area during the 1860s, see "A Young Man's Life in the West," 150–89, 202–9, 226, Folder 5, Box 1, Fourr Papers, AHS; Letter no. 4, Feb. 6, 1864, Fort Whipple, Ariz., in Nicholson, *Arizona*, 68, 70; "Reminiscences of an Old Pioneer," 1–10, Folder 2, Box 1, Brichta Papers, AHS; May 21, 1863 letter, Folder 1, Box 1, Benedict Papers, AHS; and Braatz, *Surviving*, 82–90.

51. Woody, "Woolsey Expeditions," 160–61 (emphasis mine). See also Wilson, *When the Texans Came*, 154, 178, 189; Letter no. 5, Jan. 6, 1860, Tubac, Ariz., in Altshuler, *Latest from Arizona*, 25; and Poston, *Apache-Land*, 81–83.

52. Letters no. 5, Jan. 6, 1860, and no. 30, July 18, 1860, both Tubac, Ariz., in Altshuler, *Latest from Arizona*, 25, 105–6.

53. "A Young Man's Life in the West," 194 (see also 190–95), Folder 5, Box 1, Fourr Papers, AHS (emphasis mine). See also *OR*, series 1, vol. 34, pt. 1, 121; and vol. 48, pt. 1, 901; Woody, "Woolsey Expeditions," 162–64; Letter no. 4, Feb. 6, 1864, Fort Whipple,

Ariz., in Nicholson, *Arizona*, 68, 76–77; Braatz, *Surviving*, 94; and Kuhn, *Chronicles*, 104–5.

54. *Prescott Arizona Miner*, Apr. 6, 1864, http://chroniclingamerica.loc.gov/lccn/sn82016242/1864-04-06/ed-1/seq-2/ (accessed Nov. 5, 2012). On Woolsey's campaigns, see also Woody, "Woolsey Expeditions," 164–66; *OR*, series 1, vol. 48, pt. 1, 902–3; and vol. 50, pt. 2, 835; Kuhn, *Chronicles*, 105–7; "Synopsis of Indian Scouts, 1864," Folder 8, Box 1, Bennett Papers, AHS; Letter no. 5, Mar. 16, 1864, Pima villages, Ariz., and letter no. 6, Apr. 5, 1864, Fort Whipple, Ariz., both in Nicholson, *Arizona*, 81–106; and "Reminiscences of an Old Pioneer," 4–10, Folder 2, Box 1, Brichta Papers, AHS.

55. *OR*, series 1, vol. 50, pt. 1, 368–77; and pt. 2, 870–71; Meketa and Meketa, *One Blanket*, 50–58; Kuhn, *Chronicles*, 108–10; *San Francisco Daily Alta California*, June 26, 1864.

56. Reeve, "War," 95–120, contains a diary of Woolsey's summer campaign. See also Woolsey's report in Farish, *History*, 3:258–72.

57. Browne, *Adventures*, 99–102. See also Farish, *History*, 2:215–17; Kuhn, *Chronicles*, 91; and *New York Times*, Mar. 12, 1864. For eyewitness descriptions of this and the possibility of other Apache corpses left hanging, see also Viola, *Memoirs of Charles Henry Veil*, 96–97; and Carmony, *Civil War*, 53–54.

58. Kuhn, *Chronicles*, 104–11, 331.

59. Woody, "Woolsey Expeditions," 159; Haley, *Apaches*, 247.

60. Davis, "Pioneer Days," 106–7, HL. On the use of strychnine against the Apaches, see also Bourke, *On the Border*, 118; and "A Young Man's Life in the West," 118–19, Folder 4, Box 1, Fourr Papers, AHS.

61. When the Civil War started in 1861, most Hispanics, O'odhams, and Maricopas had not shown any particular enthusiasm for the conflict. Not seeing it as their fight, the majority opted for neutrality, and Union recruiters, in their attempt to sell the war to the people, had to resort to representing the conflict either as a contest against a Texan invasion or, when the Texan threat dwindled after 1862, as a race war to suppress the Apaches (and Navajos). See *OR*, series 1, vol. 15, 230–31, 916; and Mora, *Border Dilemmas*.

62. Jacoby, *Shadows*, esp. 37–38; Russell, "Pima Indians," esp. 46; Underhill, *Papago Calendar*, esp. 26. For Anglo views, see, among others, "A Young Man's Life in the West," 146–47, Folder 4, Box 1, Fourr Papers, AHS; "Reminiscences," 29, Folder 1, Box 1, Ayer Papers, AHS; Poston, *Apache-Land*, 87–91; "Reminiscences," 16, Folder 1, Box 1, Tonge Papers, AHS; Cremony, *Life among the Apaches*, 89–107; and Letter no. 8, Apr. 20, 1864, Fort Whipple, Ariz., in Nicholson, *Arizona*, 107–14.

63. Jacoby, *Shadows*, 57–58, 171–73; Opler, "Identity," 725; Goodwin, *Social Organization*, 8, 86, 572; *OR*, series 1, vol. 50, pt. 2, 423; McCarty, *Frontier Documentary*, 50; Sheridan, *Arizona*, 37–39, 46–54; Sheridan, *Los Tucsonenses*.

64. Jacoby, *Shadows*, 81–90; *OR*, series 1, vol. 50, pt. 2, 422–23, 431–32; *Indian Tribes*, 249; *San Francisco Daily Alta California*, Sept. 11, 1863.

65. Webb, *Chronological List of Engagements*, 24–26; Kuhn, *Chronicles*, 120–24; "Arizona Volunteers: Correspondence and Reports, 1864–66," HL; Underhill, "Dr. Edward Palmer's Experiences," 52–53, 61, 66; Thrapp, *Conquest*, 35.

66. *Prescott Arizona Miner,* Apr. 11, 1866, http://chroniclingamerica.loc.gov/lccn/
sn82016242/1866-04-11/ed-1/seq-2/, and Sept. 12, 1866, http://chroniclingamerica.
loc.gov/lccn/sn82016242/1866-09-12/ed-1/seq-2/ (both accessed Jan. 29, 2014). See
also, for example, the issues of *Arizona Miner* for Feb. 28, 1866, Apr. 25, 1866, and
Aug. 22, 1866.

67. Mowry, *Arizona,* 68; Conner, *Joseph Reddeford Walker,* 219–21. The first Arizona
governor, John Goodwin, a lawyer from Maine, advocated the extermination of
the Apaches in a public meeting. Letter no. 4, Feb. 6, 1864, Fort Whipple, Ariz., in
Nicholson, *Arizona,* 76.

68. See, among many others, *ARSW* for 1867, 1868, and 1869; "Synopsis of Indian Scouts
for 1864, Department of New Mexico," Folder 8, Box 1, Bennett Papers, AHS; U.S.
Adjutant-General's Office, *Chronological List of Actions;* and Webb, *Chronological
List of Engagements.*

69. *ARSW,* 1869, 121–22 (see also 127–29); Green, "Interesting Scout," 44. See also Altshuler, *Chains.* Calls for Apache extermination can be found in *San Francisco Daily
Alta California,* for example, Aug. 10, 1862, June 8, 1864, July 31, 1864, and May 6,
1866; and *Prescott Arizona Miner,* for example, Mar. 9, 1864, July 6, 1864, Sept. 21,
1864, Oct. 26, 1864, Sept. 21, 1867.

70. Woolsey's letter from Mar. 29, 1864, is quoted in Jacoby, *Shadows,* 116. On Carleton's
orders for the campaigns against the Mescaleros, Navajos, Western Apaches, and
Comanches, in which he made it clear that no women or children would be killed
intentionally, see *OR,* series 1, vol. 15, 579–81; and vol. 34, pt. 3, 387–89; Sides, *Blood,*
339; Sonnichsen, *Mescalero Apaches,* 98–99; and Dunlay, *Kit Carson,* 329.

71. "Reminiscences of an Old Pioneer," 4, Folder 2, Box 1, Brichta Papers, AHS.

72. Burns, *Only One,* 26–29, 169. See also Brown, "John Benjamin Townsend"; and Wells,
Argonaut Tales, esp. 464.

73. *Prescott Arizona Weekly Miner,* Feb. 4, 1874, http://chroniclingamerica.loc.gov/
lccn/sn82014898/1874-02-06/ed-1/seq-1/; *Tucson Arizona Citizen,* July 8, 1871, http://
chroniclingamerica.loc.gov/lccn/sn82014896/1871-07-08/ed-1/seq-1/ (both accessed
Nov. 26, 2012); Burns, *Only One,* 169; Brown, "John Benjamin Townsend"; Thrapp,
Al Sieber, 64–77, 125 (quote on 67).

74. *OR,* series 1, vol. 50, pt. 1, 367. For the numbers, see Kuhn, *Chronicles,* 315, 319, 331.

Chapter 6

Epigraph 1: Burns, *Only One,* 51.
Epigraph 2: Bailey, *Tenderfoot,* 223.

1. Willcox quoted in Collins, *Apache Nightmare,* 90; *Prescott Weekly Arizona Miner,*
Sept. 9, 1881, http://chroniclingamerica.loc.gov/lccn/sn82014897/1881-09-09/ed-1/
seq-1/ (accessed Nov. 29, 2012). See also Lekson, *Nana's Raid;* and Robinson, *I Fought,*
329–32.

2. Lahti, "Colonized Labor."

3. Davis, *Truth,* 27–28; Diary, Feb. 7, 1886, Chrisman Papers, AHS.

4. On earlier schisms between the regular army and civilian volunteers in U.S. history, see, for instance, Foos, *Short*; Greenberg, *Wicked War*; and Winders, *Mr. Polk's Army*.

5. Sonnichsen, *Tucson*, 102 (see also 103–5). On transcontinental railroads and the Tombstone boom, see Truett, *Fugitive Landscapes*, 58, 61–64; St. John, *Line in the Sand*, 65–71; Faulk, *Tombstone*; Bailey, *"Too Tough to Die"*; and Sheridan, *Arizona*.

6. Colwell-Chanthaphonh, *Massacre*, 24–25, 64 (see also 36–37, 42–43, 65–66); William S. Oury, "Camp Grant Massacre," speech made at the Society of Arizona Pioneers, Apr. 6, 1885, Camp Grant Massacre Ephemera File, AHS. See also Record, *Big Sycamore*, 210–12, 231–42; Sherman Curley interview, 17–18, Folder 32, Box 2, and Walter Hooke interview, 43–44, Folder 34, Box 3, both in GP, ASM; and Kuhn, *Chronicles*, 176.

7. *ARCIA*, 1871, 485–91; Jacoby, *Shadows*, 129–31, 177–80; Record, *Big Sycamore*, 183–89, 191–93; Colwell-Chanthaphonh, *Massacre*, 56–58; Viola, *Memoirs of Charles Henry Veil*, 87–88. Apparently the Apache camp was such a distance away from the post that the soldiers were not alerted of the April 30 attack.

8. In early April, Whitman apparently received verbal instructions—delivered secondhand by a fellow officer—from Col. George Stoneman, commanding Arizona, to continue treating and feeding the Apaches as "prisoners of war." Record, *Big Sycamore*, 193.

9. Colwell-Chanthaphonh, *Massacre*, 42, 58–62; Record, *Big Sycamore*, 189–91, 193–215. After the massacre, Whitman was repeatedly court-martialed, usually because of drunkenness. A series of sick leaves followed, as did a divorce. Effective March 20, 1879, Whitman was retired from the army. Cunnigham, "Calamitous Career"; Altshuler, *Cavalry Yellow*, 365–66.

10. Arizona Legislative Assembly, *Memorial and Affidavits*, 6; Jacoby, *Shadows*, 180, 137 (see also 131–40 for the settlers' viewpoints and activity prior to the attack).

11. Colyer, *Peace*, 14–19, 44–45, 53–55; *ARCIA*, 1872, 533–34. For Aravaipa views on returning to the massacre site, see Walter Hooke interview, 44, Folder 34, Box 3, GP, ASM.

12. It took some nineteen minutes of deliberation for the Tucson jury to acquit the defendants. Record, *Big Sycamore*, 268–70; Jacoby, *Shadows*, 183–88, 191–96, 203–7, 220–29; Colwell-Chanthaphonh, *Massacre*, 70–72; "Extract from day book of the U.S. District Court, First Judicial District, Territory of Arizona," Camp Grant Massacre Ephemera File, AHS. On the eastern press and the Camp Grant Massacre, see, for instance, *New York Times*, May 12, 1871, May 31, 1871, July 20, 1871, and July 21, 1871.

13. On the "Peace Policy" and its further developments, see, among others, Prucha, *Great Father*; Cahill, *Federal Fathers*; and Ostler, *Plains Sioux*.

14. *ARCIA*, 1871, 431.

15. Report, June 21, 1866, Fort McDowell, Ariz., Folder 16, Box 1, Bennett Papers, AHS; Viola, *Memoirs of Charles Henry Veil*, 124–25. See also Carr, "Days of the Empire," 31; and *ARSW*, 1867, 117–19. On Apache fears, see Barney Tisle interview, 69–71, Folder 33, Box 3, and Nancy Wright interview, 12, Folder 34, Box 3, both in GP, ASM.

16. Quote from *ARSW*, 1867, 73 (see also 126). See also Altshuler, *Chains*, 70–73; and Record, *Big Sycamore*, 153.

17. Radbourne, "Great Chief," 28, 30, 32–36, 44; Davisson, "New Light," 428–34; Samuel George interview, 49, Folder 35, Box 4, GP, ASM; Green, "Interesting Scout."

18. Colyer, *Peace*, 3–7, 10–29, 44–45; *ARCIA*, 1872, 533–59, 562; Sonnichsen, *Mescalero Apaches*, 137–39.

19. Colyer, *Peace*, 6; *ARCIA*, 1872, 537.

20. *Tucson Arizona Citizen*, Oct. 14, 1871, http://chroniclingamerica.loc.gov/lccn/ sn82014896/1871-10-14/ed-1/seq-2/ (accessed Nov. 16, 2012); Crook, *His Autobiography*, 167; Bourke, *Diaries*, 51.

21. *Tucson Arizona Citizen*, May 25, 1872, http://chroniclingamerica.loc.gov/lccn/ sn82014896/1872-05-25/ed-1/seq-1/, and June 1, 1872, http://chroniclingamerica.loc. gov/lccn/sn82014896/1872-06-01/ed-1/seq-1/ (both accessed Feb. 7, 2014); *ARCIA*, 1872, 541–42; Howard, *My Life*, 160–62; Marion, "As Long"; Jacoby, *Shadows*, 192–94, 248–53; Colwell-Chanthaphonh, *Massacre*, 68–70; Walter Hooke interview, 45–46, Folder 34, Box 3, GP, ASM; Letters, Oct. 28, 1871, Dec. 7, 1871, Dec. 31, 1871, and Jan. 20, 1872, all Tucson, Ariz., Folder 1, Box 1, Letterbook of Rueben Augustine Wilbur, UASC.

22. On Eskiminzin, see Record, *Big Sycamore*, 26–38, 104–6; Jacoby, *Shadows*, 254–62; Davis, *Truth*, 61–64; Clum, "Es-kim-in-zin"; and "A Paper on Eskiminzin and His Band of Apache Indians," speech made at the Society of Arizona Pioneers, July 28, 1887, Folder 3, Box 1, Francis Goodwin Papers, AHS. For Apache Kid, see Robinson, *Apache Voices*; and McKanna, *Court-Martial*.

23. One government agent noted in 1886 that the Jicarillas "evince very little martial spirit." *ARCIA*, 1886, 419 (see also 567–68 for the Executive Orders for the Jicarilla Reservation in *ARCIA*, 1874 and 1880). See also Tiller, *Jicarilla Apache Tribe*, 61, 68–98; *ARCIA*, 1883, 52–53; *ARCIA*, 1884, 174–77; *ARCIA*, 1885, 375–79; *ARCIA*, 1887, 70–72, 249–50, 382; and *ARSW*, 1883, 143–45.

24. Minor, *Turning*, 177–78; Robinson, *I Fought*, 269–70, 277–83; Opler and Ray, "Lipan," 85; Britten, *Lipan Apaches*, 218–23.

25. Opler and Ray, "Lipan," 88–89 (see also 93–95). See also *ARCIA*, 1873, 537–41; Carter, "Raid"; Carter, *On the Border with MacKenzie*, 422–65; Wallace, *Ranald S. MacKenzie's Official Correspondence*, 161–62; U.S. Congress. House, *Texas Border Troubles*, 187–88; Britten, *Lipan Apaches*, 223–26; Wooster, "Army," 154–56; Robinson, *I Fought*, 288–95; and Smith, "U.S. Army Combat Operations," esp. 512, 519–20.

26. Robinson, *I Fought*, 290–91.

27. Britten, *Lipan Apaches*, 226–27, 230; Robinson, *I Fought*, 295–96, 320–21, 327, 366–67.

28. Sweeney, *Cochise*, 212–25; Kuhn, *Chronicles*, 102–5, 111.

29. Letter no. 15, Dec. 12, 1864, Tubac, Ariz., in Nicholson, *Arizona*, 168–69. See also *ARSW*, 1867, 96–97.

30. Sweeney, *Cochise*, 227–30; 248–49, 251–59; *ARSW*, 1867, 89–95, 97, 125, 129–30, 143–44, 161–62, 488; Kuhn, *Chronicles*, 122–46, 315, 319.

31. Letters, May 10, 1869, and July 15, 1869, both Tubac, Ariz., Folder 1, Box 1, Smith Letters, AHS. See also Altshuler, "Regulars," 120–22; "Reminiscences," 17–18, Folder 1, Box 1,

Tonge Papers, AHS; Letter no. 16, Dec. 22, 1864, Tubac, Ariz., and Letter no. 18, Jan. 3, 1865, Santa Rita, Ariz., both in Nicholson, *Arizona*, 176–80, 198; and Petra Etchells, "A Brave Woman," 2–5, Folder 6, Box 2, Wood Papers, AHS.

32. Post Returns, Fort Bowie, Oct.–Nov. 1865, Roll 129, M617, NARA; "The Apaches Past and Present," chap. 14, Folder 10, Box 1, Connell Papers, AHS; Kuhn, *Chronicles*, 118–20; Sweeney, *Cochise*, 235, 237–38, 240, 261–64.

33. *Tucson Weekly Arizonian*, Sept. 17, 1870, http://chroniclingamerica.loc.gov/lccn/sn84024829/1870-09-17/ed-1/seq-1/ (accessed Feb. 12, 2014); Arny, *Indian Agent*, 54–58; Utley, *Geronimo*, 58–60. Colyer's initial authorization called for him "to collect the wild Indians of New Mexico and Arizona to Cañada Alamosa," but en route he received instructions from Washington to use his own judgment "in locating the roving tribes in those Territories on suitable reservations." Colyer rationalized his choice by arguing that Tularosa Valley was remote enough from whites, secluded by mountains, and had good water and plenty of wood and game. Colyer, *Peace*, 7, 39, 45.

34. *ARCIA*, 1869, 537, 546–52, 689–91; *ARCIA*, 1872, 681–82, 690–91; Colyer, *Peace*, 8, 10–11, 40–42, 44–45.

35. For Howard's mission and treaty with the Chokonens, see *ARCIA*, 1872, 559–62; Sweeney, *Making Peace*; and Sweeney, *Cochise*, 356–66.

36. On Crook's campaign, see Bourke, *On the Border*, 181–84; Crook, *His Autobiography*, 174–78; Gates, "General Crook's," 312–15; and Thrapp, *Conquest*, 119–21 (quotes from 120).

37. On O'odham frustrations, see Letters, Dec. 7, 1871, Oct. 4, 1872, and Mar. 31, 1873, all Tucson, Ariz., Folder 1, Box 1, all in Letterbook of Rueben Augustine Wilbur, UASC; Cruse, *Apache Days*, 156–57; Turner, "Pima and Maricopa Villages," 368–74; De Jong, *Stealing*; and Meeks, *Border Citizens*.

38. U.S. Adjutant-General's Office, *Chronological List of Actions*, 52–53; Kuhn, *Chronicles*, 187–90; Thrapp, *Conquest*, 121–32; Braatz, *Surviving*, 137–39; Gates, "General Crook's," 316–17; Bourke, *Diaries*, 27–52; Burns, *Only One*, 4–6.

39. Crook, *His Autobiography*, 178. See also Kuhn, *Chronicles*, 190–92; and Webb, *Chronological List of Engagements*, 63–64.

40. Braatz, *Surviving*, 139–41, 145–48; Sherman Curley interview, 135–37, Folder 33, Box 3; Barney Tisle interview, 69, Folder 33, Box 3; Nancy Wright interview, 12–4, Folder 34, Box 3; John Sippi interview, 76–78, Folder 34, Box 3, Charlie Norman interview, 258–67, Folder 34, Box 3, all in GP, ASM.

41. Webb, *Chronological List of Engagements*, 67–70; U.S. Adjutant-General's Office, *Chronological List of Actions*, 55–57; Kuhn, *Chronicles*, 193–200; Thrapp, *Al Sieber*, 126–30, 135, 142–45; Thrapp, *Conquest*, 157–59; Braatz, *Surviving*, 142; King, "On Campaign"; *Prescott Arizona Weekly Miner*, Apr. 10, 1874, http://chroniclingamerica. loc.gov/lccn/sn82014898/1874-04-10/ed-1/seq-2/ (accessed Feb. 24, 2014).

42. Price, *Across the Continent*, 148; *ARSW*, 1873, 51–52; Crook, *His Autobiography*, 179; Bourke, *Diaries*, 34, 37, 45–46; Bourke, *On the Border*, 213.

43. Crook quoted in Bourke, *Diaries*, 453.

44. Haley, *Apaches*, 294–97; *ARCIA*, 1873, 657; Thrapp, *Conquest*, 147–52; Walter Hooke interview, 46–47, Folder 34, Box 3, GP, ASM.
45. *ARCIA*, 1873, 657; *Tucson Arizona Citizen*, May 31, 1873, http://chroniclingamerica.loc. gov/lccn/sn82014896/1873-05-31/ed-1/seq-2/ (accessed Feb. 24, 2014); Haley, *Apaches*, 297–98; Thrapp, *Conquest*, 152–54.
46. Letter, July 6, 1873, Schuyler Papers, HL. On the army's reservation management, see *ARSW*, 1874, 61–63; Bourke, *Diaries*, 88–91; Loring, "Report," 200–202; and Splitter, "Tour in Arizona," 86–87.
47. *ARSW*, 1874, 56, 61–63; Merritt, "Incidents," 161. See also Nickerson, "Major General," 15–17, HL; Crook, *His Autobiography*, 181–82; Corbusier, *Soldier*, 84, 192; and Walter Hooke interview, 48–49, Folder 34, Box 3, GP, ASM.
48. Bourke, *Diaries*, 134–39.
49. "Experiences with the Apaches," Reel 2, Gatewood Collection, AHS.
50. Sweeney, *From Cochise to Geronimo*, 22–25; McChristian, *Fort Bowie*, 151–57; "A Short Indian Story" typescript, 32–37; Folder 7, Box 1, Hughes Papers, AHS; Robinson, *General Crook*, 130–31; *ARSW*, 1874, 64–65; Utley, *Geronimo*, 72–77. Utley points out that, perhaps unknown to Crook, an executive order from December 14, 1872, presumably dictated by Howard, established and set the boundaries of the Chokonen Reservation.
51. *ARCIA*, 1873, 659–61; *ARCIA*, 1874, 369, 595–96; *ARCIA*, 1876, 407; U.S. Congress. House, "Estimate of Appropriation for the Indian Service in Arizona," 1–6.
52. Cochise's words were recorded in a conference between him and the army in the Dragoon Mountains on February 3, 1873. The meeting came after Crook, uncertain of Howard's peace terms and irritated by Chiricahua raiding in Mexico, prepared an offensive against the Chiricahuas, but hesitated and decided to ask Cochise of what had actually been agreed upon between him and Howard. Bourke, *Diaries*, 468–70 (emphasis mine).
53. *ARCIA*, 1876, 395–96, 407–8; Letter, June 5, 1876, Apache Pass, Ariz., Folder 5, Box 1, Hughes Papers, AHS; Utley, *Geronimo*, 74–85; Sweeney, *From Cochise to Geronimo*, 47–50.
54. Davisson, "New Light," 434–40; *ARSW*, 1875, 121–22, 135–36; *ARSW*, 1876, 99–101.
55. Summerhayes, *Vanished Arizona*, 89.
56. *ARCIA*, 1875, 717–22; *ARCIA*, 1876, 414–16; *ARCIA*, 1877, 430–31; Worcester, *Apaches*, 175–205; Haley, *Apaches*, 307–10; Dibbern, "Reputation," 202–4, 209–13, 215–17; Tate, "John P. Clum"; Clum, *Apache Agent*, esp. 250–57. Clum, a New Yorker recommended by the Reformed Church, relocated to Tombstone, where he became a successful newspaperman. He sought, futilely, reappointment as the agent at San Carlos. Carmony, *Apache Days*. On mining and San Carlos, see Hodge, *Arizona*, 115–20.
57. The army judged Camps Crittenden, abandoned in 1873, Date Creek, discarded in 1874, Goodwin, shut down in 1871, and Grant, relocated in 1873, as dangerous to the health of their occupants. See U.S. Surgeon General's Office, *Circular No. 8*; and Frazer, *Forts of the West*, 5–9.
58. Ball, *In the Days of Victorio*, 28. See also *ARCIA*, 1878, 503–4; *ARCIA*, 1879, 105, 113–14, 334; *ARSW*, 1879, 165–66; and Utley, *Geronimo*, 94–96. Upon seeing the San Carlos Agency, an army officer called the place "Hell's Forty Acres." Davis, *Truth*, 31.

59. Utley, *Geronimo*, 87; Kuhn, *Chronicles*, 209; Geronimo, *His Own Story*, 121–22; Sweeney, *From Cochise to Geronimo*, 76–77.

60. Utley, *Geronimo*, 87, 89–90, 95, 98–99; Geronimo, *His Own Story*, 105; Kuhn, *Chronicles*, 201–11, 216, 220; Fontana, *Englishman's Arizona*, 38–59.

61. Radbourne, "Juh-Geronimo Surrender," 1–18; *ARSW*, 1880, 206–7; Robinson, *Apache Voices*, 103.

62. U.S. Congress. House, *Mexican Border Troubles*, 172–74, 195; *ARSW*, 1878, 88; *New York Times*, Oct. 24, 1878, and Nov. 7, 1878; Wooster, "Army"; Minor, *Turning*, 185–90; Britten, *Lipan Apaches*, 228–30; Robinson, *I Fought*, 312–20.

63. Ball, *In the Days of Victorio*, xiii. For the closure of Ojo Caliente, see also Thrapp, *Victorio*, 187–90.

64. Watt, "Victorio's Military," 457; Chamberlain, *Victorio*, 151–58.

65. Chamberlain, *Victorio*, 159–65, 170–75; Ball, *In the Days of Victorio*, 71; Gatewood, "Campaigning," 215–18 (quote on 217); Watt, "Victorio's Military," 464; Kuhn, *Chronicles*, 224–27.

66. Robinson, *I Fought*, 284–85, 302–10, 323.

67. Chamberlain, *Victorio*, 175–82; Haley, *Apaches*, 324–25; Robinson, *Apache Voices*, 148; *ARSW*, 1880, 104, 216; Watt, "Victorio's Military," 464, 478–80; Ball, *In the Days of Victorio*, 12–15; Kuhn, *Chronicles*, 227–30; Thrapp, *Victorio*, 255–57; Gatewood, "Campaigning," 218–23.

68. Kuhn, *Chronicles*, 230–32.

69. Cruse, "From Hembrillo Canyon," esp. 263; Cruse, *Apache Days*, 71–77; Conline, "Campaign," 224–26; Laumbach, *Hembrillo*; *ARSW*, 1880, 93–95, 102, 217, 220–22; Sonnichsen, *Mescalero Apaches*, 173–78; Watt, "Victorio's Military," 480–86.

70. Haley, *Apaches*, 325–27 (quote on 326); *Tucson Weekly Arizona Citizen*, June 19, 1880, http://chroniclingamerica.loc.gov/lccn/sn82016240/1880-06-19/ed-1/seq-1/ (accessed Mar. 20, 2014); *ARSW*, 1880, 95–98 (quotes on 97 and 98), 155–57.

71. *ARSW*, 1881, 118; *ARCIA*, 1880, 118–19, 251–53; Robinson, *Apache Voices*, 147–49; Cruse, *Apache Days*, 77–80; Chamberlain, *Victorio*, 187–89; Sonnichsen, *Mescalero Apaches*, 175–85. Apaches at the Mescalero Reservation remained under military authority until March 1881.

72. Kuhn, *Chronicles*, 237; *ARSW*, 1880, 96–97, 99–100, 107–9, 217; Haley, *Apaches*, 327–28; Goodwin, *Western Apache*, 116–26; Watt, "Apaches Without and Enemies Within."

73. U.S. Adjutant-General's Office, *Chronological List of Actions*, 70–72; Webb, *Chronological List of Engagements*, 86–89.

74. *ARSW*, 1880, 157–63; Cruse, *Apache Days*, 81–85; Chamberlain, *Victorio*, 189–98; Watt, "Victorio's Military," 465–66, 475; Grierson, "Journal," FDNHS; Kuhn, *Chronicles*, 238–40; Dinges, "Victorio Campaign," 89–93.

75. Chamberlain, *Victorio*, 202–7. For Apache versions of Tres Castillos, see Ball, *In the Days of Victorio*, 88–99; and Robinson, *Apache Voices*, 17–26. Col. Buell's report, dated Nov. 20, 1880, is in Crimmins, "Col. Buell's Expedition," 135–42.

76. Splitter, "Tour in Arizona," 78, 80, 83–84.

77. Minor, *Turning*, 191; Britten, *Lipan Apaches*, 230; Lekson, *Nana's Raid*; Kuhn, *Chronicles*, 242–47.

78. *ARSW*, 1881, 126–27. See also *ARCIA*, 1881, 5–6; Lekson, *Nana's Raid*, esp. 32; Thrapp, *Conquest*, 212–16; and Sonnichsen, *Mescalero Apaches*, 211–17. For press coverage on Nana's raid, see, for example, *Baton Rouge Louisiana Capitolian*, Aug. 27, 1881, http://chroniclingamerica.loc.gov/lccn/sn88064592/1881-08-27/ed-1/seq-2/; *St. Paul (Minn.) Daily Globe*, Aug. 22, 1881, http://chroniclingamerica.loc.gov/lccn/sn83025287/1881-08-22/ed-1/seq-2/; *Daily Los Angeles Herald*, Aug. 13, 1881, http://chroniclingamerica.loc.gov/lccn/sn85042459/1881-08-13/ed-1/seq-1/; and *Washington (D.C.) National Tribune*, Aug. 27, 1881, http://chroniclingamerica.loc.gov/lccn/sn82016187/1881-08-27/ed-1/seq-1/ (all accessed Nov. 30, 2012).

79. Davisson, "New Light," 423, 440–42; Welch, Colwell-Chanthaphonh, and Altaha, "Retracing the Battle of Cibecue," 140–43; Kessel, "Battle," 125–26; "Trip to Arizona from Utah" typescript, 8–19, Folder 2, Box 1, Adams Papers, AHS; Worcester, *Apaches*, 235–37. After leaving the agency in April 1882, Tiffany faced charges. He was accused of pocketing government payments intended for the Indians, cooperation with contractors by, for instance, giving receipts for supplies that were never delivered, and sending Apaches to work on mines with government tools and wagons. The grand jury proceedings, which carried over to December 1883, could not, however, make a case for embezzlement, grand larceny, and conspiracy. Dibbern, "Reputation," 214, 216–22; Bourke, *On the Border*, 439–40.

80. Collins, *Apache Nightmare*, 45–76; Welch, Colwell-Chanthaphonh, and Altaha, "Retracing the Battle of Cibecue"; Alchisay et al., "Apache Story," 295–310; Kessel, "Battle," 130–33; Ball, *Indeh*, 52–55; *ARSW*, 1881, 120–21, 139–47, 153–55; *ARSW* 1882, 143–52; Cruse, *Apache Days*, 93–145; Carter, *From Yorktown*, 209–37; Barnes, *Apaches and Longhorns*, 50–91; Finerty, "On Campaign," 236–61.

81. Collins, *Apache Nightmare*, 70 (see also 82–89).

82. *Tucson Arizona Weekly Citizen*, Sept. 4, 1881, http://chroniclingamerica.loc.gov/lccn/sn82015133/1881-09-04/ed-1/seq-2/ (accessed Nov. 29, 2012); *New York Times*, Sept. 4, 1881; Collins, *Apache Nightmare*, 85 (Associated Press quote).

83. Bailey, *Tenderfoot*, 171 (see also 180–84, 223–24); William M. Breckenridge, "Trailing Geronimo," 1–5, Folder 4, Box 1, Wood Papers, AHS.

84. Sweeney, *From Cochise to Geronimo*, 177–84 (Naiche quote on 184); Worcester, *Apaches*, 262.

85. Collins, *Great Escape*, 59–73; Kuhn, *Chronicles*, 248–49; Sweeney, *From Cochise to Geronimo*, 186–87; *ARSW*, 1882, 146–47; Breckenridge, "Trailing Geronimo," 1–5, Folder 4, Box 1, Wood Papers, AHS.

86. Worcester, *Apaches*, 252; Sweeney, *From Cochise to Geronimo*, 187–90; Geronimo, *His Own Story*, 128; Kuhn, *Chronicles*, 249–50; Ludwig and Stute, *Battle*; Collins, *Great Escape*, esp. 73–86.

87. *ARSW*, 1882, esp. 146; Collins, *Apache Nightmare*, 88–94, 103.

88. Barnes, "Apaches' Last Stand," 267–85; *ARSW*, 1882, 150–51; Cruse, *Apache Days*, 158–72; Cruse, "From Hembrillo Canyon," 265–66; Kuhn, *Chronicles*, 257–58.

89. Robinson, *I Fought*, 333–44, 347–51.

Chapter 7

Epigraph 1: Ball, *In the Days of Victorio*, 180.

Epigraph 2: Letter, May 24, 1886, Willcox, Ariz., Sherman Miles Manuscript (in possession of the author courtesy of Robert Wooster).

1. Hanna, "With Crawford," 511–12; Elliott, "Geronimo Campaign," 431–35 (quote on 434). See also Kuhn, *Chronicles*, 275.

2. Hanna, "With Crawford," 514.

3. The number of troops in Arizona and New Mexico rose from 3,276 soldiers in 1884 to 4,803 by 1886. *ARSW*, 1884, 62–67; *ARSW*, 1886, 92–95.

4. On the economic colonization of the borderlands, see Sheridan, *Arizona*; Robbins, *Colony*; Lamar, *Far Southwest*; Truett, *Fugitive Landscapes*; Meeks, *Border Citizens*; Benton-Cohen, *Borderline Americans*; Sayre, "Cattle Boom"; and St. John, *Line in the Sand*.

5. Kuhn, *Chronicles*, 327, 331 (see also 251–92 for a summary description of each engagement from 1882 to 1886).

6. Civilians or reservation Indians killed one Chiricahua in 1885 and three in 1886. Webb, *Chronological List of Engagements*, 93–95; U.S. Adjutant-General's Office, *Chronological List of Actions*, 76–78; Kuhn, *Chronicles*, 272–82, 287, 315–19, 323.

7. See, among others, *ARSW*, 1882, 146; *ARSW*, 1883, 166–67; *ARSW*, 1886, 11–12, 72–73; Jerome, "Soldiering"; Pettit, "Apache Campaign Notes"; "Trailing Geronimo," Folder 5, Box 1, Mazzanovich Papers, AHS; and "Experiences among Apaches," Reel 2, Gatewood Collection, AHS.

8. Lamar, *Far Southwest*, 410; Faulk, *Geronimo Campaign*, 77.

9. The *New York Times*, for example, ran more than ten pieces on Apaches nearly every month between May 1885 and May 1886. On press coverage, see Stenlund, "Sota," esp. 118; Lummis, *Dateline*; and Caffey, "Theatrical Campaign."

10. *ARSW*, 1883, 167; *ARSW*, 1885, 172.

11. Most of these Chiricahuas were killed by Mexican troops south of the border. Kuhn, *Chronicles*, 319.

12. Bourke, *Apache Campaign*, 16; Davis, *Truth*, 150–52.

13. Sweeney, *From Cochise to Geronimo*, 190–206.

14. Betzinez, *I Fought*, 56.

15. Ibid., 56–64; *ARSW*, 1882, 147–48; Utley, *Geronimo*, 114–16; Goodwin, *Western Apache*, 140–47; Shapard, *Chief Loco*, 152–86. For the puberty ceremony, see Opler, *Apache Life-Way*, 82–134.

16. Forsyth, *Thrilling Days*, 79–107 (quotes on 80–81 and 105); Betzinez, *I Fought*, 62–68 (quote on 63).

17. Sweeney, *From Cochise to Geronimo*, 216–22; Thrapp, *Al Sieber*, 225–43; Thrapp, *Conquest*, 228–36; Debo, *Geronimo*, 145–49; Betzinez, *I Fought*, 68–70; *ARSW*, 1882, 148–50; Kuhn, *Chronicles*, 256.

18. Betzinez, *I Fought*, 72.

19. Robinson, *Apache Voices*, 35–44; Sweeney, *From Cochise to Geronimo*, 222–29; Debo, *Geronimo*, 149–53; Kuhn, *Chronicles*, 256; Ball, *In the Days of Victorio*, 144–45.

20. Betzinez, *I Fought*, 76.
21. Utley, *Geronimo*, 121; Roberts, *Once*, 204–5.
22. Betzinez, *I Fought*, 76–77, 81–82, 88; Ball, *Indeh*, 2–6; Apr. 7, 1883, vol. 65, Bourke Diary, AHS. At least one Anglo, Zebina Nathaniel Streeter, was also with the Chiricahuas. Robinson, *Apache Voices*, 45–48.
23. Betzinez, *I Fought*, 77–80; Thrapp, *Conquest*, 263; Kraft, *Gatewood*, 13–14.
24. Sweeney, *From Cochise to Geronimo*, 283–88; Ball, *Indeh*, 70–73; Betzinez, *I Fought*, 97–102. On Juh's death, see Sweeney, *From Cochise to Geronimo*, 331–32; Ball, *Indeh*, 75–77; and Roberts, *Once They Moved*, 216.
25. Thrapp, *General Crook*, 106–11; *ARSW*, 1883, 161, 173; Goodwin, *Western Apache*, 149–53.
26. Simmons, *Massacre*, 84–130; *ARSW*, 1883, 161–63, 173–74; Sweeney, *From Cochise to Geronimo*, 290–97; McChristian, *Fort Bowie*, 186–87; Thrapp, *Conquest*, 267–71.
27. *Tucson Arizona Daily Star*, Mar. 28, 1883, AHS; *Tombstone Republican*, Apr. 5, 1883, AHS; *Tombstone Daily Epitaph*, Mar. 25, 1883, AHS; Simmons, *Massacre*, 119, 136–61.
28. Bourke, *Apache Campaign*, 11; Thrapp, *General Crook*, 107; *ARSW*, 1883, 163.
29. *ARSW*, 1883, 166–67. See also Crook, *Resume*, 4, 20–22.
30. *ARSW*, 1883, 179–81. See also Davis, *Truth*, 30–44. Because so many of them enlisted, the White Mountain and Cibecue Apaches could return to the vicinity of Fort Apache.
31. Thrapp, *General Crook*, 118.
32. Frelinghuysen, "Mexico: Reciprocal Right."
33. For the preparation, see *ARSW*, 1883, 173–75; Bourke, *Apache Campaign*, 20–21, 39–41; Bourke, *On the Border*, 453; and Thrapp, *General Crook*, 124–29. On packtrains, see C. L. Elliott, "Pack Transportation: The Pack Train," Folder 1, Box 1, Beaumont Forsyth Papers, AHS. For "Peaches," see Peaches interview, esp. 16, Folder 35, Box 3, GP, ASM; Betzinez, *I Fought*, 117–18; Bourke, *Apache Campaign*, 14–17; and Goodwin, *Western Apache*, 149. For eyewitness descriptions of the 1883 Sierra Madre operation, see Bourke, *Apache Campaign*; Goodwin, *Western Apache*, 148–72, 197–200; Forsyth, "Diary"; and Randall, "In the Heart."
34. Betzinez, *I Fought*, 110–12. See also Sweeney, *From Cochise to Geronimo*, 302–3; Thrapp, *General Crook*, 141–42; and Kuhn, *Chronicles*, 267.
35. Bourke, *Apache Campaign*, 68–78; *ARSW*, 1883, 175–76; Kuhn, *Chronicles*, 268; Goodwin, *Western Apache*, 158–61.
36. Geronimo, *His Own Story*, 107. See also Sweeney, *From Cochise to Geronimo*, 302–4; and Simmons, *Massacre*, 158–60.
37. Bourke, *Apache Campaign*, 86; May 15, 1883, and May 22, 1883, vol. 67, Bourke Diary, AHS; Forsyth, "Diary," 392–93.
38. Roberts, *Once They Moved*, 235–38; Ball, *Indeh*, 154; Goodwin, *Western Apache*, 167; Bourke, *Apache Campaign*, 78–84.
39. For Crook's negotiation tactics, see *ARSW*, 1883, 176–78; Bourke, *Apache Campaign*, 85–88; and Forsyth, "Diary," 393.
40. For Crook's knowledge of the Garcia fight, see Crook, "Apache Affairs," 396–404.

41. Goodwin, *Western Apache*, 168–69; Thrapp, *General Crook*, 148–67.

42. *ARSW*, 1883, 166, 176–78; Thrapp, *General Crook*, 165–66. See also Bourke, *Apache Campaign*, 88–89, 102–3.

43. Bourke, *On the Border*, 453–55; Bourke, *Apache Campaign*, 104. See also *ARSW*, 1883, 178; and May 10, 1883, vol. 67, Bourke, Diary, AHS. For the Tucson reception, see *Tucson Arizona Star*, June 21, 1883, AHS. For the critique, see *Tucson Arizona Weekly Citizen*, June 30, 1883, http://chroniclingamerica.loc.gov/lccn/sn82015133/1883-06-30/ed-1/seq-1/; and *Yuma Arizona Sentinel*, July 21, 1883, http://chroniclingamerica.loc.gov/lccn/sn84021912/1883-07-21/ed-1/seq-2/ (both accessed Nov. 28, 2013).

44. On the fate of Charlie McComas, see Betzinez, *I Fought*, 118–20; *ARSW*, 1883, 176; "Dan Williamson interview," Folder 6, Box 1, Wood Manuscripts, AHS; Randall, "In the Heart," 394–95; Sweeney, *From Cochise to Geronimo*, 306–7, 333–35, 343–44, 359; Simmons, *Massacre*, 161–87; and Ball, *Indeh*, 51.

45. *ARSW*, 1885, 174–79 (quote on 175).

46. Lt. Britton Davis, Third Cavalry, first reported for duty on December 1, 1881, in Wyoming. He was transferred to Arizona in 1882. Davis, *Truth*, 7–8 (see also 77–101); Altshuler, *Cavalry Yellow*, 94–95.

47. Crook, *Resume*, 2–5; *ARSW*, 1883, 167–68, 173–77, 181–82; *ARSW*, 1884, 131–36; Davis, *Truth*, esp. 33, 122–37; Bourke, *On the Border*, 215–29.

48. Ball, *In the Days of Victorio*, 156; Sweeney, *From Cochise to Geronimo*, 368–70.

49. On tiswin, see *ARSW*, 1883, 172; *ARSW*, 1885, 177; Howard, *My Life*, 182–83, 216; Loring, "Report," 193; Carter, *From Yorktown to Santiago*, 211, 242; and Barnes, *Apaches and Longhorns*, 50–51. On nose cutting, see Bourke, *Diaries*, 92; Bourke, *On the Border*, 17; Loring, "Report," 189; and Summerhayes, *Vanished Arizona*, 84.

50. Geronimo, *His Own Story*, 129; Davis, "Difficulties," 488.

51. Ball, *In the Days of Victorio*, 164–65, 175. See also Davis, *Truth*, 124–30; Utley, *Geronimo*, 151–52; Debo, *Geronimo*, 226–28; *ARSW*, 1884, 135; and *ARSW*, 1885, 175–76. Kaytennae was brought back to Arizona for the conference at Canyon de Los Embudos in March 1886. Davis, *Truth*, 199; Crook, *Resume*, 10; Ball, *In the Days of Victorio*, 187, 190, 200.

52. It is possible that Geronimo and others had heard of the passing of a new law by Congress, the Major Crimes Act, which stated that serious offenses should be tried in civilian courts instead of tribal courts. Gatewood, *Lt. Charles Gatewood and His Apache Wars Memoir*, 7–9; Prucha, *Documents*, 166.

53. Evidently Crook never received Davis's telegram because it did not go beyond San Carlos, where Capt. Francis Pierce, who had replaced Crawford, after asking advice from the veteran scout Al Sieber, deemed the incident just another unimportant tiswin drunk and opted not to forward the message. Davis, *Truth*, 144–49 (quote on 145). See also Ball, *In the Days of Victorio*, 176; and Thrapp, *Al Sieber*, 294.

54. Geronimo, *His Own Story*, 128, 131.

55. The estimates on how many Chiricahuas actually left with Geronimo differ. Ball, *In the Days of Victorio*, 177, 181; Parker, *Old Army*, 152; *ARSW*, 1885, 169; Elliott, "Geronimo Campaign," 428.

56. Kraft, *Gatewood and Geronimo*, 88; Thrapp, *Conquest*, 322–23; *ARSW*, 1885, 161–63, 170; *ARSW*, 1886, 148.

57. Parker, *Old Army*, 152–54; Davis, *Truth*, 151; Kraft, *Gatewood and Geronimo*, 87–90; *ARSW*, 1885, 169; Ball, *In the Days of Victorio*, 177; Dinges, "Leighton Finley," 168.

58. Ball, *In the Days of Victorio*, 177–78; Ball, *Indeh*, 98.

59. Parker, *Old Army*, 154–56.

60. Ibid., 157–67; May 17–22, 1885, Notebook 4, Finley Papers, UASC.

61. For Crook's troop deployment, see Post Returns, Fort Bowie, June 1885, 326–7, Roll 130, M617, NARA; *ARSW*, 1885, 163; Crook, *Resume*; and Faulk, *Geronimo Campaign*, 61–62.

62. Bigelow, *On the Bloody Trail*, 25–109 (quote on 145).

63. Gatewood, *Lt. Charles Gatewood and His Apache Wars Memoir*, 173.

64. On the summer campaign of 1885 in Mexico, see Hanna, "With Crawford"; Elliott, "Geronimo Campaign"; Davis, *Truth*; Crawford to Capt. Charles Morton, June 10, 1885, and June 19, 1885, Folder 8, Box 1, Morton Papers, AHS; Frank West Journal, UASC; U.S. Adjutant-General's Office, *Chronological List of Actions*, 77; Webb, *Chronological List of Engagements*, 94; Sweeney, *From Cochise to Geronimo*, 444–45; and Debo, *Geronimo*, 245–47.

65. Sweeney, *From Cochise to Geronimo*, 461–64, 468–71. Geronimo's wife in question had surrendered at the Mescalero Agency in June and had been brought back to San Carlos. Those family members caught by Wirt Davis were not at the reservation. *ARSW*, 1885, 163.

66. Debo, *Geronimo*, 244. Crook wrote that Chiricahuas were selected "for the reasons that they were thoroughly familiar with the country in which they would be required to operate; they were superior to any other Indians, and fully up to the standard of the renegades." Crook, *Resume*, 6 (see also 20–22).

67. *ARSW*, 1886, 8. See also Sweeney, *From Cochise to Geronimo*, 454, 462–66, 473; and Faulk, *Geronimo Campaign*, 69–70.

68. *ARSW*, 1886, 150–51.

69. Thrapp, *Conquest*, 331; Crook, *Resume*, 7.

70. Kraft, *Gatewood and Geronimo*, 108–11; Utley, *Geronimo*, 173–74; Faulk, *Geronimo Campaign*, 70–73.

71. Sweeney, *From Cochise to Geronimo*, 479, 487–90; *ARSW*, 1886, 151; Ball, *In the Days of Victorio*, 179; Worcester, *Apaches*, 295.

72. "Resolution Adopted at Meeting of Residents of Cochise County"; *Tucson Arizona Weekly Citizen*, May 30, 1885, http://chroniclingamerica.loc.gov/lccn/sn82015133/1885-05-30/ed-1/seq-1/; *Globe Arizona Silver Belt*, May 23, 1885, http://chroniclingamerica.loc.gov/lccn/sn84021913/1885-05-23/ed-1/seq-2/ (both accessed Oct. 5, 2011). Critical toward the army, eastern papers typically blamed the Chiricahuas and included wild rumors of hundreds of indigenous men joining Geronimo. See, for example, *New York Times*, May 19, May 21, May 28, May 29, May 30, June 1, June 2, and June 9, 1885; *Washington Post*, May 21, May 28, May 29, and June 2, 1885.

73. Crook, *Resume*, 1, 7–8; Hutton, *Phil Sheridan*, 364; Utley, *Geronimo*, 175–77.

74. In the early 1880s and once more in 1885, calls for Chiricahua removal surfaced in the press, from local residents, and in the upper echelons of the government. For instance, in 1882 Tombstone judge Henry C. Dibble wrote a letter to President Chester A. Arthur and called for Chiricahuas to be exiled to the Tortugas in the Caribbean or to one of the Aleutian Islands on the Alaskan coast. Simmons, *Massacre*, 93–94. See also *ARSW*, 1883, 169; *ARSW*, 1886, 6–7; and "Resolution Adopted at Meeting of Residents of Cochise County."

75. Davis, *Truth*, 86, 159–63, 184–88; Daly, "Geronimo Campaign," 485; Wright, "In the Days of Geronimo," 500; Shipp, "Captain Crawford's Last Expedition," 521; Hanna, "With Crawford," 512; Elliott, "Geronimo Campaign"; Utley, *Geronimo*, 168–69.

76. Ball, *In the Days of Victorio*, 80, 154–67, 175–80; Ball, *Indeh*, 47, 251–52; Kenoi, "Chiricahua Apache's Account," 72.

77. *ARSW*, 1886, 6–9, 71; Hutton, *Phil Sheridan*, 364–66; Robinson, *General Crook*, 277.

78. According to U.S. reports, the Mexicans opened fire on Crawford's Apache soldiers. Crawford, thinking his soldiers had been mistaken as independent Chiricahuas, tried to stop the fight. As he stood up to parley with the Mexicans, he was shot and later died. Retaliating, the Apache soldiers gunned down several of the Mexican command, driving it away. After the guns paused, Lt. Marion Maus, Crawford's second in command, temporarily became a prisoner when talking with the Mexicans. A heated diplomatic exchange between the two countries followed. See, for example, *ARSW*, 1886, 152–53, 155–64; Utley, *Geronimo*, 177–81; Bowen-Hatfield, *Chasing Shadows*, 84–99; Roberts, *Once They Moved*, 265–67; Daly, "Geronimo Campaign"; Shipp, "Crawford's Last Expedition"; and "Historical Sketch of the Third U.S. Cavalry," typescript, 37–38, Folder 5, Box 1, Morton Papers, AHS (see also Folder 9 for correspondence of family, friends, and colleagues concerning Crawford's passing). For the Mexican perspective, see also the papers in Folders 17–22, Box 2, Mexican Government Documents, UASC.

79. Extracts from the conference transcripts are reprinted in Davis, *Truth*, 198–212 (see also 213–14). See also Crook, *Resume*, 8–15; Bourke, *On the Border*, 472–79; *ARSW*, 1886, 153; Debo, *Geronimo*, 252–63; Utley, *Geronimo*, 182–88; and Sweeney, *From Cochise to Geronimo*, 516–27. Geronimo escaped with twenty men, but two changed their minds and returned.

80. Sheridan wrote Crook, "It seems strange that Geronimo and party could have escaped without the knowledge of the scouts" and that "the offensive campaign against him [Geronimo and the Chiricahuas] with scouts has failed." Crook replied, "There can be no question that the scouts were thoroughly loyal and would have prevented the hostiles leaving had it been possible." He also stated, "I believe that the plan upon which I have conducted operations is the one most likely to prove successful in the end. It may be however that I am too much wedded to my own views in this matter, and as I have spent nearly eight years of the hardest work of my life in this Department, I respectfully request that I may be now relieved from its command." Crook, *Resume*, 12–16. After departing Arizona, Crook soon enjoyed extended hunting trips in his new command in Nebraska. Two years later he even gained a coveted, and controversial, promotion to the rank of a major general. He died from heart failure in 1890.

81. R. C. Drum to Miles, Apr. 3, 1886, in *General Miles and the Surrender of Geronimo*, 2.

82. Generally jealous of West Point graduates, Miles, a Civil War volunteer, saw Crook as overrated, insisting he had flopped in the Sioux wars of 1876–77. Miles was also one of those who saw Crook's two-grade promotion in 1873 as grossly unfair. Although he denied it publicly, it is possible that Miles had been gunning for Crook's Arizona command for quite some time. At least from January 1886, there circulated rumors in the press of Miles replacing Crook. Wooster, *Nelson A. Miles*, 80–85, 91–97; Hutton, *Phil Sheridan*, 135–38.

83. Letter, Apr. 11, 1886, Fort Bowie, Ariz. See also Letters Apr. 12, 1886, Ft. Bowie, Ariz., May 8, 1886, Nogales, Ariz., May 25, 1886, Willcox, Ariz., June 7, 1886, Calabasas, Ariz., June 24, 1886, Deming, N.Mex., and July 23, 1886, Fort Bowie, Ariz., all in Sherman Miles Manuscript; Miles, *Personal Recollections*, 477–79.

84. General Orders No. 76, Department of Arizona, Apr. 20, 1886, in *General Miles and the Surrender of Geronimo*, 2–3; ARSW, 1886, 164–67; Miles, *Personal Recollections*, 481–87; Wooster, *Nelson A. Miles*, 145–47.

85. Gale, "Lebo," 11–24; Gale, "Hatfield," 453–63; Utley, *Geronimo*, 193–98; Kuhn, *Chronicles*, 286–87. After two months on the move with the Chiricahuas, Trinidad Verdin was hit by a bullet in a small clash with Mexican troops in June. Recaptured by the Mexican force, she was handed over to Captain Lawton's command prior to return to Arizona. McCarty, "Trinidad Verdin."

86. Radbourne, "Last Raid"; Sweeney, *From Cochise to Geronimo*, 531–51; Kuhn, *Chronicles*, 289–90.

87. Lawton's report, dated Sept. 9, 1886, is in *General Miles and the Surrender of Geronimo*, 45–48. See also Wood, *Chasing Geronimo*; Wood, "On Campaign"; Parker, *Old Army*, 176–78; and Benson, "Geronimo Campaign," 552–56.

88. Robinson, *Apache Voices*, 49–52. See also Utley, *Geronimo*, 200–202, 205–7; Ball, *In the Days of Victorio*, 185–87; and Letters, June 8, 1886, Calabasas, Ariz., June 15, 1886, Fort Huachuca, Ariz., and Aug. 4, 1886, Headquarters in the Field, Ariz., all in Sherman Miles Manuscript.

89. Utley, *Geronimo*, 207–11; Ball, *Indeh*, 106–14; Gatewood, "Surrender," 53–70; Martine and Kayitah, "The Final Surrender of Geronimo," Reel 1, Gatewood Collection, AHS; Debo, *Geronimo*, 282–91.

90. Utley, *Geronimo*, 213–20; Faulk, *Geronimo Campaign*; Wood, *Chasing Geronimo*, 103–10; Debo, *Geronimo*, 279–94; Worcester, *Apaches*, 301–7.

91. Miles suggested that the Chiricahuas be sent to the Indian Territory. However, in 1879, Congress, as demanded by the people from the adjoining states, had prohibited the removal to Indian Territory of any Arizona and New Mexico Indians. ARSW, 1886, 170–71; Debo, *Geronimo*, 271–79, 299–312; Faulk, *Geronimo Campaign*, 152–75. On the removal, see *General Miles and the Surrender of Geronimo*, 4–7, 49–77.

Epilogue

1. Gardner, "Escorting," 567–68. See also Utley, *Geronimo*, 223, 226–29.

2. Kenoi, "Chiricahua Apache's Account," 83–84. See also Ball, *In the Days of Victorio*, 191–94; Opler, *Apache Odyssey*, 49–50; and Ball, *Indeh*, 122–36.

3. Cleveland to Acting Secretary of War, Aug. 23, 1886, and Sept. 7, 1886, in *General Miles and the Surrender of Geronimo*, 4, 8.

4. See *General Miles and the Surrender of Geronimo*, 3–34, especially Howard to President, Sept. 24, 1886, 18; Drum to Miles, Sept. 25, 1886, 20; Miles to Drum, Sept. 29, 1886, 20–21; and Stanley to Drum, Oct. 27, 1886, 29–30.

5. Utley, *Geronimo*, 228; Kuhn, *Chronicles*, 292.

6. Miles to Adjutant General, July 7, 1886, in *General Miles and the Surrender of Geronimo*, 51. See also Sonnichsen, *Tucson*, 118–21.

7. Bourke, *On the Border*, 485; Crook, *Resume*; Utley, *Geronimo*, esp. 230–34.

8. Robinson, *Apache Voices*, 33.

9. Ball, *Indeh*, 34.

BIBLIOGRAPHY

Archival Sources

Arizona Historical Society, Tucson (AHS)
David Edward Adams Papers
Edward E. Ayer Papers
Natalie Beaumont Forsyth Papers
Albert Case Benedict Papers
Clarence E. Bennett Papers
John G. Bourke Diary
Augustus C. Brichta Papers
Clarence Chrisman Papers
Charles T. Connell Papers
Fort Lowell Records
William Fourr Papers
Charles Gatewood Collection
James Glover Papers
Francis Goodwin Papers
Guy Howard Papers
Fred Hughes Papers
Indians of North America—Apache—Camp Grant Massacre Ephemera File
Anton Mazzanovich Papers
Charles Morton Papers
Gustav van Hemert Schneider Papers
    Joseph P. Widney Letters
John T. Smith Letters
Phylena Tonge Papers
Charles Morgan Wood Manuscripts
Charles Morgan Wood Papers
James Worthington Letters
Arizona State Library, Archives, and Public Records, Phoenix
Charles Poston Collection
Arizona State Museum, Tucson (ASM)
Grenville Goodwin Papers (GP)

Center for Southwest Research, Albuquerque, New Mexico (CSR)
 Frank Reeve Papers
 Michael Steck Papers
Fort Davis National Historic Site, Fort Davis, Texas (FDNHS)
 Gordon W. Geldard, "The Lost Patrol"
 Robert K. Grierson, "Journal Kept on the Victorio Campaign in 1880"
Henry E. Huntington Library, San Marino, California (HL)
 "Arizona Volunteers: Correspondence and Reports, 1864–66"
 Alonzo E. Davis, "Pioneer Days in Arizona by One Who Was There"
 Azor H. Nickerson, "Major General George Crook and the Indians"
 Walter Scribner Schuyler Papers
 Thomas T. Tidball Diary
Sherman Miles Manuscript, in possession of the author
National Archives and Records Administration, Washington, D.C. (NARA)
 M617, Returns from U.S. Military Posts, 1800–1916
  Roll 33, Fort Apache, Arizona
  Rolls 87–88, Fort Bayard, New Mexico
  Rolls 129–130, Fort Bowie, Arizona
  Roll 156, Fort Buchanan, New Mexico
  Roll 261, Fort Craig, New Mexico
  Rolls 414–415, Fort Grant, Arizona
  Roll 1407, Fort Webster, New Mexico
  Rolls 1216–1218, Fort Stanton, New Mexico
  Roll 1265, Fort Thomas, Arizona
  Roll 1325, Fort Verde, Arizona
 M744, Returns from Regular Cavalry Regiments
  Rolls 88–89, Ninth Cavalry
University of Arizona Special Collections, Tucson (UASC)
 Thomas Akers Diary
 Alexander Grayson Bowman Diary
 Joseph Corson Reminiscences
 Leighton Finley Papers
 Mexican Government Documents
 Edward D. Tuttle Papers
 Frank West Journal
 Letterbook of Rueben Augustine Wilbur

Government Publications

Abel, Annie Heloise, ed. *The Official Correspondence of James S. Calhoun while Indian Agent at Santa Fe and Superintendent of Indian Affairs in New Mexico.* Washington, D.C.: Government Printing Office, 1915.
Arizona Legislative Assembly. *Memorial and Affidavits Showing the Outrages Perpetrated by the Apache Indians, in the Territory of Arizona, during the Years of 1869 and 1870.*

San Francisco: Francis and Valentine Printers, 1871.

Colyer, Vincent. *Peace with the Apaches of New Mexico and Arizona: Report of Vincent Colyer, Member of the Board of Indian Commissioners, 1871.* Washington, D.C.: Government Printing Office, 1872.

Cooke, Philip St. George, *Journal of the March of the Mormon Battalion.* Sen. Ex. Doc. No. 2, 30th Cong., Special Session, Serial 547.

Crook, George. *Resume of Operations against Apache Indians, 1882–1886.* Washington, D.C.: Government Printing Office, 1887.

Emory, William H. *Notes of a Military Reconnaissance from Fort Leavenworth, in Missouri, to San Diego, in California.* Washington, D.C.: Wendell and Van Benthuysen, 1848.

———. *Report on the United States and Mexican Boundary Survey.* 2 vols. Washington, D.C.: A. O. P. Nicholson, 1857–1859.

Kappler, Charles J., ed. *Indian Affairs: Laws and Treaties.* Washington, D.C.: Government Printing Office, 1904.

Miller, Hunter, ed. *Treaties and Other International Acts of the United States of America.* 8 vols. Washington, D.C.: Government Printing Office, 1931–1948.

Parke, John G., and William H. Emory. *Report of Explorations for that Portion of a Railway Route Near the 32d Parallel of Latitude, Lying between Dona Ana, on the Rio Grande, and Pimas Villages, on the Gila, 1855.* Washington, D.C.: Corps of Topographical Engineers, 1859.

Russell, Frank. "The Pima Indians." In *Twenty-Sixth Annual Report of the Bureau of American Ethnology, 1904–05.* Washington, D.C.: Government Printing Office, 1908.

Statistical Report on the Sickness and Mortality in the Army of the United States . . . 1855 to 1860. Senate Ex. Doc. No. 52, 36th Cong., 1st sess., Serial 1035.

U.S. Adjutant-General's Office. *Chronological List of Actions &c., With Indians from January 15, 1837 to January, 1891.* Fort Collins, Colo.: Old Army Press, 1979.

U.S. Census Office. *Statistics of the Population of the United States at the Ninth Census.* Washington, D.C.: Government Printing Office, 1872.

U.S. Commissioner of Indian Affairs. *Annual Reports (ARCIA)*
1853: House Ex. Doc. No. 1, 33d Cong., 1st sess. Serial 710.
1855: Senate Ex. Doc. No. 1, 34th Cong., 1st sess. Serial 810.
1856: Senate Ex. Doc. No. 5, 34th Cong., 3d sess. Serial 875.
1857: Senate Ex. Doc. No. 11, 35th Cong., 1st sess. Serial 919.
1859: Senate Ex. Doc. No. 2, 36th Cong., 1st sess. Serial 1023.
1862: House Ex. Doc. No. 1, 37th Cong., 3d sess. Serial 1156.
1863: House Ex. Doc. No. 1, 38th Cong., 1st sess. Serial 1182.
1864: House Ex. Doc. No. 1, 38th Cong., 2d sess. Serial 1220.
1865: House Ex. Doc. No. 1, 39th Cong., 1st sess. Serial 1248.
1866: House Ex. Doc. No. 1, 39th Cong., 2d sess. Serial 1284.
1867: House Ex. Doc. No. 1, 40th Cong., 2d sess. Serial 1326.
1868: House Ex. Doc. No. 1, 40th Cong., 3d sess. Serial 1366.
1869: House Ex. Doc. No. 1, 41st Cong., 2d sess. Serial 1414.
1871: House Ex. Doc. No. 1, 42d Cong., 2d sess. Serial 1505.
1872: House Ex. Doc. No. 1, 42d Cong., 3d sess. Serial 1560.

1873: House Ex. Doc. No. 1, 43d Cong., 1st sess. Serial 1601.

1874: House Ex. Doc. No. 1, 43d Cong., 2d sess. Serial 1639.

1875: House Ex. Doc. No. 1, 44th Cong., 1st sess. Serial 1680.

1876: House Ex. Doc. No. 1, 44th Cong., 2d sess. Serial 1749.

1877: House Ex. Doc. No. 1, 45th Cong., 2d sess. Serial 1800.

1878: House Ex. Doc. No. 1, 45th Cong., 3d sess. Serial 1850.

1879: House Ex. Doc. No. 1, 46th Cong., 2d sess. Serial 1910.

1880: House Ex. Doc. No. 1, 46th Cong., 3d sess. Serial 1959.

1881: House Ex. Doc. No. 1, 47th Cong., 1st sess. Serial 2018.

1883: House Ex. Doc. No. 1, 48th Cong., 1st sess. Serial 2191.

1884: House Ex. Doc. No. 1, 48th Cong., 2d sess. Serial 2287.

1885: House Ex. Doc. No. 1, 49th Cong., 1st sess. Serial 2379.

1886: House Ex. Doc. No. 1, 49th Cong., 2d sess. Serial 2467.

1887: House Ex. Doc. No. 1, 50th Cong., 1st sess. Serial 2542.

U.S. Congress. House. "An Estimate of Appropriation for the Indian Service in Arizona." House Misc. Doc. No. 172, 44th Cong., 1st sess., Serial 1698.

———. *Mexican Border Troubles.* House Ex. Doc. No. 13, 45th Cong., 1st sess., Serial 1773.

———. *Reorganization of the Army.* House Mis. Doc. No. 56, 45th Cong., 2d sess., Serial 1818.

———. *Texas Border Troubles.* House Misc. Doc. No. 64, 45th Cong., 2d sess., Serial 1820.

U.S. Secretary of War. *Annual Reports (ARSW).*

1846: House Ex. Doc. No. 4, 28th Cong., 1st sess. Serial 497.

1849: House Ex. Doc. No. 5, 31st Cong., 1st sess. Serial 569.

1850: House Ex. Doc. No. 1, 31st Cong., 2d sess. Serial 595.

1851: House Ex. Doc. No. 2, 32d Cong., 1st sess. Serial 633.

1852: House Ex. Doc. No. 1, 32d Cong., 2d sess. Serial 673.

1854: Senate Ex. Doc. No. 1, 33d Cong., 2d sess. Serial 746.

1855: Senate Ex. Doc. No. 1, 34th Cong., 1st sess. Serial 810.

1857: Senate Ex. Doc. No. 11, 35th Cong., 1st sess. Serial 919.

1859: Senate Ex. Doc. No. 2, 36th Cong., 1st sess. Serial 1023.

1867: House Ex. Doc. No. 1, 40th Cong., 2d sess. Serial 1324 and 1325.

1868: House Ex. Doc. No. 1, 40th Cong., 3d sess. Serial 1367.

1869: House Ex. Doc. No. 1, 41st Cong., 2d sess. Serial 1412.

1871: House Ex. Doc. No. 1, 42d Cong., 2d sess. Serial 1503.

1873: House Ex. Doc. No. 1, 43d Cong., 1st sess. Serial 1597.

1874: House Ex. Doc. No. 1, 43d Cong., 2d sess. Serial 1635.

1875: House Ex. Doc. No. 1, 44th Cong., 1st sess. Serial 1674.

1876: House Ex. Doc. No. 1, 44th Cong., 2d sess. Serial 1742.

1878: House Ex. Doc. No. 1, 45th Cong., 3d sess. Serial 1843.

1879: House Ex. Doc. No. 1, 46th Cong., 2d sess. Serial 1903.

1880: House Ex. Doc. No. 1, 46th Cong., 3d sess. Serial 1952.

1881: House Ex. Doc. No. 1, 47th Cong., 1st sess. Serial 2010.

1882: House Ex. Doc. No. 1, 47th Cong., 2d sess. Serial 2091.

1883: House Ex. Doc. No. 1, 48th Cong., 1st sess. Serial 2182.

1884: House Ex. Doc. No. 1, 48th Cong., 2d sess. Serial 2277.

1885: House Ex. Doc. No. 1, 49th Cong., 1st sess. Serial 2369.

1886: House Ex. Doc. No. 1, 49th Cong., 2d sess. Serial 2461.

U.S. Senate. *General Miles and the Surrender of Geronimo in 1886.* Senate Ex. Doc. No. 117, 49th Cong., 2d sess., Serial 2449.

———. *Indian Tribes and Their Treatment.* Sen. Rep. No. 156, 39th Cong., 2d sess., Serial 1279.

U.S. Surgeon General's Office. *Circular No. 8, A Report on the Hygiene of the United States Army, with Descriptions of Military Posts.* Washington, D.C.: Government Printing Office, 1875.

The War of the Rebellion: A Compilation of the Official Records of the Union and Confederate Armies. 139 vols. Washington, D.C.: Government Printing Office, 1880–1901.

Winfrey, Dorman H., and James M. Day, eds. *Texas Indian Papers.* 5 vols. Austin: Texas State Library, 1959–1961.

Published Sources

Adams, Kevin. *Class and Race in the Frontier Army: Military Life in the West, 1870–1890.* Norman: University of Oklahoma Press, 2009.

Adelman, Jeremy, and Stephen Aron. "From Borderlands to Borders: Empires, Nation-States, and the Peoples in Between in North American History." *American Historical Review* 104 (June 1999): 814–41.

Alberts, Don E., ed. *Rebels on the Rio Grande: The Civil War Journal of A. B. Peticolas.* Albuquerque: University of New Mexico Press, 1984.

Alchisay, Peter, and Peter Cozzeus. "The Apache Story of the Cibicue." In Cozzens, *Eyewitnesses,* 295–310.

Alonso, Ana Maria. *Thread of Blood: Colonialism, Revolution, and Gender on Mexico's Northern Frontier.* Tucson: University of Arizona Press, 1995.

Altshuler, Constance Wynn. *Cavalry Yellow and Infantry Blue: Army Officers in Arizona between 1851–1886.* Tucson: Arizona Historical Society, 1991.

———. *Chains of Command: Arizona and the Army, 1856–1875.* Tucson: Arizona Historical Society, 1981.

———, ed. *Latest from Arizona! The Hesperian Letters, 1859–61.* Tucson: Arizona Historical Society, 1969.

———. "The Regulars in Arizona in 1866: Interviews with Henry I. Yohn." *Journal of Arizona History* 16 (Summer 1975): 119–126.

Anderson, Fred, and Andrew Cayton. *The Dominion of War: Empire and Liberty in North America, 1500–2000.* New York: Viking, 2005.

Anderson, Gary Clayton. *The Conquest of Texas: Ethnic Cleansing in the Promised Land, 1820–1875.* Norman: University of Oklahoma Press, 2005.

———. *Ethnic Cleansing and the Indian: The Crime That Should Haunt America.* Norman: University of Oklahoma Press, 2014.

———. *The Indian Southwest: Ethnogenesis and Reinvention.* Norman: University of Oklahoma Press, 1999.

Anderson, Hattie M., ed. "Mining and Indian Fighting in New Mexico, 1858–1861: Memoirs of Hank Smith." *Panhandle Plains Historical Review* 1 (1928): 67–115.

Arny, W. F. M. *Indian Agent in New Mexico: The Journal of Special Agent W. F. M. Arny, 1870.* Santa Fe: Stagecoach Press, 1967.

Averell, William Woods. *Ten Years in the Saddle: The Memoir of William Woods Averell, 1851–1862.* Edited by Edward K. Eckert and Nicholas J. Amato. San Rafael, Calif.: Presidio Press, 1978.

Bailey, Lynn R., ed. *A Tenderfoot in Tombstone, the Private Journal of George Whitwell Parksons: The Turbulent Years, 1880–82.* Tucson: Westernlore Press, 2010.

———. *"Too Tough to Die": The Rise, Fall, and Resurrection of a Silver Camp, 1878 to 1990.* Tucson: Westernlore Press, 2004.

Ball, Durwood. *Army Regulars on the Western Frontier, 1848–1861.* Norman: University of Oklahoma Press, 2001.

———. "Fort Craig, New Mexico, and the Southwest Indian Wars, 1854–1884." *New Mexico Historical Review* 73 (April 1998): 153–73.

Ball, Eve, with Nora Henn and Lynda Sanchez. *Indeh: An Apache Odyssey.* Provo, Utah: Brigham Young University Press, 1980.

———. *In the Days of Victorio: Recollections of a Warm Springs Apache.* Tucson: University of Arizona Press, 1970.

Barnes, Will C. *Apaches and Longhorns: The Reminiscences of Will C. Barnes.* Los Angeles: Ward Ritchie Press, 1941.

———. "The Apaches' Last Stand in Arizona: The Battle of Big Dry Wash." In Cozzens, *Eyewitnesses,* 267–85.

———. "In the Apache Country." In Cozzens, *Eyewitnesses,* 615–24.

Barr, Juliana. *Peace Came in the Form of a Woman: Indians and Spaniards in the Texas Borderlands.* Chapel Hill: University of North Carolina Press, 2007.

Bartlett, John Russell. *Personal Narrative of Explorations and Incidents in Texas, New Mexico, California, Sonora, and Chihuahua, 1850–1853.* 2 vols. New York: D. Appleton, 1854.

Basehart, Harry W. "Mescalero Apache Band Organization and Leadership." *Southwestern Journal of Anthropology* 26 (Spring 1970): 87–106.

Bauer, Jack K. *The Mexican War, 1846–1848.* New York: Macmillan, 1974.

Baylor, George Wythe. *Into the Far, Wild Country: True Tales of the Old Southwest.* Edited by Jerry D. Thompson. El Paso: Texas Western Press, 1996.

Belich, James. *Replenishing the Earth: The Settler Revolution and the Rise of the Angloworld.* New York: Oxford University Press, 2011.

Bellesiles, Michael A. *Arming America: The Origins of National Gun Culture.* New York: Knopf, 2000.

Bender, Averam B. *The March of Empire: Frontier Defense in the Southwest, 1848–1860* Lawrence: University Press of Kansas, 1952.

Bender, Thomas. *A Nation among Nations: America's Place in World History.* New York: Hill and Wang, 2006.

Bennett, James A. *Forts and Forays: A Dragoon in New Mexico, 1850–1856.* Edited by Clinton E. Brooks and Frank D. Reeve. Albuquerque: University of New Mexico Press, 1996.

Benson, Harry C. "The Geronimo Campaign." In Cozzens, *Eyewitnesses,* 552–56.

Benton-Cohen, Katherine. *Borderline Americans: Racial Division and Labor in the Arizona Borderlands.* Cambridge, Mass.: Harvard University Press, 2009.

Betzinez, Jason, with Wilbur Sturtevant Nye. *I Fought with Geronimo.* 1959. Reprint, Lincoln: University of Nebraska Press, 1987.

Bieber, Ralph P., ed. *Journal of a Soldier under Kearny and Doniphan, 1846–1847.* Glendale, Calif.: Arthur H. Clark, 1935.

———, ed. "Letters of William Carr Lane, 1852–1854." *New Mexico Historical Review* 3 (April 1928): 179–203.

Bigelow, John, Jr. *On the Bloody Trail of Geronimo.* Tucson: Westernlore Press, 1986.

Black, Jeremy. *The Age of Total War, 1860–1945.* Westport, Conn.: Praeger, 2006.

———. *Fighting for America: The Struggle for Mastery in North America, 1519–1871.* Bloomington: Indiana University Press, 2011.

———. *Rethinking Military History.* London: Routledge, 2004.

Blackhawk, Ned. *Violence over the Land: Indians and Empires in the Early American West.* Cambridge, Mass.: Harvard University Press, 2006.

Blyth, Lance R. *Chiricahua and Janos: Communities of Violence in the Southwest Borderlands, 1680–1880.* Lincoln: University of Nebraska Press, 2012.

Bode, Emil A. *A Dose of Frontier Soldiering: The Memoirs of Corporal E.A. Bode, Frontier Regular Infantry, 1877–1882.* Edited by Thomas T. Smith. Lincoln: University of Nebraska Press, 1994.

Bourke John G. *An Apache Campaign in the Sierra Madre.* 1886. Reprint, Lincoln: University of Nebraska Press, 1987.

———. *The Diaries of John Gregory Bourke.* Vol. 1, *November 20, 1872–July 28, 1876.* Edited by Charles M. Robinson III. Denton: University of North Texas Press, 2003.

———. *On the Border with Crook.* New York: Charles Scribner's Sons, 1891.

Bowen-Hatfield, Shelley. *Chasing Shadows: Apaches and Yaquis along the United States-Mexico Border, 1876–1911.* Albuquerque: University of New Mexico Press, 1998.

Boyd, Mrs. Orsemus Bronson. *Cavalry Life in Tent and Field.* Lincoln: University of Nebraska Press, 1982.

Boyer, Ruth McDonald, and Narcissus Duffy Gayton. *Apache Mothers and Daughters: Four Generations of a Family.* Norman: University of Oklahoma Press, 1992.

Braatz, Timothy. *Surviving Conquest: A History of the Yavapai Peoples.* Lincoln: University of Nebraska Press, 2003.

Brady, Lisa M. *War upon the Land: Military Strategy and the Transformation of Southern Landscapes during the American Civil War.* Athens: Georgia University Press, 2012.

Brinckerhoff, Sidney B., and Pierce Chamberlin. "The Army's Search for a Repeating Rifle: 1873–1903." *Military Affairs* 32 (Spring 1968): 20–30.

Britten, Thomas A. *The Lipan Apaches: People of Wind and Lighting.* Albuquerque: University of New Mexico Press, 2009.

Brooks, James F. *Captives and Cousins: Slavery, Kinship, and Community in the Southwest Borderlands.* Chapel Hill: University of North Carolina Press, 2002.

Brown, Lenard E. "John Benjamin Townsend: The Arizona Cherokee." *Arizoniana* 2 (Fall 1961): 29–31.

Browne, J. Ross. *Adventures in the Apache Country: A Tour through Arizona and Sonora with Notes on the Silver Regions of Nevada.* New York: Harper, 1869.

Buckelew, Frank M. *Life of F. M. Buckelew: The Indian Captive.* Bandera, Tex.: Hunter's Printing House, 1925.

Burbank, Jane, and Frederick Cooper. *Empires in World History: Power and the Politics of Difference.* Princeton: Princeton University Press, 2011.

Burns, Mike. *The Only One Living to Tell: The Autobiography of a Yavapai Indian.* Edited by Gregory McNamee. Tucson: University of Arizona Press, 2012.

Caffey, James R. "A Theatrical Campaign." In Cozzens, *Eyewitnesses,* 562–66.

Cahill, Cathleen D. *Federal Fathers and Mothers: A Social History of the United States Indian Service, 1869–1933.* Chapel Hill: University of North Carolina Press, 2011.

Carmony, Neil, B., ed. *Apache Days and Tombstone Nights: John Clum's Autobiography, 1877–1887.* Silver City, N.Mex.: High Lonesome Books, 1997.

———, ed. *The Civil War in Apacheland: Sergeant George Hand's Diary.* Silver City, N.Mex.: High-Lonesome Books, 1996.

Carr, Camillo C. C. "The Days of the Empire—Arizona, 1866–1869." In Cozzens, *Eyewitnesses,* 18–35.

Carson, William G. B., ed. "William Carr Lane Diary." *New Mexico Historical Review* 39 (July–October 1964): 181–234, 274–332.

Carter, Robert G. *On the Border with MacKenzie; or, Winning West Texas from the Comanches.* 1935. Reprint, New York: Antiquarian Press, 1961.

———. "Raid into Mexico." *Outing* (April 1888): 1–9.

Carter, W. H. *From Yorktown to Santiago with the Sixth U.S. Cavalry.* Austin: State House Press, 1989.

Castetter, Edward Franklin, and Morris E. Opler. *The Ethnobiology of the Chiricahua and Mescalero Apache.* Albuquerque: University of New Mexico Press, 1936.

Chamberlain, Kathleen P. *Victorio: Apache Warrior and Chief.* Norman: University of Oklahoma Press, 2007.

Chance, Joseph E., ed. *My Life in the Old Army: The Reminiscences of Abner Doubleday from the Collection of the New York Historical Society.* Fort Worth: Texas Christian University Press, 1998.

Chávez, Thomas E. *New Mexico Past and Future.* Albuquerque: University of New Mexico Press, 2006.

Citino, Robert M. "Military Histories Old and New: A Reintroduction." *American Historical Review* 112 (October 2007): 1070–90.

Clarke, Dwight L., ed. *The Original Journals of Henry Smith Turner with Stephen Watts Kearny to New Mexico and California, 1846–1847.* Norman: University of Oklahoma Press, 1966.

Clarke, Powhatan H. "A Hot Trail." In Cozzens, *Eyewitnesses,* 630–41.

Clum, John P. "Es-kim-in-zin." Pts. 1 and 2. *New Mexico Historical Review* 3 (October 1928): 399–420; 4 (January 1929): 1–27.

Clum, Woodworth. *Apache Agent: The Story of John P. Clum.* New York: Houghton Mifflin, 1936.

Coffman, Edward M. *The Old Army: A Portrait of the American Army in Peacetime, 1784–1898.* New York: Oxford University Press, 1986.

Cole, D. C. *Chiricahua Apache, 1846–1876: From War to Reservation.* Albuquerque: University of New Mexico Press, 1988.

Collins, Charles. *Apache Nightmare: The Battle at Cibecue Creek.* Norman: University of Oklahoma Press, 1999.

———. *The Great Escape: The Apache Outbreak of 1881.* Tucson: Westernlore Press, 1994.

Colwell-Chanthaphonh, Chip. *Massacre at Camp Grant: Forgetting and Remembering Apache History.* Tucson: University of Arizona Press, 2007.

Conline, John. "The Campaign of 1880 against Victorio." In Cozzens, *Eyewitnesses,* 224–26.

Conner, Daniel E. *Joseph Reddeford Walker and the Arizona Adventure.* Norman: University of Oklahoma Press, 1956.

Cooke, Philip St. George. *The Conquest of New Mexico and California: An Historical and Personal Narrative.* New York: Putnam's Sons, 1878.

Cooper, Fredrick, and Ann Laura Stoler, eds. *Tensions of Empire: Colonial Cultures in a Bourgeois World.* Berkeley: University of California Press, 1997

Cooper, Jerry M. *The Army and Civil Disorder: Federal Military Intervention in Labor Disputes, 1877–1900.* Westport, Conn.: Greenwood Press, 1980.

———. *The Rise of the National Guard: The Evolution of the American Militia, 1865–1920.* Lincoln: University of Nebraska Press, 2002.

Corbusier, William Henry. *Soldier, Surgeon, Scholar: The Memoirs of William Henry Corbusier, 1844–1930.* Edited by Robert Wooster. Norman: University of Oklahoma Press, 2003.

Cozzens, Peter, ed. *Eyewitnesses to the Indian Wars, 1865–1890.* Vol. 1, *The Struggle for Apacheria.* Mechanicsburg, Pa.: Stackpole Books, 2001.

Cozzens, Samuel. *The Marvelous Country.* London: Low, Marston, Low, and Searle, 1875.

Cremony, John. C. *Life among the Apaches.* 1868. Reprint, Lincoln: University of Nebraska Press, 1983.

Crimmins, Martin L. "Col. Buell's Expedition into Mexico in 1880." *New Mexico Historical Review* 10 (April 1935): 133–42.

Cronon, William. *Nature's Metropolis: Chicago and the Great West.* New York: Norton, 1991.

Crook, George. "Apache Affairs: An Interview with General Crook," *New York Herald,* July 9, 1883. In Cozzens, *Eyewitnesses,* 396–404.

———. *His Autobiography.* Edited by Martin F. Schmitt. Norman: University of Oklahoma Press, 1960.

Cruse, Thomas. *Apache Days and After.* 1941. Reprint, Lincoln: University of Nebraska Press, 1987.

———. "From Hembrillo Canyon to Chevelon's Fork." In Cozzens, *Eyewitnesses,* 262–66.

Cumings, Bruce. *Dominion from Sea to Sea: Pacific Ascendancy and American Power.* New Haven: Yale University Press, 2010.

Cunningham, Bob. "The Calamitous Career of Lt. Royal E. Whitman." *Journal of Arizona History* 29 (Summer 1988): 149–62.

Cutts, James Madison. *The Conquest of California and New Mexico*. Philadelphia: Carey and Hart, 1847.

Daly, Henry W. "The Geronimo Campaign." In Cozzens, *Eyewitnesses*, 447–87.

Davis, Britton. "The Difficulties of Indian Warfare." In Cozzens, *Eyewitnesses*, 488–94.

———. *The Truth about Geronimo*. 1929. Reprint, Lincoln: University of Nebraska Press, 1976.

Davisson, Lori. "New Light on the Cibecue Fight: Untangling Apache Identities." *Journal of Arizona History* 20 (Winter 1979): 423–44.

Day, David. *Conquest: How Societies Overwhelm Others*. Oxford: Oxford University Press, 2008.

Debo, Angie. *Geronimo: The Man, His Time, His Place*. Norman: University of Oklahoma Press, 1976.

De Jong, David H. "'Good Samaritans of the Desert': The Pima-Maricopa Villages as Described in California Emigrant Journals, 1846–1852." *Journal of the Southwest* 47 (Autumn 2005): 457–96.

———. *Stealing the Gila: The Pima Agricultural Economy and Water Deprivation, 1848–1921*. Tucson: University of Arizona Press, 2009.

DeLay, Brian. "Independent Indians and the U.S.-Mexican War." *American Historical Review* 112 (February 2007): 35–68.

———. *War of a Thousand Deserts: Indian Raids and the U.S.-Mexican War*. New Haven: Yale University Press, 2008.

Dibbern, John. "The Reputation of Indian Agents: A Reappraisal of John P. Clum and Joseph C. Tiffany." *Journal of the Southwest* 39 (Summer 1997): 201–38.

Dinges, Bruce J. "Leighton Finley: A Forgotten Soldier of the Apache Wars." *Journal of Arizona History* 29 (Summer 1988): 163–84.

———, ed. "A New York Private in Arizona Territory: The Letters of George H. Cranston, 1867–1870." *Journal of Arizona History* 26 (Spring 1985): 53–76.

———. "The Victorio Campaign of 1880: Cooperation and Conflict on the United States-Mexico Border." *New Mexico Historical Review* 62 (January 1987): 81–94.

Dixon, David. *Hero of Beecher Island: The Life and Military Career of George A. Forsyth*. Lincoln: University of Nebraska Press, 1994.

Dobak, William A., and Thomas D. Phillips. *The Black Regulars, 1866–1898*. Norman: University of Oklahoma Press, 2001.

Dobyns, Henry F. "Military Transculturation of Northern Piman Indians, 1782–1821." *Ethnohistory* 19 (Fall 1972): 323–343.

Dunlay, Thomas W. *Kit Carson and the Indians*. Lincoln: University of Nebraska Press, 2005.

———. *Wolves for the Blue Soldiers: Indian Scouts and Auxiliaries with the United States Army, 1860–90*. Lincoln: University of Nebraska Press, 1982.

Duval, John C. *The Adventures of Big-Foot Wallace*. Macon, Ga.: J. W. Burke, 1921.

DuVal, Kathleen. *The Native Ground: Indians and Colonists in the Heart of the Continent*. Philadelphia: University of Pennsylvania Press, 2006.

"Early Days in Arizona with the Fifth U.S. Cavalry." In Cozzens, *Eyewitnesses*, 141–43.

Eaton, George O. "A String for the Bow." In Cozzens, *Eyewitnesses*, 177–81.

Edwards, Frank S. *A Campaign in New Mexico with Colonel Doniphan*. Philadelphia: Carey and Hart, 1847.

Elliott, Charles P. "The Geronimo Campaign of 1885–1886." In Cozzens, *Eyewitnesses*, 427–46.

Evans, Robert K. "The Indian Question in Arizona." In Cozzens, *Eyewitnesses*, 604–14.

Farish, Thomas Edwin. *History of Arizona*. 8 vols. Phoenix: Filmer Brothers, 1915–1918.

Faulk, Odie B. *The Geronimo Campaign*. New York: Oxford University Press, 1969.

———. *Tombstone: Myth and Reality*. New York: Oxford University Press, 1972.

Finerty, John F. "On Campaign after Cibicue Creek." In Cozzens, *Eyewitnesses*, 236–61.

Fontana, Bernard L., ed. *An Englishman's Arizona: The Ranching Letters of Herbert R. Hislop, 1876–1878*. Tucson: Overland Press, 1965.

Foos, Paul. *A Short, Offhand, Killing Affair: Soldiers and Social Conflict during the Mexican-American War*. Chapel Hill: University of North Carolina Press, 2002.

Forbes, Archibald. "The United States Army." *North American Review* 135 (August 1882): 127–45.

Forbes, Jack D. *Apache, Navaho and Spaniard*. Norman: University of Oklahoma Press, 1960.

Forsyth, George A. *The Story of the Soldier*. New York: D. Appleton and Co., 1900.

———. *Thrilling Days in Army Life*. 1900. Reprint, Lincoln: University of Nebraska Press, 1994.

Forsyth, William W. "A Diary of the Sierra Madre Campaign." In Cozzens, *Eyewitnesses*, 391–94.

Fowler, O. S. *Human Science*. N.p., 1873.

Frazer, Robert W. *Forts and Supplies: The Role of the Army in the Economy of the Southwest, 1846–1861*. Albuquerque: University of New Mexico Press, 1983.

———. *Forts of the West*. Norman: University of Oklahoma Press, 1965.

———, ed. *Mansfield on the Condition of Western Forts, 1853–54*. Norman: University of Oklahoma Press, 1963.

Frazier, Donald S. *Blood and Treasure: Confederate Empire in the Southwest*. College Station: Texas A&M University Press, 1995.

Frelinghuysen, Frederick T. "Mexico: Reciprocal Right to Pursue Savage Indians across the Boundary Line." In Cozzens, *Eyewitnesses*, 343–45.

Gale, Jack C. "Hatfield under Fire, May 15, 1886: An Episode of the Geronimo Campaigns." *Journal of Arizona History* 18 (Winter 1977): 447–68.

———. "Lebo in Pursuit." *Journal of Arizona History* 21 (Spring 1980): 11–24.

Gálvez, Bernardo de. *Instructions for Governing the Interior Provinces of New Spain, 1786*. Edited and translated by Donald E. Worcester. Berkeley, Calif.: Quivira Society, 1951.

Gardner, John P. "Escorting Chihuahua's Band to Florida." In Cozzens, *Eyewitnesses*, 567–68.

"Gashuntz." "On the March to Fort Yuma." In Cozzens, *Eyewitnesses*, 53–56.

Gates, John. "General Crook's First Apache Campaign." *Journal of the West* 6 (April 1967): 310–18.

Gatewood, Charles B. "Campaigning against Victorio in 1879." In Cozzens, *Eyewitnesses*, 213–23.

———. *Lt. Charles Gatewood and His Apache Wars Memoir*. Edited by Louis Kraft. Lincoln: University of Nebraska Press, 2005.

———. "The Surrender of Geronimo." In *Geronimo and the End of the Apache Wars*, edited by C. L. Sonnichsen, 53–70. Lincoln: University of Nebraska Press, 1990.

Geronimo. *His Own Story*. Edited by Frederick Turner. 1906. Reprint, New York: Meridian, 1996.

Go, Julian. *Patterns of Empire: The British and American Empire, 1688 to Present*. Cambridge: Cambridge University Press, 2011.

Goddard, Pliny Earle. *Jicarilla Apache Texts*. New York: Trustees of the American Museum of Natural History, 1911.

———. "Myths and Tales from the San Carlos Apache." *Anthropological Papers of the American Museum of Natural History* 24 (1918): 1–86.

———. *San Carlos Apache Texts*. New York: Trustees of the American Museum of Natural History, 1919.

Goetzmann, William H. *Army Exploration in the American West, 1803–1863*. New Haven: Yale University Press, 1959.

González, Deena J. *Refusing the Favor: The Spanish-Mexican Women of Santa Fe, 1820–1880*. New York: Oxford University Press, 1999.

Goodwin, Grenville. "The Characteristics and Function of Clan in a Southern Athapascan Culture." *American Anthropologist* 39 (July–September 1937): 394–407.

———. "The Social Divisions and Economic Life of the Western Apache." *American Anthropologist* 37 (January–March 1935): 55–64.

———. *The Social Organization of the Western Apache*. Chicago: University of Chicago Press, 1942.

———. *Western Apache Raiding and Warfare*. Edited by Keith H. Basso. Tucson: University of Arizona Press, 1971.

Goodwin, Grenville, and Neil Goodwin. *The Apache Diaries: A Father-Son Journey*. Lincoln: University of Nebraska Press, 2000.

Green, John. "Interesting Scout among White Mountain Apaches Some of Whom Sue for Peace and a Reservation." In Cozzens, *Eyewitnesses*, 40–48.

Greenberg, Amy S. *Manifest Manhood: and the Antebellum American Empire*. Cambridge: Cambridge University Press, 2005.

———. *Wicked War: Polk, Clay, Lincoln, and the 1846 U.S. Invasion of Mexico*. New York: Knopf, 2012.

Gressley, Gene M., ed. "A Soldier with Crook: The Letters of Henry R. Porter." *Montana: The Magazine of Western History* 8 (July 1958): 33–47.

Griffen, William B. *Apaches at War and Peace: The Janos Presidio, 1750–1858*. Norman: University of Oklahoma Press, 1998.

Griswold del Castillo, Richard. *The Treaty of Guadalupe Hidalgo: A Legacy of Conflict*. Norman: University of Oklahoma Press, 1990.

Gunnerson, Dolores A. *The Jicarilla Apaches: A Study in Survival*. DeKalb: Northern Illinois University Press, 1974.

Gustafson, A. M., ed. *John Spring's Arizona.* Tucson: University of Arizona Press, 1966.

Haas, Oscar. "The Diary of Julius Giesecke, 1861–1862." *Military History of the Southwest* 18 (Spring 1988): 49–92.

Haley, James L. *Apaches: A History and Culture Portrait.* New York: Doubleday, 1981.

Hall, Martin H. *The Confederate Army of New Mexico.* Austin: Presidial Press, 1978.

———. "Thomas J. Mastin's 'Arizona Guards.'" *New Mexico Historical Review* 49 (April 1974): 143–51.

Hämäläinen, Pekka. *The Comanche Empire.* New Haven: Yale University Press, 2008.

Hammond, George P., ed. *Campaigns in the West, 1856–1861: The Journal and Letters of Colonel John Van Deusen Du Bois.* Tucson: Arizona Pioneers Historical Society, 1949.

Hanna, Robert. "With Crawford in Mexico." In Cozzens, *Eyewitnesses,* 509–15.

Hanson, Victor David. *Carnage and Culture: Landmark Battles in the Rise of Western Power.* New York: Doubleday, 2001.

———. *The Western Way of War: Infantry Battle in Classical Greece.* New York: Knopf, 1989.

Haskell, J. Loring. *Southern Athapaskan Migration, a.d. 200–1750.* Tsaile, Ariz.: Navajo Community College Press, 1987.

Hays, Kelly R. "General Garland's War: The Mescalero Apache Campaigns, 1854–1855." *New Mexico Historical Review* 67 (July 1992): 251–68.

Henry, Guy V. "Cavalry Life in Arizona." In Cozzens, *Eyewitnesses,* 96–106.

Herrera, Ricardo A. "Self-Governance and the American Citizen as Soldier, 1775–1861." *Journal of Military History* 65 (January 2001): 21–52.

Hicks, Elijah. "The Journal of Elijah Hicks." *Chronicles of Oklahoma* 13 (March 1935): 68–99.

Hixson, Walter L. *American Settler Colonialism: A History.* New York: Palgrave Macmillan, 2013.

Hodge, Hiram C. *Arizona as It Is; or, The Coming Country.* New York: Hurd and Houghton, 1877.

Holtby, David. *Forty-Seventh Star: New Mexico's Struggle for Statehood.* Norman: University of Oklahoma Press, 2012.

Hook, Jason, and Martin Pegler. *To Live and Die in the West: The American Indian Wars.* Chicago: Fitzroy Dearborn, 2001.

Horsman, Reginald. *Race and Manifest Destiny: The Origins of American Racial Anglo-Saxonism.* Cambridge, Mass.: Harvard University Press, 1981.

Howard, Oliver O. *My Life and Experiences among Our Hostile Indians.* New York: Da Capo Press, 1972.

Huggard, Christopher J., and Terrence M. Humble. *Santa Rita del Cobre: A Copper Mining Community in New Mexico.* Boulder: University Press of Colorado, 2012.

Hughes, John T. *Doniphan's Expedition.* Cincinnati: U. P. James, 1847.

Hunt, Aurora. *Major General James Henry Carleton, 1814–1873: Western Frontier Dragoon.* Glendale, Calif.: Arthur H. Clark, 1958.

Hutton, Paul Andrew. *Phil Sheridan and His Army.* Lincoln: University of Nebraska Press, 1985.

Hutton, Paul Andrew, and Durwood Ball, eds. *Soldiers West: Biographies from the Military Frontier*, 2nd ed. Norman: University of Oklahoma Press, 2009.

Jacobs, Margaret D. *White Mother to a Dark Race: Settler Colonialism, Maternalism, and the Removal of Indigenous Children in the American West and Australia, 1880–1940*. Lincoln: University of Nebraska Press, 2009.

Jacoby, Karl. "'The Broad Platform of Extermination': Nature and Violence in the Nineteenth Century North American Borderlands." *Journal of Genocide Research* 10 (June 2008): 249–67.

———. *Shadows at Dawn: An Apache Massacre and the Violence of History*. New York: Penguin, 2008.

Janda, Lance. "Shutting the Gates of Mercy: The American Origins of Total War, 1860–1880." *Journal of Military History* 59 (January 1995): 7–26.

Jastrzembski, Joseph C. "Treacherous Towns in Mexico: Chiricahua Apache Personal Narratives of Horror." *Western Folklore* 54 (July 1995): 169–96.

Jerome, Lawrence R. "Soldiering and Suffering in the Geronimo Campaign." Edited by Joseph A. Stout Jr. *Journal of the West* 11 (January 1972): 154–69.

Jett, William B. "Engagement in Guadalupe Canyon." In Cozzens, *Eyewitnesses*, 495–96.

Johannsen, Robert W. *To the Halls of the Montezumas: The Mexican War in the American Imagination*. Oxford: Oxford University Press, 1985.

John, Elizabeth A. H. *Storms Brewed in Other Men's Worlds: The Confrontation of Indians, Spanish, and French in the Southwest, 1540–1795*. College Station: Texas A&M University Press, 1975.

Josephy, Alvin M., Jr. *Civil War in the American West*. New York: Vintage, 1993.

Kane, Adam. "James H. Carleton." In *Soldiers West: Biographies from the Military Frontier*, edited by Paul Andrew Hutton and Durwood Ball, 122–48. 2nd ed. Norman: University of Oklahoma Press, 2009.

Kaplan, Amy. *The Anarchy of Empire in the Making of U.S. Culture*. Cambridge, Mass.: Harvard University Press, 2002.

Kaut, Charles. "The Clan System as an Epiphenomenal Element of Western Apache Social Organization." *Ethnology* 13 (January 1974): 45–70.

Keegan, John. *The Face of Battle*. London: Jonathan Cape, 1976.

———. *A History of Warfare*. New York: Vintage, 1994.

Kelly, Lawrence C., ed. *Navajo Roundup: Selected Correspondence of Kit Carson's Expedition against the Navajo, 1863–1865*. Boulder, Colo.: Pruett, 1970.

Kenoi, Samuel L. "A Chiricahua Apache's Account of the Geronimo Campaign of 1886." In *Geronimo and the End of the Apache Wars*, edited by C. L. Sonnichsen, 71–90. Lincoln: University of Nebraska Press, 1990.

Kessell, John L. *Friars, Soldiers, and Reformers: Hispanic Arizona and the Sonora Mission Frontier, 1767–1856*. Tucson: University of Arizona Press, 1976.

———. *Spain in the Southwest: A Narrative History of Colonial New Mexico, Arizona, Texas, and California*. Norman: University of Oklahoma Press, 2002.

Kessel, William B. "The Battle of Cibecue and Its Aftermath: A White Mountain Apache's Account." *Ethnohistory* 21 (Spring 1974): 123–34.

King, Charles. "On Campaign in Arizona." In *Cozzens, Eyewitnesses*, 162–76.

Kiser, William S. *Dragoons in Apacheland: Conquest and Resistance in Southern New Mexico, 1846–1861*. Norman: University of Oklahoma Press, 2012.

———. *Turmoil on the Rio Grande: The Territorial History of the Mesilla Valley, 1846–1865*. College Station: Texas A&M University Press, 2011.

Kraemer, Paul. "Sickliest Post in the Territory of New Mexico: Fort Thorn and Malaria, 1853–1860." *New Mexico Historical Review* 71 (July 1996): 221–36.

Kraft, Louis. *Gatewood and Geronimo*. Albuquerque: University of New Mexico Press, 2000.

Kramer, Paul A. *The Blood of Government: Race, Empire, the United States and the Philippines*. Chapel Hill: University of North Carolina Press, 2006.

———. "Power and Connections: Imperial Histories of the United States in the World." *American Historical Review* 116 (December 2011): 1348–82.

Kuhn, Berndt. *Chronicles of War: Apache and Yavapai Resistance in the Southwestern United States and Northern Mexico, 1821–1937*. Tucson: Arizona Historical Society, 2014.

Lahti, Janne. "Colonized Labor: Apaches and Pawnees as Army Workers." *Western Historical Quarterly* 39 (Autumn 2008): 283–302.

———. *Cultural Construction of Empire: The U.S. Army in Arizona and New Mexico*. Lincoln: University of Nebraska Press, 2012.

———. "Journey to the 'Outside': The U.S. Army on the Road to the Southwest." *New Mexico Historical Review* 85 (Fall 2010): 349–74.

———. "Silver Screen Savages: Images of Apaches in Motion Pictures." *Journal of Arizona History* 54 (Spring 2013): 51–84.

———, ed. *Soldiers in the Southwest Borderlands, 1848–1886*. Norman: University of Oklahoma Press, 2017.

Lamar, Howard R. *The Far Southwest, 1846–1912: A Territorial History*. New Haven: Yale University Press, 1966.

Lane, Lydia Spencer. *I Married a Soldier*. Philadelphia: J. B. Lippincott, 1893.

Latorre, Felipe A., and Dolores L. Latorre. *The Mexican Kickapoo Indians*. New York: Dover, 1991.

Laumbach, Karl. W. *Hembrillo: An Apache Battlefield of the Victorio War*. Tularosa, N.Mex.: Human Systems Research, 2000.

Lee, Wayne E. "Mind and Matter—Cultural Analysis in American Military History: A Look at the State of the Field." *Journal of American History* 93 (March 2007): 1116–42.

———. "Warfare and Culture." In *Warfare and Culture in World History*, edited by Wayne E. Lee, 1–12. New York: New York University Press, 2011.

Lekson, Stephen H. *Nana's Raid: Apache Warfare in Southern New Mexico, 1881*. El Paso: Texas Western Press, 1987.

Lindsay, Brendan C. *Murder State: California's Native American Genocide, 1846–1873*. Lincoln: University of Nebraska Press, 2012.

Linn, Brian M. "'The American Way of War' Revisited." *Journal of Military History* 66 (April 2002): 501–33.

———. *The Echo of Battle: The Army's Way of War*. Cambridge, Mass.: Harvard University Press, 2009.

Lynn, John A. *Battle: A History of Combat and Culture*. Cambridge, Mass.: Westview, 2003.

Lockwood, Frank C. *The Apache Indians*. 1938. Reprint, Lincoln: University of Nebraska Press, 1987.

Loring, L. Y. "Report on the Coyotero Apaches." In Cozzens, *Eyewitnesses*, 182–202.

Ludwig, Larry L., and James L. Stute. *The Battle of K-H Butte*. Tucson: Westernlore Press, 1993.

Lummis, Charles. *Dateline Fort Bowie: Charles Fletcher Lummis Reports on an Apache War*. Norman: University of Oklahoma Press, 1979.

Madley, Benjamin. "Reexamining the American Genocide Debate: Meaning, Historiography, and New Methods." *American Historical Review* 120 (February 2015): 98–139.

Magoffin, Susan. *Down the Santa Fe Trail and into Mexico: The Diary of Susan Shelby Magoffin, 1846–1847*. Edited by Stella M. Drummond. 1926. Reprint, Lincoln: University of Nebraska Press, 1982.

Mahan, Alfred Thayer. *The Influence of Sea Power upon History, 1660–1783*. Boston: Little, Brown, 1898.

Mahon, John K. *History of the Second Seminole War, 1834–1842*. Rev. ed. Gainesville: University Press of Florida, 2010.

Maier, Charles. *Among Empires: American Ascendancy and Its Predecessors*. Cambridge, Mass.: Harvard University Press, 2006.

Mangum, Neil. "The Mays Fight: A Reappraisal of a Neglected Action." *Journal of Big Bend Studies* 9 (1997): 45–56.

Mapp, Paul W. *The Elusive West and the Contest for Empire, 1713–1763*. Chapel Hill: University of North Carolina Press, 2011.

Marion, Jeanie. "'As Long as the Stone Lasts': General O. O. Howard's 1872 Peace Conference." *Journal of Arizona History* 35 (Summer 1994): 109–40.

Masich, Andrew E. *The Civil War in Arizona: The Story of the California Volunteers, 1861–1865*. Norman: University of Oklahoma Press, 2006.

McCall, George A. *New Mexico in 1850: A Military View*. Edited by Robert W. Frazer. Norman: University of Oklahoma Press, 1968.

McCarty, Kieran, ed. and trans. *A Frontier Documentary: Sonora and Tucson, 1821–1848*. Tucson: University of Arizona Press, 1997.

———, ed. and trans. "Trinidad Verdin and the 'Truth' of History." *Journal of Arizona History* 14 (Summer 1973): 149–64.

McChristian, Douglas C. *Fort Bowie, Arizona: Combat Post of the Southwest, 1858–1894*. Norman: University of Oklahoma Press, 2005.

———. *The U.S. Army in the West, 1870–1880: Uniforms, Weapons, and Equipment*. Norman: University of Oklahoma Press, 1995.

McGinty, Brian. *The Oatman Massacre: A Tale of Desert Captivity and Survival*. Norman: University of Oklahoma Press, 2005.

McKanna, Clare V., Jr. *Court-Martial of Apache Kid: The Renegade of Renegades*. Lubbock: Texas Tech University Press, 2009.

Meed, Douglas V. *They Never Surrendered: Bronco Apaches of the Sierra Madres, 1890–1935*. Tucson: Westernlore Press, 1993.

Meeks, Eric V. *Border Citizens: The Making of Indians, Mexicans, and Anglos in Arizona.* Austin: University of Texas Press, 2007.

Meketa, Charles, and Jacqueline Meketa. *One Blanket and Ten Days Rations.* Globe: Southwest Parks and Monuments Association, 1980.

Merritt, Wesley. "Incidents of Indian Campaigning in Arizona." In Cozzens, *Eyewitnesses,* 155–61.

Mifflin, Margot. *The Blue Tattoo: The Life of Olive Oatman.* Lincoln: University of Nebraska Press, 2011.

Miles, Nelson A. *Personal Recollections and Observations of General Nelson A. Miles.* 2 vols. Lincoln: University of Nebraska Press, 1992.

Miller, Darlis A. *The California Column in New Mexico.* Albuquerque: University of New Mexico Press, 1982.

———. *Soldiers and Settlers: Military Supply in the Southwest, 1861–1885.* Albuquerque: University of New Mexico Press, 1989.

Miller, Susan A. *Coacoochee's Bones: A Seminole Saga.* Lawrence: University Press of Kansas, 2003.

Mills, Anson. *My Story.* Washington, D.C.: published by author, 1918.

Minor, McCown Nancy. *Turning Adversity to Advantage: A History of the Lipan Apaches of Texas and Northern Mexico.* Lanham, Md.: University Press of America, 2009.

Missall, John, and Mary Lou Missall. *The Seminole Wars: America's Longest Indian Conflict.* Gainesville: University Press of Florida, 2004.

Moorhead, Max L. *The Apache Frontier: Jacobo Ugarte and Spanish-Indian Relations in Northern New Spain, 1769–1791.* Norman: University of Oklahoma Press, 1968.

———. *The Presidio: Bastion of the Spanish Borderlands.* Norman: University of Oklahoma Press, 1975.

Mora, Anthony P. *Border Dilemmas: Racial and National Uncertainties in New Mexico, 1848–1912.* Durham, N.C.: Duke University Press, 2011.

Morillo, Stephen, with Michael F. Pavkovic. *What Is Military History?* Cambridge: Polity, 2006.

Mort, Terry. *The Wrath of Cochise: The Bascom Affair and the Origins of Apache Wars.* New York: Pegasus: 2013.

Moses, A. Dirk, ed. *Empire, Colony, Genocide: Conquest, Occupation and Subaltern Resistance in World History.* New York: Berghahn Books, 2008.

Mowry, Sylvester. *Arizona and Sonora: The Geography, History, and Resources of the Silver Region of North America.* New York: Harper, 1866.

Moyar, Mark. "The Current State of Military History." *The Historical Journal* 50 (March 2007): 225–40.

Nicholson, John, ed. *The Arizona of Joseph Pratt Allyn. Letters from a Pioneer Judge: Observations and Travels, 1863–1866.* Tucson: University of Arizona Press, 1974.

Nickerson, Azor H. "An Apache Raid, and a Long Distance Ride." In Cozzens, *Eyewitnesses,* 107–12.

Nugent, Walter. *Habits of Empire: A History of American Expansion.* New York: Knopf, 2008.

Ogle, Ralph H. *Federal Control of the Western Apaches.* 1949. Reprint, Albuquerque: University of New Mexico Press, 1970.

Olmstead, Frederick Law. *Journey through Texas.* New York: Mason Brothers, 1857.

Opler, Morris E. *An Apache Life-Way: The Economic, Social and Religious Institutions of the Chiricahua Indians.* 1941. Reprint, Lincoln: University of Nebraska Press, 1996.

———. *Apache Odyssey: A Journey between Two Worlds.* 1969. Reprint, Lincoln: University of Nebraska Press, 2002.

———. *Childhood and Youth in Jicarilla Apache Society.* Los Angeles: Southwest Museum, 1946.

———, ed. *Grenville Goodwin among the Apaches: Letters from the Field.* Tucson: University of Arizona Press, 1973.

———. "The Identity of the Apache Mansos." *American Anthropologist* 44 (October–December 1942): 725.

———. "Jicarilla Apache Territory, Economy, and Society in 1850." *Southwestern Journal of Anthropology* 27 (Winter 1971): 309–29.

———. *Myths and Tales of the Chiricahua Apache Indians.* 1942. Reprint, Lincoln: University of Nebraska Press, 1994.

———. *Myths and Tales of the Jicarilla Apache Indians.* New York: American Folklore Society, 1938.

———. "A Summary of Jicarilla Apache Culture." *American Anthropologist* 38 (April–June 1936): 202–23.

Opler, Morris E., and Harry Hoijer. "The Raid and War-Path Language of the Chiricahua Apache." *American Anthropologist* 42 (October–December 1940): 617–34.

Opler, Morris E., and Verne Frederick Ray. "The Lipan and Mescalero Apache in Texas." In *An Ethnohistorical Analysis of Documents Regarding the Apaches in Texas.* New York: Garland Publishing, 1975.

Ostler, Jeffrey. *The Plains Sioux and U.S. Colonialism from Lewis and Clark to Wounded Knee.* Cambridge: Cambridge University Press, 2004.

Parker, James. *Old Army: Memories, 1872–1918.* Mechanicsburg, Pa.: Stackpole Books, 2003.

Parker, William T. *Annals of Old Fort Cummings.* Northampton, Mass.: Privately published, 1916.

Pattie, James O. *The Personal Narrative of James O. Pattie.* Cincinnati: John H. Wood, 1831.

Peers, Douglas M., ed. *Warfare and Empires: Contact and Conflict between European and Non-European Military and Maritime Forces and Cultures.* London: Variorum, 1997.

Perry, Richard J. *Apache Reservation: Indigenous Peoples and the American State.* Austin: University of Texas Press, 1993.

———. "The Apachean Transition from the Subarctic to the Southwest." *Plains Anthropologist* 25 (November 1980): 279–96.

Pettis, George H. *The California Column.* Santa Fe: New Mexican Printing, 1908.

Pettit, James S. "Apache Campaign Notes—1886." In Cozzens, *Eyewitnesses,* 532–35.

Platten, Fred. *Ten Years on the Trail of the Redskins.* Edited by Thomas E. Way. Williams, Ariz.: Williams News Press, 1963.

Porter, Bernard. *Empire and Superempire: Britain, America and the World.* New Haven: Yale University Press, 2006.

Porter, Joseph C. *Paper Medicine Man: John Gregory Bourke and His American West.* Norman: University of Oklahoma Press, 1986.

Poston, Charles. *Apache-Land.* San Francisco: A. L. Bancroft, 1878.

————. *Building a State in Apache Land.* Tempe, Ariz.: Aztec Press, 1963.

Price, George F. *Across the Continent with the Fifth Cavalry.* New York: D. Van Nostrand, 1883.

Prucha, Francis Paul, ed. *Documents of United States Indian Policy.* Lincoln: University of Nebraska Press, 1975.

————. *The Great Father: The United States Government and the American Indians.* Lincoln: University of Nebraska Press, 1984.

————. *The Sword of the Republic: The United States Army on the Frontier, 1783–1846.* 1969. Reprint, Bloomington: Indiana University Press, 1977.

Pumpelly, Raphael. *Travels and Adventures.* New York: Henry Holt, 1920.

Radbourne, Allan. *The Battle for Apache Pass: Reports of the California Volunteers.* London: English Westerners' Society, 2001.

————. "Geronimo's Last Raid into Arizona." *True West* 41 (March 1994): 22–29.

————. "Great Chief: Hashkeedasillaa of the White Mountain Apaches." *Journal of Arizona History* 50 (Spring 2009): 1–58.

————. "The Juh-Geronimo Surrender of 1879." *English Westerners Brand Book* 21 (1983): 1–18.

————. *Mickey Free: Apache Captive, Interpreter, and Indian Scout.* Tucson: Arizona Historical Society, 2005.

Radding, Cynthia. *Wandering Peoples: Colonialism, Ethnic Spaces, and Ecological Frontiers in Northwestern Mexico, 1700–1850.* Durham, N.C.: Duke University Press, 1997.

Randall, A. Franklin. "In the Heart of the Sierra Madre." In Cozzens, *Eyewitnesses,* 394–95.

Record, Ian W. *Big Sycamore Stands Alone: The Western Apaches, Aravaipa, and the Struggle for Place.* Norman: University of Oklahoma Press, 2008.

Reeve, Frank D., ed. "Frederick E. Phelps: A Soldier's Memoirs." *New Mexico Historical Review* 25 (1950): 37–56, 109–35, 187–221, and 305–27.

————, ed. "Puritan and Apache: A Diary." *New Mexico Historical Review* 23 (October 1948): 269–301; 24 (January 1949): 12–50.

————, ed. "War and Peace: Two Arizona Diaries." *New Mexico Historical Review* 24 (April 1949): 95–129.

Reid, John C. *Reid's Tramp, or a Journal of the Incidents of Ten Months Travel through Texas, New Mexico, Arizona, Sonora, and California.* Austin: Steck, 1935.

Resendez, Andres. *Changing National Identities at the Frontier: Texas and New Mexico, 1800–1850.* Cambridge: Cambridge University Press, 2005.

"Resolution Adopted at Meeting of Residents of Cochise County, Arizona, Regarding Outbreak of Indians from San Carlos Reservation." In Cozzens, *Eyewitnesses,* 414–24.

Rice, Michael M. "Across Apache Land." In Cozzens, *Eyewitnesses,* 502–508.

Richardson, William H. *Journal of William H. Richardson, A Private Soldier in the Campaign of New and Old Mexico.* Baltimore: John W. Woods, 1848.

Richter, Daniel K. *Facing East from Indian Country: A Native History of Early America.* Cambridge, Mass.: Harvard University Press, 2003.

Rickey, Don, Jr. *Forty Miles a Day on Beans and Hay: The Enlisted Soldier Fighting the Indian Wars.* Norman: University of Oklahoma Press, 1963.

Robbins, William G. *Colony and Empire: The Capitalist Transformation of the American West.* Lawrence: University Press of Kansas, 1994.

Roberts, David. *Once They Moved Like the Wind: Cochise, Geronimo, and the Apache Wars.* New York: Simon and Schuster, 1993.

Robinson, Charles M., III. *Bad Hand: A Biography of General Ranald S. Mackenzie.* Austin: State House Press, 1993.

———. *General Crook and the Western Frontier.* Norman: University of Oklahoma Press, 2001.

Robinson, Sherry. *Apache Voices: Their Stories of Survival as told to Eve Ball.* Albuquerque: University of New Mexico Press, 2000.

———. *I Fought a Good Fight: A History of the Lipan Apaches.* Denton: University of North Texas Press, 2013.

Ryan, Andrew. *News from Fort Craig, New Mexico, 1863: Civil War Letters of Andrew Ryan with the First California Volunteers.* Edited by Ernest Marchand. Santa Fe: Stagecoach, 1966.

Ryan, John P. *Fort Stanton and Its Community.* Las Cruces: Yucca Tree, 1998.

Santiago, Mark. *The Jar of Severed Hands: The Spanish Deportation of Apache Prisoners of War, 1770–1810.* Norman: University of Oklahoma Press, 2011.

Sayre, Nathan. "The Cattle Boom in Southern Arizona: Towards a Critical Political Ecology." *Journal of the Southwest* 41 (Summer 1999): 239–71.

Schreier, Jim, ed. "For This I Had Left Civilization: Julia Davis at Camp McDowell, 1869–1870." *Journal of Arizona History* 29 (Summer 1988): 185–98.

Schrier, Konrad F., Jr. "The California Column in the Civil War: Hazen's Civil War Diary." *Journal of San Diego History* 22 (Spring 1976): 31–47.

Scott, Kim Allen. "'Whiskey Is the Most Formidable Enemy in This Campaign,' Capt. Gustavus Cheney Doane's Fight with Boredom and Vice during the Geronimo Pursuit." *Journal of Arizona History* 48 (Spring 2007): 31–52.

Shapard, Bud. *Chief Loco: Apache Peacemaker.* Norman: University of Oklahoma Press, 2010.

Sheridan, Thomas E. *Arizona: A History.* Tucson: University of Arizona Press, 1995.

———. *Los Tucsonenses: The Mexican Community in Tucson, 1854–1941.* Tucson: University of Arizona Press, 1986.

Shipp, William E. "Captain Crawford's Last Expedition." In Cozzens, *Eyewitnesses,* 516–31.

Sides, Hampton. *Blood and Thunder: An Epic of the American West.* New York: Doubleday, 2006.

Simmons, Marc. *Massacre on the Lordsburg Road: A Tragedy of the Apache Wars.* College Station: Texas A&M University Press, 1997.

Sjoberg, Andrée F. "Lipan Apache Culture in Historical Perspective." *Southwestern Journal of Anthropology* 9 (Spring 1953): 76–98.

Skelton, William B. *An American Profession of Arms: The Army Officers Corps, 1784–1860.* Lawrence: University Press of Kansas, 1992.

Smith, F. Todd. *From Dominance to Disappearance: The Indians of Texas and the Near Southwest, 1786–1859.* Lincoln: University of Nebraska Press, 2005.

Smith, Ralph A. *Borderlander: The Life of James Kirker, 1793–1852.* Norman: University of Oklahoma Press, 1999.

———. "John Joel Glanton, Lord of the Scalp Range." *Smoke Signal* 6 (Fall 1962): 9–16.

———. "The Scalp Hunt in Chihuahua, 1849." *New Mexico Historical Review* 40 (April 1965): 117–40.

Smith, Sherry L. *The View From Officers' Row: Army Perceptions of Western Indians.* Tucson: University of Arizona Press, 1990.

Smith, Thomas T. *Fort Inge: Sharps, Spurs, and Sabers on the Texas Frontier, 1849–1869.* Austin: Eakin Press, 1993.

———. "U.S. Army Combat Operations in the Indian Wars of Texas, 1849–1881." *Southwestern Historical Quarterly* 99 (April 1996): 501–31.

———. "West Point and the Indian Wars, 1802–1891." *Military History of the West* 24 (Spring 1994): 25–55.

Smith, Victoria. *Captive Arizona, 1851–1900.* Lincoln: University of Nebraska Press, 2009.

Smith-Rosenberg, Carroll. *This Violent Empire: The Birth of an American National Identity.* Chapel Hill: University of North Carolina Press, 2010.

Smits, David D. "Fighting Fire with Fire: The Frontier Army's Use of Indian Scouts and Allies in the Trans-Mississippi Campaigns, 1860–1890." *American Indian Culture and Research Journal* 22 (Spring 1998): 73–116.

———. "The Frontier Army and the Destruction of the Buffalo, 1865–1883." *Western Historical Quarterly* 25 (Autumn 1994): 313–38.

Sonnichsen, C. L. *The Mescalero Apaches.* Norman: University of Oklahoma Press, 1958.

———. *Tucson: The Life and Times of an American City.* Norman: University of Oklahoma Press, 1982.

Spicer, Edward H. *Cycles of Conquest: The Impact of Spain, Mexico, and the United States on the Indians of the Southwest, 1533–1960.* Tucson: University of Arizona Press, 1962.

Splitter, Henry Winfred, ed. "Tour in Arizona: Footprints of an Army Officer." *Journal of the West* 1 (July 1962): 74–97.

St. John, Rachel. *Line in the Sand: A History of the Western U.S.-Mexico Border.* Princeton: Princeton University Press, 2011.

Stephenson, Anders. *Manifest Destiny: American Expansion and the Empire of Right.* New York: Hill and Wang, 1995.

Stoler, Ann Laura. *Carnal Knowledge and Imperial Power: Race and the Intimate in Colonial Rule.* Berkeley: University of California Press, 2002.

———, ed. *Haunted by Empire: Geographies of Intimacy in North American History.* Durham, N.C.: Duke University Press, 2006.

Storms, C. Gilbert. *Reconnaissance in Sonora: Charles D. Poston's 1854 Exploration of Mexico and the Gadsden Purchase.* Tucson: University of Arizona Press, 2015.

Strickland, Rex W. "The Birth and Death of a Legend: The Johnson Massacre of 1837." *Arizona and the West* 18 (Autumn 1976): 257–86

Stratton, Royal B. *The Captivity of the Oatman Girls.* 1857. Reprint, Lincoln: University of Nebraska Press, 1983.

Summerhayes, Martha. *Vanished Arizona: Recollections of the Army Life of a New England Woman.* Lincoln: University of Nebraska Press, 1979.

Sweeney, Edwin R. "Cochise and the Prelude to the Bascom Affair." *New Mexico Historical Review* 64 (October 1989): 427–46.

———. *Cochise: Chiricahua Apache Chief.* Norman: University of Oklahoma Press, 1991.

———. *From Cochise to Geronimo: The Chiricahua Apaches, 1874–1886.* Norman: University of Oklahoma Press, 2010.

———, ed. *Making Peace with Cochise: The 1872 Journal of Captain Joseph Alton Sladen.* Norman: University of Oklahoma Press, 1997.

———. *Mangas Coloradas: Chief of the Chiricahua Apaches.* Norman: University of Oklahoma Press, 1998.

———. *Merejildo Grijalva: Apache Captive, Army Scout.* El Paso: Texas Western Press, 1992.

Tate, Michael L. *The Frontier Army in the Settlement of the West.* Norman: University of Oklahoma Press, 1999.

———. "John P. Clum and the Origins of an Apache Constabulary, 1874–1877." *American Indian Quarterly* 3 (Summer 1977): 99–120.

Taylor, John. *Bloody Valverde: A Civil War Battle on the Rio Grande.* Albuquerque: University of New Mexico Press, 1995.

Taylor, Morris F. "Campaigns against the Jicarilla Apache, 1854." *New Mexico Historical Review* 44 (October 1969): 269–91.

———. "Campaigns against the Jicarilla Apache, 1855." *New Mexico Historical Review* 45 (April 1970): 119–36.

Tevis, James H. *Arizona in the 50's.* Albuquerque: University of New Mexico Press, 1954.

Thompson, Gerald. *The Army and the Navajo: The Bosque Redondo Reservation Experiment, 1863–1868.* Tucson: University of Arizona Press, 1976.

Thompson, Jerry. *Civil War to the Bloody End: The Life and Times of Major General Samuel P. Heintzelman.* College Station: Texas A&M University Press, 2006.

———. *Confederate General of the West: Henry Hopkins Sibley.* 1987. Reprint, College Station: Texas A&M University Press, 1996.

———. *Desert Tiger: Captain Paddy Graydon and the Civil War in the Far Southwest.* El Paso: Texas Western Press, 1992.

———, ed. "'Is This to Be the Glory of Our Brave Men?': The New Mexico Civil War Journal and Letters of Dr. Henry Jacob 'Hal' Hunter." *New Mexico Historical Review* 75 (October 2000): 535–603.

———, ed. *New Mexico Territory during the Civil War: Wallen and Evans Inspection Reports, 1862–1863.* Albuquerque: University of New Mexico Press, 2008.

———, ed. *Westward the Texans: The Civil War Journal of Private William Randolph Howell.* El Paso: Texas Western Press, 1990.

———, ed. "With the Third Infantry in New Mexico, 1851–1853: The Lost Diary of Private Sylvester W. Matson." *Journal of Arizona History* 31 (Winter 1990): 349–404.

Thrapp, Dan L. *Al Sieber: Chief of Scouts.* Norman: University of Oklahoma Press, 1964.

———. *The Conquest of Apacheria.* Norman: University of Oklahoma Press, 1967.

———. *General Crook and the Sierra Madre Adventure.* Norman: University of Oklahoma Press, 1971.

———. *Victorio and the Mimbres Apaches.* Norman: University of Oklahoma Press, 1974.

Tiller, Veronica E. Velarde. *The Jicarilla Apache Tribe: A History, 1846–1970.* Lincoln: University of Nebraska Press, 1983.

Truett, Samuel. *Fugitive Landscapes: The Forgotten History of the U.S.-Mexico Borderlands.* New Haven: Yale University Press, 2006.

Truett, Samuel, and Elliott Young, eds. *Continental Crossroads: Remapping U.S.-Mexico Borderlands History.* Durham: Duke University Press, 2004.

Turner, James E. "The Pima and Maricopa Villages, Oasis at a Cultural Crossroads, 1846–1873." *Journal of Arizona History* 39 (Winter 1998): 345–78.

Underhill, Lonnie, ed. "Dr. Edward Palmer's Experiences with the Arizona Volunteers, 1865–1866." *Arizona and the West* 26 (Spring 1984): 43–68.

Underhill, Ruth M. *A Papago Calendar Record.* Albuquerque: University of New Mexico Press, 1938.

———. *Social Organization of the Papago Indians.* New York: Columbia University Press, 1946.

Upham, Frank K. "Incidents of Regular Army Life in Time of Peace." In Cozzens, *Eyewitnesses*, 85–93.

Upton, Emory. *Armies of Asia and Europe.* New York: D. Appleton, 1878.

———. *The Military Policy of the United States.* Washington, D.C.: Government Printing Office, 1917.

Utley, Robert M. "Captain John Pope's Plan of 1853 for the Frontier Defense of New Mexico." *Arizona and the West* 5 (Summer 1963): 149–63.

———. *Frontier Regulars: The United States Army and the Indian, 1866–1891.* 1973. Reprint, Lincoln: University of Nebraska Press, 1984.

———. *Frontiersmen in Blue: The United States Army and the Indian, 1848–1865.* New York: Macmillan, 1967.

———. *Geronimo.* New Haven: Yale University Press, 2012.

Vandervort, Bruce. *Indian Wars of Mexico, Canada and the United States, 1812–1900.* New York: Routledge, 2006.

———. *Wars of Imperial Conquest in Africa, 1830–1914.* Bloomington: Indiana University Press, 2009.

Velasco, José Francisco. *Sonora: Its Extent, Population, Natural Productions, Indian Tribes, Mines, Mineral Lands, etc.* San Francisco: H. H. Bancroft, 1861.

Veracini, Lorenzo. *Settler Colonialism: A Theoretical Overview.* New York: Palgrave Macmillan, 2010.

Viola, Herman J., ed. *The Memoirs of Charles Henry Veil: A Soldier's Recollections of the Civil War and Arizona Territory.* New York: Orion Books, 1993.

Voss, Stuart F. *On the Periphery of Nineteenth-Century Mexico: Sonora and Sinaloa, 1810–1877.* Tucson: University of Arizona Press, 1982.

Waghelstein, John D. "Preparing the U.S. Army for the Wrong War: Educational and Doctrinal Failure, 1865–1891." *Small Wars and Insurgencies* 10 (Winter 1999): 1–33.

Walde, Dale A. "Avonlea and Athabaskan Migrations: A Reconsideration." *Plains Anthro-pologist* 51 (May 2006): 185–97.

Walker, Henry P. "Freighting from Guaymas to Tucson, 1850–1880." *Western Historical Quarterly* 1 (July 1970): 291–304.

———, ed. "The Reluctant Corporal: The Autobiography of William Bladen Jett." *Journal of Arizona History* 12 (Spring 1971): 1–50.

———, ed. "Soldier in the California Column: The Diary of John W. Teal." *Arizona and the West* 13 (Spring 1971): 33–82.

Wallace, Andrew, and Richard H. Hevly, eds. *From Texas to San Diego in 1851: The Overland Journal Dr. S. W. Woodhouse, Surgeon-Naturalist of the Sitgreaves Expedition.* Lubbock: Texas Tech University Press, 2007.

Wallace, Ernest, ed. *Ranald S. MacKenzie's Official Correspondence Relating to Texas.* Lubbock: West Texas Museum Association, 1967.

Watt, Robert N. "Apaches Without and Enemies Within: The U.S. Army in New Mexico, 1879–1881." *War in History* 18 (April 2011): 148–83.

———. *Apache Tactics.* Botley, Oxford: Osprey Publishing, 2012.

———. "Victorio's Military and Political Leadership of the Warm Springs Apaches." *War in History* 18 (November 2011): 457–94.

Webb, George A. *Chronological List of Engagements.* 1939. Reprint, New York: AMS Press, 1976.

Weber, David J. *Barbaros: Spaniards and their Savages in the Age of Enlightenment.* New Haven: Yale University Press, 2006.

———. *The Mexican Frontier, 1821–1846: The American Southwest Under Mexico.* Albu-querque: University of New Mexico Press, 1982.

———. *The Spanish Frontier in North America.* New Haven: Yale University Press, 1992.

———. *The Taos Trappers: The Fur Trade in the Far Southwest, 1540–1846.* Norman: University of Oklahoma Press, 1971.

Weigley, Russell F. *The American Way of War: A History of United States Military Strategy and Policy.* 1973. Reprint, Bloomington: Indiana University Press, 1977.

———. *History of the United States Army.* Bloomington: Indiana University Press, 1984.

Welch, John R., Chip Colwell-Chanthaphonh, and Mark Altaha. "Retracing the Battle of Cibecue: Western Apache, Documentary, and Archaeological Interpretations." *Kiva* 71 (2005): 133–63.

Wells, Edmund. *Argonaut Tales.* New York: Grafton Press, 1927.

Werne, Joseph Richard. *The Imaginary Line: A History of the United States and Mexican Boundary Survey, 1848–1857.* Fort Worth: Texas Christian University Press, 2007.

Wetherington, Ronald K., and Frances Levine, eds. *Battles and Massacres on the South-western Frontier: Historical and Archeological Perspectives.* Norman: University of Oklahoma Press, 2014.

White, Richard. *"It's Your Misfortune and None of My Own": A New History of the American West.* Norman: University of Oklahoma Press, 1991.

———. *The Middle Ground: Indians, Empires, and Republics in the Great Lakes Region, 1650–1815.* Cambridge: Cambridge University Press, 1991.

Williams, William Appleman. *Empire as a Way of Life*. Oxford: Oxford University Press, 1980.

Wilson, H. Clyde. *Jicarilla Apache Political and Economic Structures*. Berkeley: University of California Press, 1964.

Wilson, John P., ed. *From Western Deserts to Carolina Swamps: A Civil War Soldier's Journal and Letters Home*. Albuquerque: University of New Mexico Press, 2012.

———. *When the Texans Came: Missing Records from the Civil War in the Southwest, 1861–1862*. Albuquerque: University of New Mexico Press, 2001.

Wilson, Peter H. "Defining Military Culture." *Journal of Military History* 72 (January 2008): 11–42.

Winders, Richard Bruce. *Mr. Polk's Army: The American Military Experience in the Mexican War*. College Station: Texas A&M University Press, 1997.

Wislizenus, A. *Memoir of a Tour to Northern Mexico*. Washington, D.C.: Tippin and Streeper, 1848.

Wolfe, Patrick. "Settler Colonialism and the Elimination of the Native." *Journal of Genocide Research* 8 (December 2006): 387–409.

Wood, Leonard. *Chasing Geronimo: The Journal of Leonard Wood, May-September 1886*. Jack Lane, ed. Albuquerque: University of New Mexico Press, 1970.

———. "On Campaign in Sonora." In Cozzens, *Eyewitnesses*, 546–52.

Woody, Clara T. "The Woolsey Expeditions of 1864." *Arizona and the West* 4 (Summer 1962): 157–76.

Wooster, Robert. *The American Military Frontiers: The United States Army in the West, 1783–1900*. Albuquerque: University of New Mexico Press, 2009.

———. "The Army and the Politics of Expansion: Texas and the Southwestern Borderlands, 1870–1886." *Southwestern Historical Quarterly* 93 (October 1989): 151–67.

———. "'A Difficult and Forlorn Country': The Military Looks at the American Southwest, 1850–1890." *Arizona and the West* 28 (Winter 1986): 339–356.

———. *The Military and United States Indian Policy, 1865–1903*. New Haven: Yale University Press, 1988.

———. *Nelson A. Miles and the Twilight of the Frontier Army*. Lincoln: University of Nebraska Press, 1993.

Worcester, Donald E. *The Apaches: Eagles of the Southwest*. Norman: University of Oklahoma Press, 1979.

Wright, Harry R. "In the Days of Geronimo." In Cozzens, *Eyewitnesses*, 497–501.

Dissertations and Theses

Babcock, Matthew M. "Turning Apaches into Spaniards: North America's Forgotten Indian Reservations." PhD diss., Southern Methodist University, 2008.

Bruhl, Taborri I. "The Primacy of Method over Technology in the Subjugation of the Chiricahua Apaches of the American Southwest: 1848–1886." Master's thesis, California State University, Dominquez Hills, 2004.

Harte, John Bret. "The San Carlos Indian Reservation, 1872–1886: An Administrative History." PhD diss., University of Arizona, 1972.

Jastrzembski, Joseph Curtis. "An Enemy's Ethnography: The 'Mexican' in Nineteenth Century Chiricahua Apache Ethnographic Practice." PhD diss., University of Chicago, 1994.

Rockwell, Susan L. "The Autobiography of Mike Burns, Yavapai Apache." PhD diss., Arizona State University, 2001.

Smith, Victoria. "White Eyes, Red Heart, Blue Coat: The Life and Times of Mickey Free." PhD diss., Arizona State University, 2002.

Stenlund, Pekka. "Sota Yhdysvaltain pahinta intiaania vastaan: Yhdysvallat ja Geronimo-sotaretki 1885–1886." Master's thesis, University of Tampere, Finland, 2011.

Newspapers

Baton Rouge Louisiana Capitolian
Daily Los Angeles Herald
Globe Arizona Silver Belt
Las Cruces Rio Grande Republican
Mesilla (N.Mex.) Times
New York Herald
New York Times
New York Tribune
Prescott Arizona Miner (1864–68)
Prescott Arizona Weekly Miner (1874–77)
Prescott Weekly Arizona Miner (1868–74; 1877–85)
San Francisco Daily Alta California
Santa Fe Gazette (1859–64)
Santa Fe Weekly Gazette (?–1859)
St. Paul (Minn.) Daily Globe
Tombstone Daily Epitaph
Tombstone Republican
Tucson Arizona Citizen (1870–80)
Tucson Arizona Daily Star
Tucson Arizona Star
Tucson Arizona Weekly Citizen (1881–1901)
Tucson Weekly Arizona Citizen (April–December 1880)
Tucson Weekly Arizonian
Washington (D.C.) National Tribune
Washington Post
Yuma Arizona Sentinel

INDEX

Page numbers in *italics* indicate illustrations.